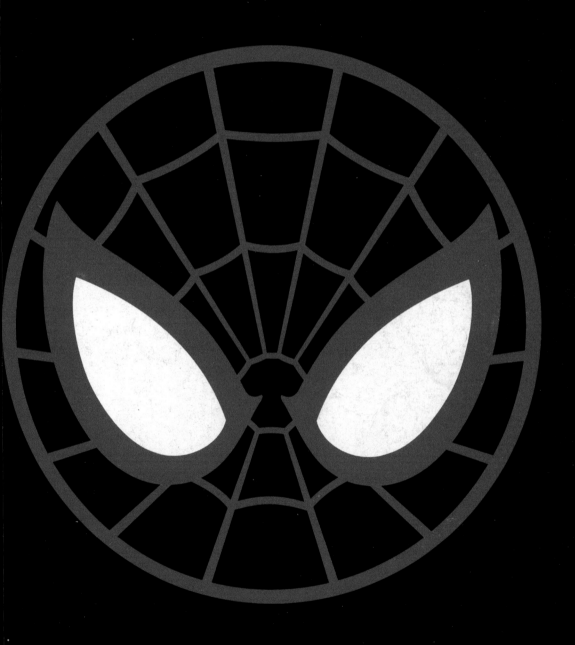

SPIDER-MAN

SPIDER-MAN: MILES MORALES VOL. 3. Contains material originally published in magazine form as SPIDER-MAN #15-21. First printing 2017. ISBN# 978-1-302-90597-2. Published by MARVEL WORLDWIDE, INC., a subsidiary of MARVEL ENTERTAINMENT, LLC. OFFICE OF PUBLICATION: 135 West 50th Street, New York, NY 10020. Copyright © 2017 MARVEL. No similarity between any of the names, characters, persons, and/or institutions in this magazine with those of any living or dead person or institution is intended, and any such similarity which may exist is purely coincidental. **Printed in the U.S.A.** DAN BUCKLEY, President, Marvel Entertainment; JOE QUESADA, Chief Creative Officer; TOM BREVOORT, SVP of Publishing; DAVID BOGART, SVP of Business Affairs & Operations, Publishing & Partnership; C.B. CEBULSKI, VP of Brand Management & Development, Asia; DAVID GABRIEL, SVP of Sales & Marketing, Publishing; JEFF YOUNGQUIST, VP of Production & Special Projects; DAN CARR, Executive Director of Publishing Technology; ALEX MORALES, Director of Publishing Operations; SUSAN CRESPI, Production Manager; STAN LEE, Chairman Emeritus. For information regarding advertising in Marvel Comics or on Marvel.com, please contact Vit DeBellis, Integrated Sales Manager, at vdebellis@marvel.com. For Marvel subscription inquiries, please call 888-511-5480. **Manufactured between 8/25/2017 and 9/26/2017 by QUAD/GRAPHICS WASECA, WASECA, MN, USA.**

10 9 8 7 6 5 4 3 2 1

MILES MORALES

BRIAN MICHAEL BENDIS
writer

issue #15

SZYMON KUDRANSKI
artist

JUSTIN PONSOR
color artist

issues #16-19

OSCAR BAZALDUA
artist

JUSTIN PONSOR (#16-18) &
JASON KEITH (#19) WITH RAIN BEREDO (#18)
color artists

issues #20-21

NICO LEON
artist

JUSTIN PONSOR
WITH JASON KEITH (#21)
color artists

VC's CORY PETIT
letterer

PATRICK BROWN
cover art

ALLISON STOCK & KATHLEEN WISNESKI
assistant editors

DEVIN LEWIS
associate editor

NICK LOWE
editor

special thanks to JUAN VLASCO

collection editor JENNIFER GRÜNWALD
assistant editor CAITLIN O'CONNELL
associate managing editor KATERI WOODY
editor special projects MARK D. BEAZLEY

editor in chief AXEL ALONSO
chief creative officer JOE QUESADA
president DAN BUCKLEY
executive producer ALAN FINE

SPIDER-MAN created by
STAN LEE & STEVE DITKO

PREVIOUSLY

High schooler Miles Morales was bitten by a genetically altered spider that granted him incredible arachnid-like powers. This is a secret he has shared only with his best friend Ganke, Fabio Medina (A.K.A. Goldballs) and his father, Jefferson.

Concerned about his son, Jefferson approached his old employers at the intelligence agency S.H.I.E.L.D., offering to return to active duty in exchange for Miles' protection. This is a secret he has shared with no one.

Neither Miles nor Jefferson have shared their secrets with Miles' mom, Rio.

After an epic dimension-hopping adventure with Spider-Gwen, Miles and Jefferson returned home triumphant, tired and hungry.

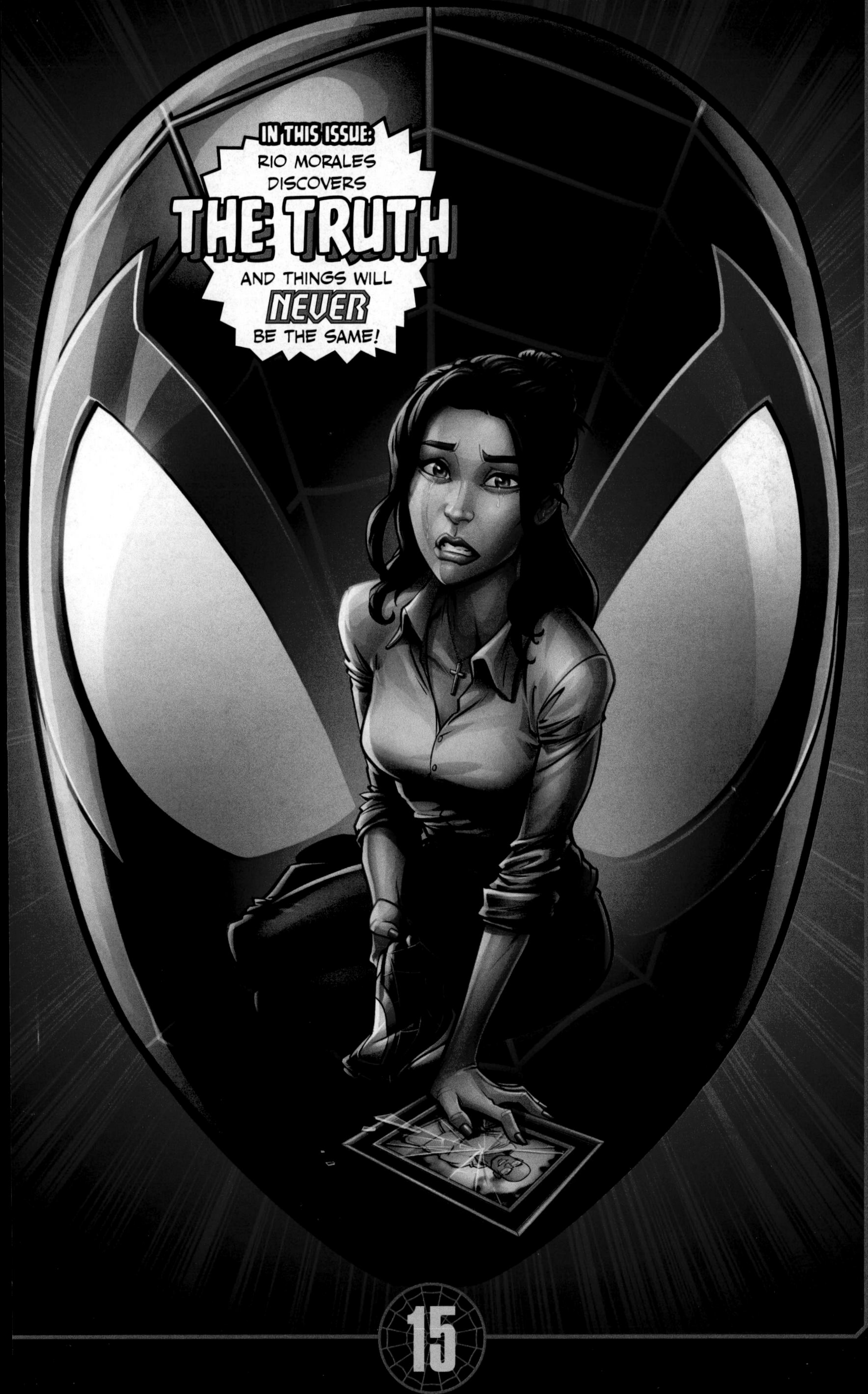
IN THIS ISSUE:
RIO MORALES DISCOVERS
THE TRUTH
AND THINGS WILL
NEVER
BE THE SAME!
15

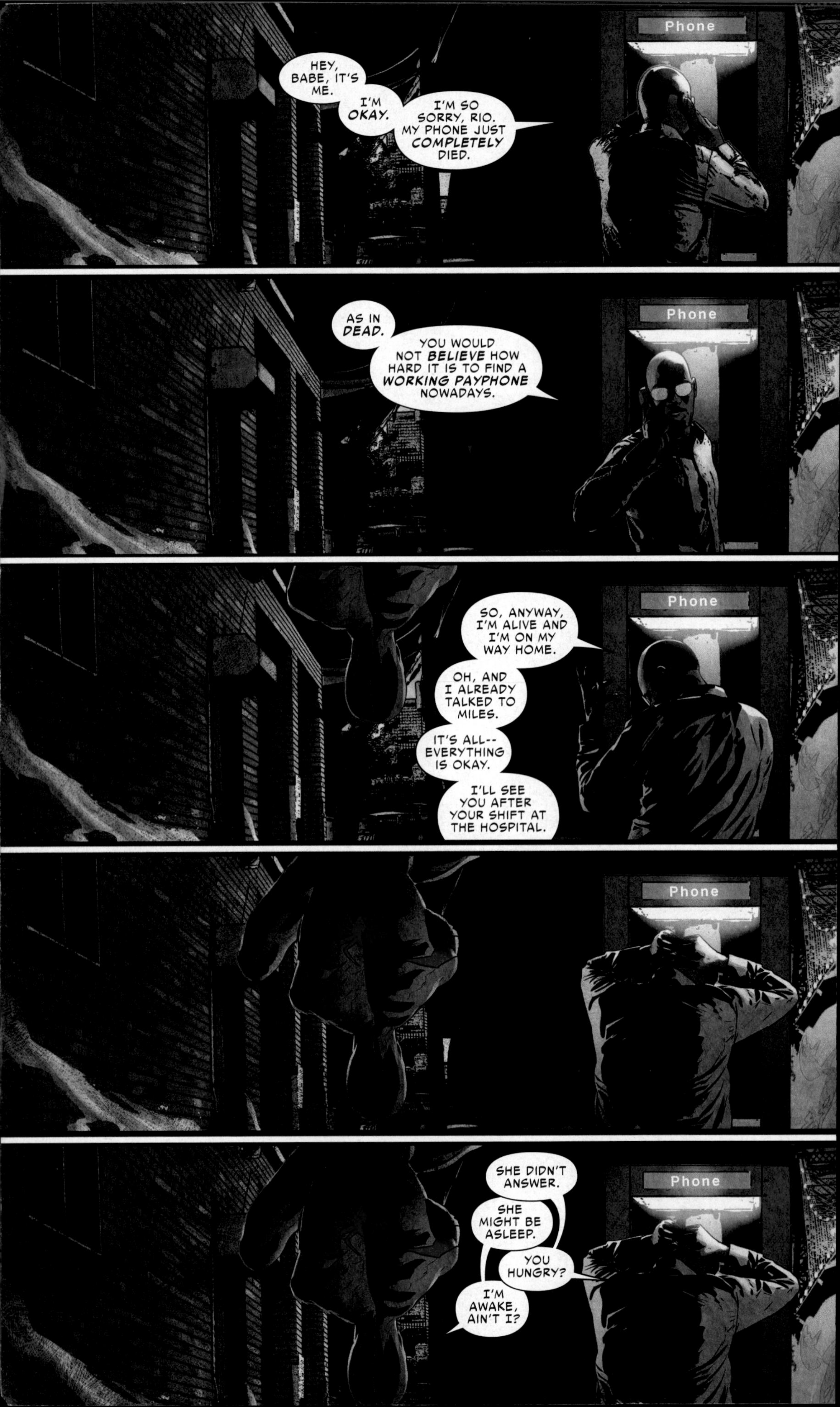
HEY, BABE, IT'S ME.
I'M OKAY.
I'M SO SORRY, RIO. MY PHONE JUST COMPLETELY DIED.
AS IN DEAD.
YOU WOULD NOT BELIEVE HOW HARD IT IS TO FIND A WORKING PAYPHONE NOWADAYS.
SO, ANYWAY, I'M ALIVE AND I'M ON MY WAY HOME.
OH, AND I ALREADY TALKED TO MILES.
IT'S ALL-- EVERYTHING IS OKAY.
I'LL SEE YOU AFTER YOUR SHIFT AT THE HOSPITAL.
SHE DIDN'T ANSWER.
SHE MIGHT BE ASLEEP.
YOU HUNGRY?
I'M AWAKE, AIN'T I?

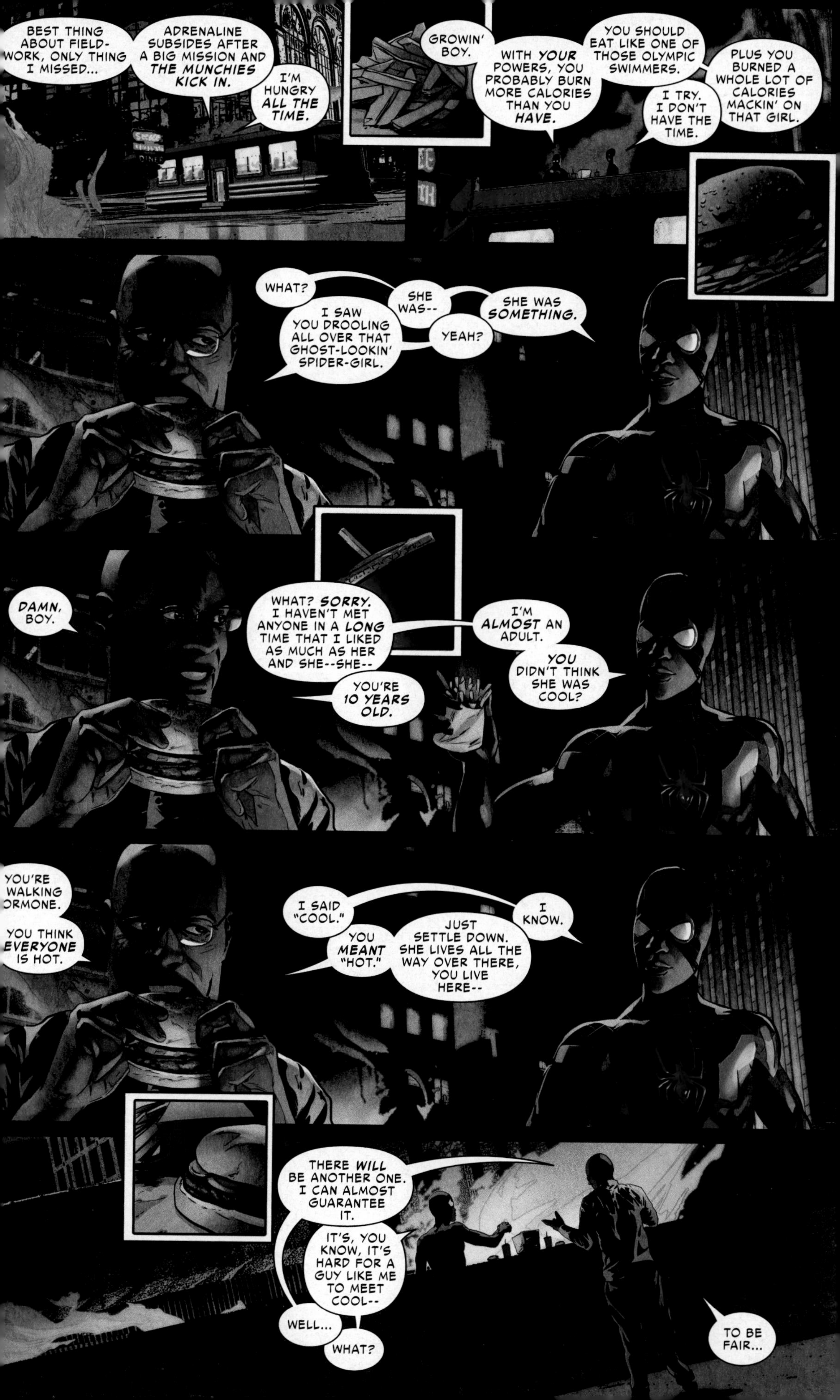
BEST THING ABOUT FIELD-WORK, ONLY THING I MISSED...
ADRENALINE SUBSIDES AFTER A BIG MISSION AND THE MUNCHIES KICK IN.
I'M HUNGRY ALL THE TIME.
GROWIN' BOY.
WITH YOUR POWERS, YOU PROBABLY BURN MORE CALORIES THAN YOU HAVE.
YOU SHOULD EAT LIKE ONE OF THOSE OLYMPIC SWIMMERS.
I TRY. I DON'T HAVE THE TIME.
PLUS YOU BURNED A WHOLE LOT OF CALORIES MACKIN' ON THAT GIRL.
WHAT?
I SAW YOU DROOLING ALL OVER THAT GHOST-LOOKIN' SPIDER-GIRL.
SHE WAS--
YEAH?
SHE WAS SOMETHING.
DAMN, BOY.
WHAT? SORRY. I HAVEN'T MET ANYONE IN A LONG TIME THAT I LIKED AS MUCH AS HER AND SHE--SHE--
YOU'RE 10 YEARS OLD.
I'M ALMOST AN ADULT.
YOU DIDN'T THINK SHE WAS COOL?
YOU'RE WALKING ORMONE.
YOU THINK EVERYONE IS HOT.
I SAID "COOL."
YOU MEANT "HOT."
I KNOW.
JUST SETTLE DOWN. SHE LIVES ALL THE WAY OVER THERE, YOU LIVE HERE--
THERE WILL BE ANOTHER ONE. I CAN ALMOST GUARANTEE IT.
IT'S, YOU KNOW, IT'S HARD FOR A GUY LIKE ME TO MEET COOL--
WELL...
WHAT?
TO BE FAIR...

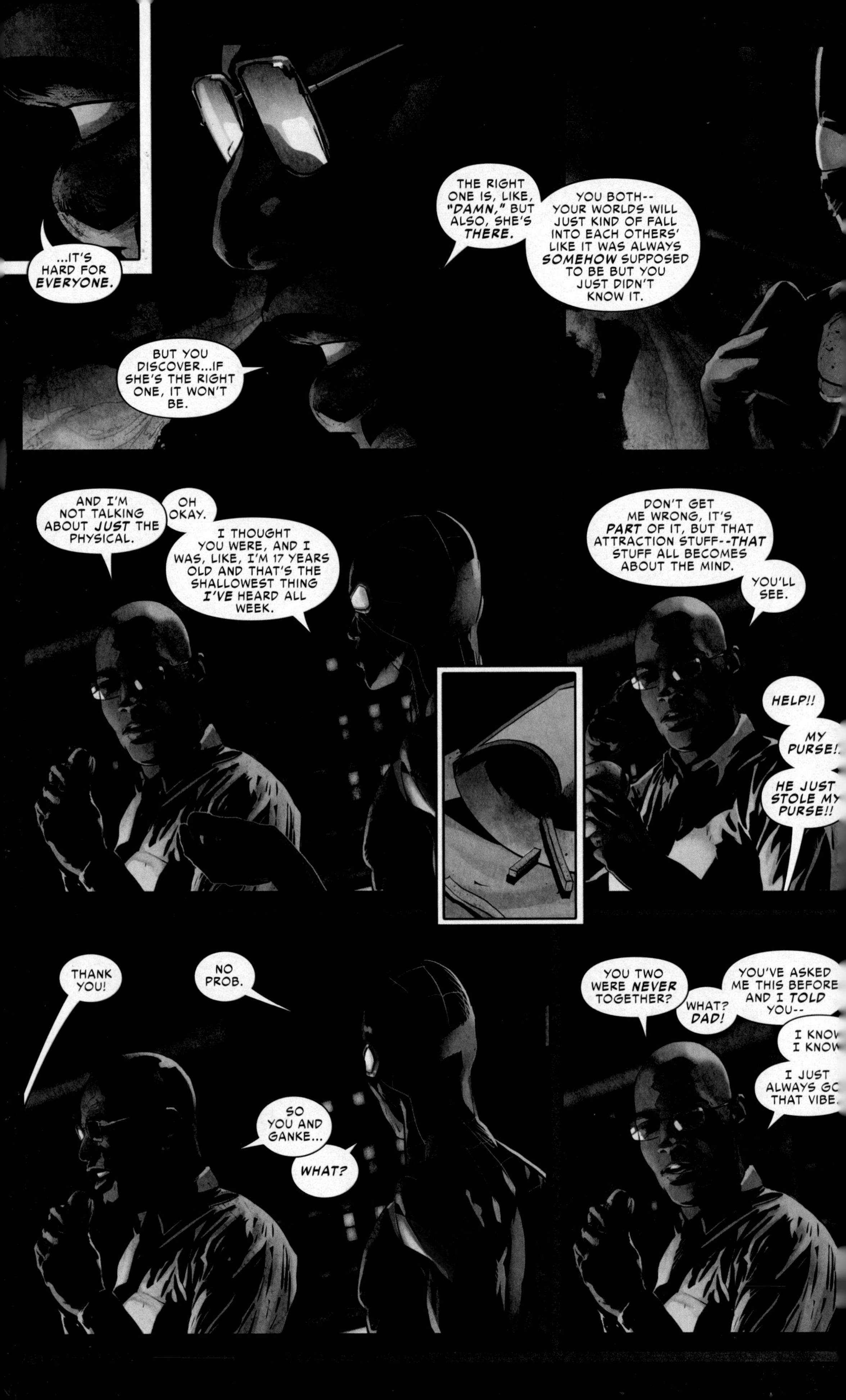
...IT'S HARD FOR EVERYONE.
BUT YOU DISCOVER...IF SHE'S THE RIGHT ONE, IT WON'T BE.
THE RIGHT ONE IS, LIKE, "DAMN," BUT ALSO, SHE'S THERE.
YOU BOTH-- YOUR WORLDS WILL JUST KIND OF FALL INTO EACH OTHERS' LIKE IT WAS ALWAYS SOMEHOW SUPPOSED TO BE BUT YOU JUST DIDN'T KNOW IT.
AND I'M NOT TALKING ABOUT JUST THE PHYSICAL.
OH OKAY.
I THOUGHT YOU WERE, AND I WAS, LIKE, I'M 17 YEARS OLD AND THAT'S THE SHALLOWEST THING I'VE HEARD ALL WEEK.
DON'T GET ME WRONG, IT'S PART OF IT, BUT THAT ATTRACTION STUFF--THAT STUFF ALL BECOMES ABOUT THE MIND.
YOU'LL SEE.
HELP!!
MY PURSE!
HE JUST STOLE MY PURSE!!
THANK YOU!
NO PROB.
SO YOU AND GANKE...
WHAT?
YOU TWO WERE NEVER TOGETHER?
WHAT? DAD!
YOU'VE ASKED ME THIS BEFORE AND I TOLD YOU--
I KNOW I KNOW
I JUST ALWAYS GOT THAT VIBE.

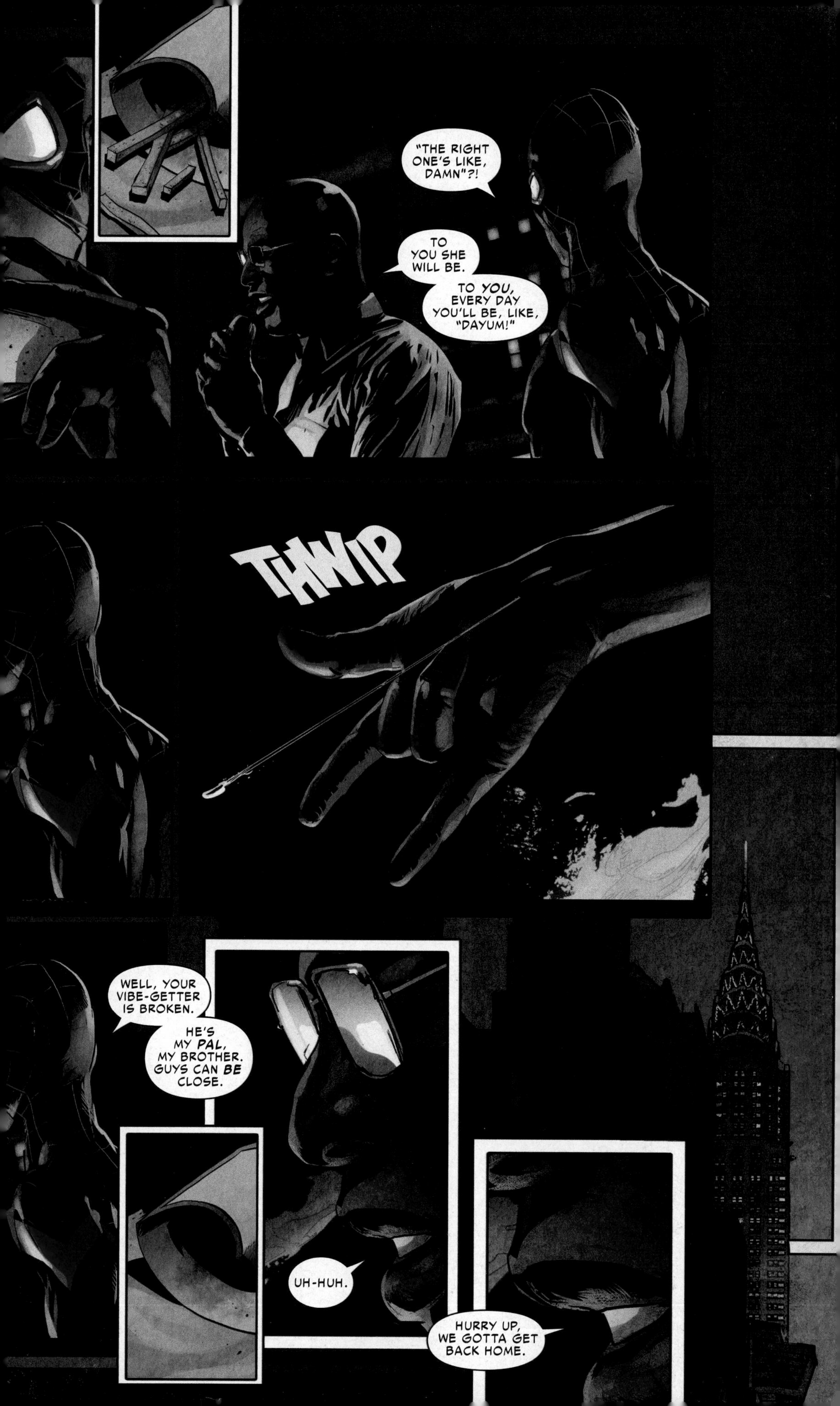

"THE RIGHT ONE'S LIKE, DAMN"?!
TO YOU SHE WILL BE.
TO YOU, EVERY DAY YOU'LL BE, LIKE, "DAYUM!"
THWIP
WELL, YOUR VIBE-GETTER IS BROKEN.
HE'S MY PAL, MY BROTHER. GUYS CAN BE CLOSE.
UH-HUH.
HURRY UP, WE GOTTA GET BACK HOME.

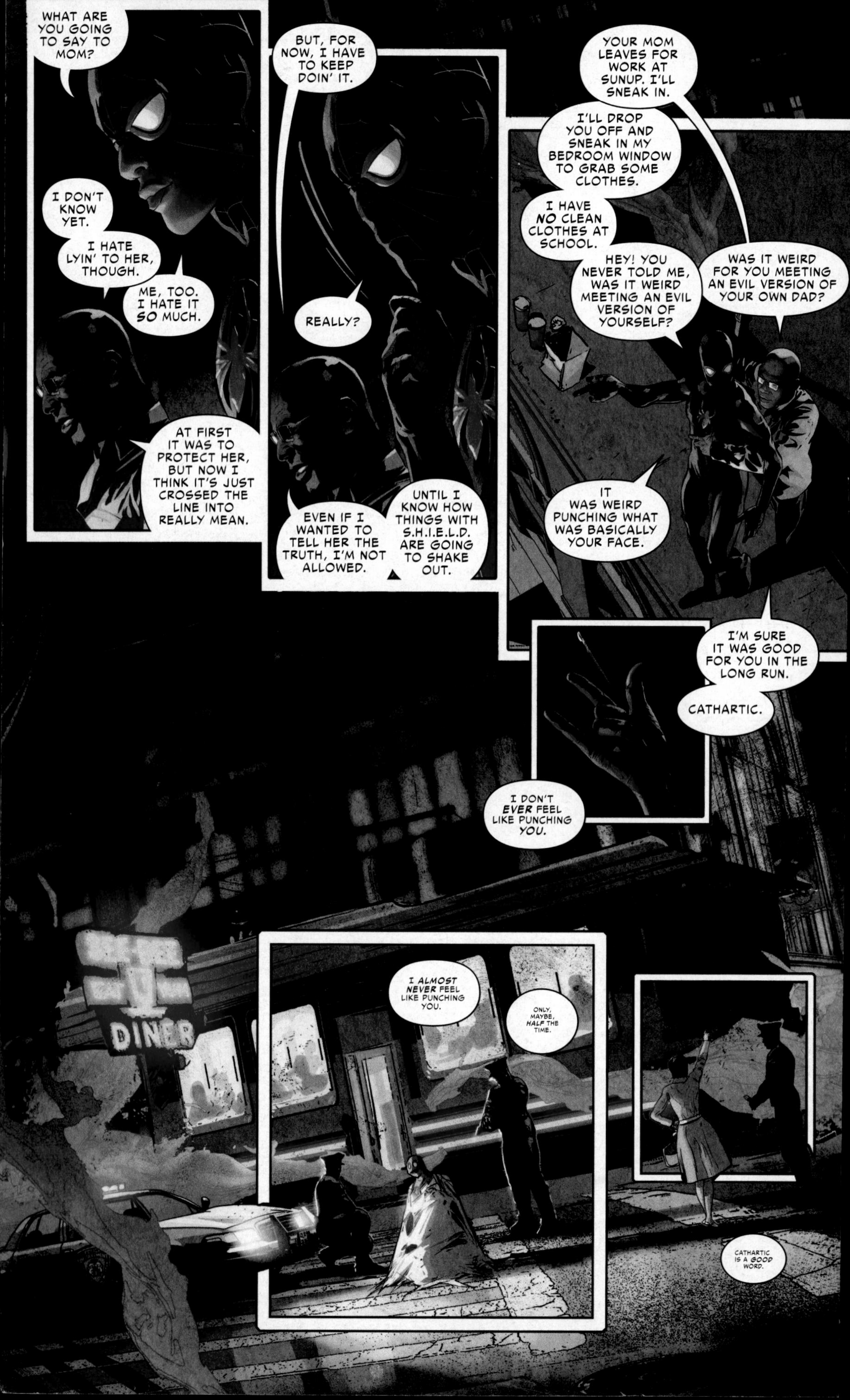
WHAT ARE YOU GOING TO SAY TO MOM?
I DON'T KNOW YET.
I HATE LYIN' TO HER, THOUGH.
ME, TOO. I HATE IT SO MUCH.
AT FIRST IT WAS TO PROTECT HER, BUT NOW I THINK IT'S JUST CROSSED THE LINE INTO REALLY MEAN.
BUT, FOR NOW, I HAVE TO KEEP DOIN' IT.
REALLY?
EVEN IF I WANTED TO TELL HER THE TRUTH, I'M NOT ALLOWED.
UNTIL I KNOW HOW THINGS WITH S.H.I.E.L.D. ARE GOING TO SHAKE OUT.
YOUR MOM LEAVES FOR WORK AT SUNUP. I'LL SNEAK IN.
I'LL DROP YOU OFF AND SNEAK IN MY BEDROOM WINDOW TO GRAB SOME CLOTHES.
I HAVE NO CLEAN CLOTHES AT SCHOOL.
HEY! YOU NEVER TOLD ME, WAS IT WEIRD MEETING AN EVIL VERSION OF YOURSELF?
WAS IT WEIRD FOR YOU MEETING AN EVIL VERSION OF YOUR OWN DAD?
IT WAS WEIRD PUNCHING WHAT WAS BASICALLY YOUR FACE.
I'M SURE IT WAS GOOD FOR YOU IN THE LONG RUN.
CATHARTIC.
I DON'T EVER FEEL LIKE PUNCHING YOU.
DINER
I ALMOST NEVER FEEL LIKE PUNCHING YOU.
ONLY, MAYBE, HALF THE TIME.
CATHARTIC IS A GOOD WORD.

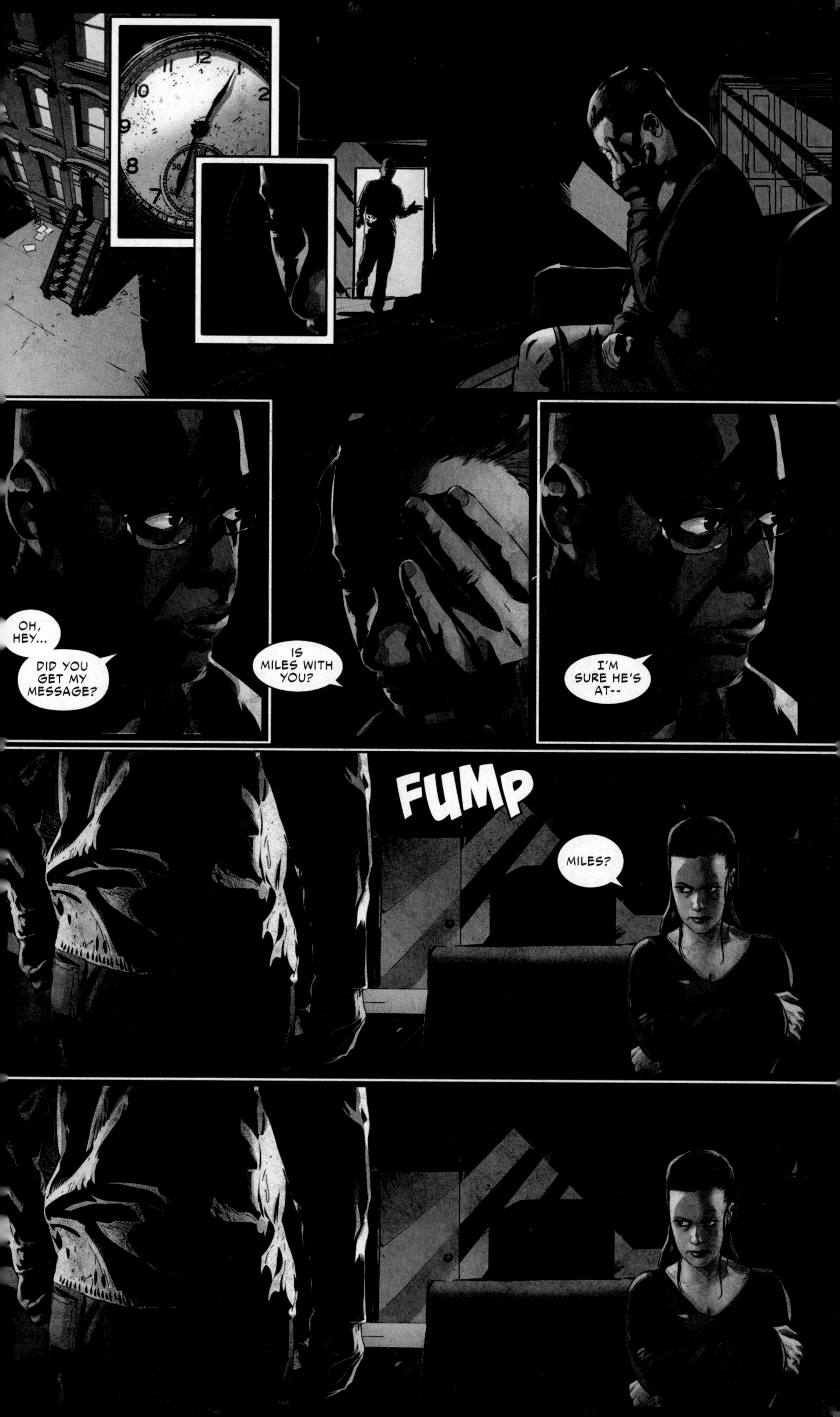

OH, HEY...
DID YOU GET MY MESSAGE?
IS MILES WITH YOU?
I'M SURE HE'S AT--
FUMP
MILES?

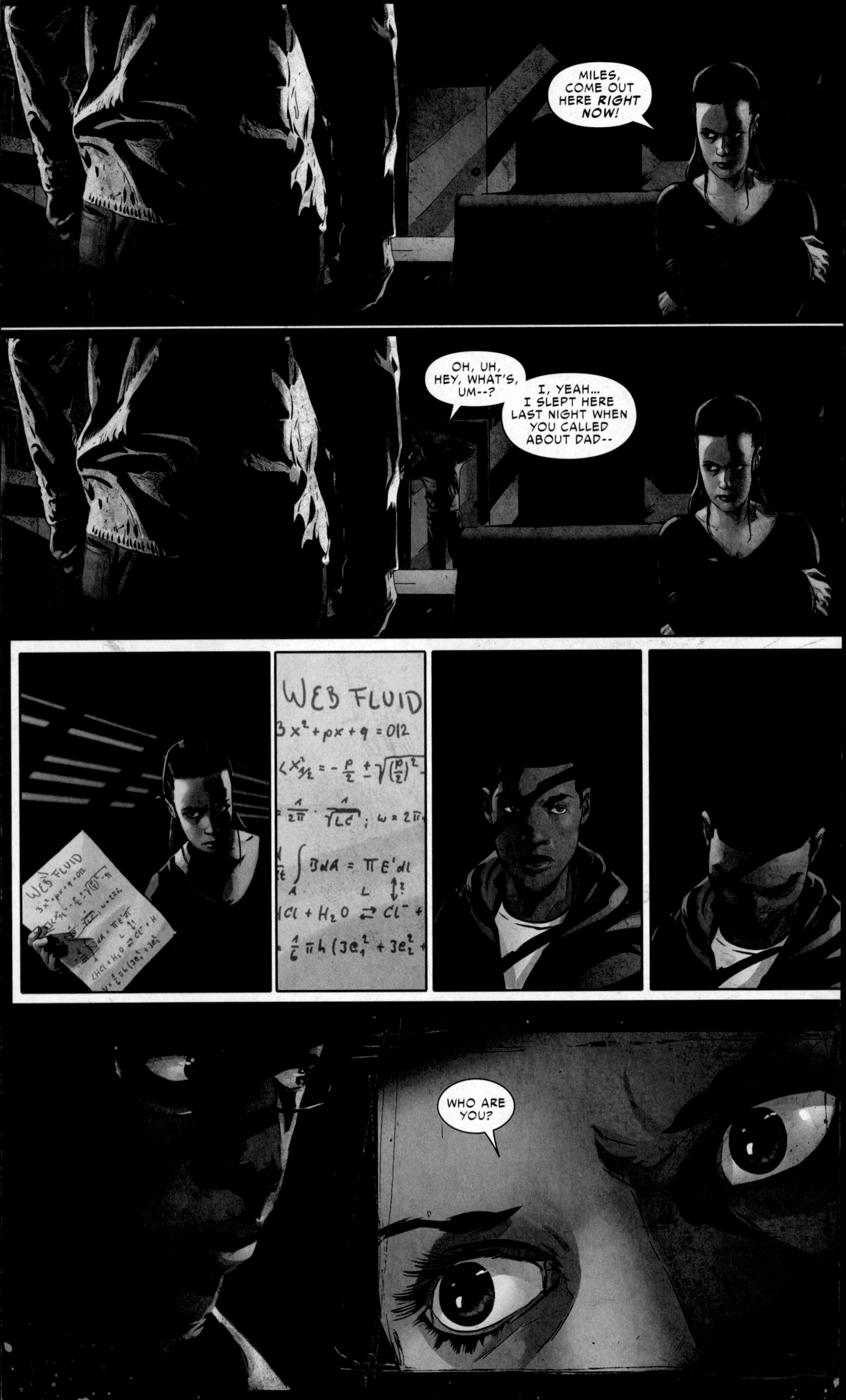
MILES, COME OUT HERE RIGHT NOW!
OH, UH, HEY, WHAT'S, UM--?
I, YEAH... I SLEPT HERE LAST NIGHT WHEN YOU CALLED ABOUT DAD--
WEB FLUID
WHO ARE YOU?

MOM.

BOY, DON'T YOU *LIE* TO ME.

NOT ONE MORE LIE. NOT EVEN A LITTLE ONE.

RIO, JUST-- JUST LET THE BOY--

LOOKING FOR CLUES TO WHERE MY SON AND HUSBAND HAVE MYSTERIOUSLY DISAPPEARED TO...

...I FOUND THAT. AND *THIS.*

THIS VERY STRANGE PHONE THAT I DIDN'T KNOW MY HUSBAND EVEN HAD.

SO STRANGE.

THEN I NOTICED IT DIDN'T HAVE A LOGO ON IT. NOT APPLE. NOT STARK.

AND OF COURSE IT'S *LOCKED,* SO I CAN'T SEE WHAT IT'S ACTUALLY *USED* FOR.

I WENT ONLINE AND FOUND OUT THIS IS NOT A PHONE THAT YOU CAN BUY.

MY HUSBAND HAS A PHONE THAT CANNOT BE PURCHASED.

WHERE WOULD MY HUSBAND GET A PHONE THAT CANNOT BE BOUGHT, BY HUMANS, ON THIS PLANET?

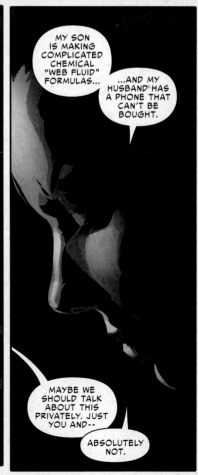

MY SON IS MAKING COMPLICATED CHEMICAL "WEB FLUID" FORMULAS...

...AND MY HUSBAND HAS A PHONE THAT CAN'T BE BOUGHT.

MAYBE WE SHOULD TALK ABOUT THIS PRIVATELY. JUST YOU AND--

ABSOLUTELY NOT.

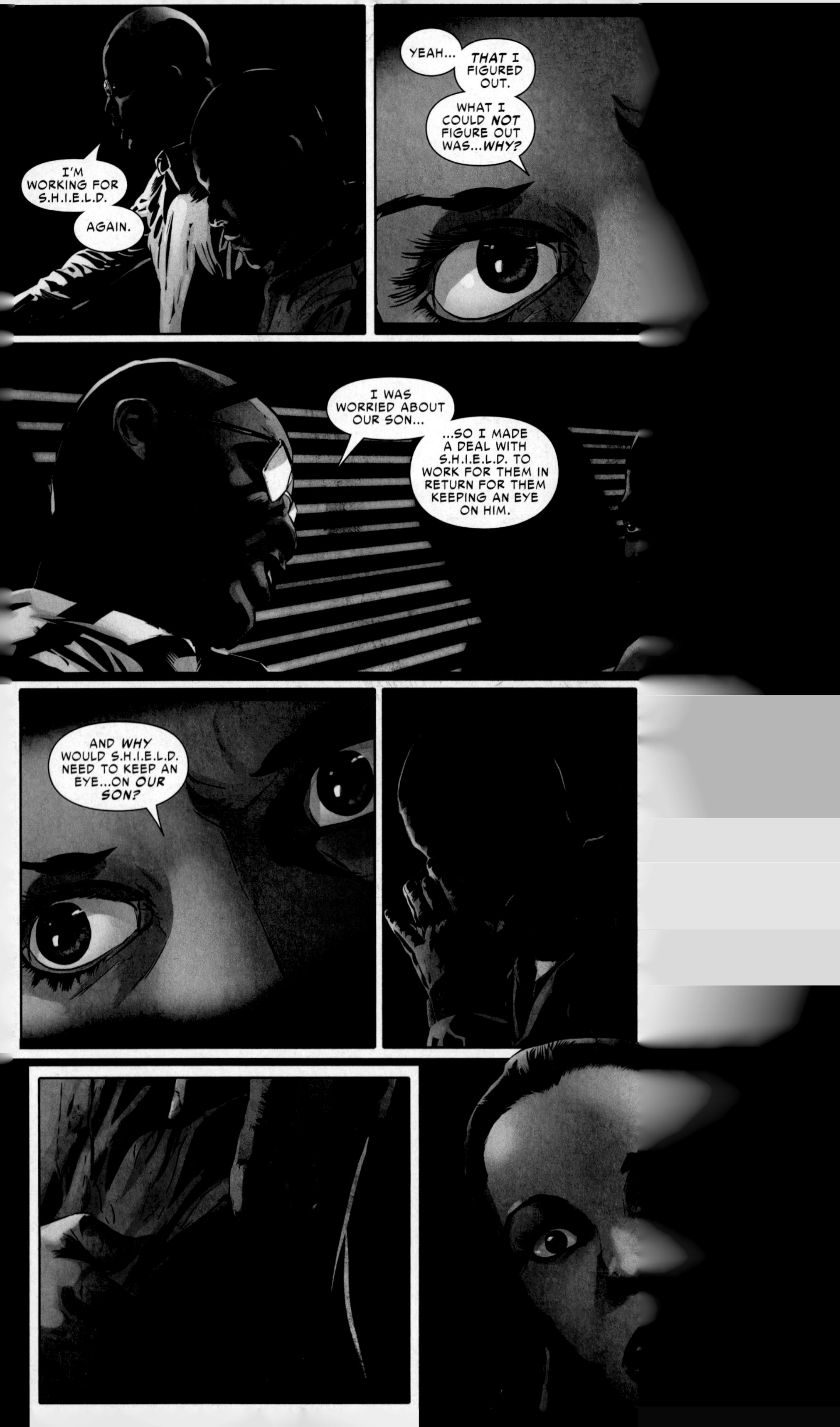
I'M WORKING FOR S.H.I.E.L.D.
AGAIN.
YEAH... THAT I FIGURED OUT.
WHAT I COULD NOT FIGURE OUT WAS...WHY?
I WAS WORRIED ABOUT OUR SON...
...SO I MADE A DEAL WITH S.H.I.E.L.D. TO WORK FOR THEM IN RETURN FOR THEM KEEPING AN EYE ON HIM.
AND WHY WOULD S.H.I.E.L.D. NEED TO KEEP AN EYE...ON OUR SON?

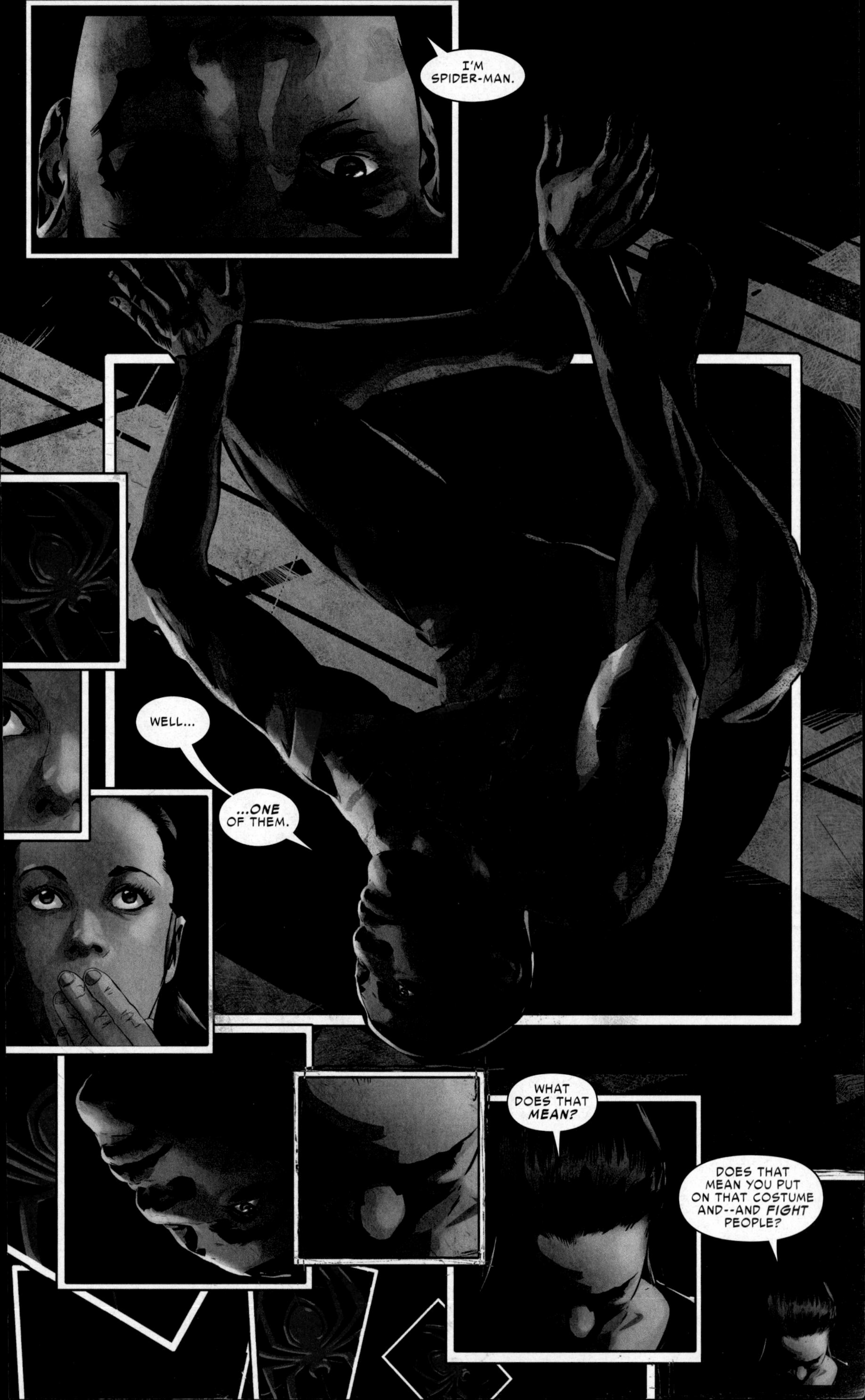
I'M SPIDER-MAN.
WELL...
...ONE OF THEM.
WHAT DOES THAT MEAN?
DOES THAT MEAN YOU PUT ON THAT COSTUME AND--AND FIGHT PEOPLE?

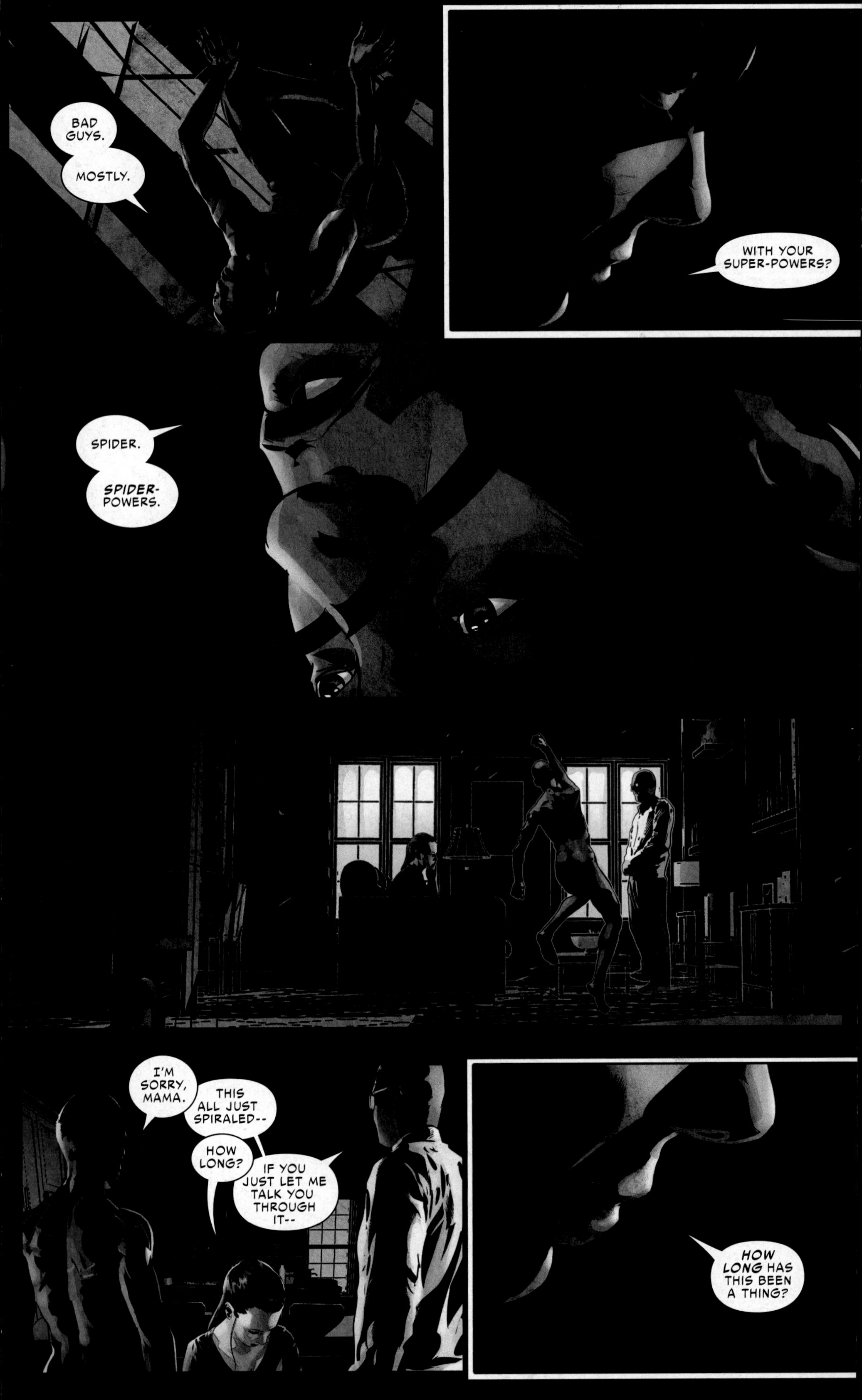

BAD GUYS.
MOSTLY.
WITH YOUR SUPER-POWERS?
SPIDER.
SPIDER-POWERS.
I'M SORRY, MAMA.
THIS ALL JUST SPIRALED--
HOW LONG?
IF YOU JUST LET ME TALK YOU THROUGH IT--
HOW LONG HAS THIS BEEN A THING?

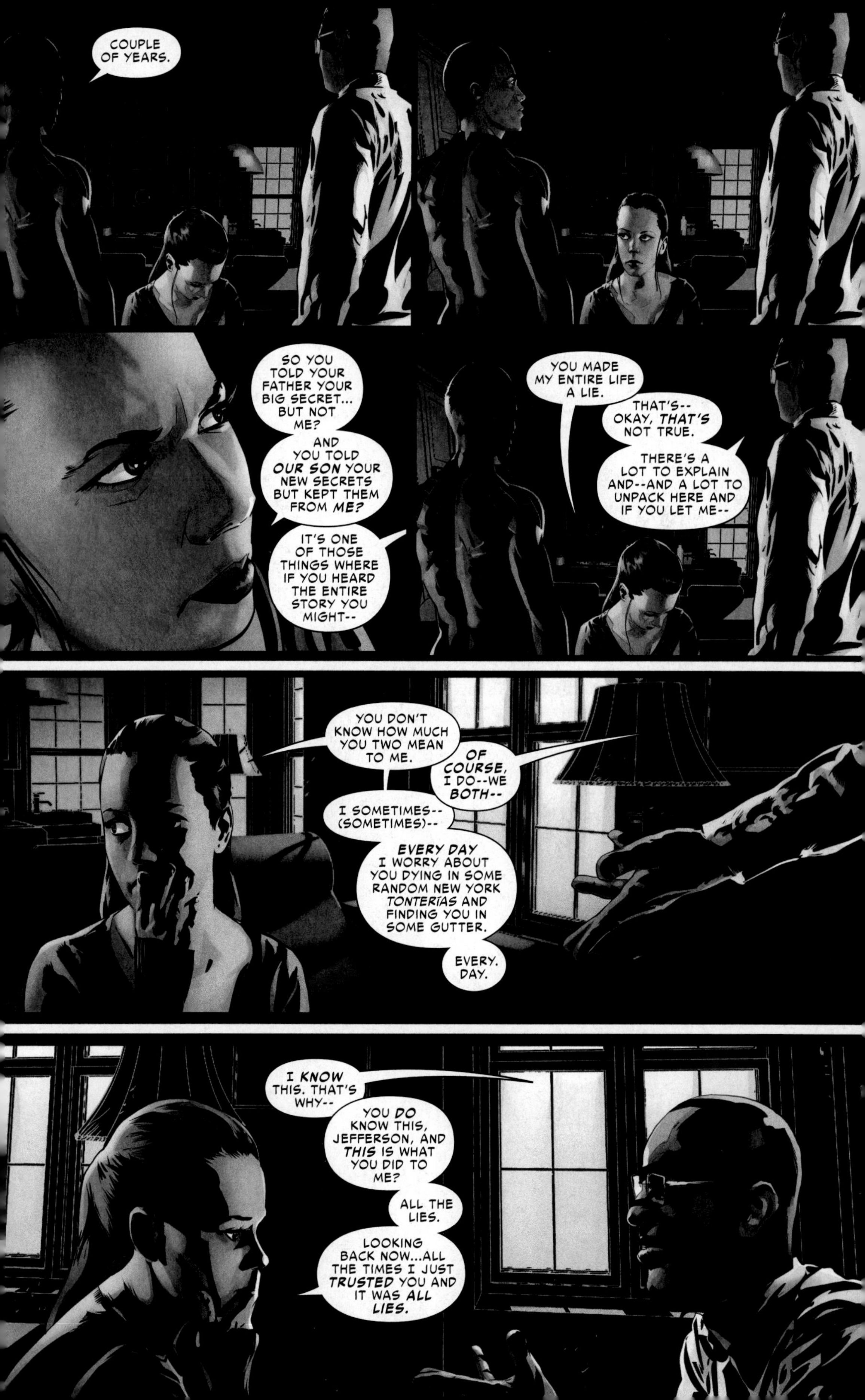
COUPLE OF YEARS.
SO YOU TOLD YOUR FATHER YOUR BIG SECRET... BUT NOT ME?
AND YOU TOLD *OUR SON* YOUR NEW SECRETS BUT KEPT THEM FROM *ME?*
IT'S ONE OF THOSE THINGS WHERE IF YOU HEARD THE ENTIRE STORY YOU MIGHT--
YOU MADE MY ENTIRE LIFE A LIE.
THAT'S-- OKAY, *THAT'S* NOT TRUE.
THERE'S A LOT TO EXPLAIN AND--AND A LOT TO UNPACK HERE AND IF YOU LET ME--
YOU DON'T KNOW HOW MUCH YOU TWO MEAN TO ME.
OF COURSE, I DO--WE *BOTH*--
I SOMETIMES-- (SOMETIMES)--
EVERY DAY I WORRY ABOUT YOU DYING IN SOME RANDOM NEW YORK *TONTERÍAS* AND FINDING YOU IN SOME GUTTER.
EVERY. DAY.
I *KNOW* THIS. THAT'S WHY--
YOU *DO* KNOW THIS, JEFFERSON, AND *THIS* IS WHAT YOU DID TO ME?
ALL THE LIES.
LOOKING BACK NOW...ALL THE TIMES I JUST *TRUSTED* YOU AND IT WAS *ALL LIES.*

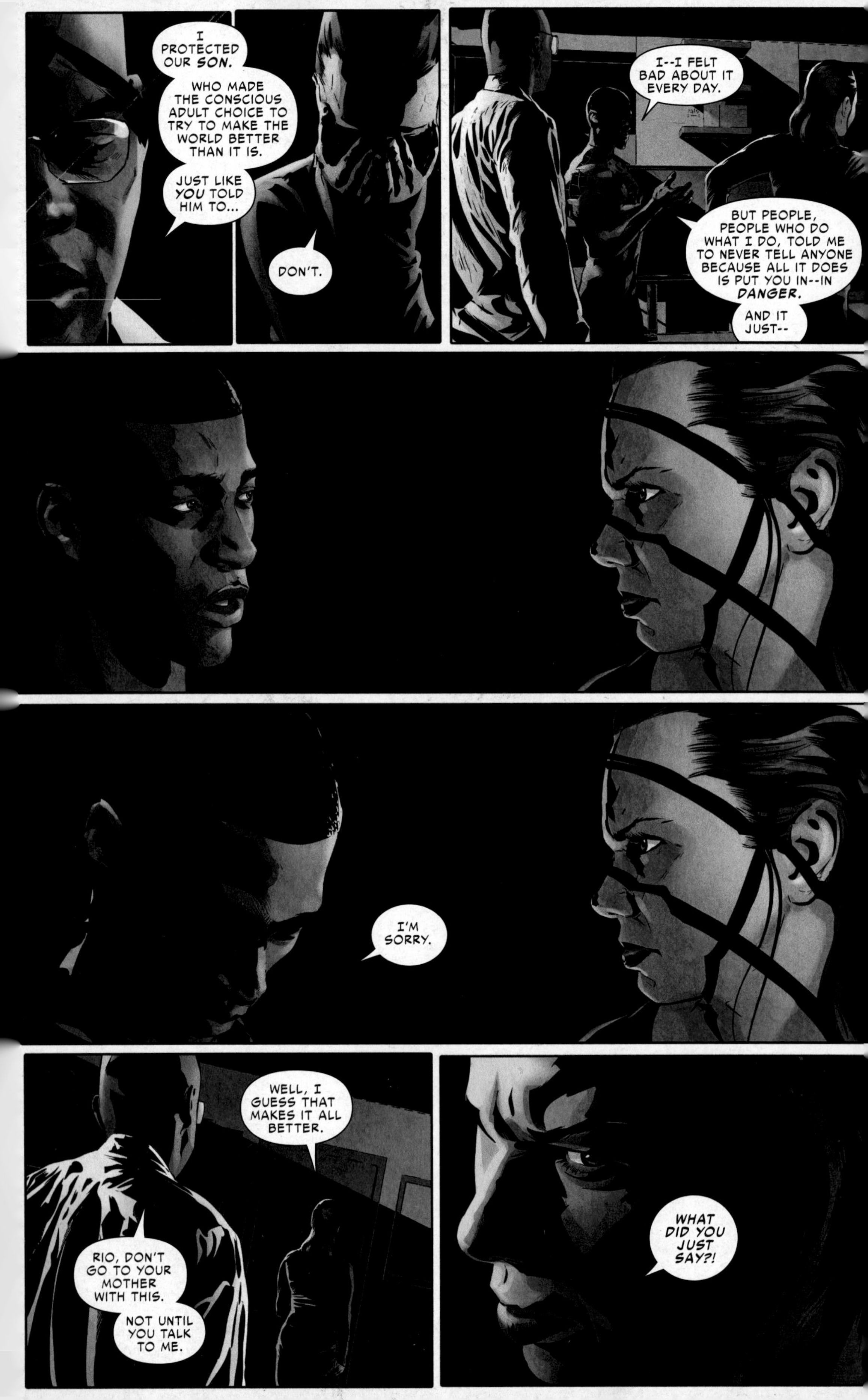
I PROTECTED OUR SON.
WHO MADE THE CONSCIOUS ADULT CHOICE TO TRY TO MAKE THE WORLD BETTER THAN IT IS.
JUST LIKE YOU TOLD HIM TO...
DON'T.
I--I FELT BAD ABOUT IT EVERY DAY.
BUT PEOPLE, PEOPLE WHO DO WHAT I DO, TOLD ME TO NEVER TELL ANYONE BECAUSE ALL IT DOES IS PUT YOU IN--IN DANGER.
AND IT JUST--
I'M SORRY.
WELL, I GUESS THAT MAKES IT ALL BETTER.
RIO, DON'T GO TO YOUR MOTHER WITH THIS.
NOT UNTIL YOU TALK TO ME.
WHAT DID YOU JUST SAY?!

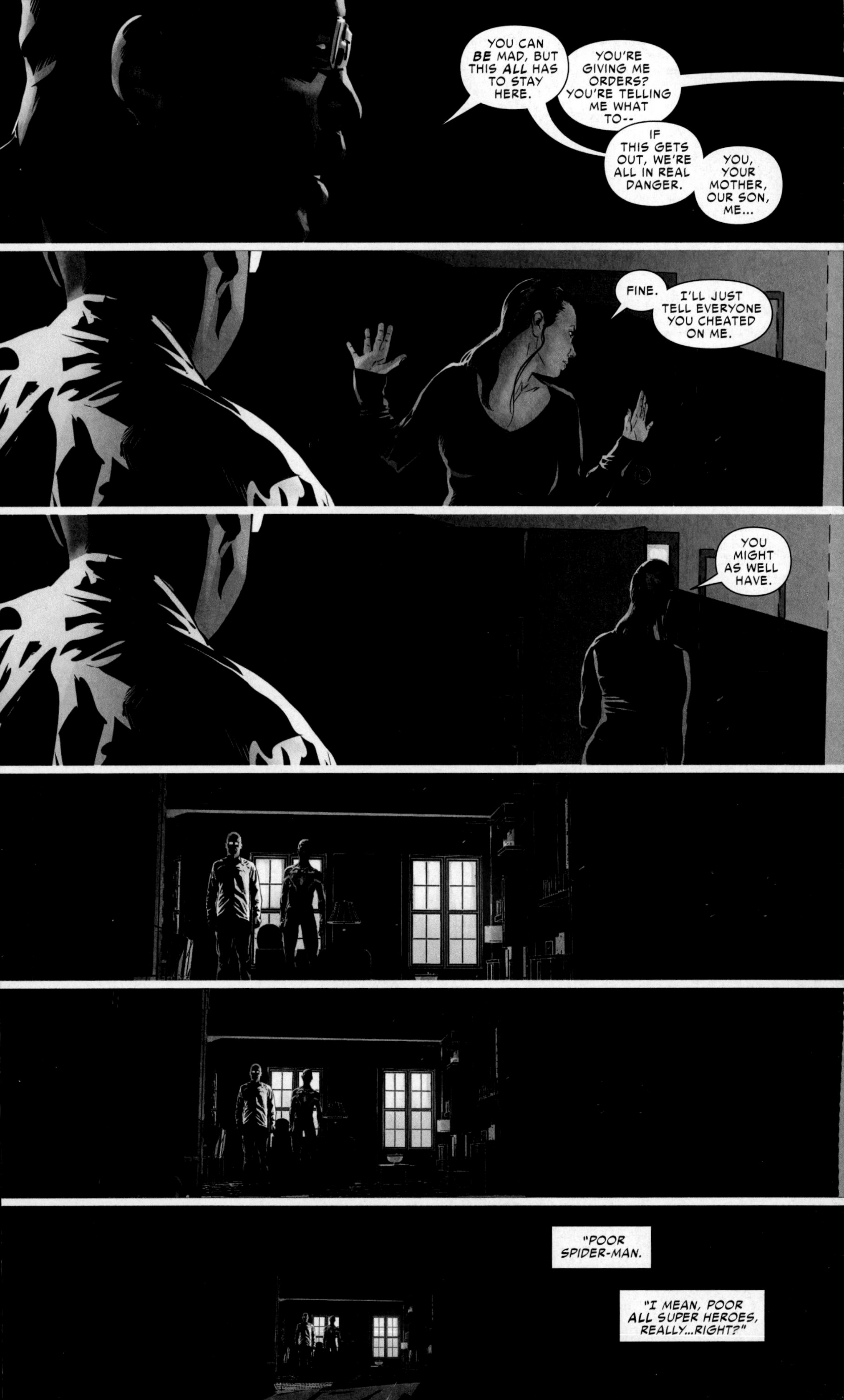
YOU CAN BE MAD, BUT THIS ALL HAS TO STAY HERE.
YOU'RE GIVING ME ORDERS? YOU'RE TELLING ME WHAT TO--
IF THIS GETS OUT, WE'RE ALL IN REAL DANGER.
YOU, YOUR MOTHER, OUR SON, ME...
FINE.
I'LL JUST TELL EVERYONE YOU CHEATED ON ME.
YOU MIGHT AS WELL HAVE.
"POOR SPIDER-MAN.
"I MEAN, POOR ALL SUPER HEROES, REALLY...RIGHT?"

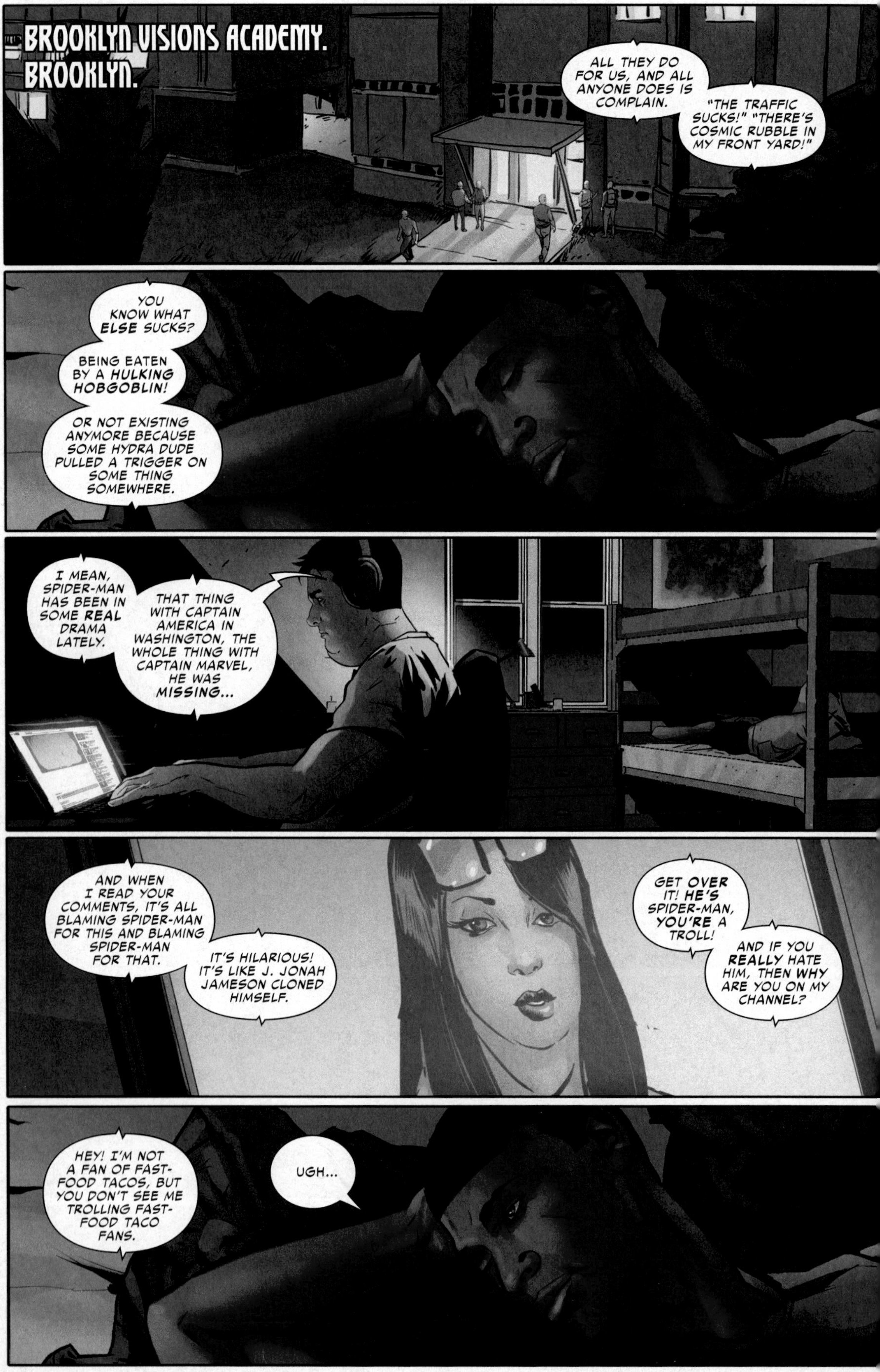
BROOKLYN VISIONS ACADEMY. BROOKLYN.
ALL THEY DO FOR US, AND ALL ANYONE DOES IS COMPLAIN.
"THE TRAFFIC SUCKS!" "THERE'S COSMIC RUBBLE IN MY FRONT YARD!"
YOU KNOW WHAT ELSE SUCKS?
BEING EATEN BY A HULKING HOBGOBLIN!
OR NOT EXISTING ANYMORE BECAUSE SOME HYDRA DUDE PULLED A TRIGGER ON SOME THING SOMEWHERE.
I MEAN, SPIDER-MAN HAS BEEN IN SOME REAL DRAMA LATELY.
THAT THING WITH CAPTAIN AMERICA IN WASHINGTON, THE WHOLE THING WITH CAPTAIN MARVEL, HE WAS MISSING...
AND WHEN I READ YOUR COMMENTS, IT'S ALL BLAMING SPIDER-MAN FOR THIS AND BLAMING SPIDER-MAN FOR THAT.
IT'S HILARIOUS! IT'S LIKE J. JONAH JAMESON CLONED HIMSELF.
GET OVER IT! HE'S SPIDER-MAN, YOU'RE A TROLL!
AND IF YOU REALLY HATE HIM, THEN WHY ARE YOU ON MY CHANNEL?
HEY! I'M NOT A FAN OF FAST-FOOD TACOS, BUT YOU DON'T SEE ME TROLLING FAST-FOOD TACO FANS.
UGH...

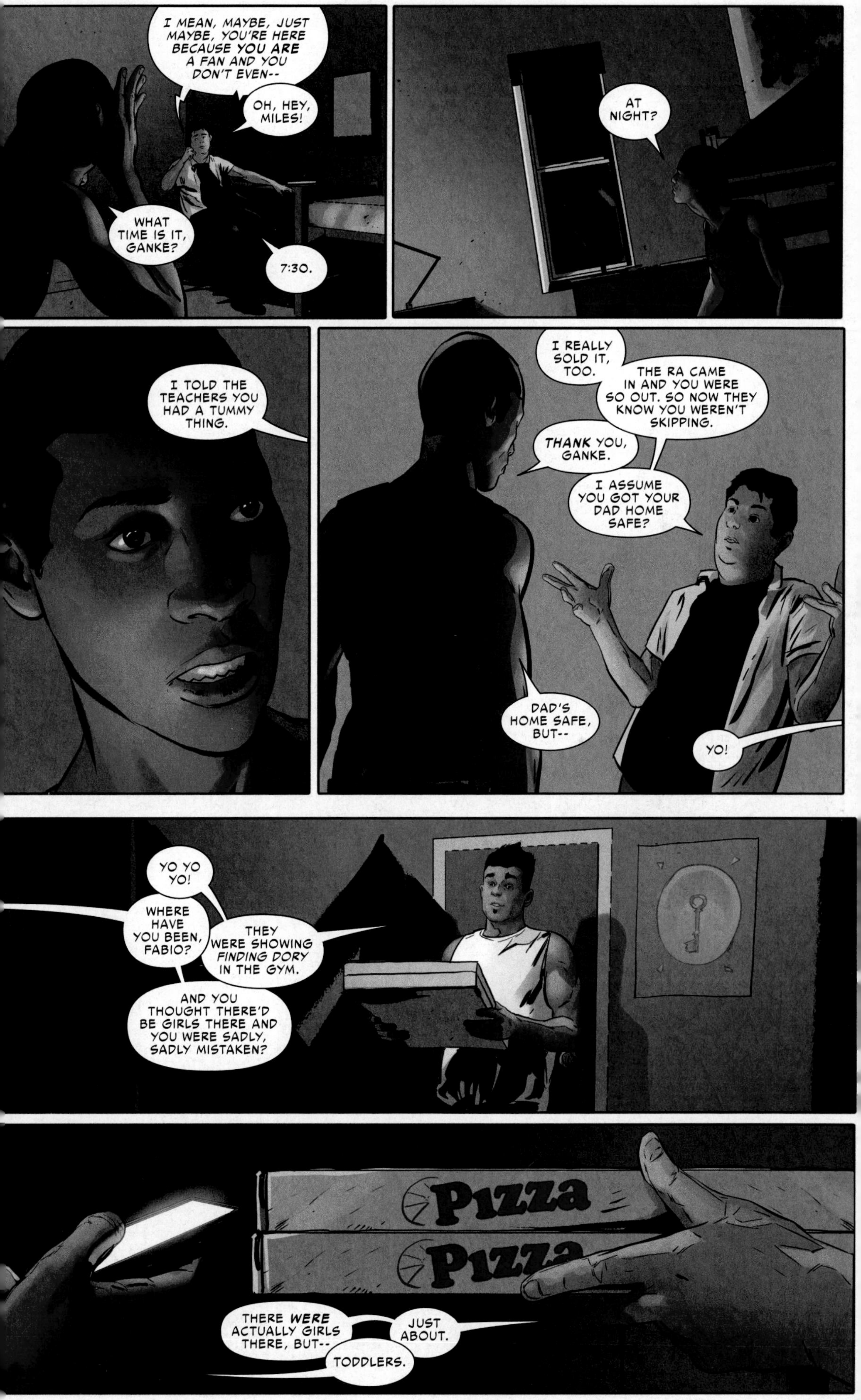

I MEAN, MAYBE, JUST MAYBE, YOU'RE HERE BECAUSE YOU ARE A FAN AND YOU DON'T EVEN--
OH, HEY, MILES!
WHAT TIME IS IT, GANKE?
7:30.
AT NIGHT?
I TOLD THE TEACHERS YOU HAD A TUMMY THING.
I REALLY SOLD IT, TOO.
THE RA CAME IN AND YOU WERE SO OUT. SO NOW THEY KNOW YOU WEREN'T SKIPPING.
THANK YOU, GANKE.
I ASSUME YOU GOT YOUR DAD HOME SAFE?
DAD'S HOME SAFE, BUT--
YO!
YO YO YO!
WHERE HAVE YOU BEEN, FABIO?
THEY WERE SHOWING FINDING DORY IN THE GYM.
AND YOU THOUGHT THERE'D BE GIRLS THERE AND YOU WERE SADLY, SADLY MISTAKEN?
PIZZA
PIZZA
THERE WERE ACTUALLY GIRLS THERE, BUT--
JUST ABOUT.
TODDLERS.

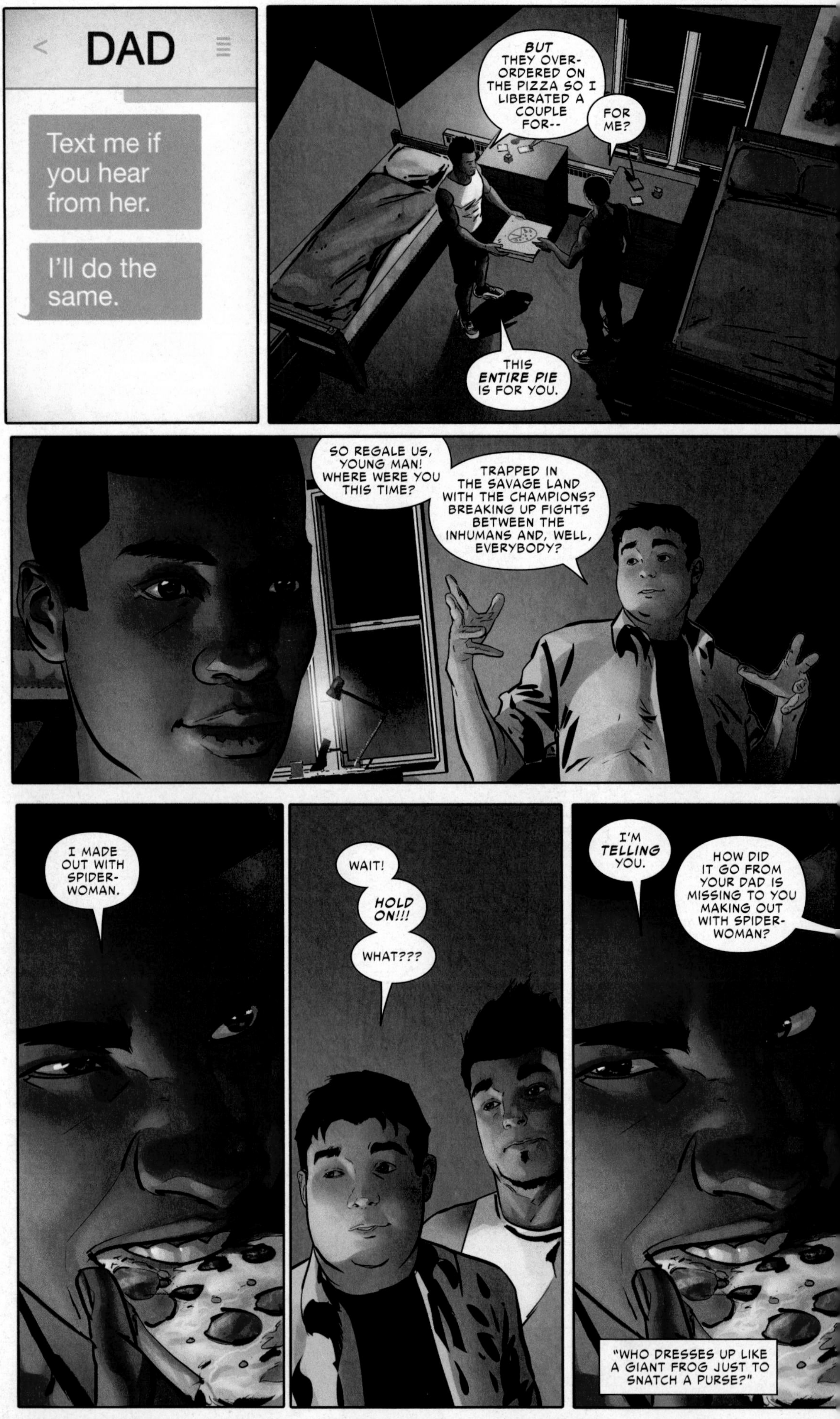
DAD
Text me if you hear from her.
I'll do the same.
BUT THEY OVER-ORDERED ON THE PIZZA SO I LIBERATED A COUPLE FOR--
FOR ME?
THIS ENTIRE PIE IS FOR YOU.
SO REGALE US, YOUNG MAN! WHERE WERE YOU THIS TIME?
TRAPPED IN THE SAVAGE LAND WITH THE CHAMPIONS? BREAKING UP FIGHTS BETWEEN THE INHUMANS AND, WELL, EVERYBODY?
I MADE OUT WITH SPIDER-WOMAN.
WAIT!
HOLD ON!!!
WHAT???
I'M TELLING YOU.
HOW DID IT GO FROM YOUR DAD IS MISSING TO YOU MAKING OUT WITH SPIDER-WOMAN?
"WHO DRESSES UP LIKE A GIANT FROG JUST TO SNATCH A PURSE?"

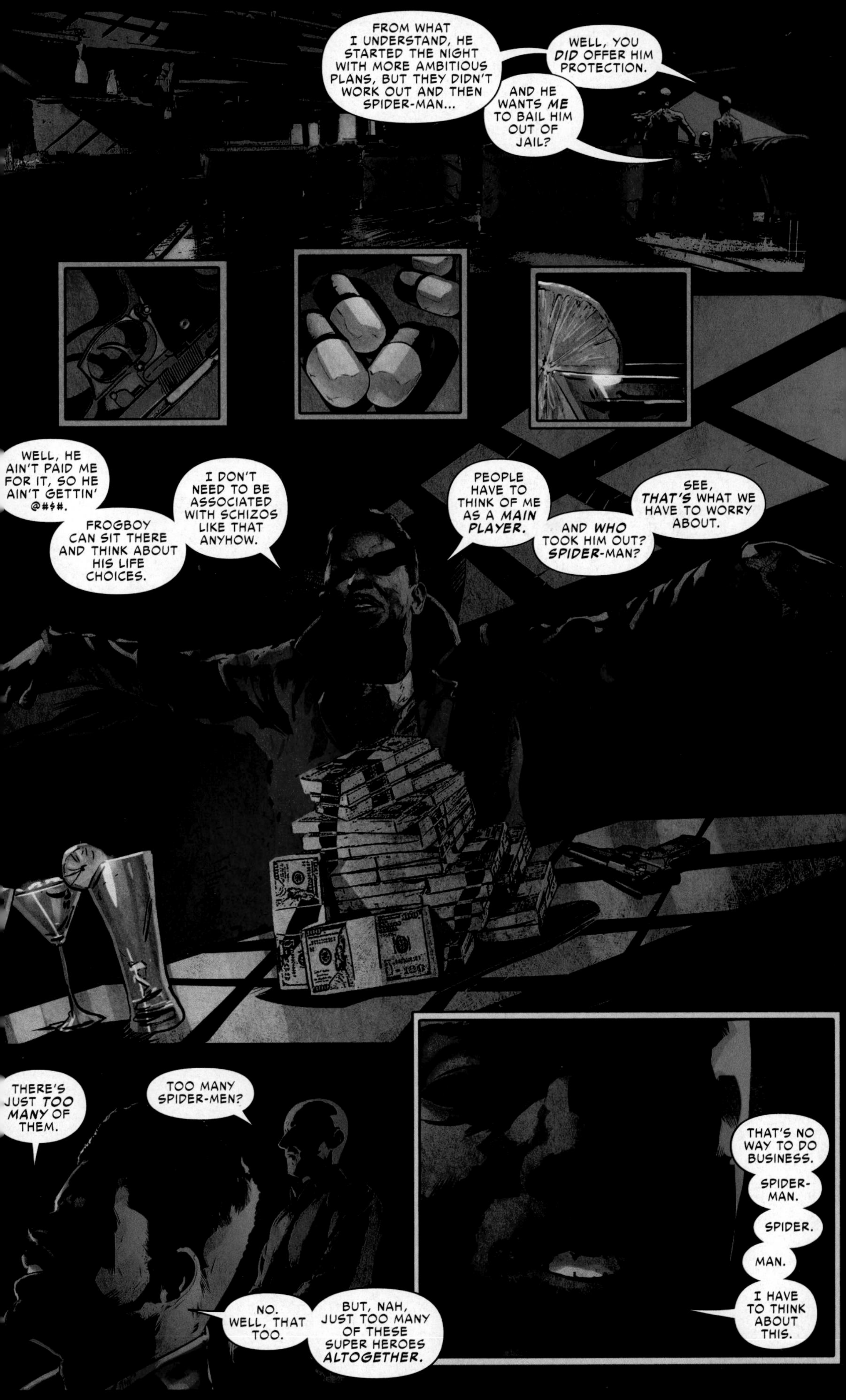
FROM WHAT I UNDERSTAND, HE STARTED THE NIGHT WITH MORE AMBITIOUS PLANS, BUT THEY DIDN'T WORK OUT AND THEN SPIDER-MAN...
WELL, YOU DID OFFER HIM PROTECTION.
AND HE WANTS ME TO BAIL HIM OUT OF JAIL?
WELL, HE AIN'T PAID ME FOR IT, SO HE AIN'T GETTIN' @#$#.
FROGBOY CAN SIT THERE AND THINK ABOUT HIS LIFE CHOICES.
I DON'T NEED TO BE ASSOCIATED WITH SCHIZOS LIKE THAT ANYHOW.
PEOPLE HAVE TO THINK OF ME AS A MAIN PLAYER.
AND WHO TOOK HIM OUT? SPIDER-MAN?
SEE, THAT'S WHAT WE HAVE TO WORRY ABOUT.
THERE'S JUST TOO MANY OF THEM.
TOO MANY SPIDER-MEN?
NO. WELL, THAT TOO.
BUT, NAH, JUST TOO MANY OF THESE SUPER HEROES ALTOGETHER.
THAT'S NO WAY TO DO BUSINESS.
SPIDER-MAN.
SPIDER.
MAN.
I HAVE TO THINK ABOUT THIS.

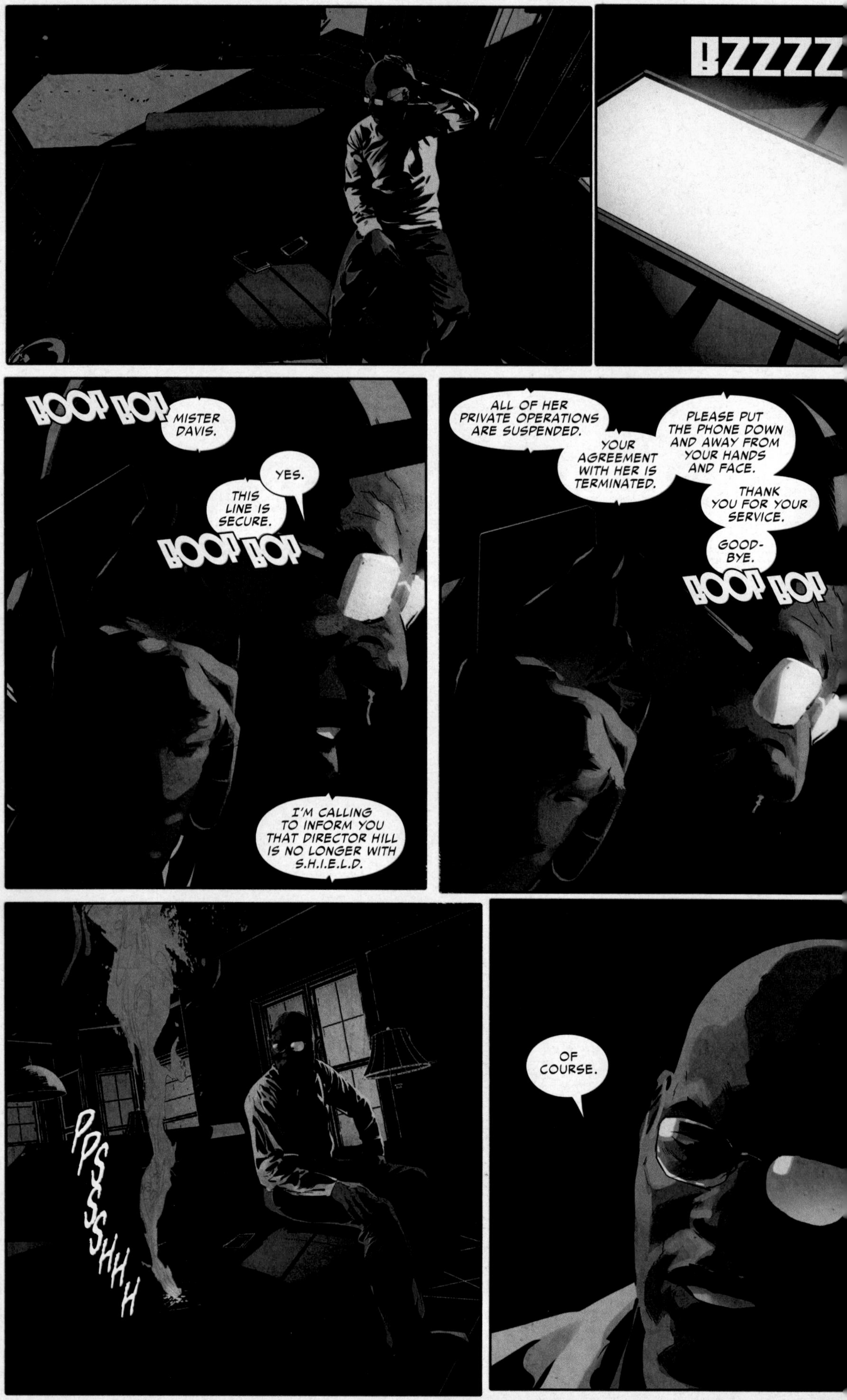
BZZZZ
BOOP BOP
MISTER DAVIS.
YES.
THIS LINE IS SECURE.
BOOP BOP
I'M CALLING TO INFORM YOU THAT DIRECTOR HILL IS NO LONGER WITH S.H.I.E.L.D.
ALL OF HER PRIVATE OPERATIONS ARE SUSPENDED.
YOUR AGREEMENT WITH HER IS TERMINATED.
PLEASE PUT THE PHONE DOWN AND AWAY FROM YOUR HANDS AND FACE.
THANK YOU FOR YOUR SERVICE.
GOOD-BYE.
BOOP BOP
PPSSSHHH
OF COURSE.

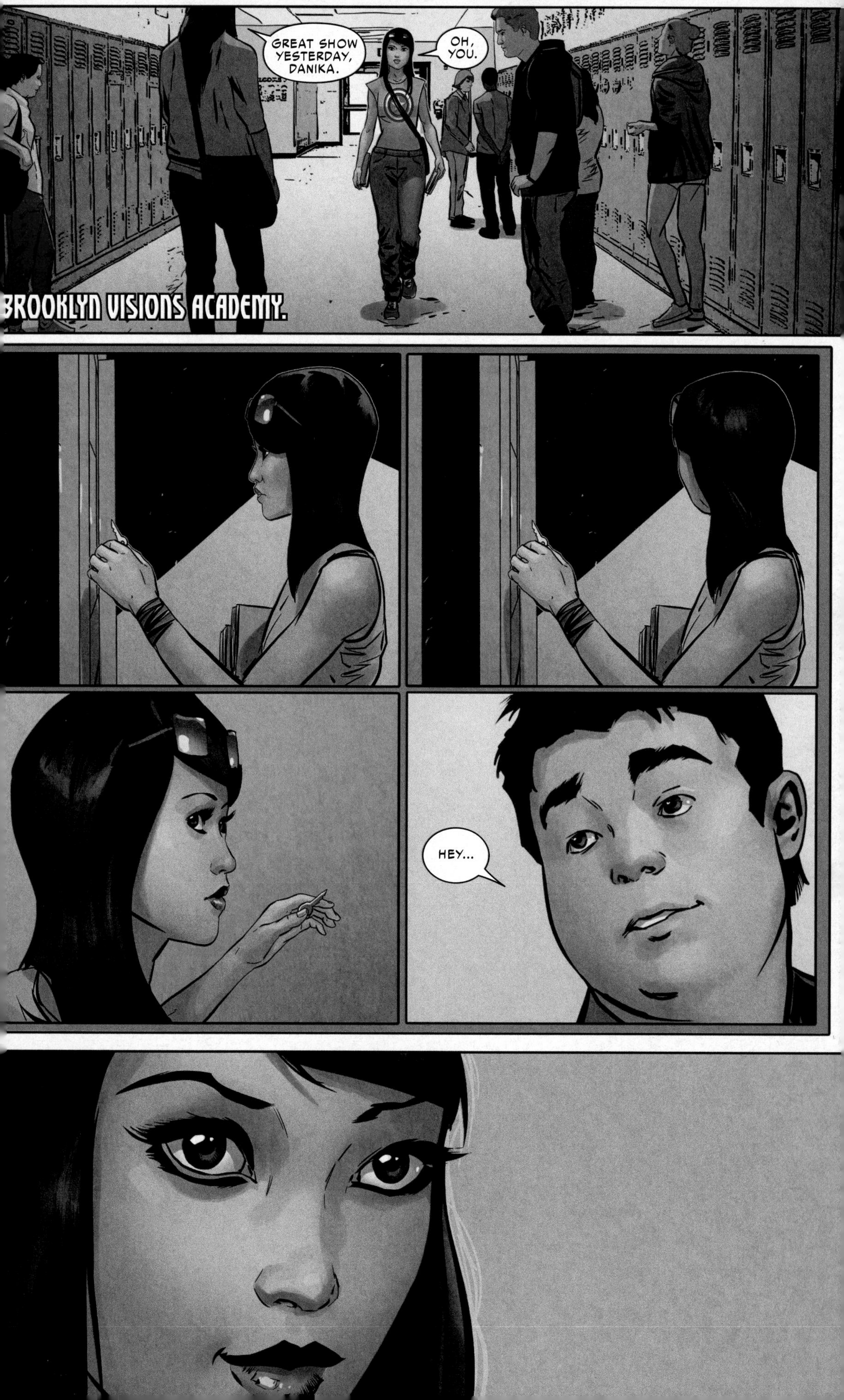
GREAT SHOW YESTERDAY, DANIKA.
OH, YOU.
BROOKLYN VISIONS ACADEMY.
HEY...

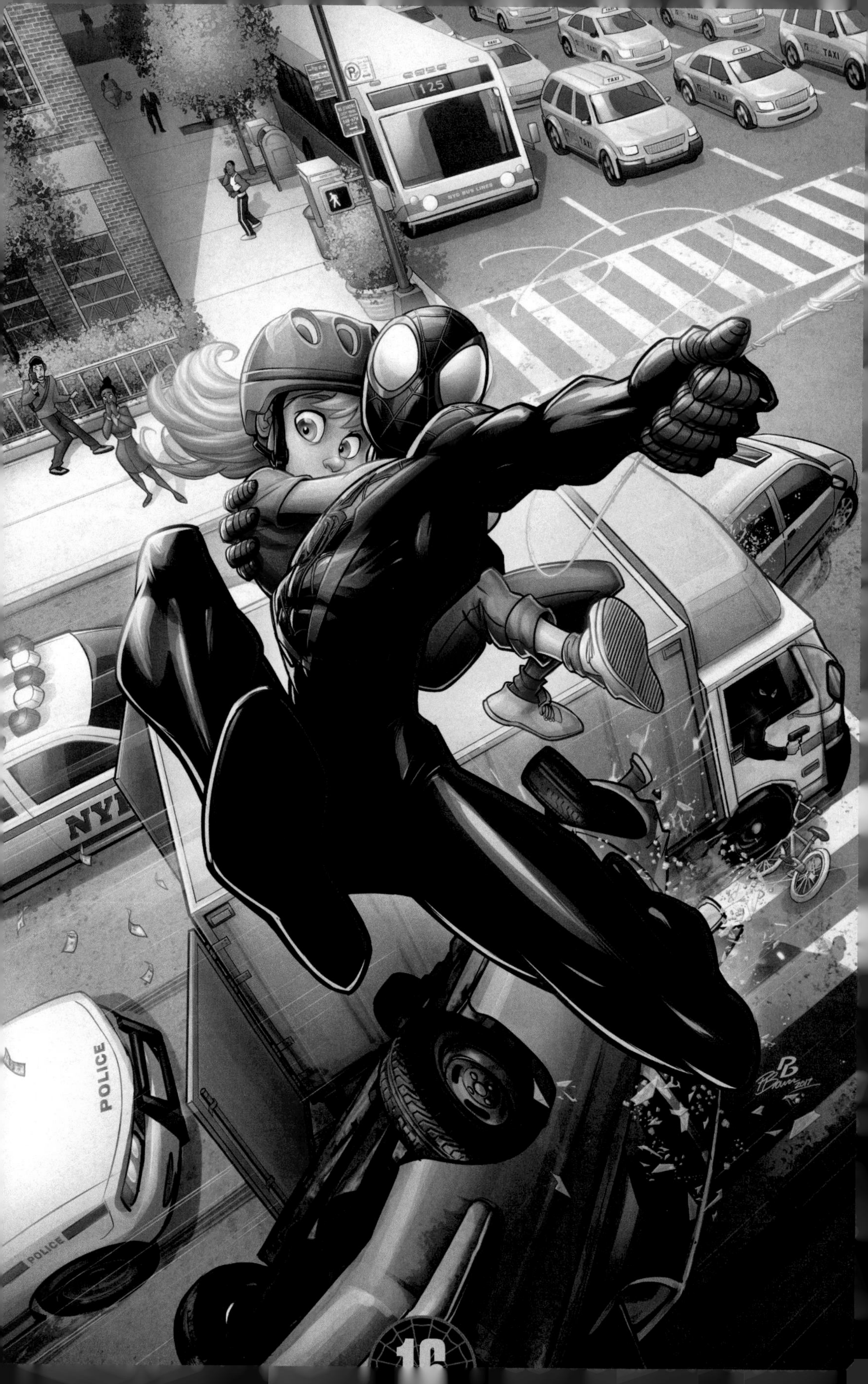
125
TAXI
NY
POLICE
POLICE

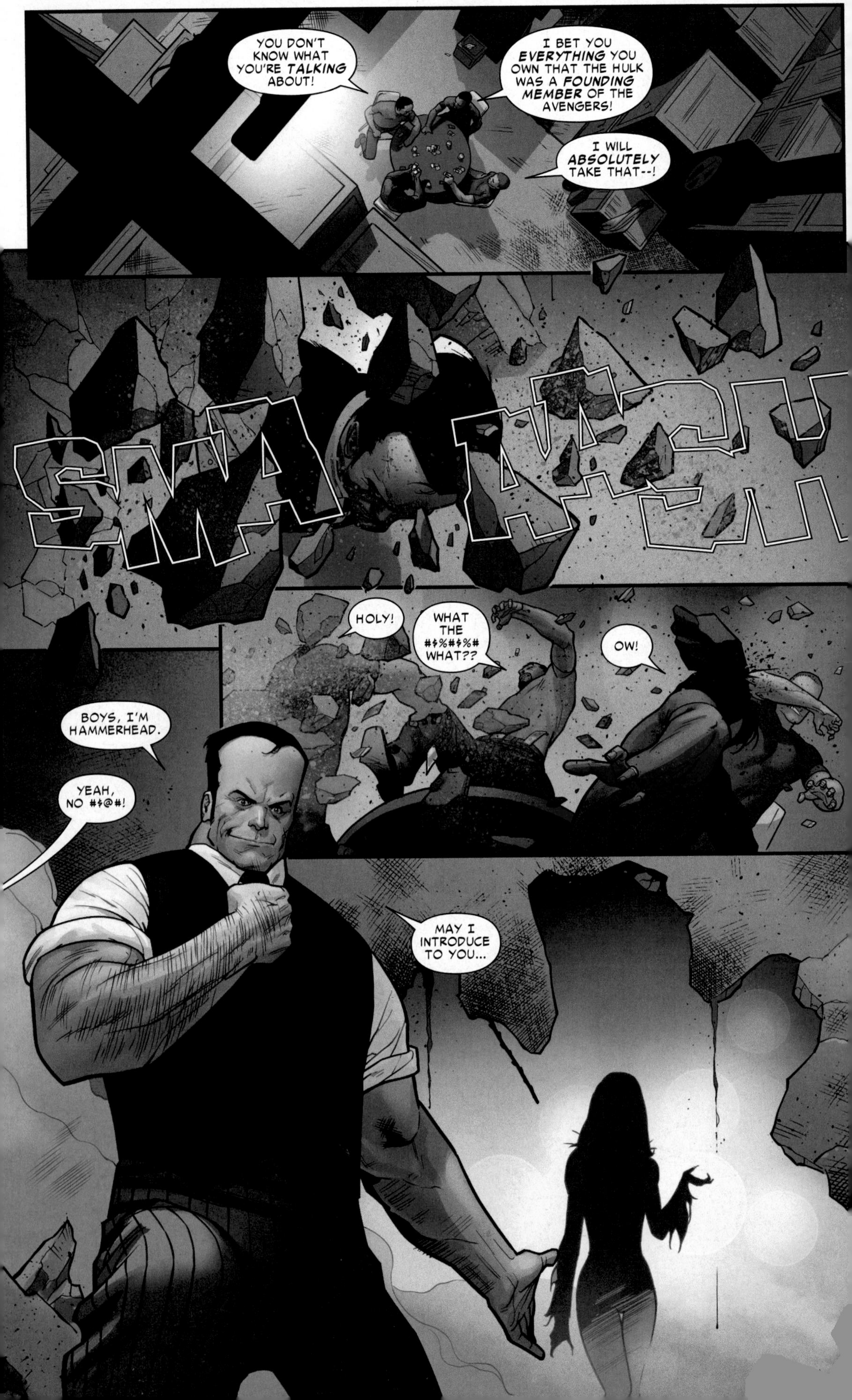
YOU DON'T KNOW WHAT YOU'RE TALKING ABOUT!
I BET YOU EVERYTHING YOU OWN THAT THE HULK WAS A FOUNDING MEMBER OF THE AVENGERS!
I WILL ABSOLUTELY TAKE THAT--!
SMASH
HOLY!
WHAT THE #$%#$%# WHAT??
OW!
BOYS, I'M HAMMERHEAD.
YEAH, NO #$@#!
MAY I INTRODUCE TO YOU...

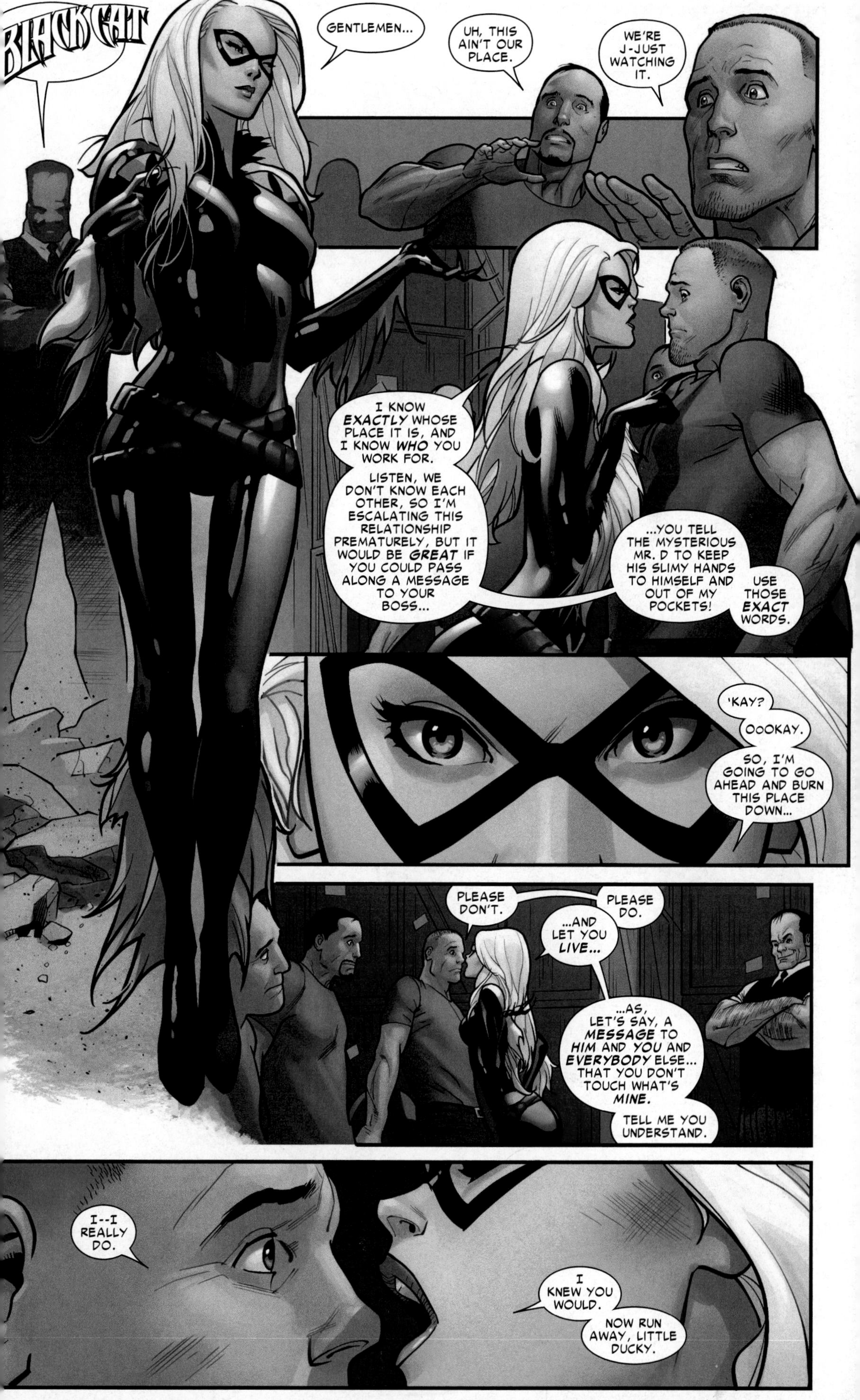
BLACK CAT
GENTLEMEN...
UH, THIS AIN'T OUR PLACE.
WE'RE J-JUST WATCHING IT.
I KNOW EXACTLY WHOSE PLACE IT IS, AND I KNOW WHO YOU WORK FOR.
LISTEN, WE DON'T KNOW EACH OTHER, SO I'M ESCALATING THIS RELATIONSHIP PREMATURELY, BUT IT WOULD BE GREAT IF YOU COULD PASS ALONG A MESSAGE TO YOUR BOSS...
...YOU TELL THE MYSTERIOUS MR. D TO KEEP HIS SLIMY HANDS TO HIMSELF AND OUT OF MY POCKETS!
USE THOSE EXACT WORDS.
'KAY?
OOOKAY.
SO, I'M GOING TO GO AHEAD AND BURN THIS PLACE DOWN...
PLEASE DON'T.
PLEASE DO.
...AND LET YOU LIVE...
...AS, LET'S SAY, A MESSAGE TO HIM AND YOU AND EVERYBODY ELSE... THAT YOU DON'T TOUCH WHAT'S MINE.
TELL ME YOU UNDERSTAND.
I--I REALLY DO.
I KNEW YOU WOULD.
NOW RUN AWAY, LITTLE DUCKY.

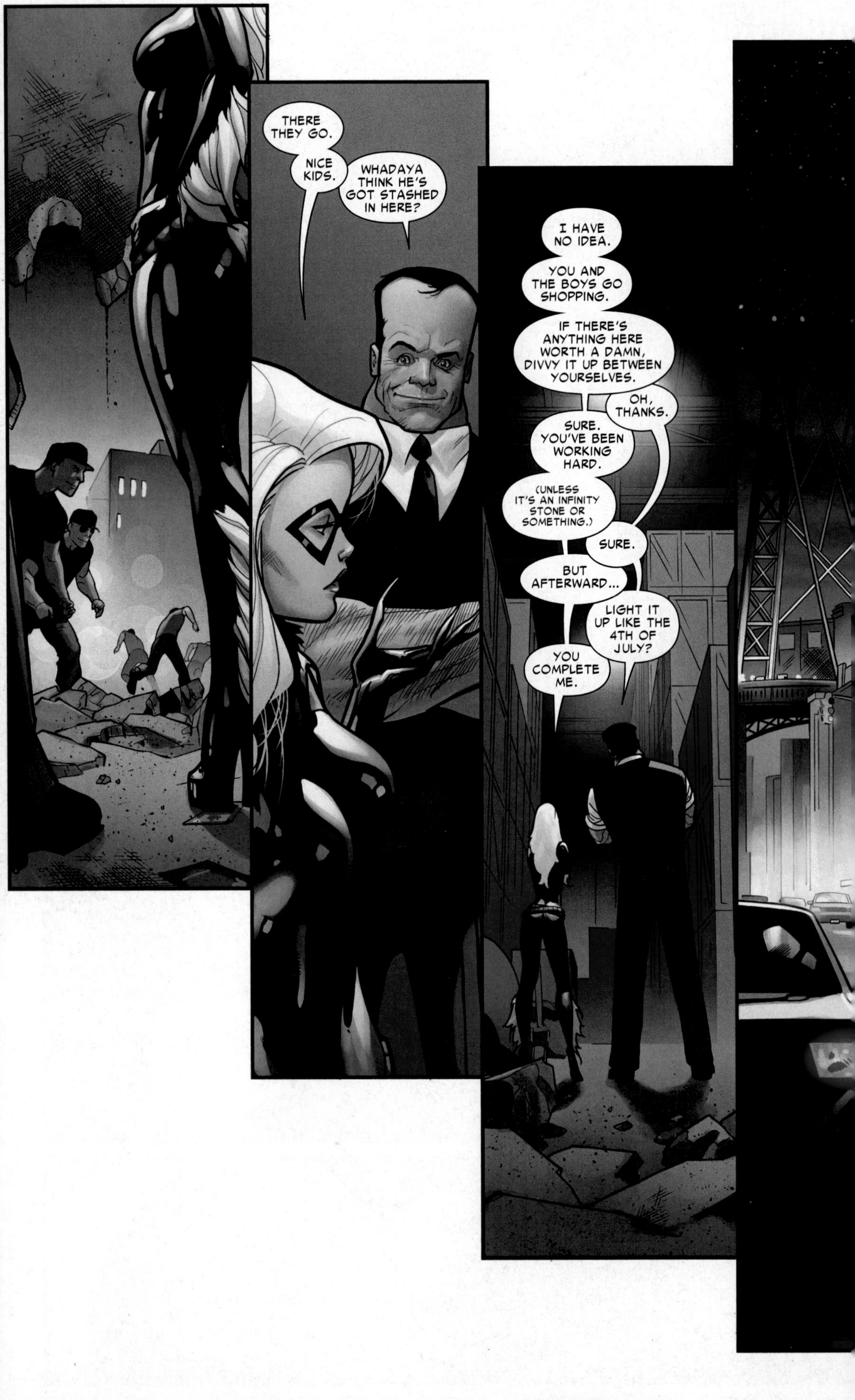
THERE THEY GO.
NICE KIDS.
WHADAYA THINK HE'S GOT STASHED IN HERE?
I HAVE NO IDEA.
YOU AND THE BOYS GO SHOPPING.
IF THERE'S ANYTHING HERE WORTH A DAMN, DIVVY IT UP BETWEEN YOURSELVES.
OH, THANKS.
SURE. YOU'VE BEEN WORKING HARD.
(UNLESS IT'S AN INFINITY STONE OR SOMETHING.)
SURE.
BUT AFTERWARD...
LIGHT IT UP LIKE THE 4TH OF JULY?
YOU COMPLETE ME.

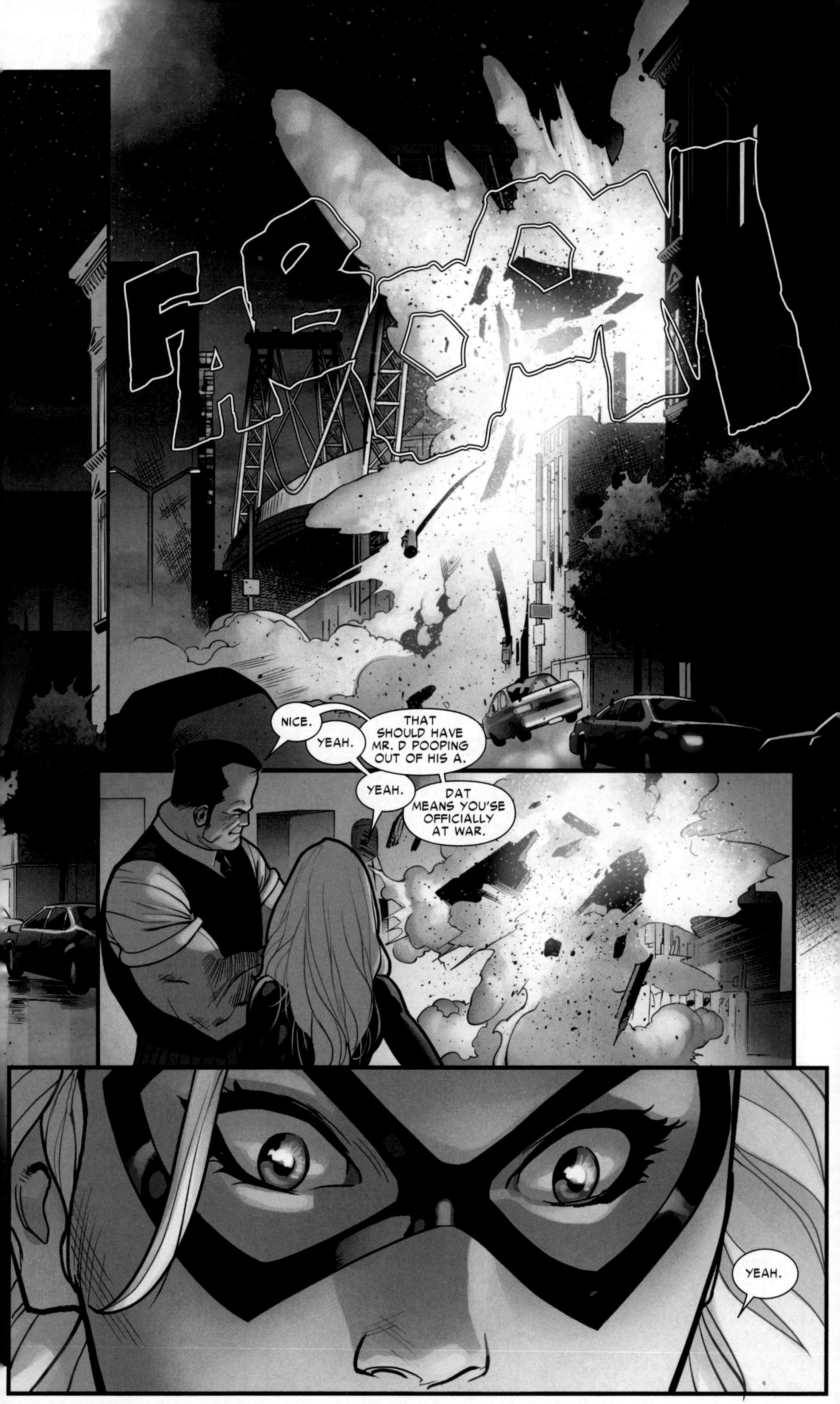
FRA-BOOM
NICE.
YEAH.
THAT SHOULD HAVE MR. D POOPING OUT OF HIS A.
YEAH.
DAT MEANS YOU'SE OFFICIALLY AT WAR.
YEAH.

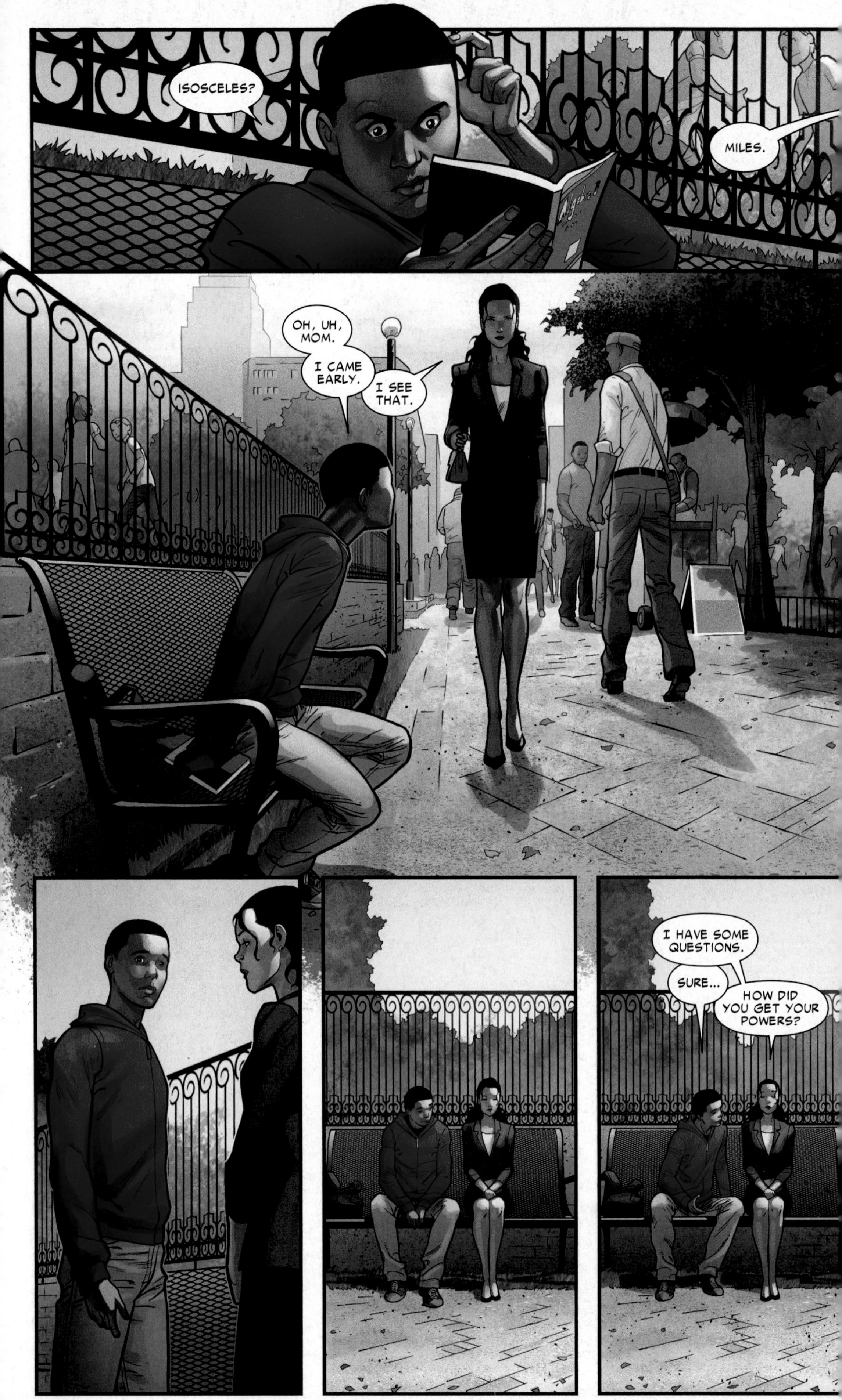
ISOSCELES?
MILES.
OH, UH, MOM.
I CAME EARLY.
I SEE THAT.
I HAVE SOME QUESTIONS.
SURE...
HOW DID YOU GET YOUR POWERS?

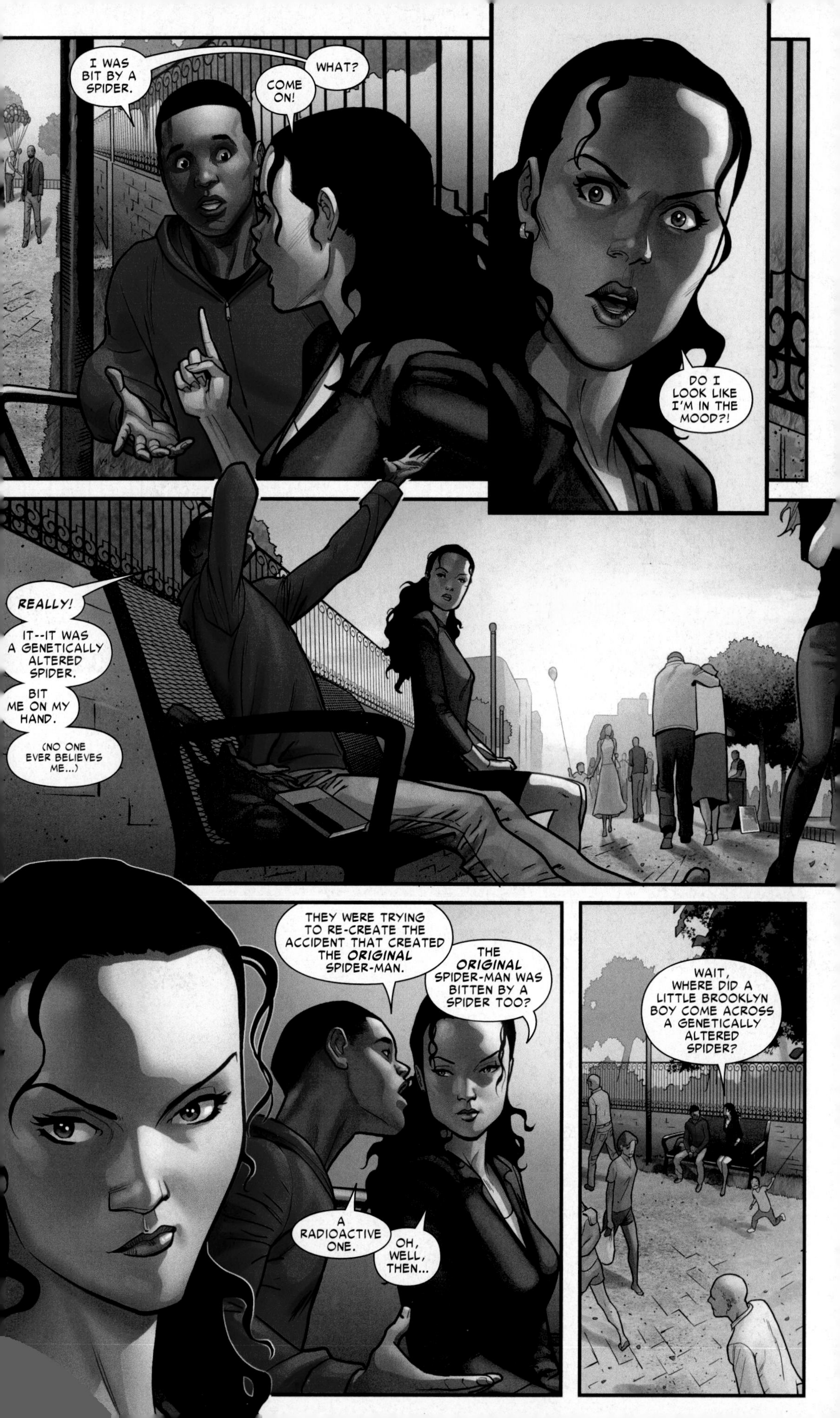
I WAS BIT BY A SPIDER.
WHAT?
COME ON!
DO I LOOK LIKE I'M IN THE MOOD?!
REALLY!
IT--IT WAS A GENETICALLY ALTERED SPIDER.
BIT ME ON MY HAND.
(NO ONE EVER BELIEVES ME...)
THEY WERE TRYING TO RE-CREATE THE ACCIDENT THAT CREATED THE *ORIGINAL* SPIDER-MAN.
THE *ORIGINAL* SPIDER-MAN WAS BITTEN BY A SPIDER TOO?
A RADIOACTIVE ONE.
OH, WELL, THEN...
WAIT, WHERE DID A LITTLE BROOKLYN BOY COME ACROSS A GENETICALLY ALTERED SPIDER?

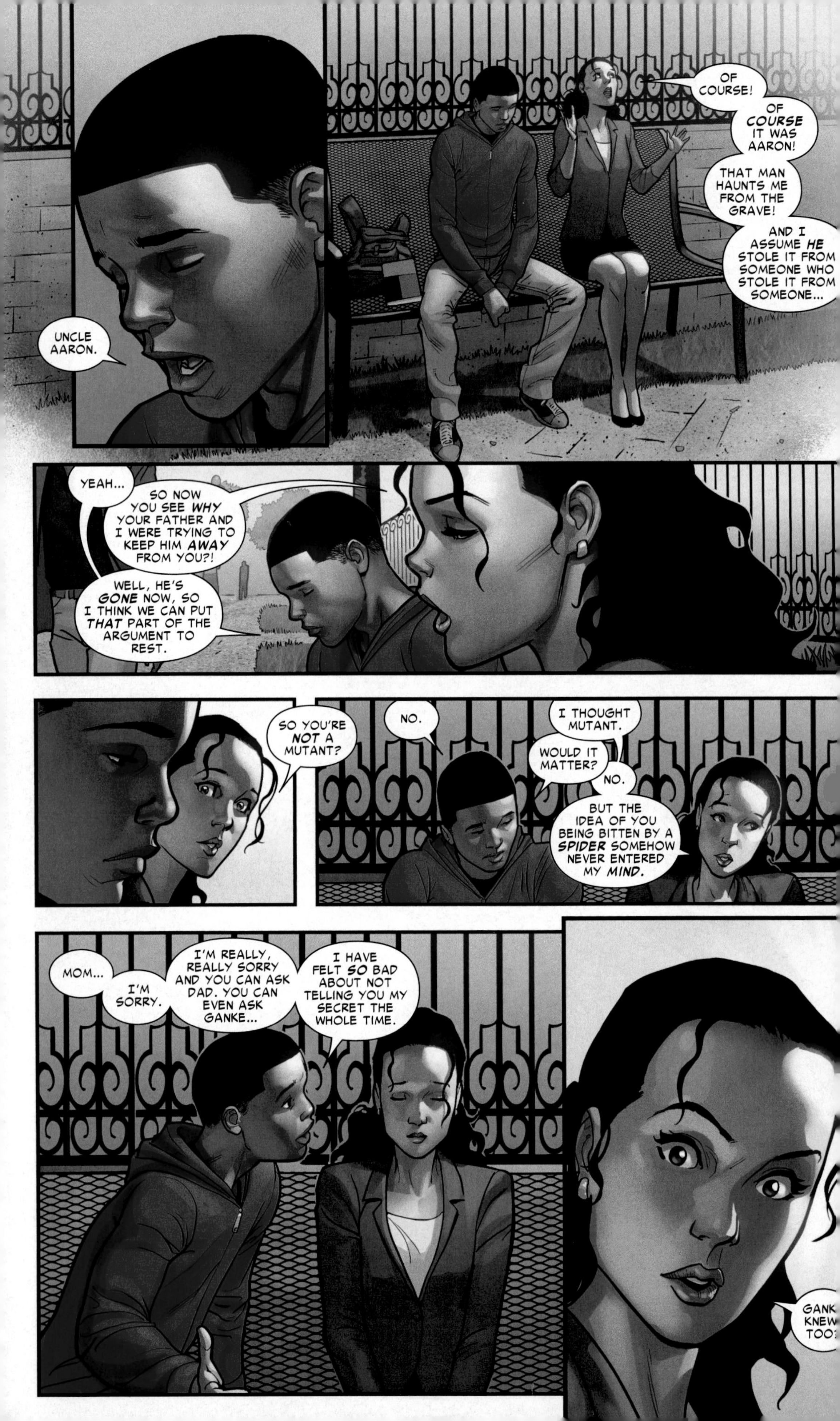
UNCLE AARON.
OF COURSE!
OF COURSE IT WAS AARON!
THAT MAN HAUNTS ME FROM THE GRAVE!
AND I ASSUME HE STOLE IT FROM SOMEONE WHO STOLE IT FROM SOMEONE...
YEAH...
SO NOW YOU SEE WHY YOUR FATHER AND I WERE TRYING TO KEEP HIM AWAY FROM YOU?!
WELL, HE'S GONE NOW, SO I THINK WE CAN PUT THAT PART OF THE ARGUMENT TO REST.
SO YOU'RE NOT A MUTANT?
NO.
I THOUGHT MUTANT.
WOULD IT MATTER?
NO.
BUT THE IDEA OF YOU BEING BITTEN BY A SPIDER SOMEHOW NEVER ENTERED MY MIND.
MOM...
I'M SORRY.
I'M REALLY, REALLY SORRY AND YOU CAN ASK DAD. YOU CAN EVEN ASK GANKE...
I HAVE FELT SO BAD ABOUT NOT TELLING YOU MY SECRET THE WHOLE TIME.
GANK KNEW TOO

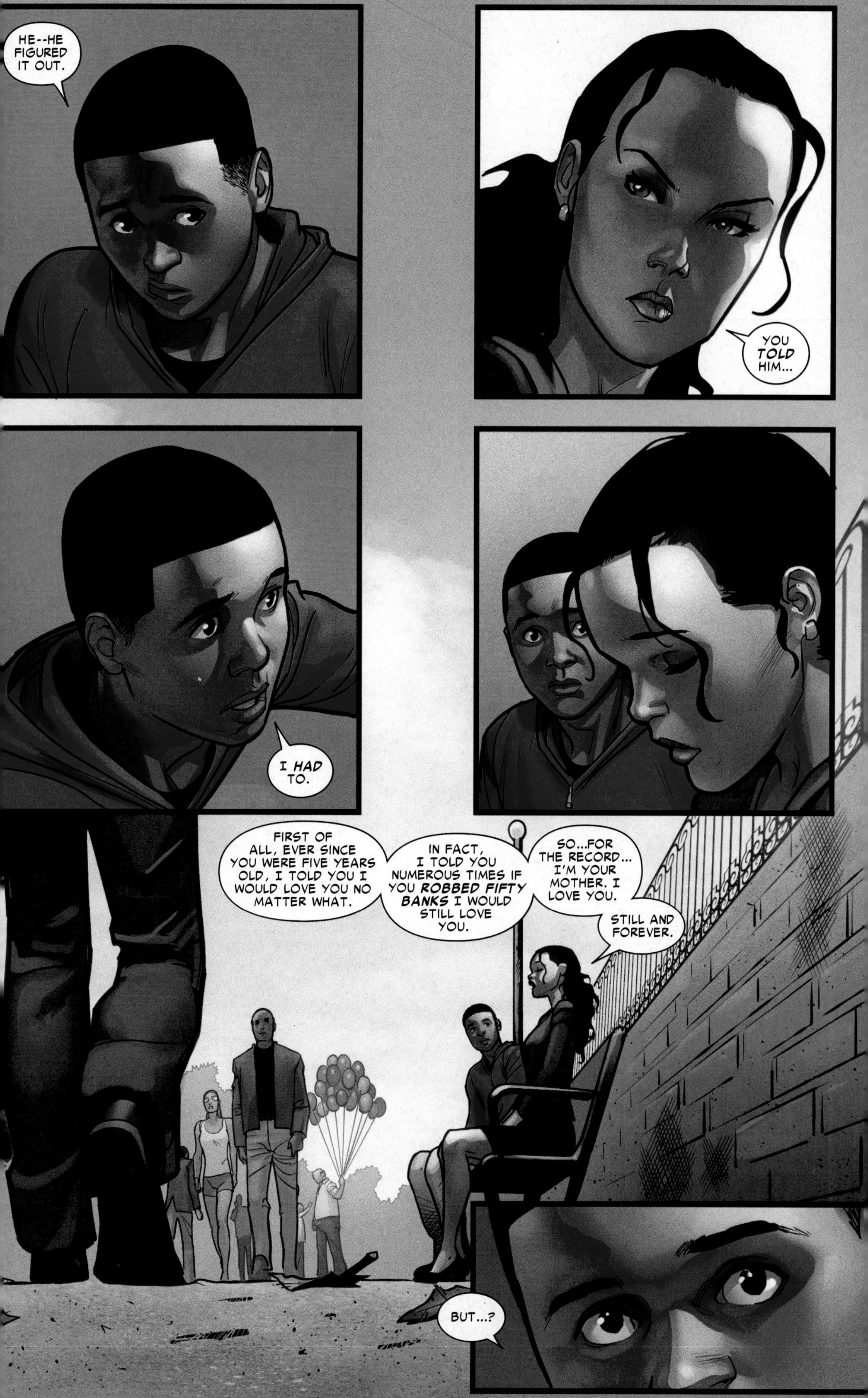
HE--HE FIGURED IT OUT.
YOU TOLD HIM...
I HAD TO.
FIRST OF ALL, EVER SINCE YOU WERE FIVE YEARS OLD, I TOLD YOU I WOULD LOVE YOU NO MATTER WHAT.
IN FACT, I TOLD YOU NUMEROUS TIMES IF YOU ROBBED FIFTY BANKS I WOULD STILL LOVE YOU.
SO...FOR THE RECORD... I'M YOUR MOTHER. I LOVE YOU.
STILL AND FOREVER.
BUT...?

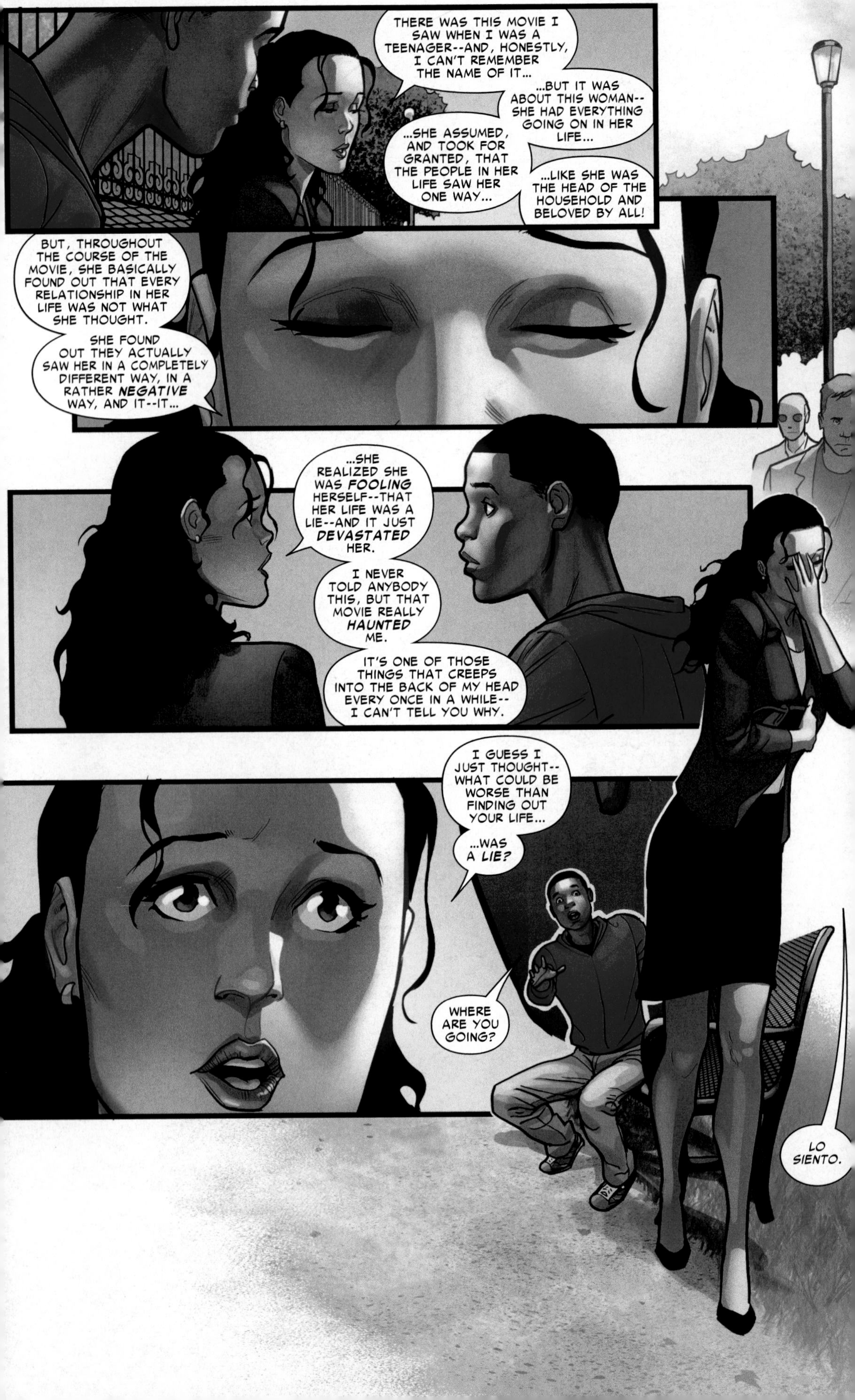

THERE WAS THIS MOVIE I SAW WHEN I WAS A TEENAGER--AND, HONESTLY, I CAN'T REMEMBER THE NAME OF IT...
...BUT IT WAS ABOUT THIS WOMAN--SHE HAD EVERYTHING GOING ON IN HER LIFE...
...LIKE SHE WAS THE HEAD OF THE HOUSEHOLD AND BELOVED BY ALL!
...SHE ASSUMED, AND TOOK FOR GRANTED, THAT THE PEOPLE IN HER LIFE SAW HER ONE WAY...
BUT, THROUGHOUT THE COURSE OF THE MOVIE, SHE BASICALLY FOUND OUT THAT EVERY RELATIONSHIP IN HER LIFE WAS NOT WHAT SHE THOUGHT.
SHE FOUND OUT THEY ACTUALLY SAW HER IN A COMPLETELY DIFFERENT WAY, IN A RATHER *NEGATIVE* WAY, AND IT--IT...
...SHE REALIZED SHE WAS *FOOLING* HERSELF--THAT HER LIFE WAS A LIE--AND IT JUST *DEVASTATED* HER.
I NEVER TOLD ANYBODY THIS, BUT THAT MOVIE REALLY *HAUNTED* ME.
IT'S ONE OF THOSE THINGS THAT CREEPS INTO THE BACK OF MY HEAD EVERY ONCE IN A WHILE--I CAN'T TELL YOU WHY.
I GUESS I JUST THOUGHT--WHAT COULD BE WORSE THAN FINDING OUT YOUR LIFE...
...WAS A *LIE?*
WHERE ARE YOU GOING?
LO SIENTO.

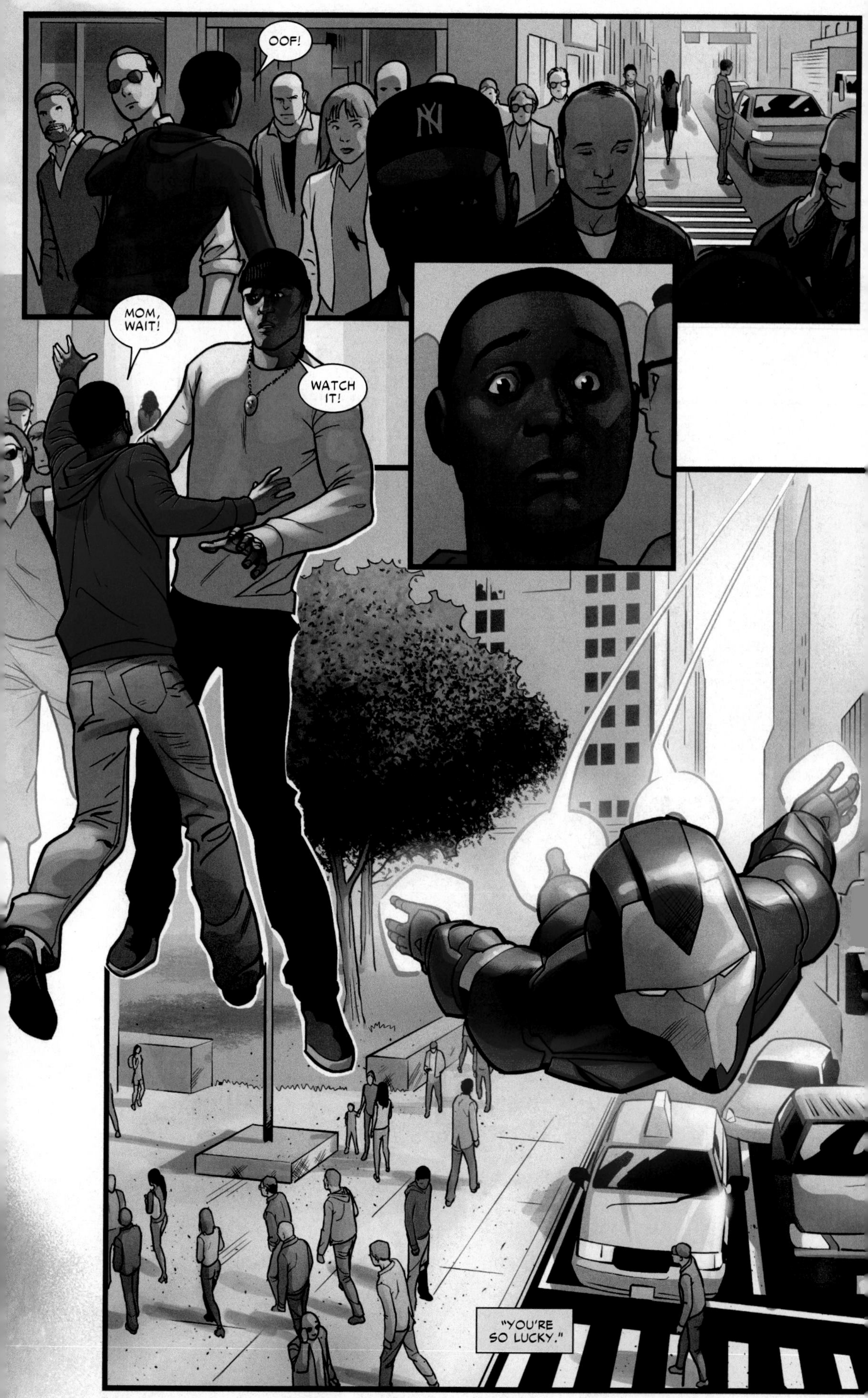
OOF!
MOM, WAIT!
WATCH IT!
"YOU'RE SO LUCKY."

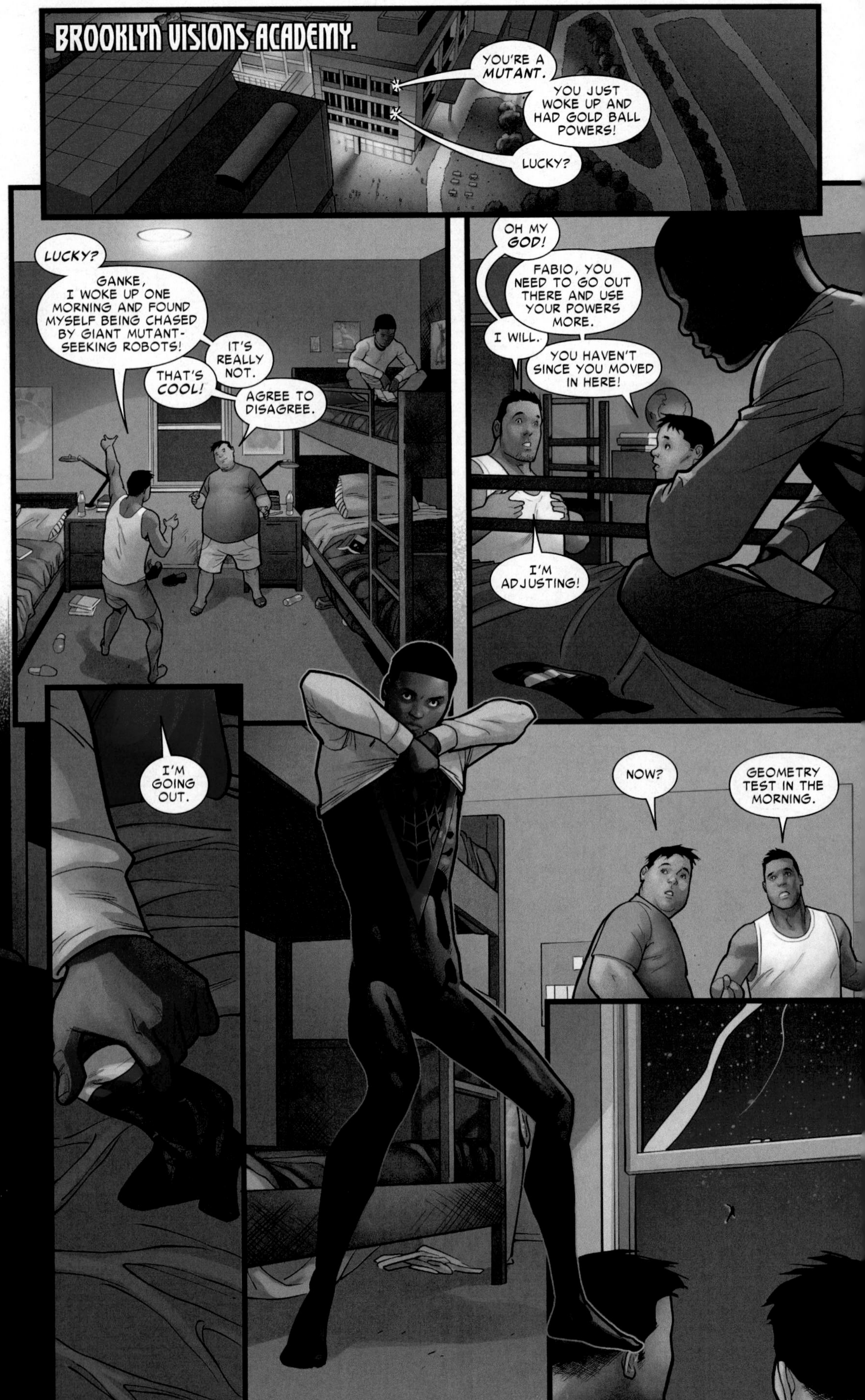
BROOKLYN VISIONS ACADEMY.
YOU'RE A MUTANT.
YOU JUST WOKE UP AND HAD GOLD BALL POWERS!
LUCKY?
LUCKY?
GANKE, I WOKE UP ONE MORNING AND FOUND MYSELF BEING CHASED BY GIANT MUTANT-SEEKING ROBOTS!
IT'S REALLY NOT.
THAT'S COOL!
AGREE TO DISAGREE.
OH MY GOD!
FABIO, YOU NEED TO GO OUT THERE AND USE YOUR POWERS MORE.
I WILL.
YOU HAVEN'T SINCE YOU MOVED IN HERE!
I'M ADJUSTING!
I'M GOING OUT.
NOW?
GEOMETRY TEST IN THE MORNING.

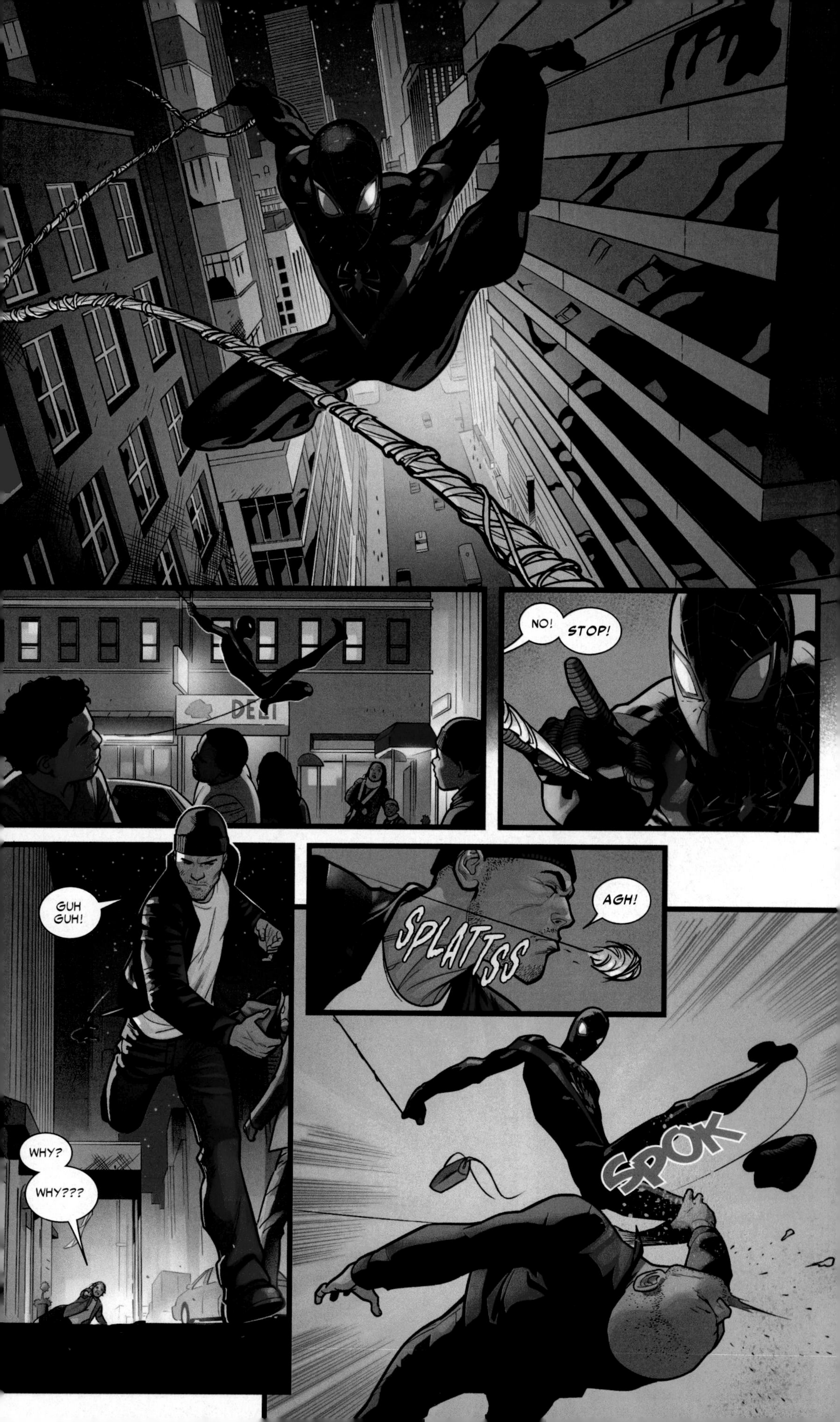

NO!
STOP!
GUH GUH!
SPLATTSS
AGH!
WHY?
WHY???
SPOK

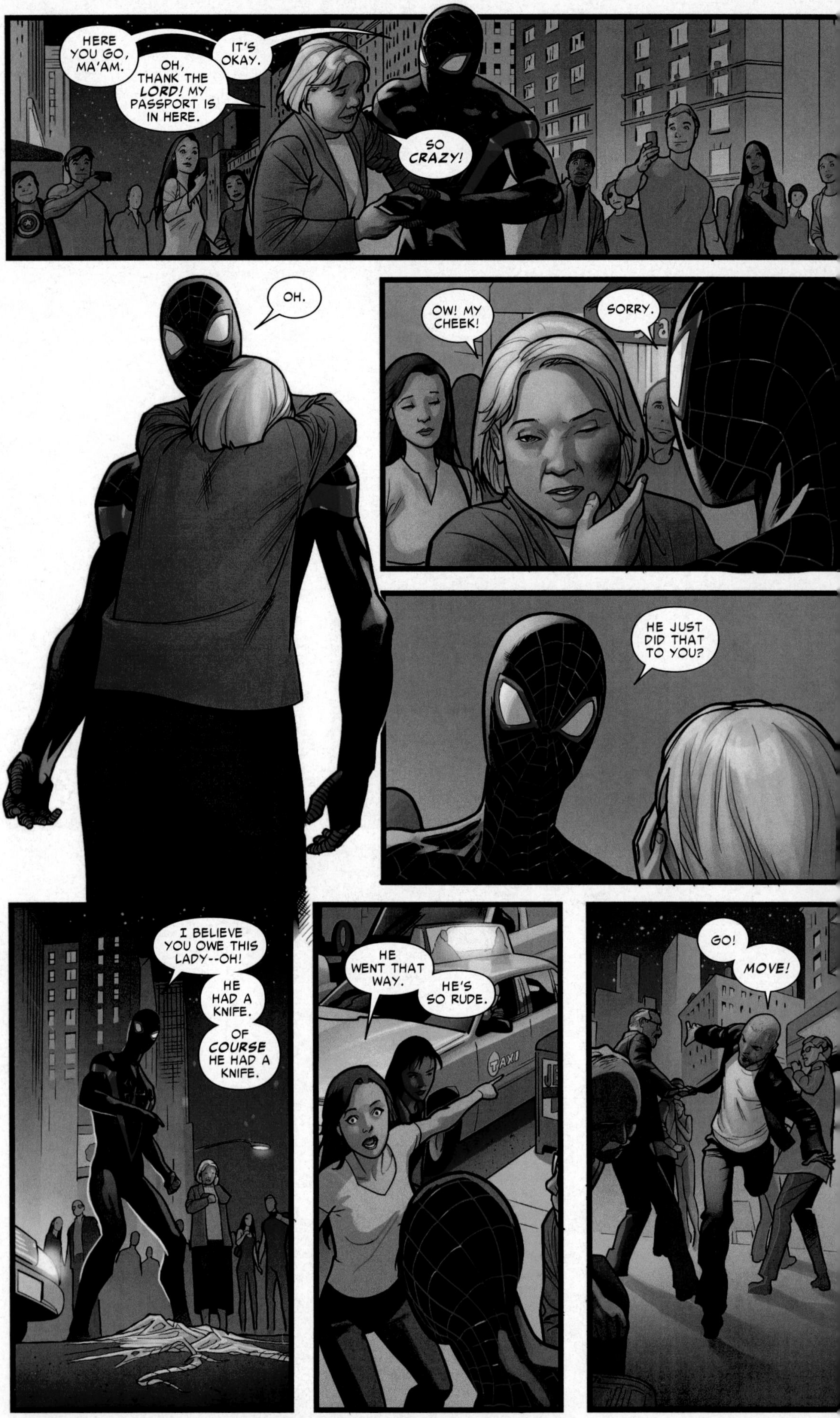
HERE YOU GO, MA'AM.
IT'S OKAY.
OH, THANK THE LORD! MY PASSPORT IS IN HERE.
SO CRAZY!
OH.
OW! MY CHEEK!
SORRY.
HE JUST DID THAT TO YOU?
I BELIEVE YOU OWE THIS LADY--OH!
HE HAD A KNIFE.
OF COURSE HE HAD A KNIFE.
HE WENT THAT WAY.
HE'S SO RUDE.
TAXI
GO!
MOVE!

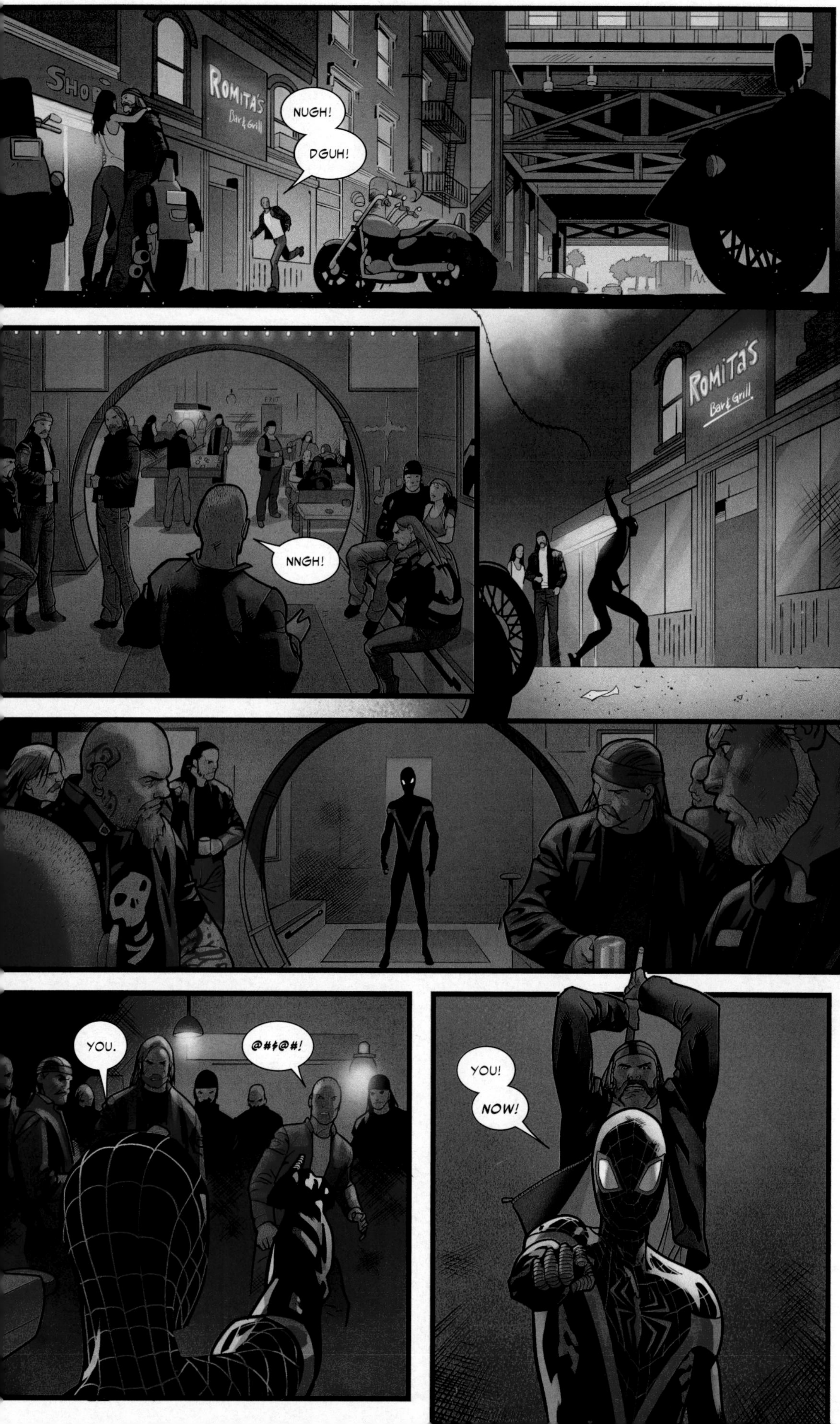
ROMITA'S Bar & Grill
NUGH!
DGUH!
NNGH!
Romita's Bar & Grill
YOU.
@#$@#!
YOU!
NOW!

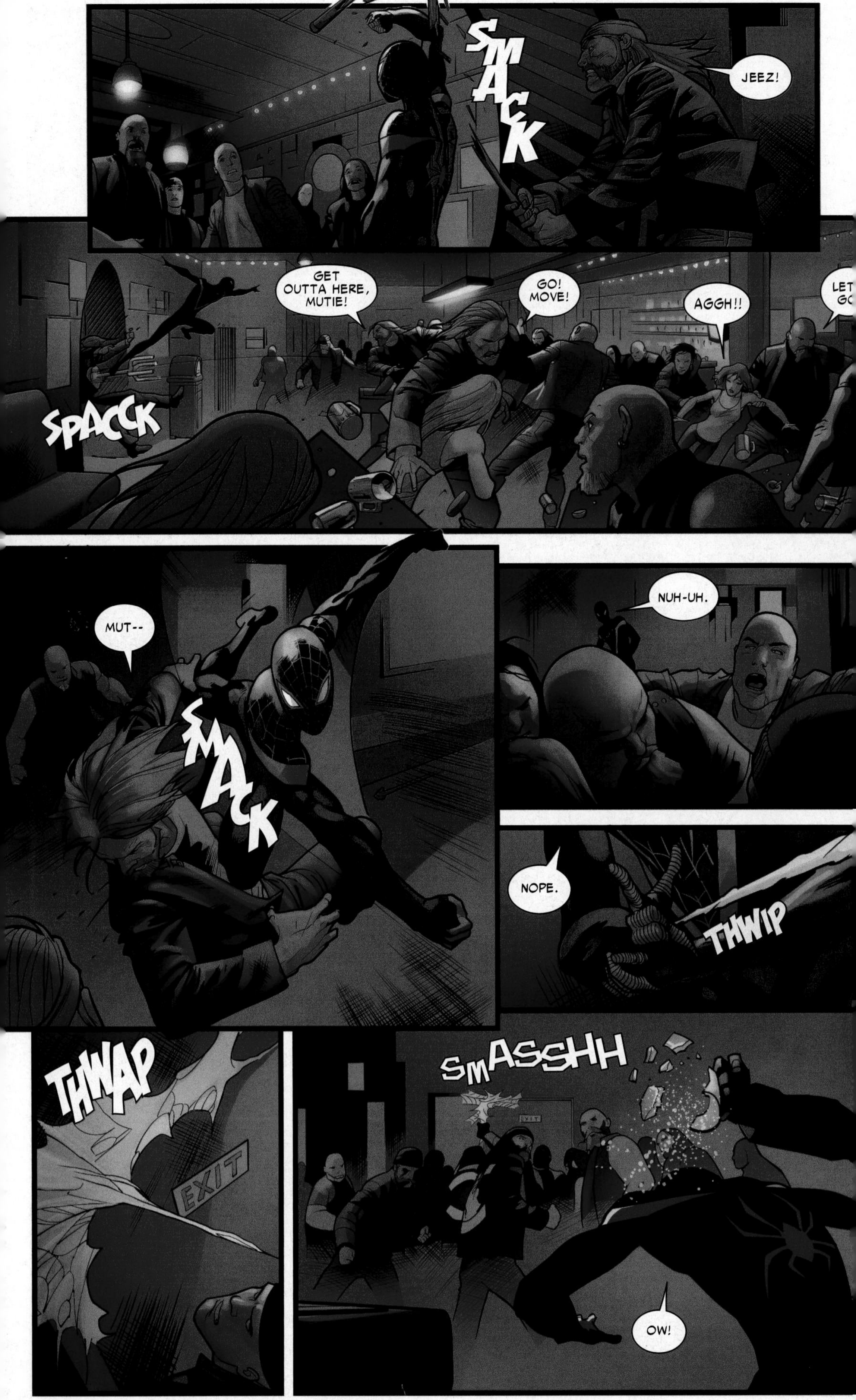
SMACK
JEEZ!
SPACCK
GET OUTTA HERE, MUTIE!
GO! MOVE!
AGGH!!
MUT--
SMACK
NUH-UH.
NOPE.
THWIP
THWAP
EXIT
SMASSHH
OW!

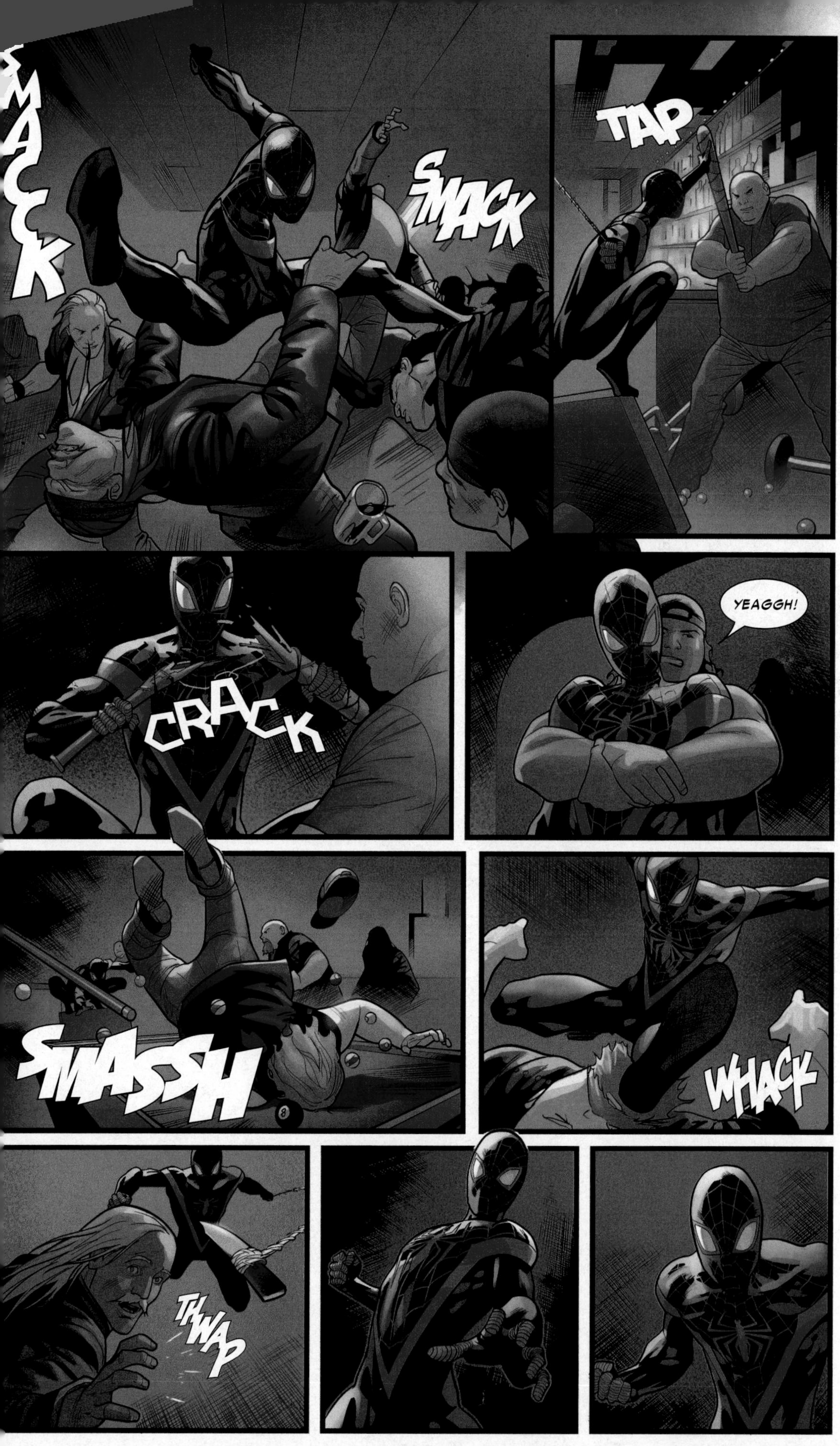
SMACK
SMACK
TAP
CRACK
YEAGGH!
SMASSH
WHACK
THWAP

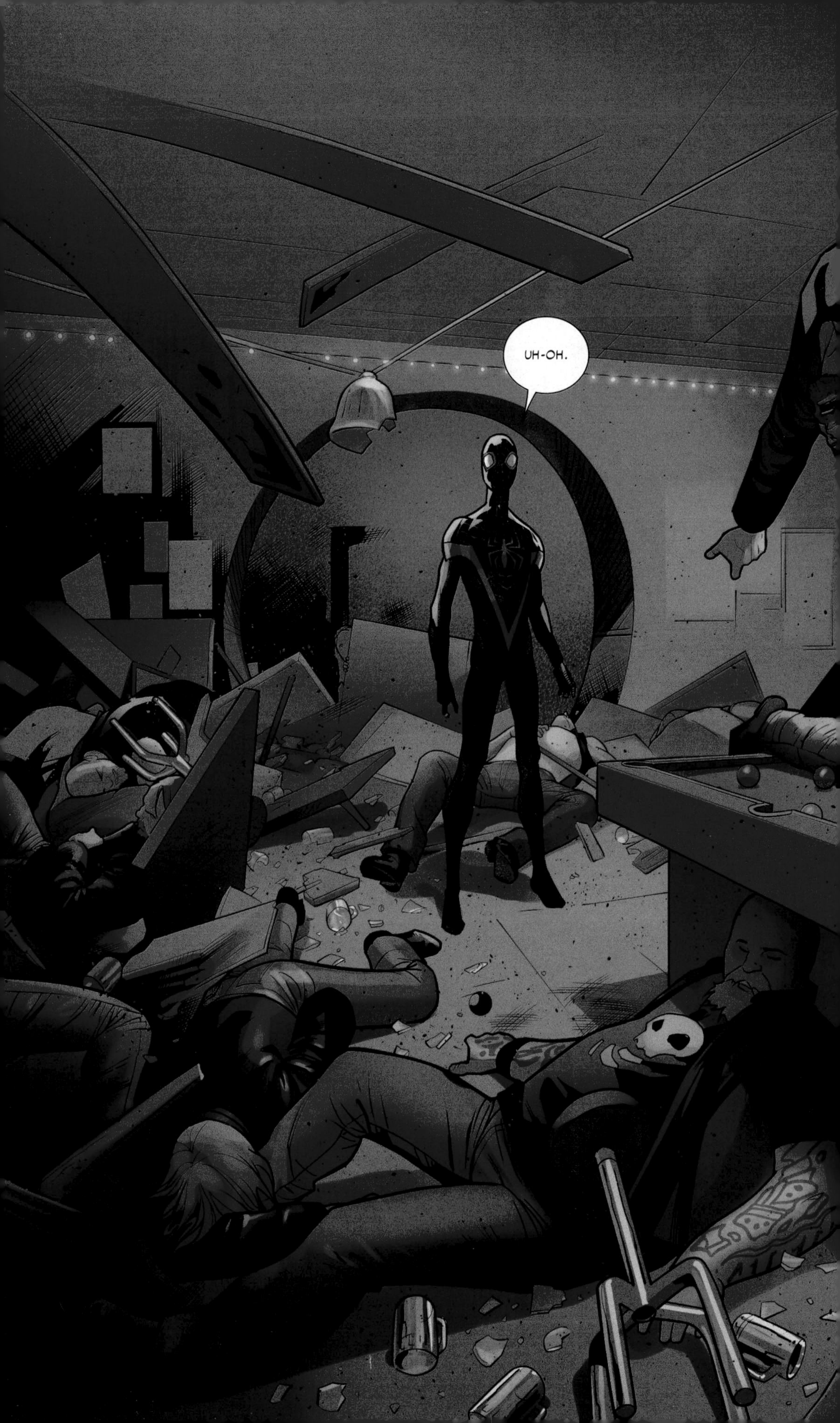
UH-OH.

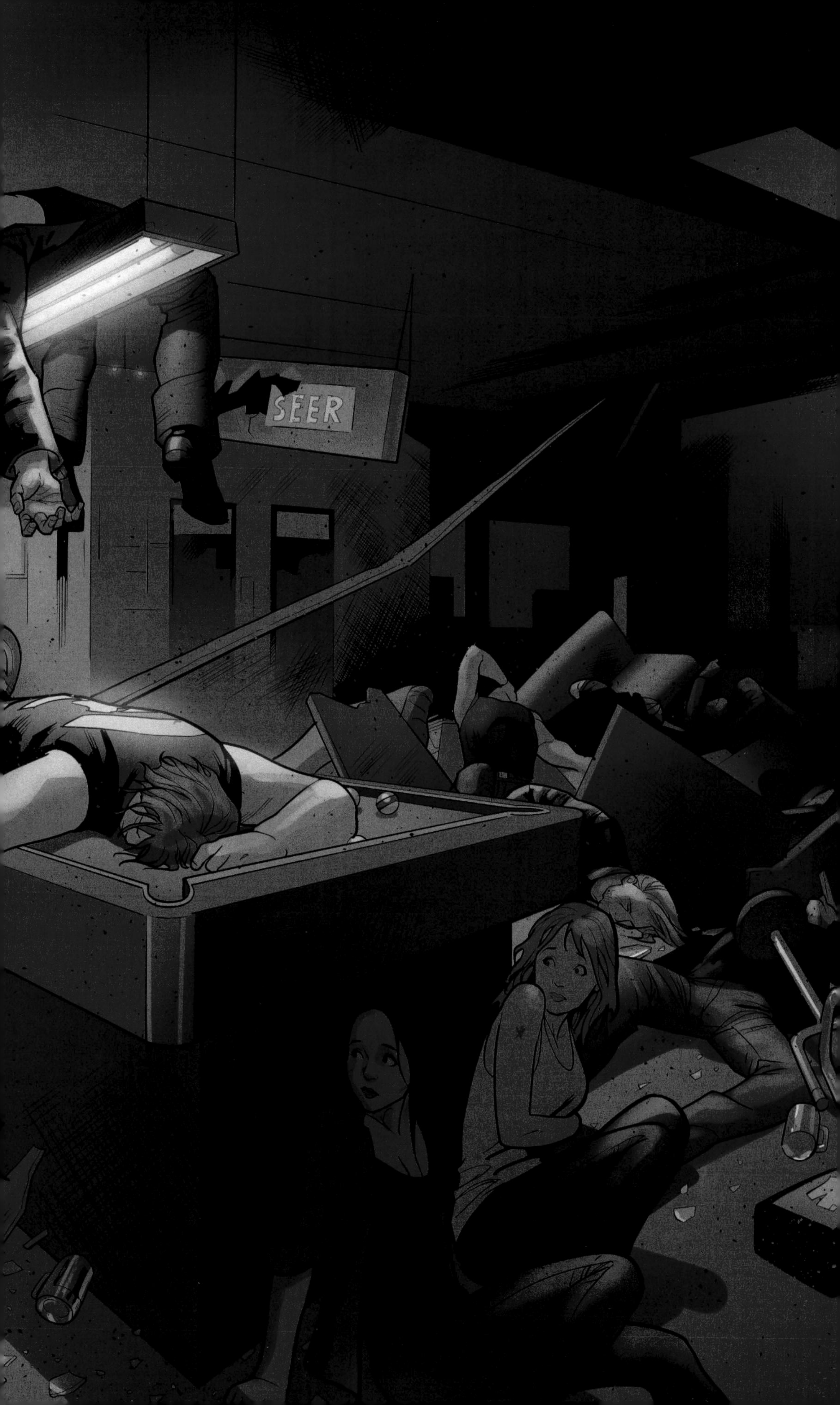
SEER

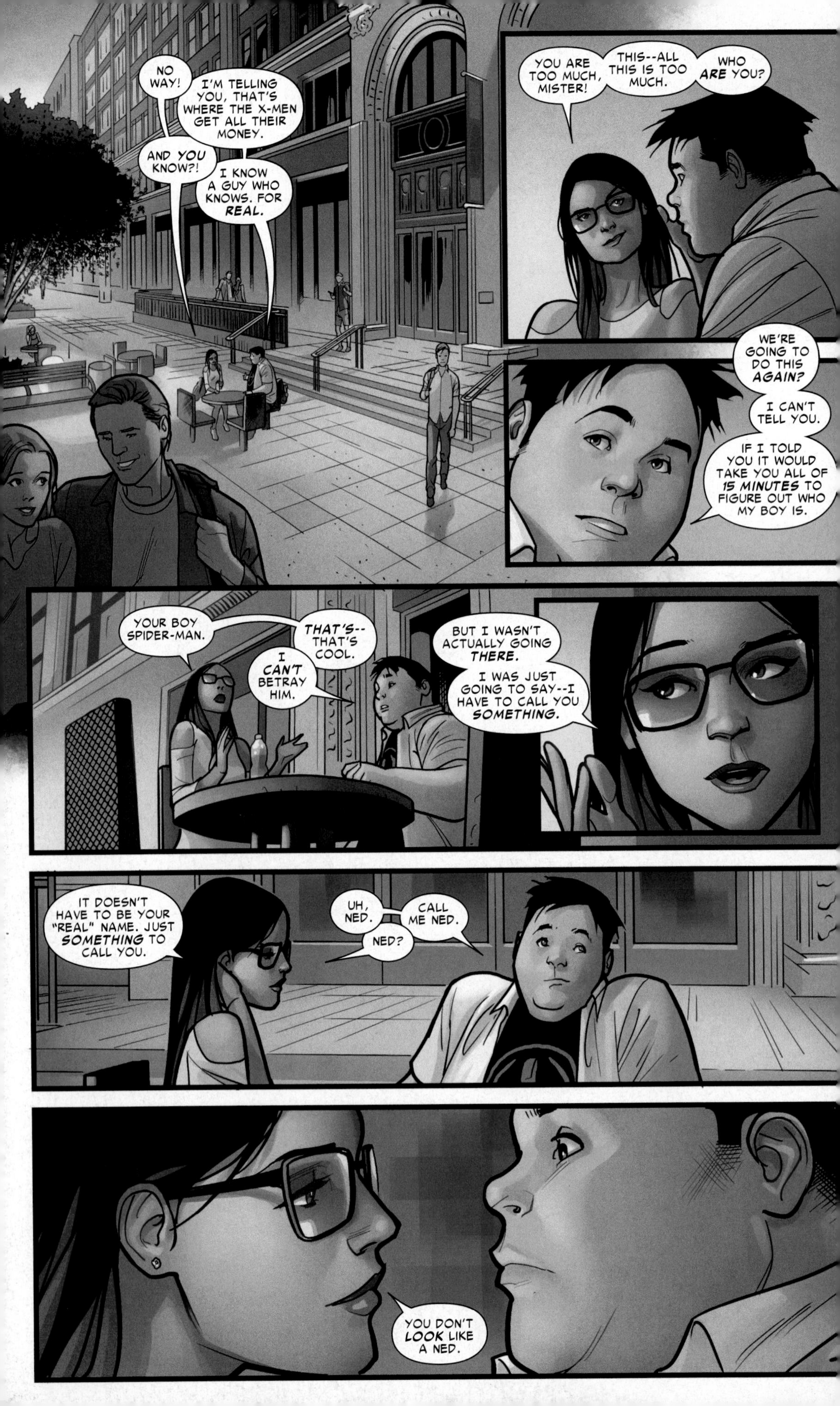

NO WAY!
I'M TELLING YOU, THAT'S WHERE THE X-MEN GET ALL THEIR MONEY.
AND YOU KNOW?!
I KNOW A GUY WHO KNOWS. FOR REAL.
YOU ARE TOO MUCH, MISTER!
THIS--ALL THIS IS TOO MUCH.
WHO ARE YOU?
WE'RE GOING TO DO THIS AGAIN?
I CAN'T TELL YOU.
IF I TOLD YOU IT WOULD TAKE YOU ALL OF 15 MINUTES TO FIGURE OUT WHO MY BOY IS.
YOUR BOY SPIDER-MAN.
THAT'S--THAT'S COOL.
I CAN'T BETRAY HIM.
BUT I WASN'T ACTUALLY GOING THERE.
I WAS JUST GOING TO SAY--I HAVE TO CALL YOU SOMETHING.
IT DOESN'T HAVE TO BE YOUR "REAL" NAME. JUST SOMETHING TO CALL YOU.
UH, NED.
CALL ME NED.
NED?
YOU DON'T LOOK LIKE A NED.

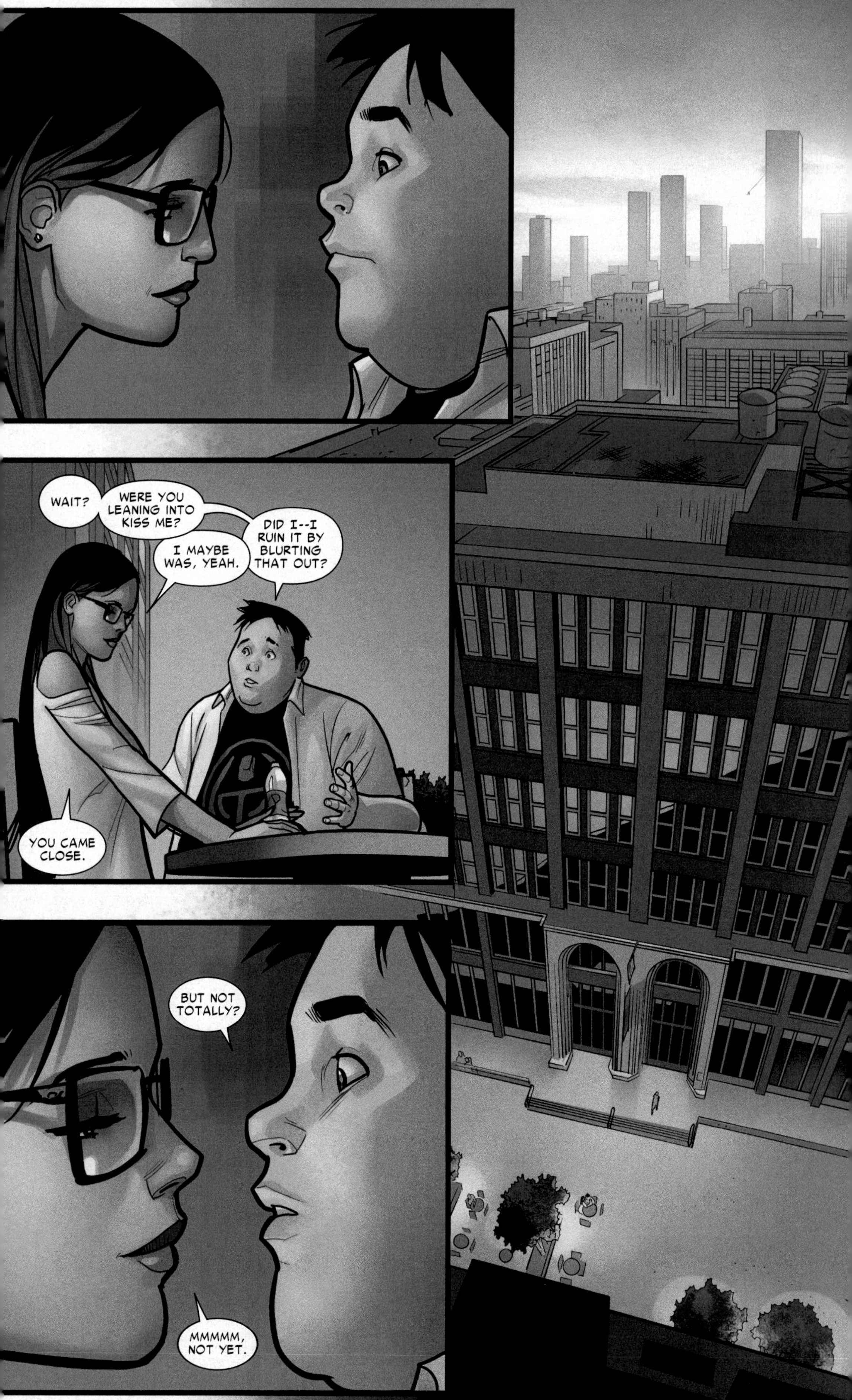
WAIT?
WERE YOU LEANING INTO KISS ME?
I MAYBE WAS, YEAH.
DID I--I RUIN IT BY BLURTING THAT OUT?
YOU CAME CLOSE.
BUT NOT TOTALLY?
MMMMM, NOT YET.

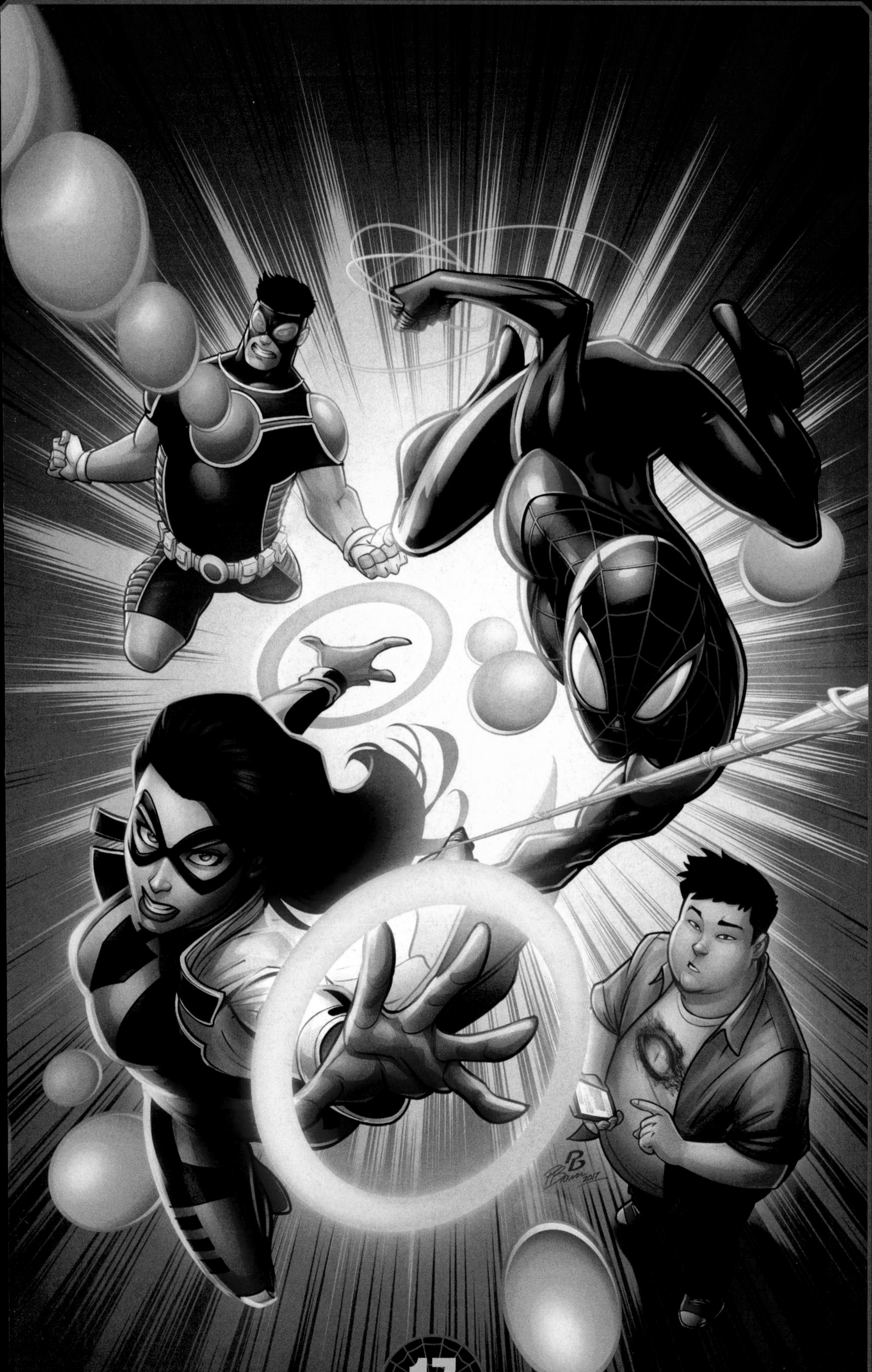

17

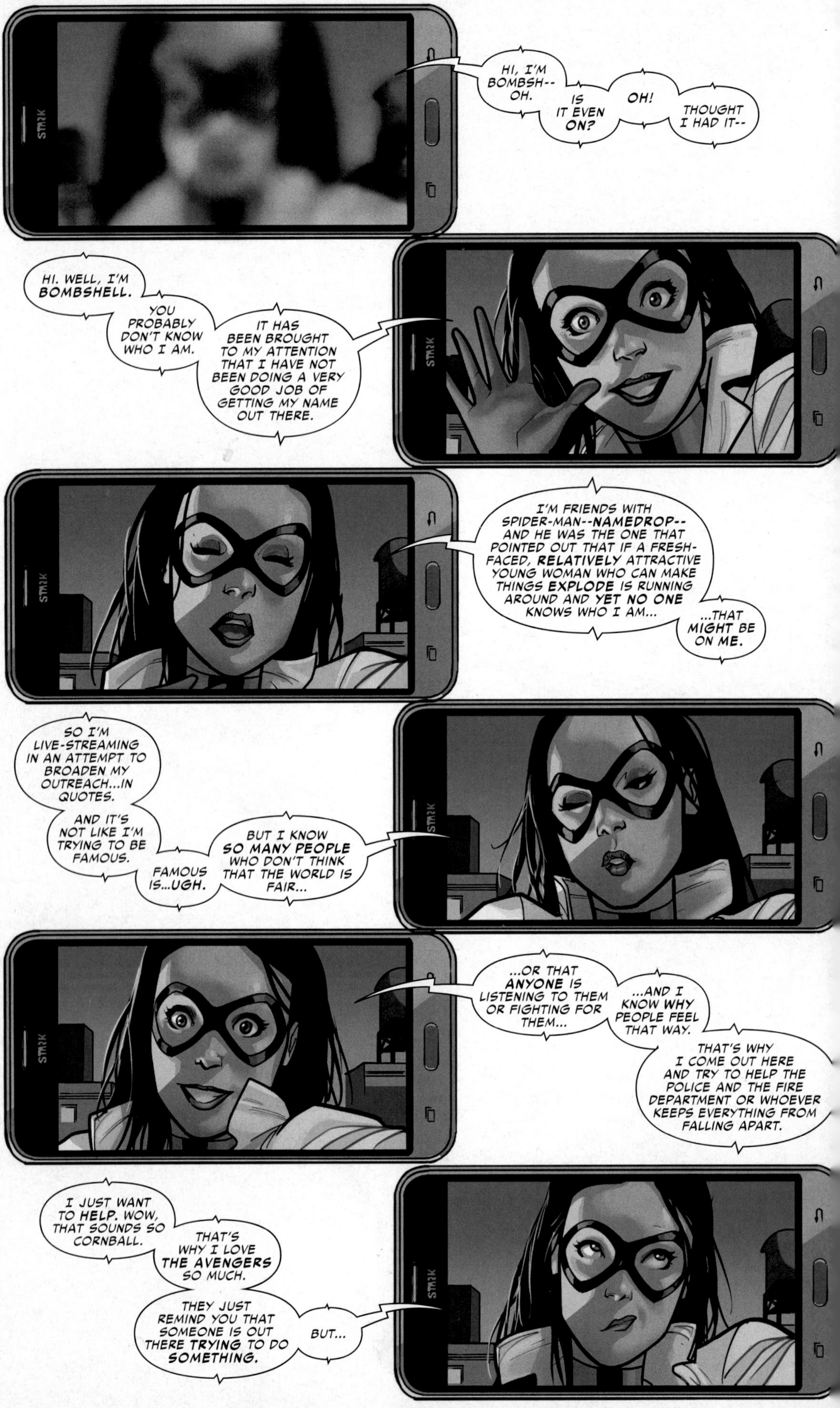

HI, I'M BOMBSH-- OH.
IS IT EVEN ON?
OH!
THOUGHT I HAD IT--
HI. WELL, I'M BOMBSHELL.
YOU PROBABLY DON'T KNOW WHO I AM.
IT HAS BEEN BROUGHT TO MY ATTENTION THAT I HAVE NOT BEEN DOING A VERY GOOD JOB OF GETTING MY NAME OUT THERE.
I'M FRIENDS WITH SPIDER-MAN--NAMEDROP-- AND HE WAS THE ONE THAT POINTED OUT THAT IF A FRESH-FACED, RELATIVELY ATTRACTIVE YOUNG WOMAN WHO CAN MAKE THINGS EXPLODE IS RUNNING AROUND AND YET NO ONE KNOWS WHO I AM...
...THAT MIGHT BE ON ME.
SO I'M LIVE-STREAMING IN AN ATTEMPT TO BROADEN MY OUTREACH...IN QUOTES.
AND IT'S NOT LIKE I'M TRYING TO BE FAMOUS.
FAMOUS IS...UGH.
BUT I KNOW SO MANY PEOPLE WHO DON'T THINK THAT THE WORLD IS FAIR...
...OR THAT ANYONE IS LISTENING TO THEM OR FIGHTING FOR THEM...
...AND I KNOW WHY PEOPLE FEEL THAT WAY.
THAT'S WHY I COME OUT HERE AND TRY TO HELP THE POLICE AND THE FIRE DEPARTMENT OR WHOEVER KEEPS EVERYTHING FROM FALLING APART.
I JUST WANT TO HELP. WOW, THAT SOUNDS SO CORNBALL.
THAT'S WHY I LOVE THE AVENGERS SO MUCH.
THEY JUST REMIND YOU THAT SOMEONE IS OUT THERE TRYING TO DO SOMETHING.
BUT...

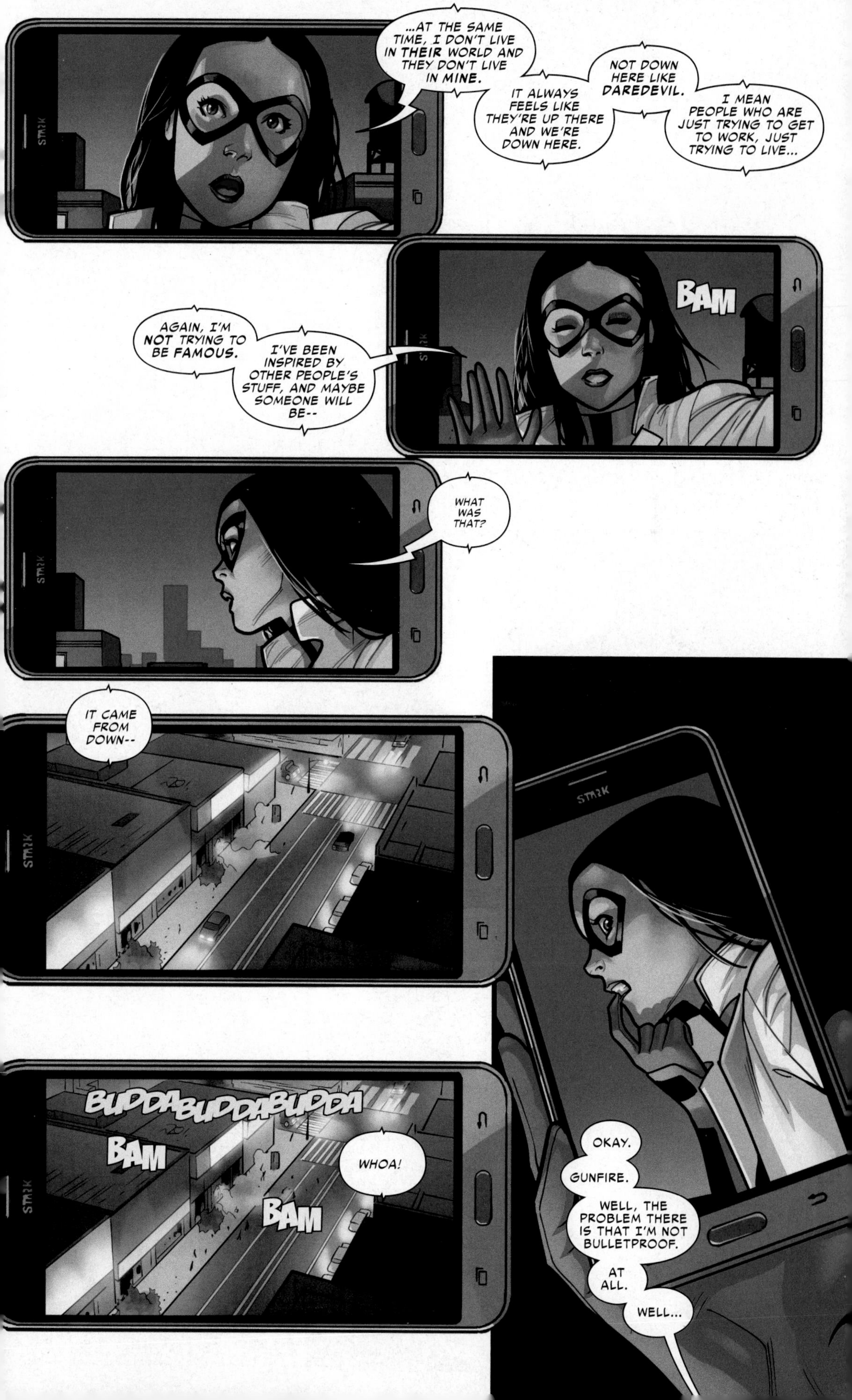

...AT THE SAME TIME, I DON'T LIVE IN THEIR WORLD AND THEY DON'T LIVE IN MINE.
IT ALWAYS FEELS LIKE THEY'RE UP THERE AND WE'RE DOWN HERE.
NOT DOWN HERE LIKE DAREDEVIL.
I MEAN PEOPLE WHO ARE JUST TRYING TO GET TO WORK, JUST TRYING TO LIVE...
STARK
BAM
AGAIN, I'M NOT TRYING TO BE FAMOUS.
I'VE BEEN INSPIRED BY OTHER PEOPLE'S STUFF, AND MAYBE SOMEONE WILL BE--
STARK
WHAT WAS THAT?
STARK
IT CAME FROM DOWN--
STARK
STARK
BUDDABUDDABUDDA
BAM
BAM
WHOA!
STARK
OKAY.
GUNFIRE.
WELL, THE PROBLEM THERE IS THAT I'M NOT BULLETPROOF.
AT ALL.
WELL...

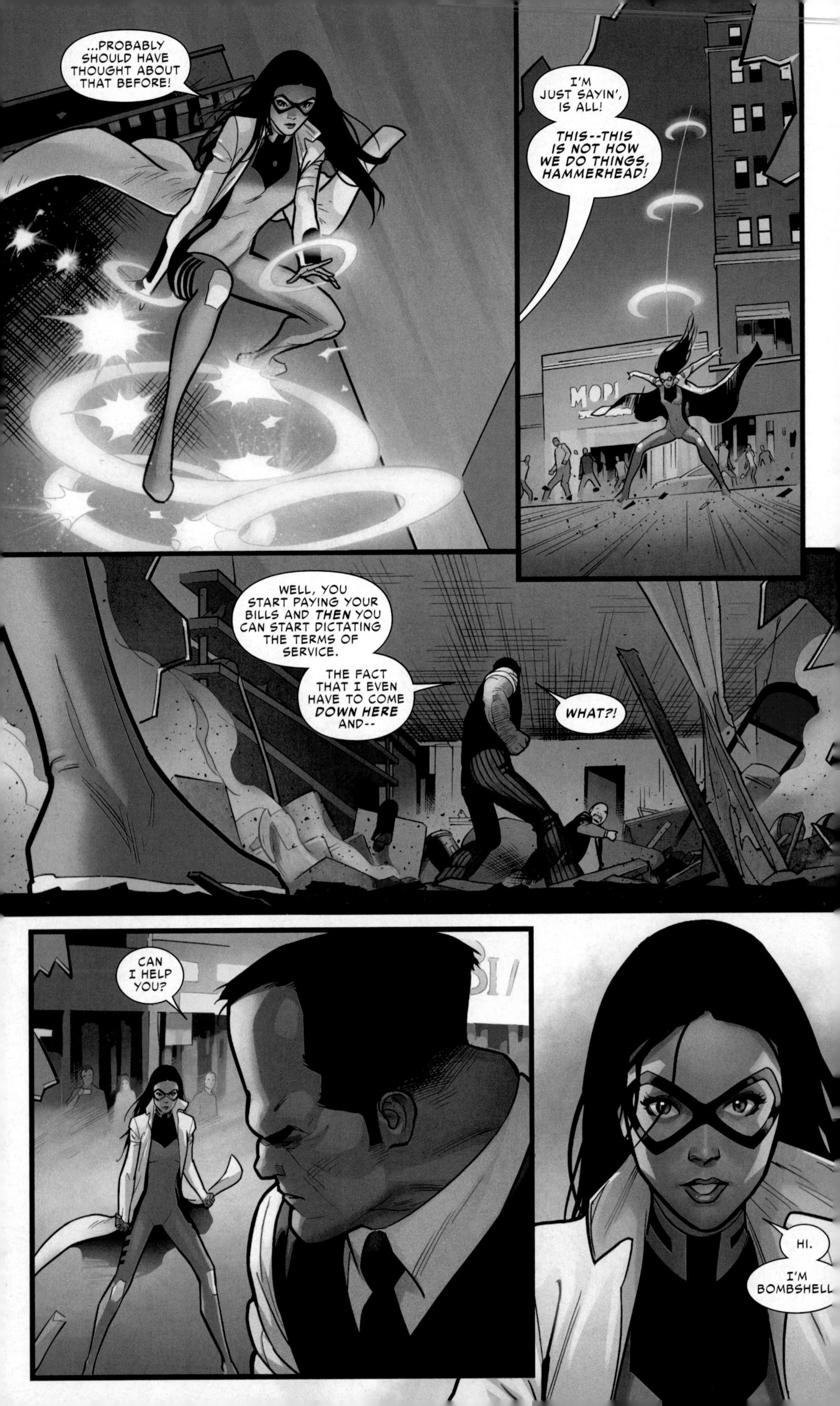
...PROBABLY SHOULD HAVE THOUGHT ABOUT THAT BEFORE!
I'M JUST SAYIN', IS ALL!
THIS--THIS IS NOT HOW WE DO THINGS, HAMMERHEAD!
WELL, YOU START PAYING YOUR BILLS AND THEN YOU CAN START DICTATING THE TERMS OF SERVICE.
THE FACT THAT I EVEN HAVE TO COME DOWN HERE AND--
WHAT?!
CAN I HELP YOU?
HI.
I'M BOMBSHELL

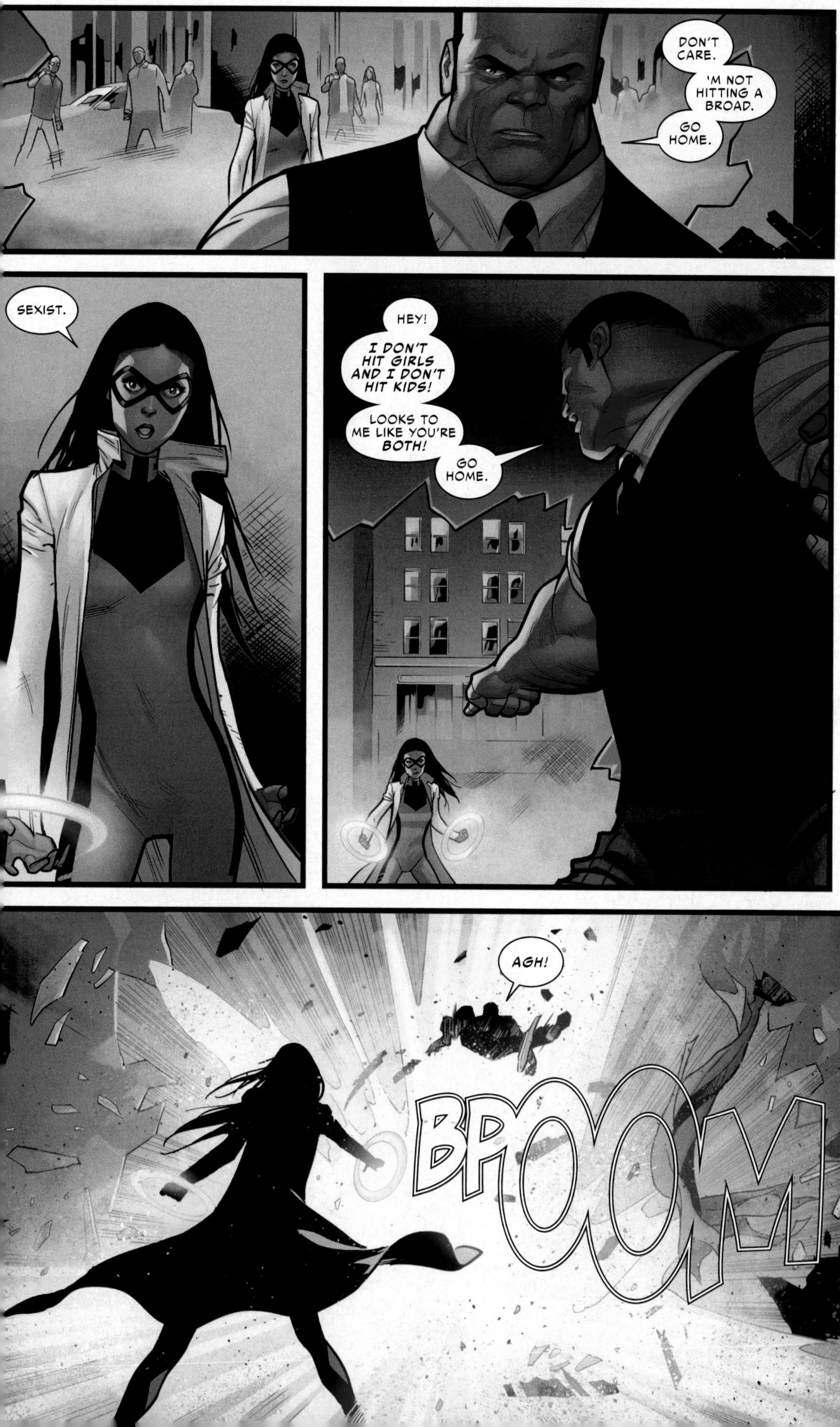
DON'T CARE.
'M NOT HITTING A BROAD.
GO HOME.
SEXIST.
HEY!
I DON'T HIT GIRLS AND I DON'T HIT KIDS!
LOOKS TO ME LIKE YOU'RE BOTH!
GO HOME.
AGH!
BPOOOM

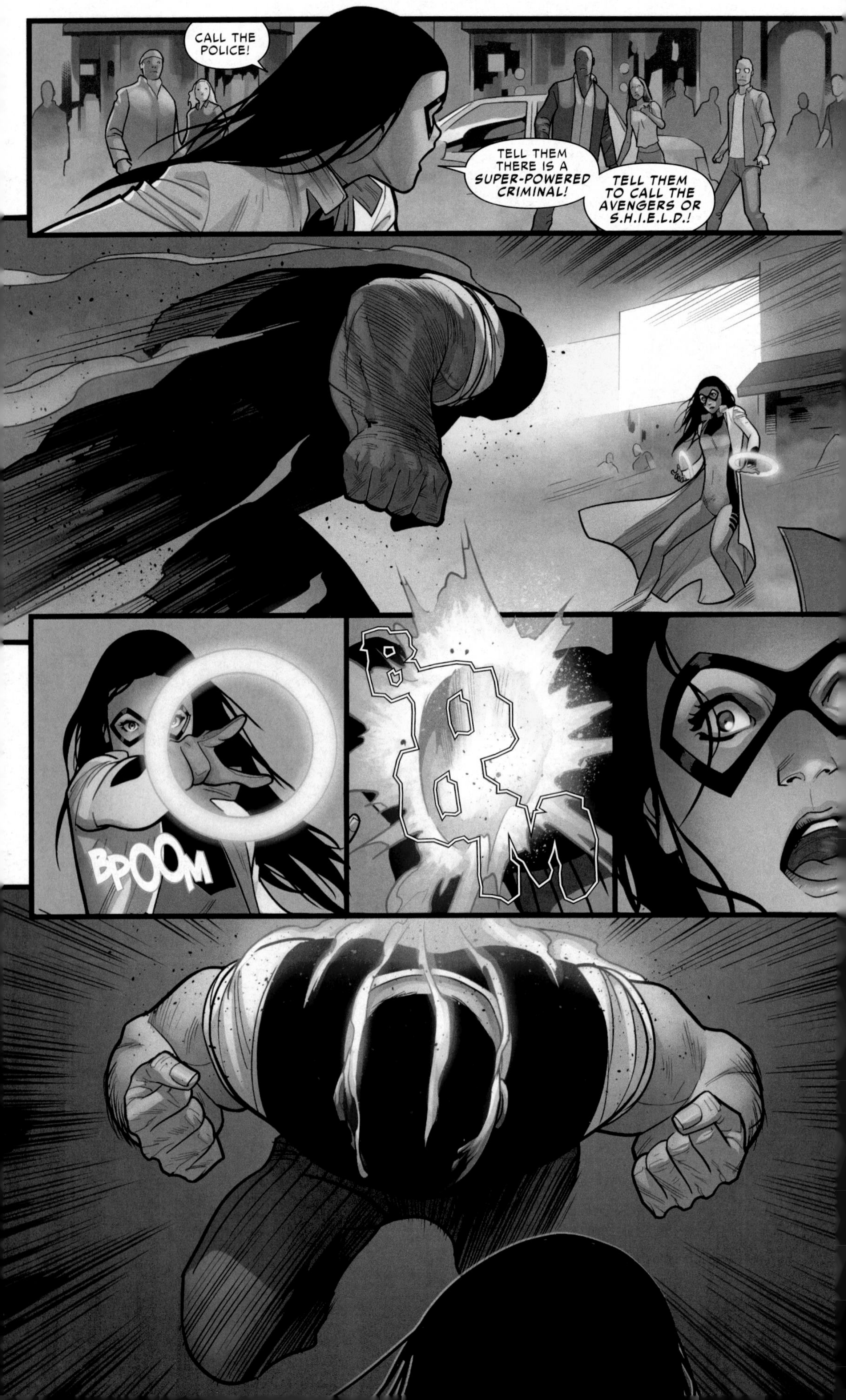

CALL THE POLICE!
TELL THEM THERE IS A SUPER-POWERED CRIMINAL!
TELL THEM TO CALL THE AVENGERS OR S.H.I.E.L.D.!
BPOOM

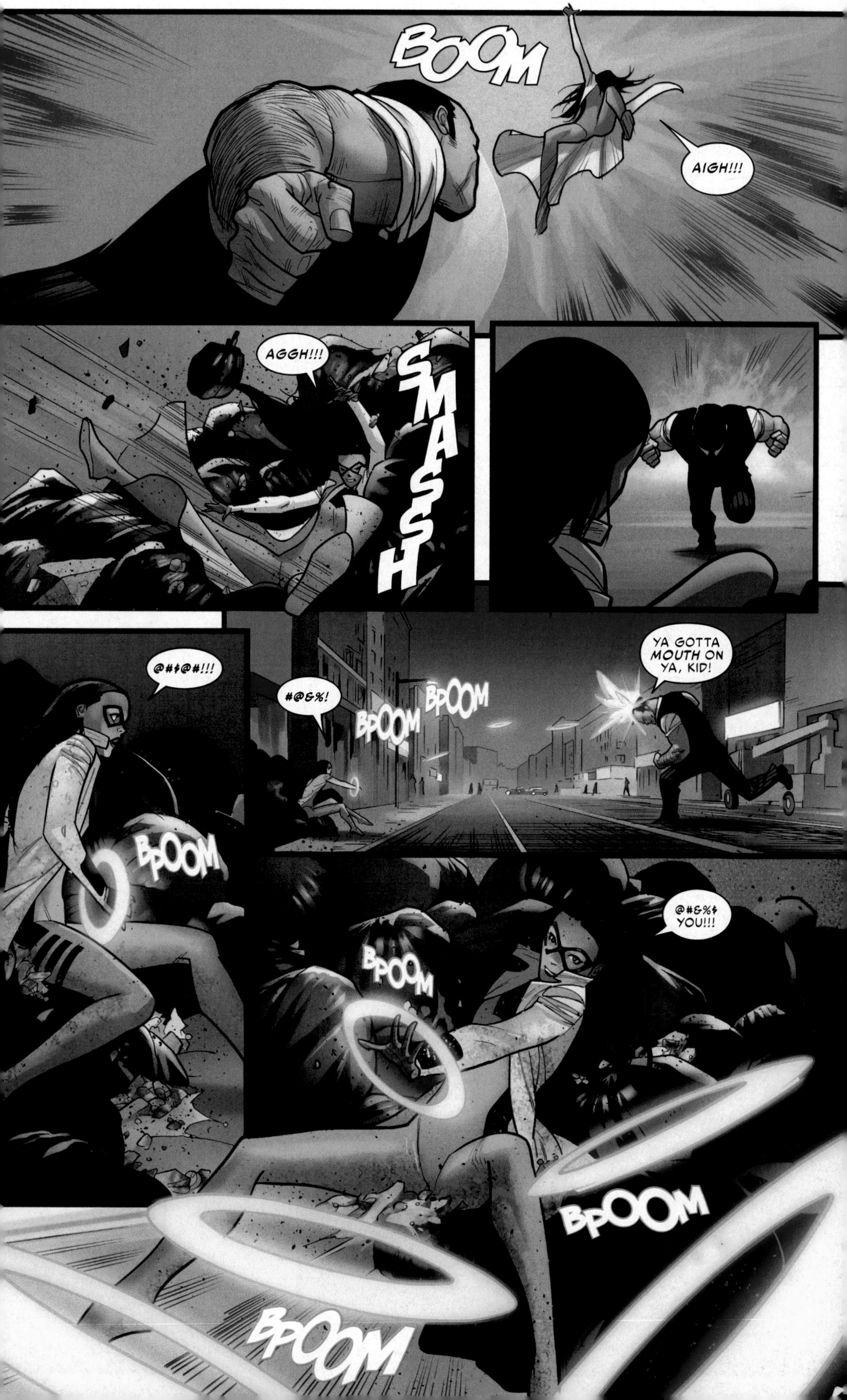
BOOM
AIGH!!!
AGGH!!!
SMASSH
@#$@#!!!
#@&%!
BPOOM
BPOOM
YA GOTTA MOUTH ON YA, KID!
BPOOM
@#&%$ YOU!!!
BPOOM
BPOOM
BPOOM

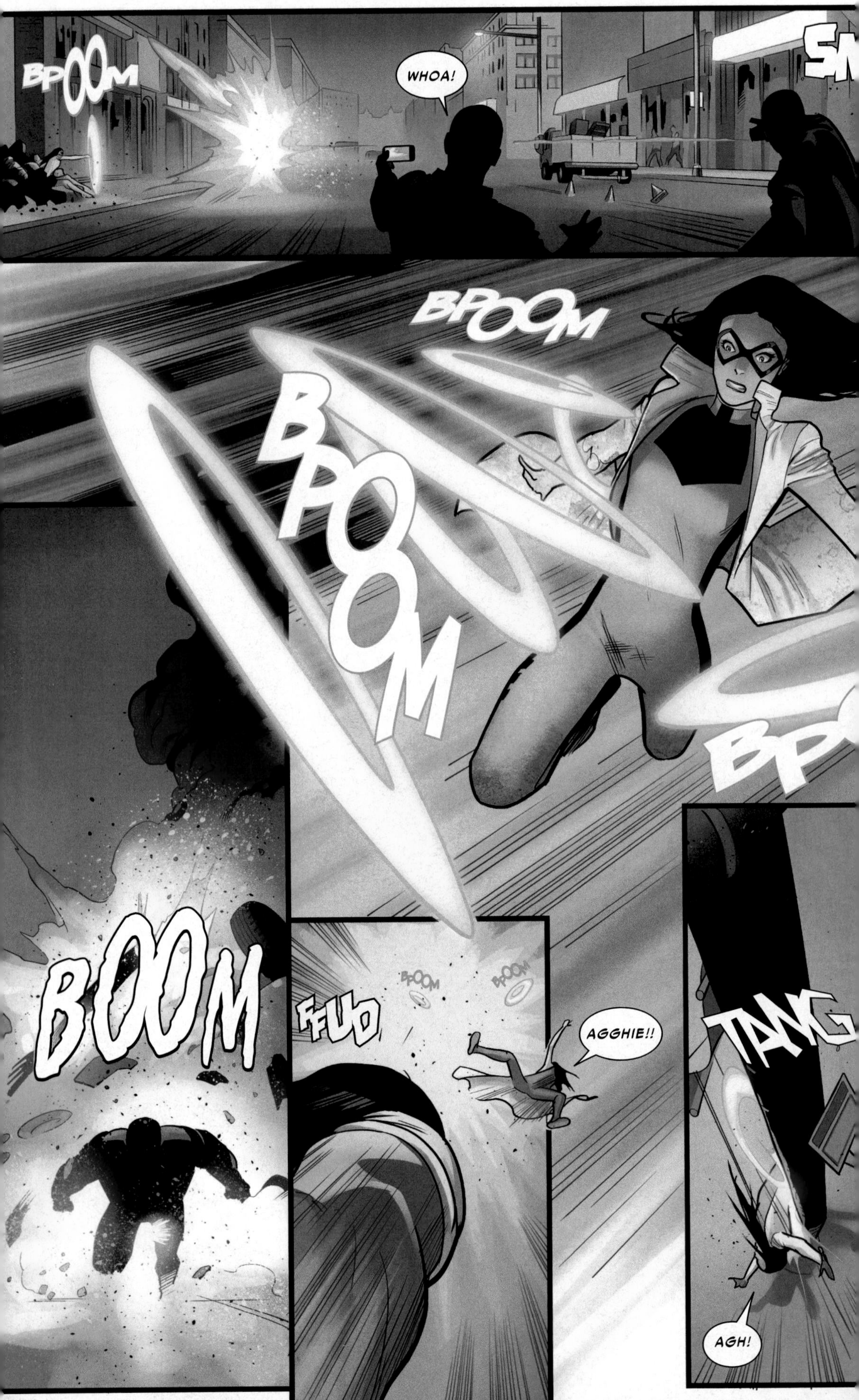
BPOOM
WHOA!
BPOOM
BPOOM
BOOM
FFUD
BPOOM
BPOOM
AGGHIE!!
TANG
AGH!

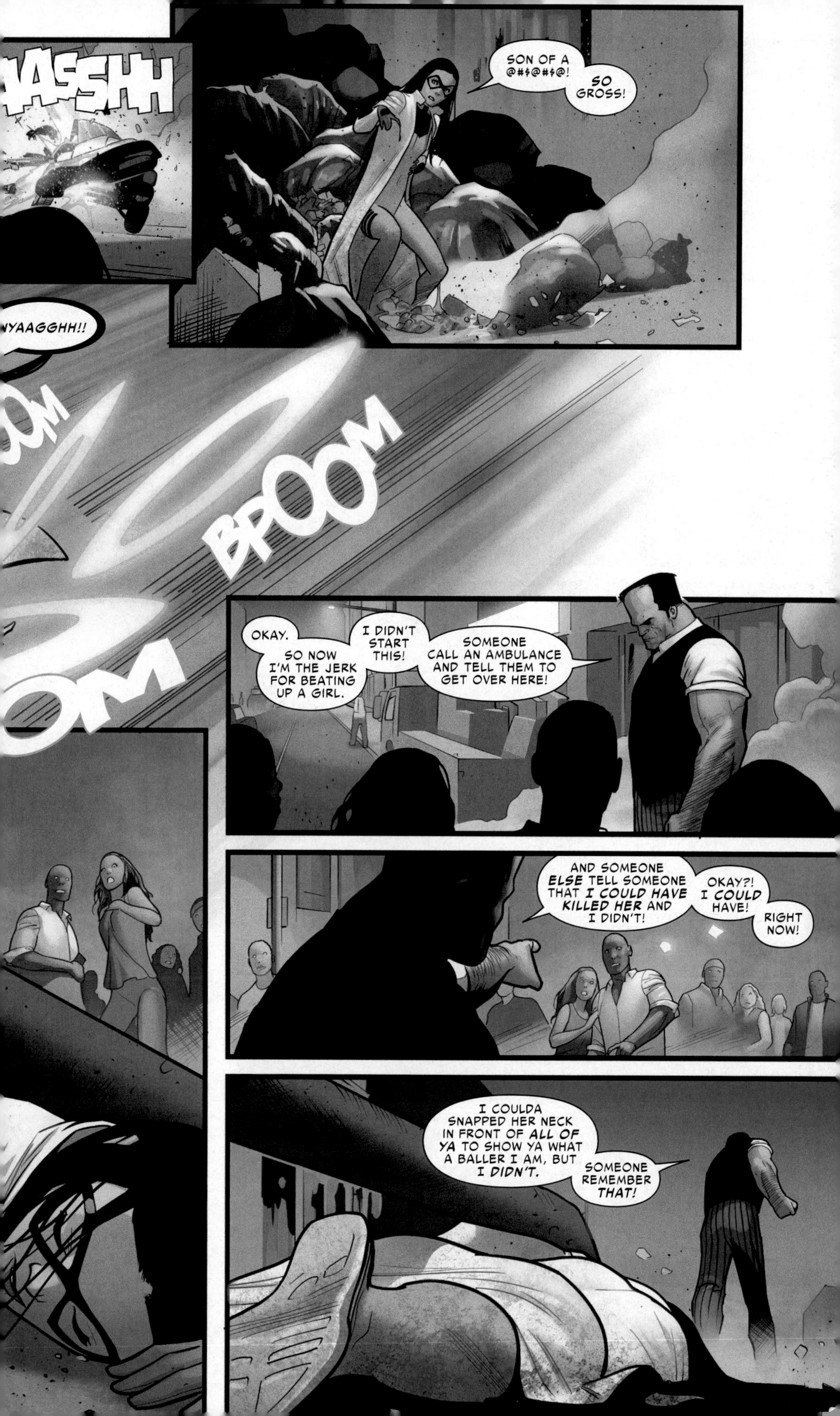

SHASSHH
SON OF A @#$@#$@!
SO GROSS!
NYAAGGHH!!
BROOM
BROOM
BROOM
OKAY.
SO NOW I'M THE JERK FOR BEATING UP A GIRL.
I DIDN'T START THIS!
SOMEONE CALL AN AMBULANCE AND TELL THEM TO GET OVER HERE!
AND SOMEONE ELSE TELL SOMEONE THAT I COULD HAVE KILLED HER AND I DIDN'T!
OKAY?! I COULD HAVE!
RIGHT NOW!
I COULDA SNAPPED HER NECK IN FRONT OF ALL OF YA TO SHOW YA WHAT A BALLER I AM, BUT I DIDN'T.
SOMEONE REMEMBER THAT!

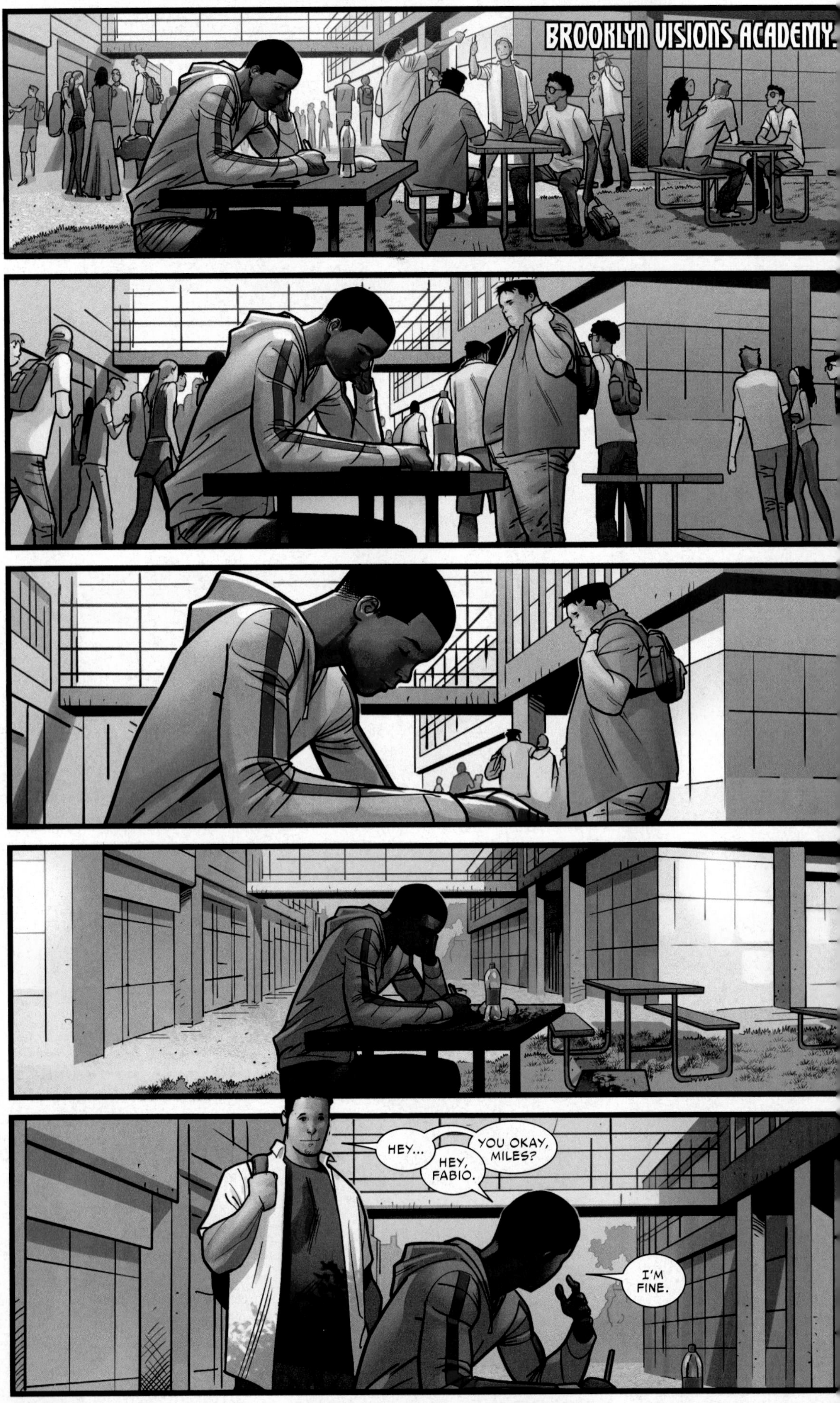
BROOKLYN VISIONS ACADEMY.
HEY...
YOU OKAY, MILES?
HEY, FABIO.
I'M FINE.

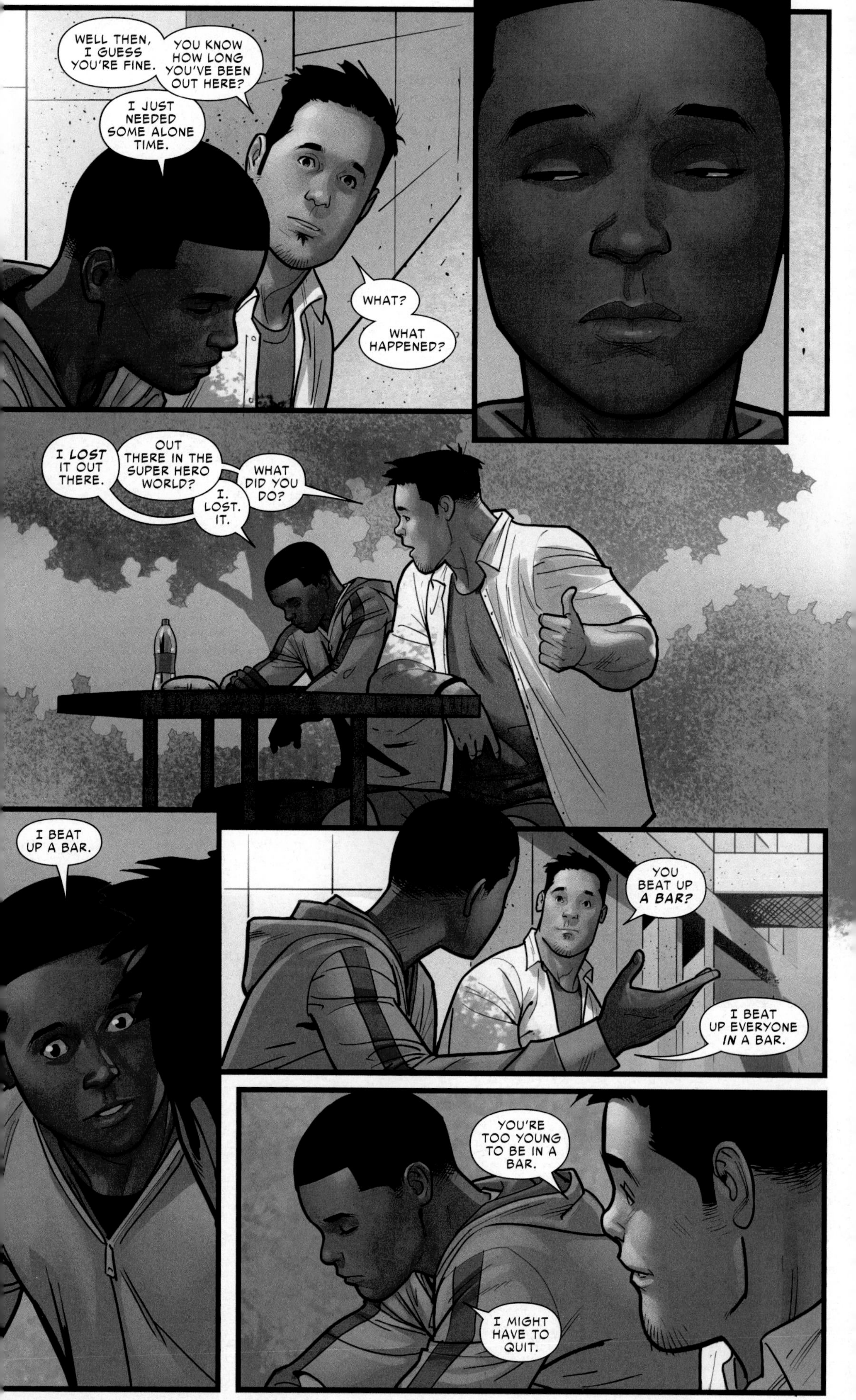
WELL THEN, I GUESS YOU'RE FINE.
YOU KNOW HOW LONG YOU'VE BEEN OUT HERE?
I JUST NEEDED SOME ALONE TIME.
WHAT?
WHAT HAPPENED?
I *LOST* IT OUT THERE.
OUT THERE IN THE SUPER HERO WORLD?
WHAT DID YOU DO?
I. LOST. IT.
I BEAT UP A BAR.
YOU BEAT UP *A BAR?*
I BEAT UP EVERYONE *IN* A BAR.
YOU'RE TOO YOUNG TO BE IN A BAR.
I MIGHT HAVE TO QUIT.

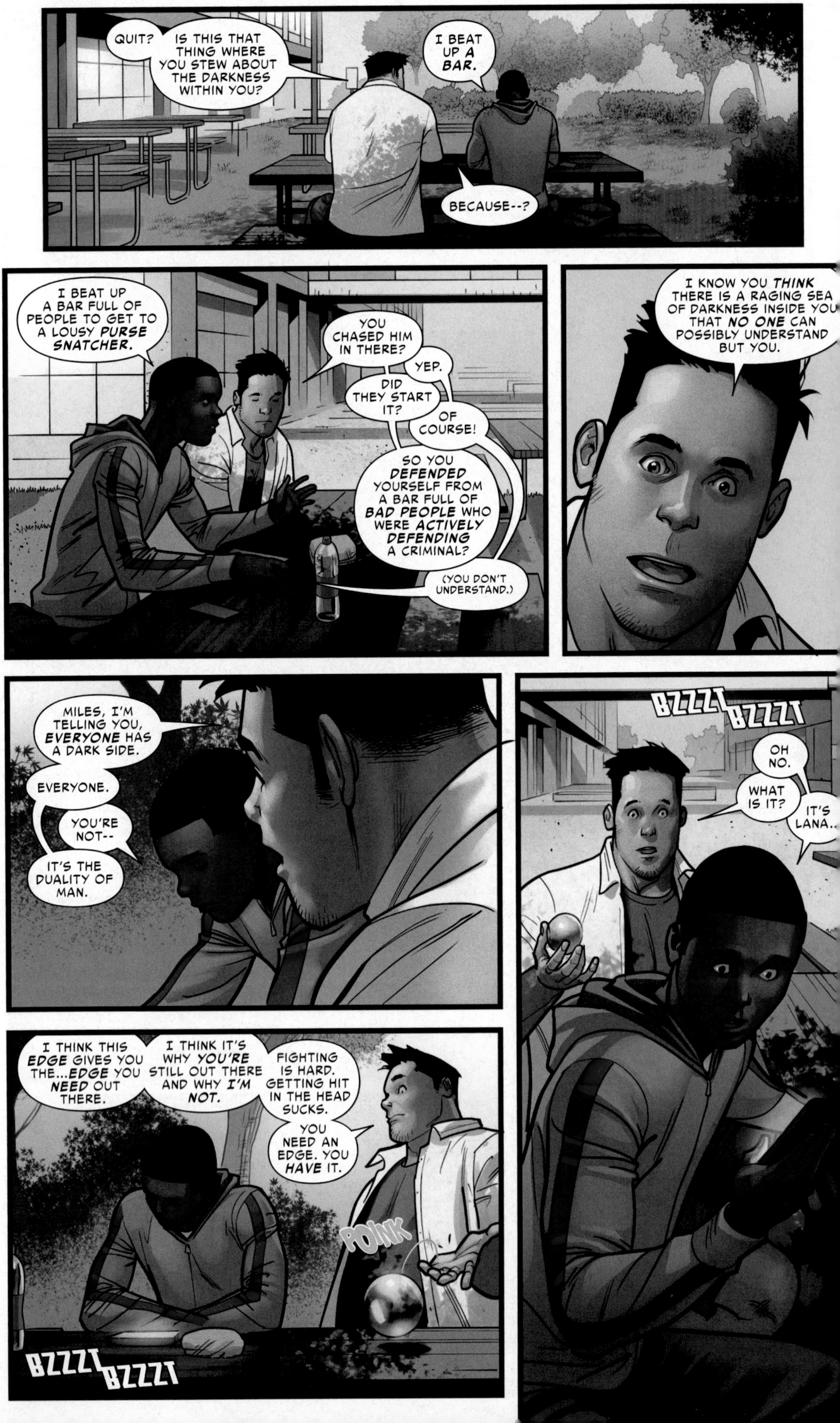
QUIT?
IS THIS THAT THING WHERE YOU STEW ABOUT THE DARKNESS WITHIN YOU?
I BEAT UP A BAR.
BECAUSE--?
I BEAT UP A BAR FULL OF PEOPLE TO GET TO A LOUSY PURSE SNATCHER.
YOU CHASED HIM IN THERE?
YEP.
DID THEY START IT?
OF COURSE!
SO YOU DEFENDED YOURSELF FROM A BAR FULL OF BAD PEOPLE WHO WERE ACTIVELY DEFENDING A CRIMINAL?
(YOU DON'T UNDERSTAND.)
I KNOW YOU THINK THERE IS A RAGING SEA OF DARKNESS INSIDE YOU THAT NO ONE CAN POSSIBLY UNDERSTAND BUT YOU.
MILES, I'M TELLING YOU, EVERYONE HAS A DARK SIDE.
EVERYONE.
YOU'RE NOT--
IT'S THE DUALITY OF MAN.
I THINK THIS EDGE GIVES YOU THE...EDGE YOU NEED OUT THERE.
I THINK IT'S WHY YOU'RE STILL OUT THERE AND WHY I'M NOT.
FIGHTING IS HARD. GETTING HIT IN THE HEAD SUCKS.
YOU NEED AN EDGE. YOU HAVE IT.
POINK
BZZZT BZZZT
BZZZT BZZZT
OH NO.
WHAT IS IT?
IT'S LANA...

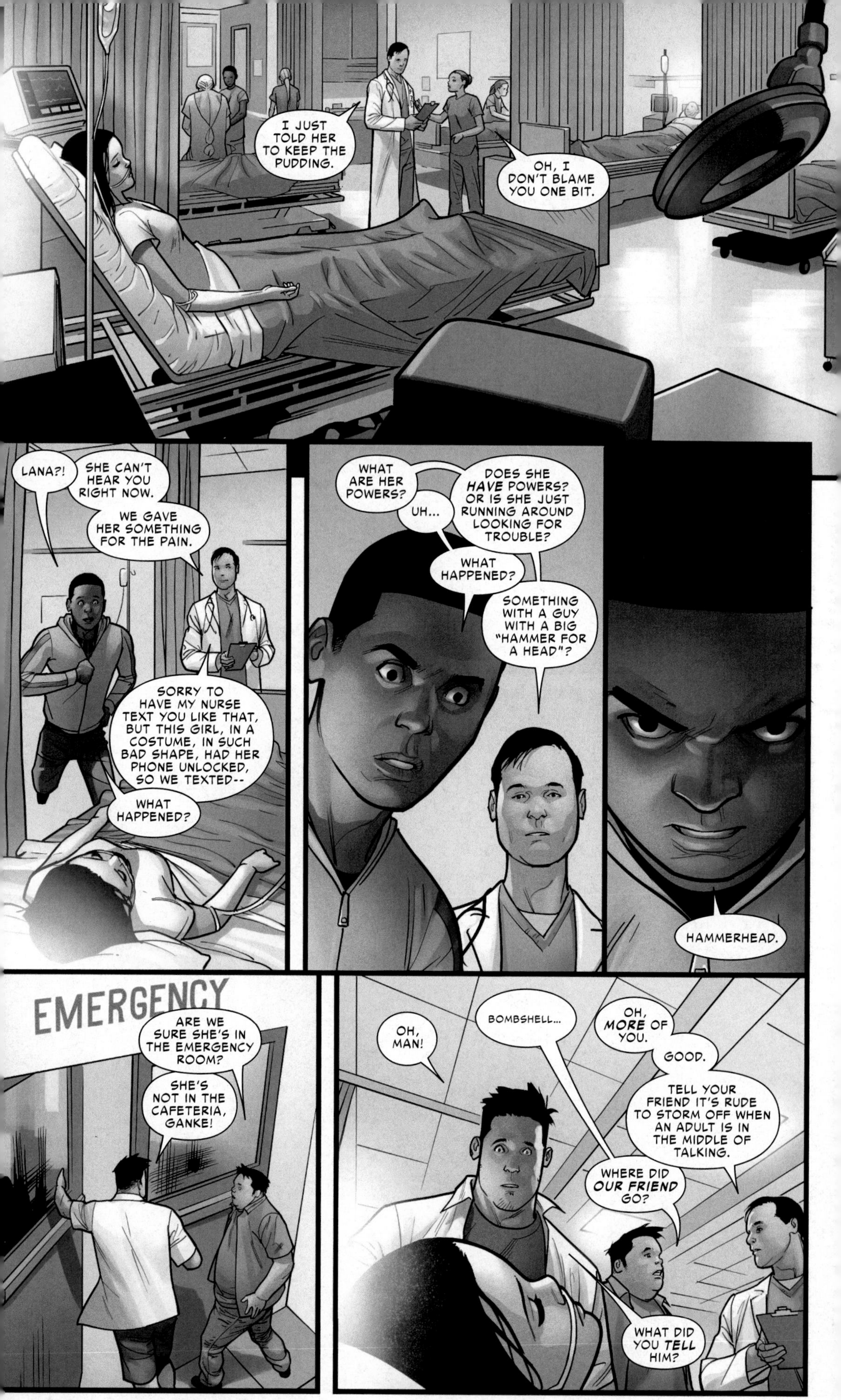
I JUST TOLD HER TO KEEP THE PUDDING.
OH, I DON'T BLAME YOU ONE BIT.
LANA?!
SHE CAN'T HEAR YOU RIGHT NOW.
WE GAVE HER SOMETHING FOR THE PAIN.
SORRY TO HAVE MY NURSE TEXT YOU LIKE THAT, BUT THIS GIRL, IN A COSTUME, IN SUCH BAD SHAPE, HAD HER PHONE UNLOCKED, SO WE TEXTED--
WHAT HAPPENED?
WHAT ARE HER POWERS?
DOES SHE HAVE POWERS? OR IS SHE JUST RUNNING AROUND LOOKING FOR TROUBLE?
UH...
WHAT HAPPENED?
SOMETHING WITH A GUY WITH A BIG "HAMMER FOR A HEAD"?
HAMMERHEAD.
EMERGENCY
ARE WE SURE SHE'S IN THE EMERGENCY ROOM?
SHE'S NOT IN THE CAFETERIA, GANKE!
OH, MAN!
BOMBSHELL...
OH, MORE OF YOU.
GOOD.
TELL YOUR FRIEND IT'S RUDE TO STORM OFF WHEN AN ADULT IS IN THE MIDDLE OF TALKING.
WHERE DID OUR FRIEND GO?
WHAT DID YOU TELL HIM?

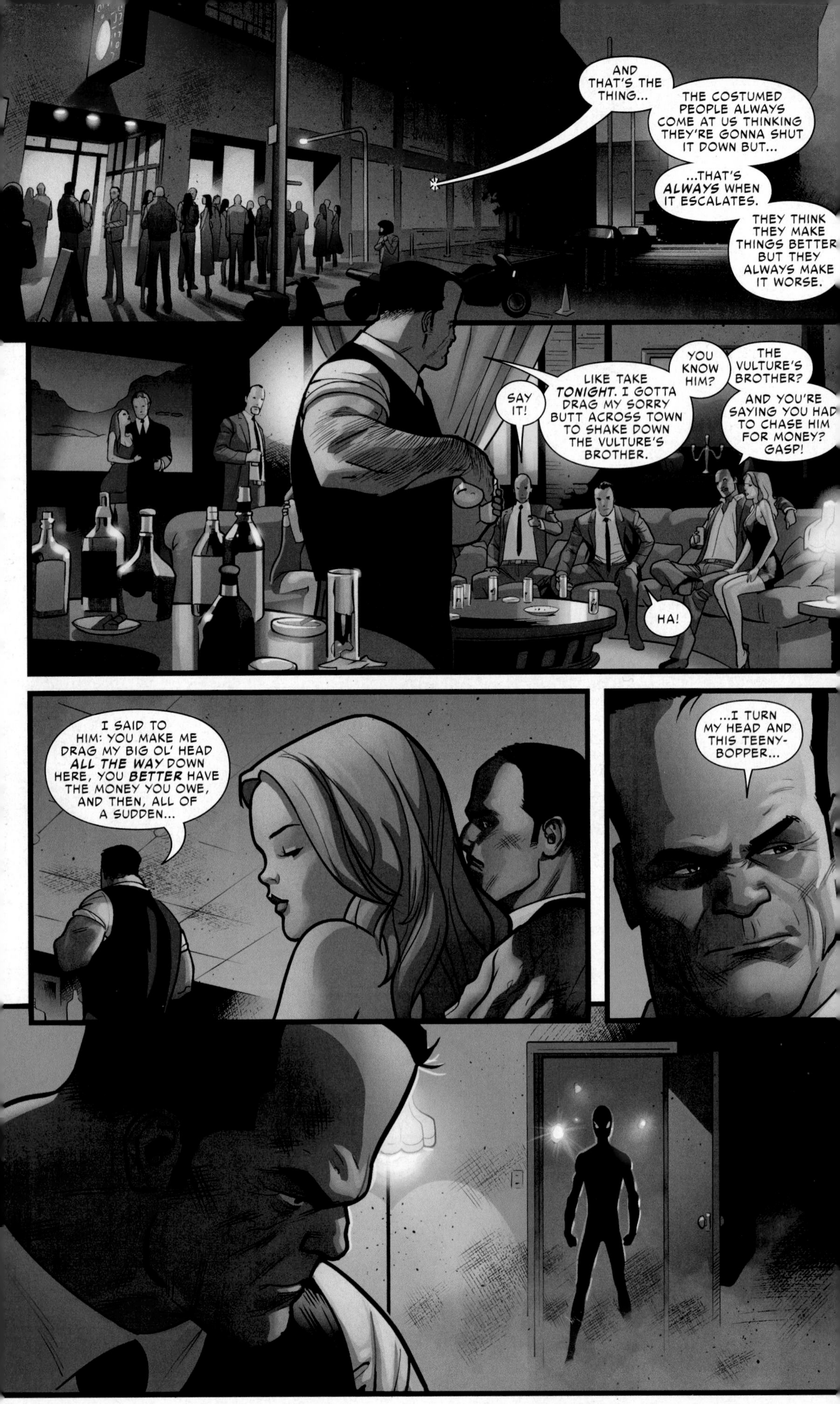
AND THAT'S THE THING...
THE COSTUMED PEOPLE ALWAYS COME AT US THINKING THEY'RE GONNA SHUT IT DOWN BUT...
...THAT'S ALWAYS WHEN IT ESCALATES.
THEY THINK THEY MAKE THINGS BETTER BUT THEY ALWAYS MAKE IT WORSE.
SAY IT!
LIKE TAKE TONIGHT. I GOTTA DRAG MY SORRY BUTT ACROSS TOWN TO SHAKE DOWN THE VULTURE'S BROTHER.
YOU KNOW HIM?
THE VULTURE'S BROTHER?
AND YOU'RE SAYING YOU HAD TO CHASE HIM FOR MONEY? GASP!
HA!
I SAID TO HIM: YOU MAKE ME DRAG MY BIG OL' HEAD ALL THE WAY DOWN HERE, YOU BETTER HAVE THE MONEY YOU OWE, AND THEN, ALL OF A SUDDEN...
...I TURN MY HEAD AND THIS TEENY-BOPPER...

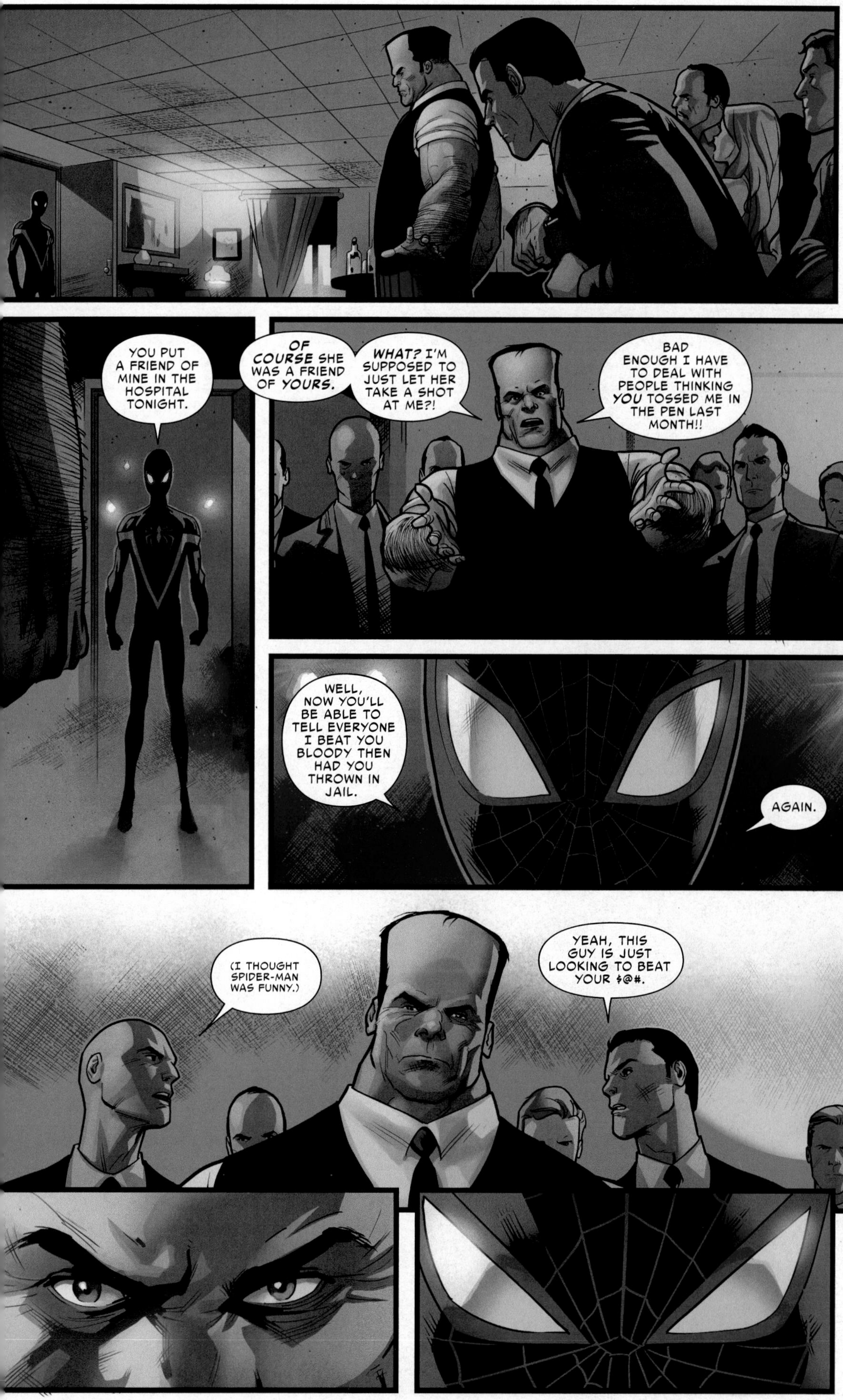

YOU PUT A FRIEND OF MINE IN THE HOSPITAL TONIGHT.
OF COURSE SHE WAS A FRIEND OF YOURS.
WHAT? I'M SUPPOSED TO JUST LET HER TAKE A SHOT AT ME?!
BAD ENOUGH I HAVE TO DEAL WITH PEOPLE THINKING YOU TOSSED ME IN THE PEN LAST MONTH!!
WELL, NOW YOU'LL BE ABLE TO TELL EVERYONE I BEAT YOU BLOODY THEN HAD YOU THROWN IN JAIL.
AGAIN.
(I THOUGHT SPIDER-MAN WAS FUNNY.)
YEAH, THIS GUY IS JUST LOOKING TO BEAT YOUR $@#.

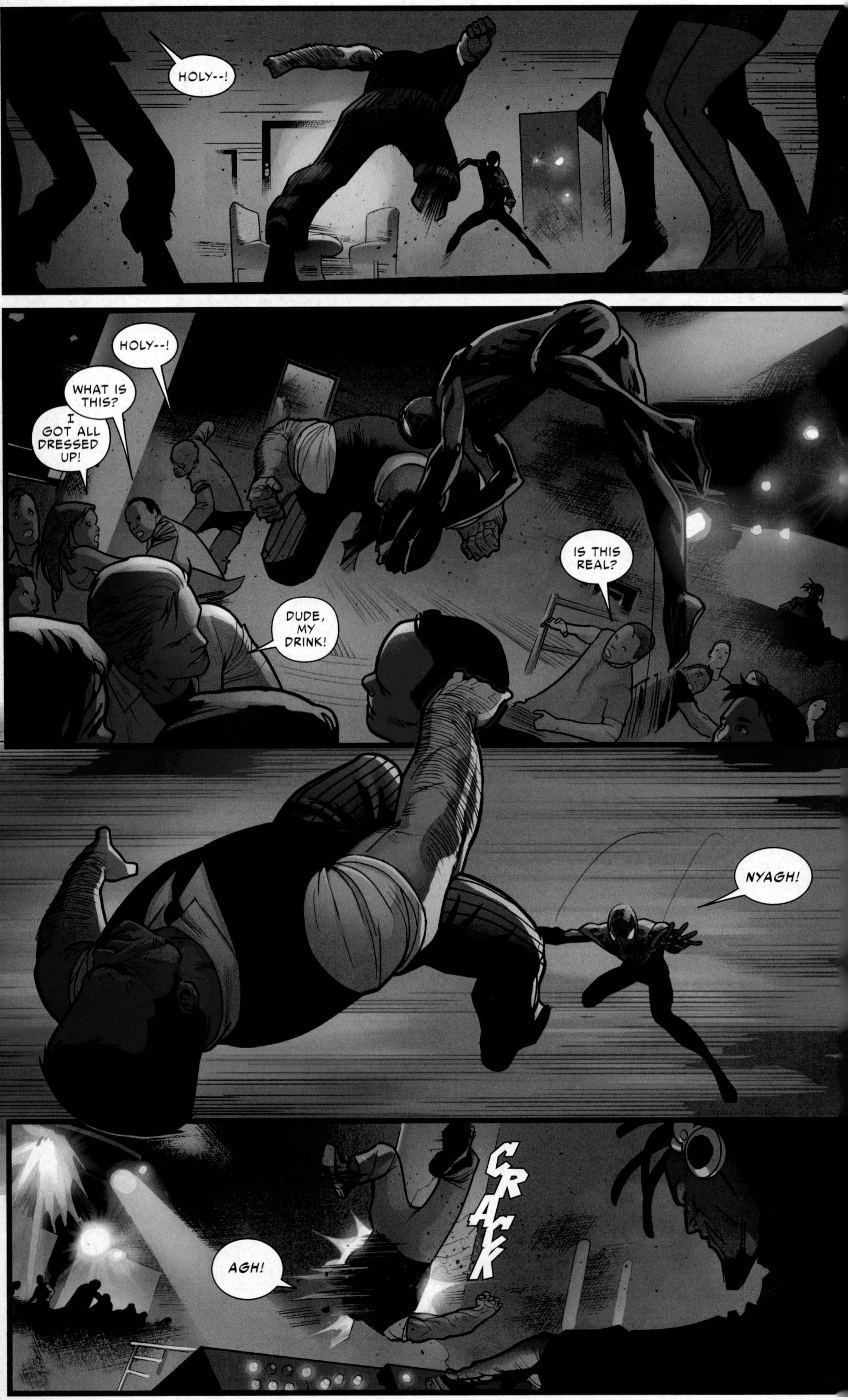
HOLY--!
HOLY--!
WHAT IS THIS?
I GOT ALL DRESSED UP!
IS THIS REAL?
DUDE, MY DRINK!
NYAGH!
CRACK
AGH!

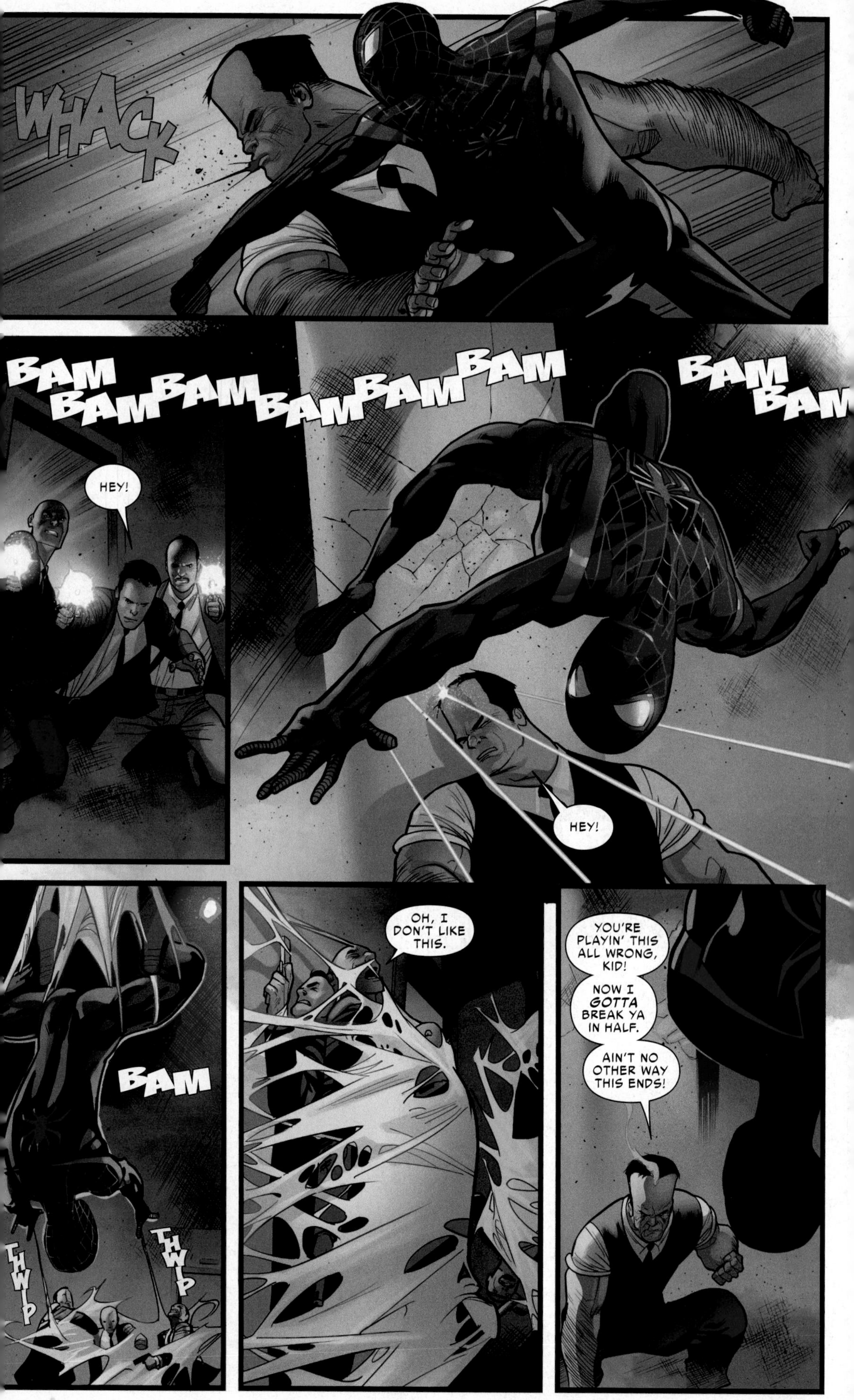
WHACK
BAM
BAM BAM BAM BAM BAM
HEY!
BAM
BAM
BAM BAM
HEY!
BAM
THWIP
THWIP
OH, I DON'T LIKE THIS.
YOU'RE PLAYIN' THIS ALL WRONG, KID!
NOW I *GOTTA* BREAK YA IN HALF.
AIN'T NO OTHER WAY THIS ENDS!

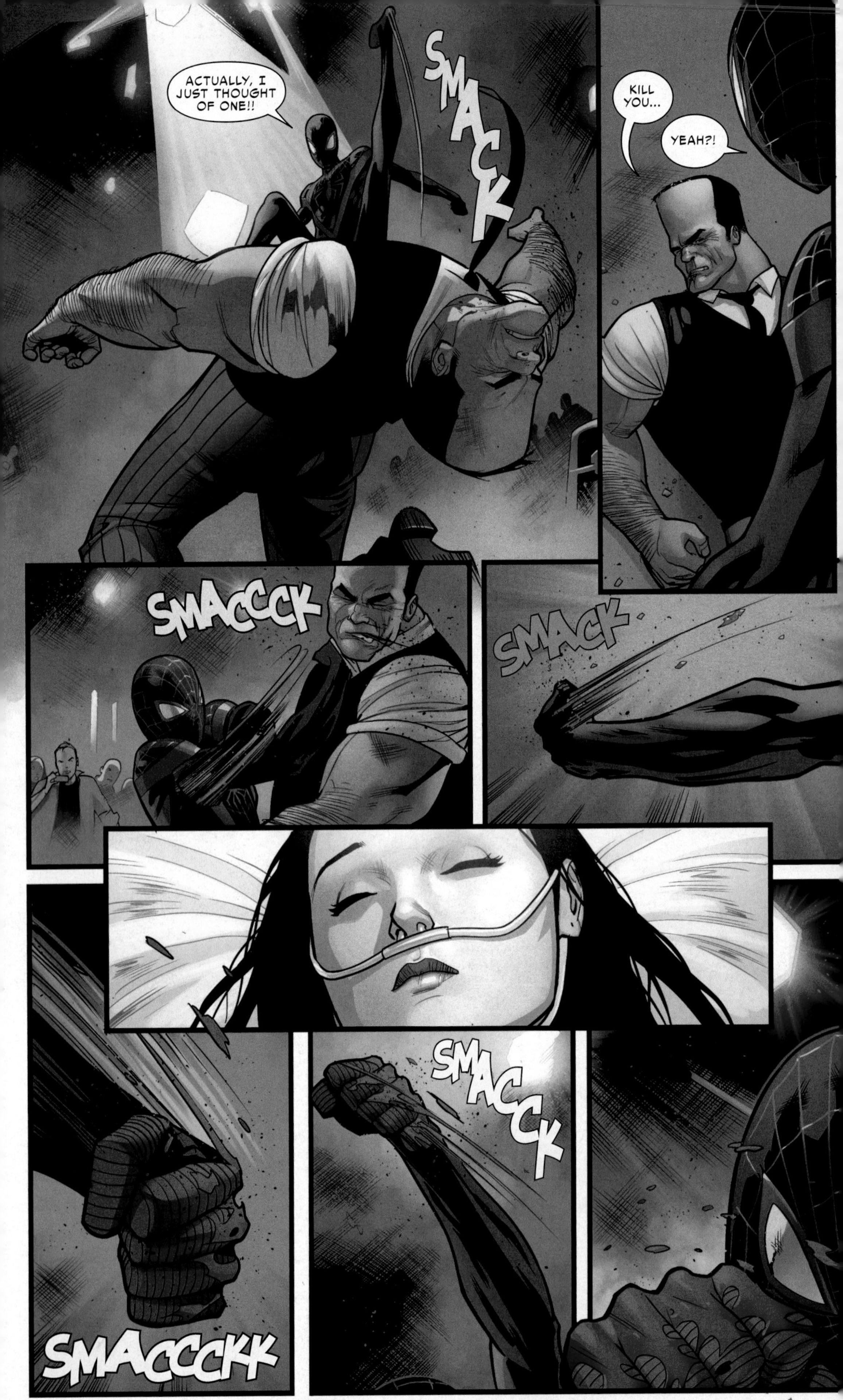
ACTUALLY, I JUST THOUGHT OF ONE!!
SMACK
KILL YOU...
YEAH?!
SMACCCK
SMACK
SMACCCK
SMACCCKK

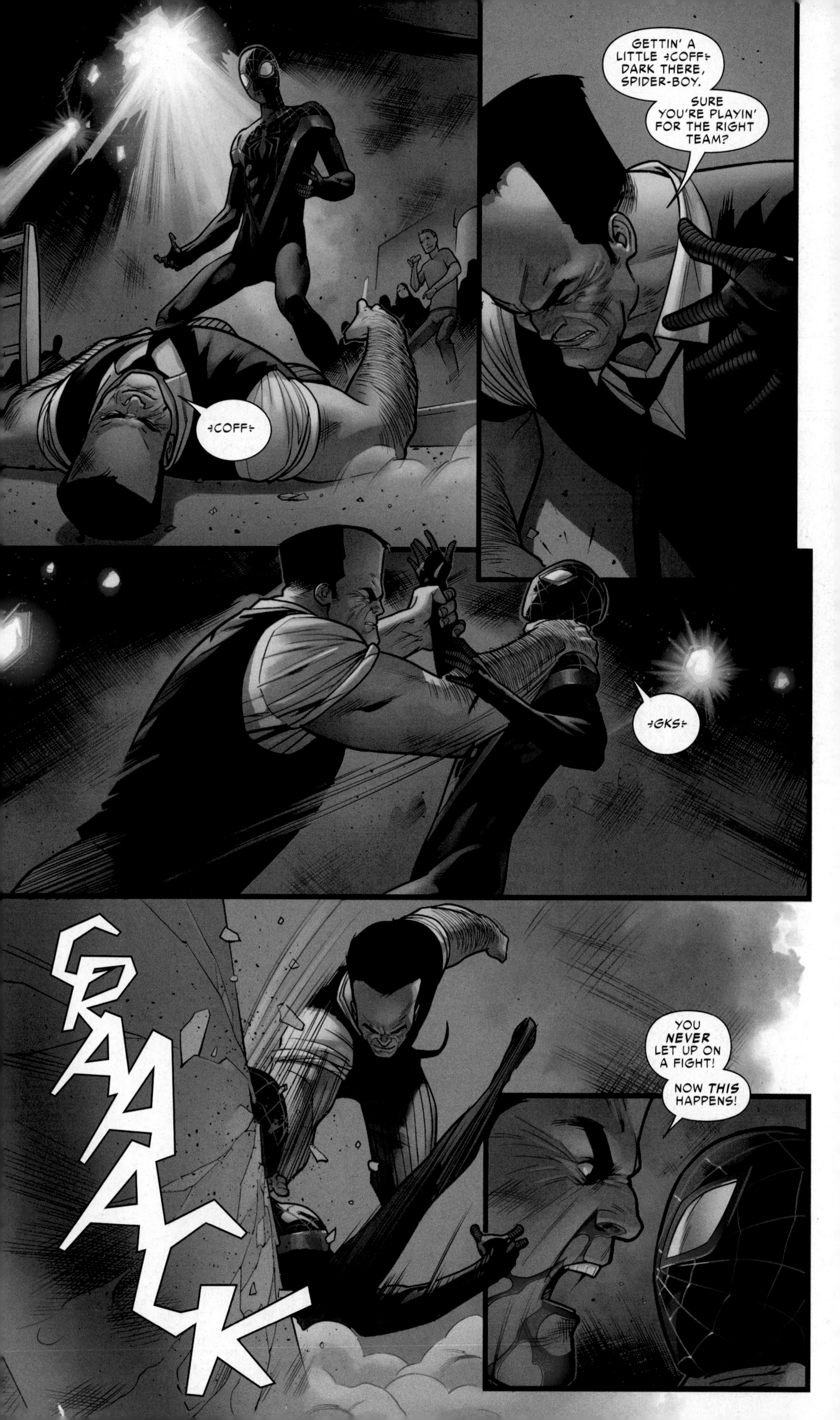

≑COFF≑
GETTIN' A LITTLE ≑COFF≑ DARK THERE, SPIDER-BOY.
SURE YOU'RE PLAYIN' FOR THE RIGHT TEAM?
≑GKS≑
CRAAACK
YOU **NEVER** LET UP ON A FIGHT!
NOW **THIS** HAPPENS!

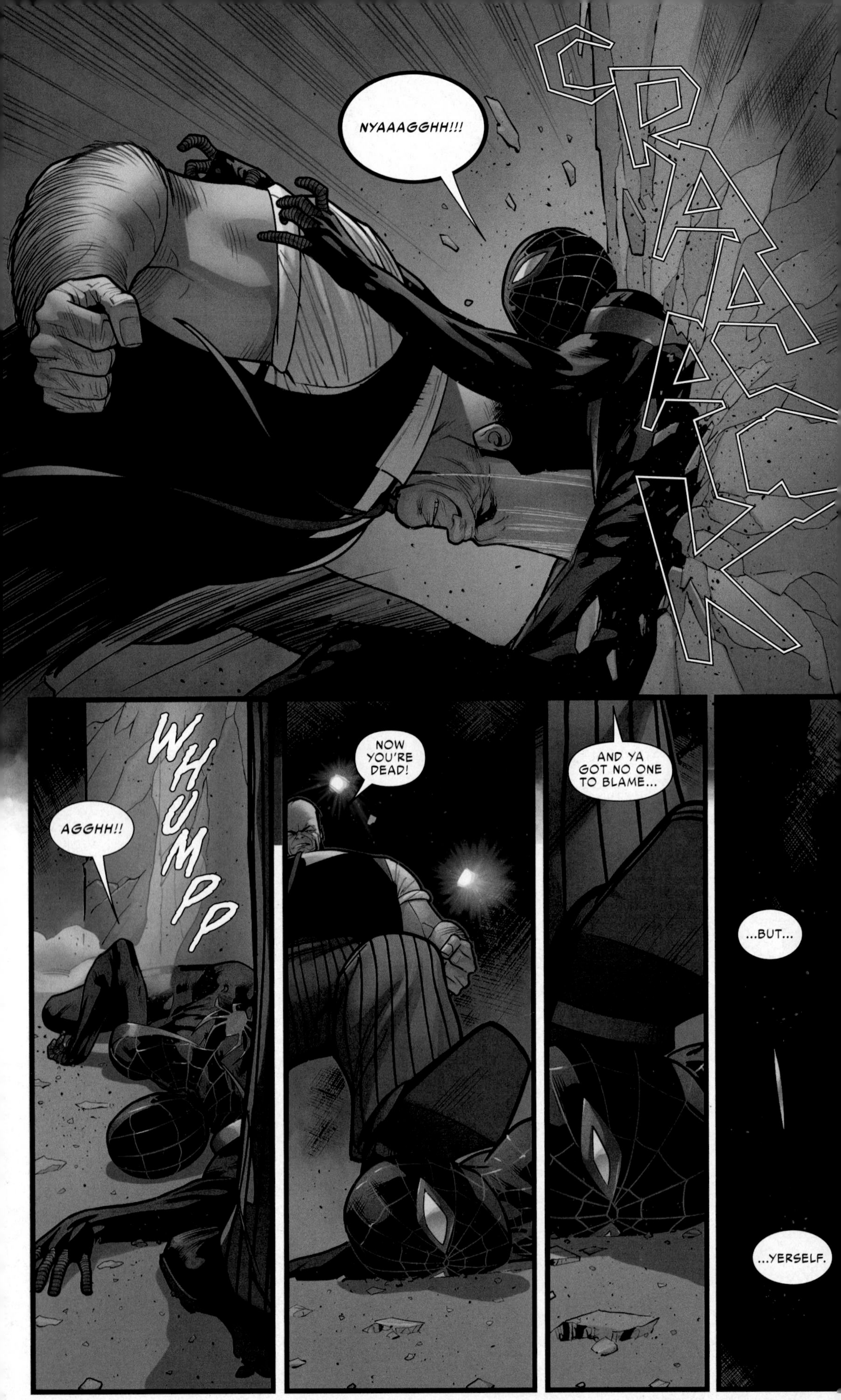
CRRAAACK
NYAAAGGHH!!!
WHUMPP
AGGHH!!
NOW YOU'RE DEAD!
AND YA GOT NO ONE TO BLAME...
...BUT...
...YERSELF.

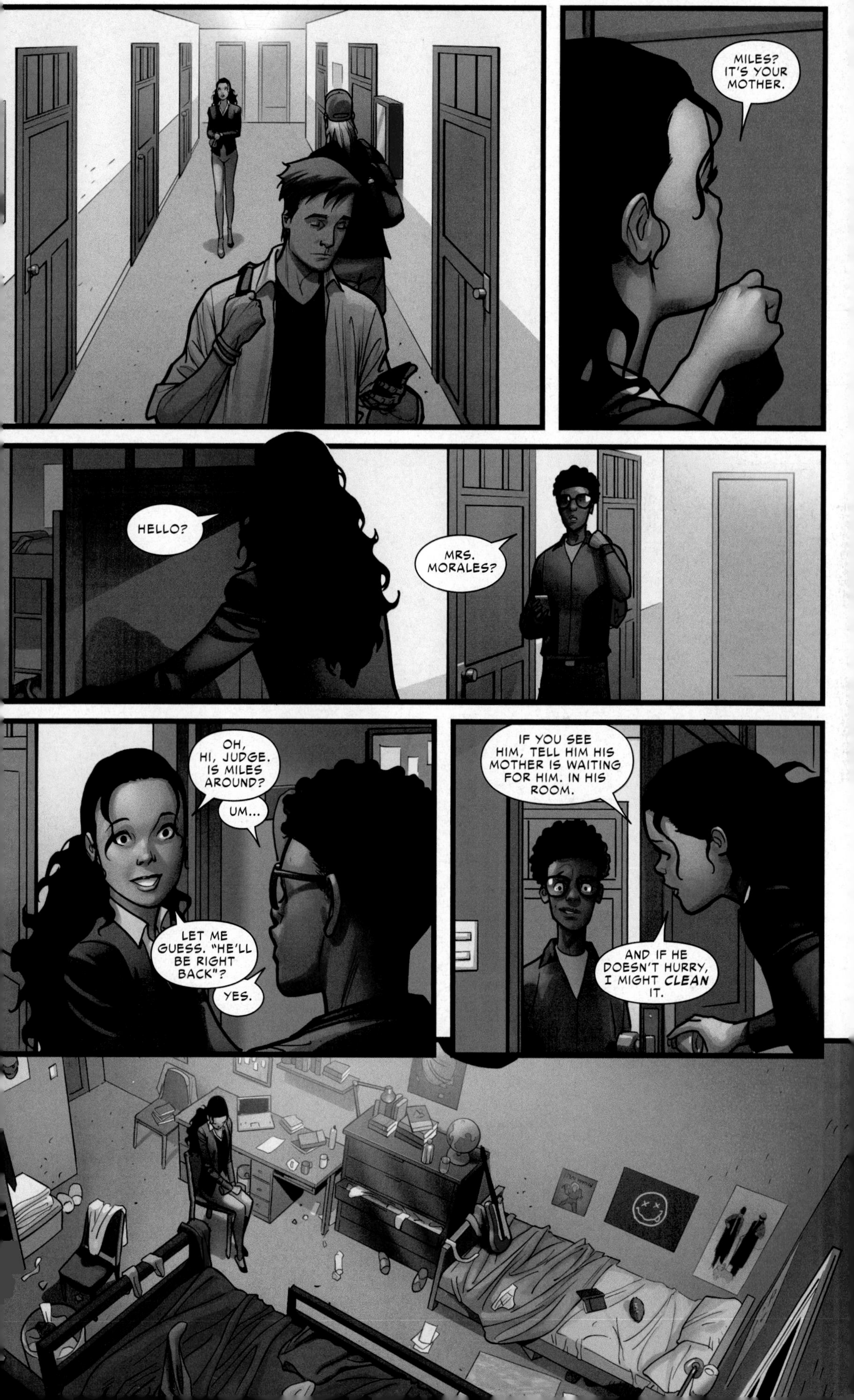

MILES? IT'S YOUR MOTHER.
HELLO?
MRS. MORALES?
OH, HI, JUDGE. IS MILES AROUND?
UM...
LET ME GUESS. "HE'LL BE RIGHT BACK"?
YES.
IF YOU SEE HIM, TELL HIM HIS MOTHER IS WAITING FOR HIM. IN HIS ROOM.
AND IF HE DOESN'T HURRY, I MIGHT *CLEAN* IT.

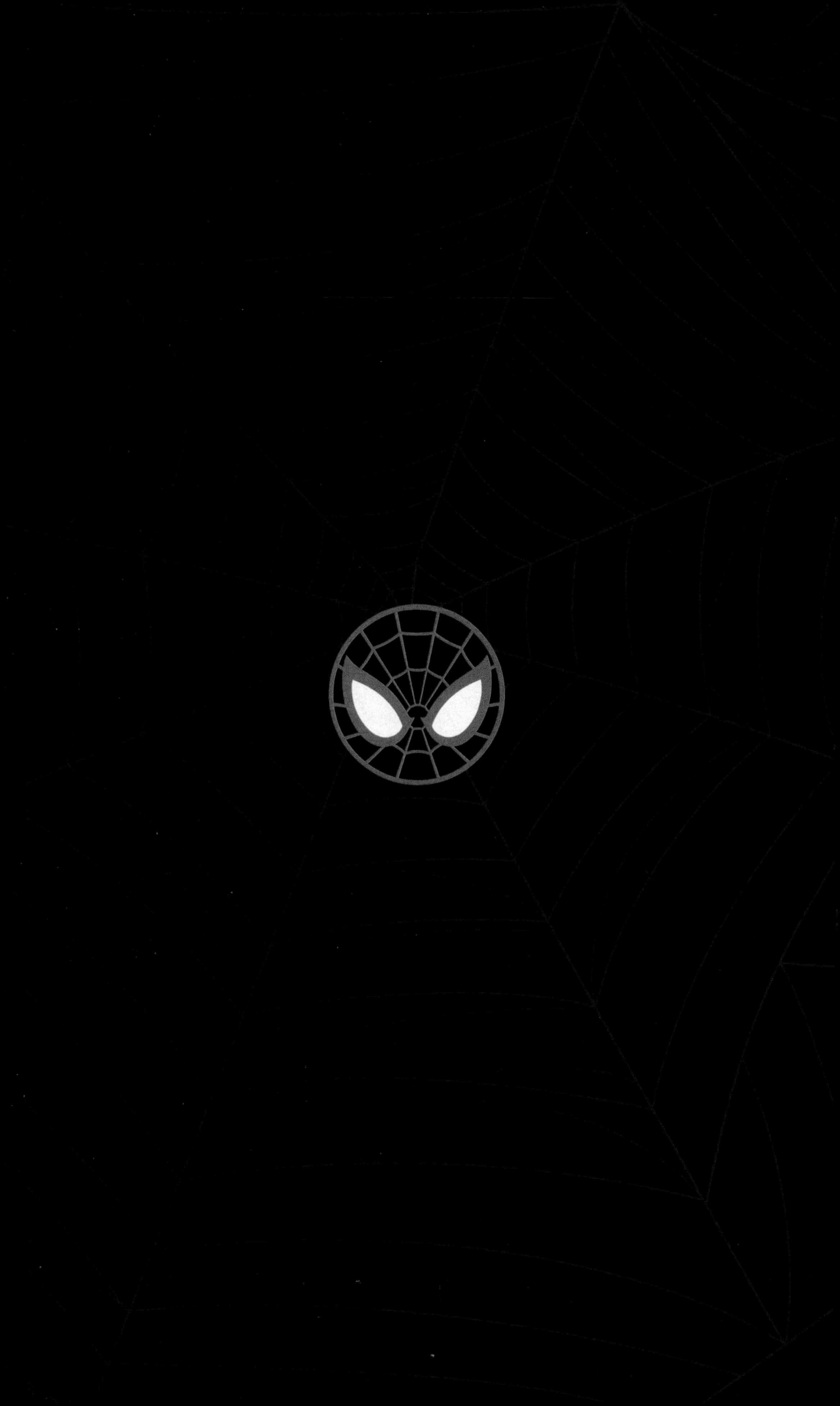

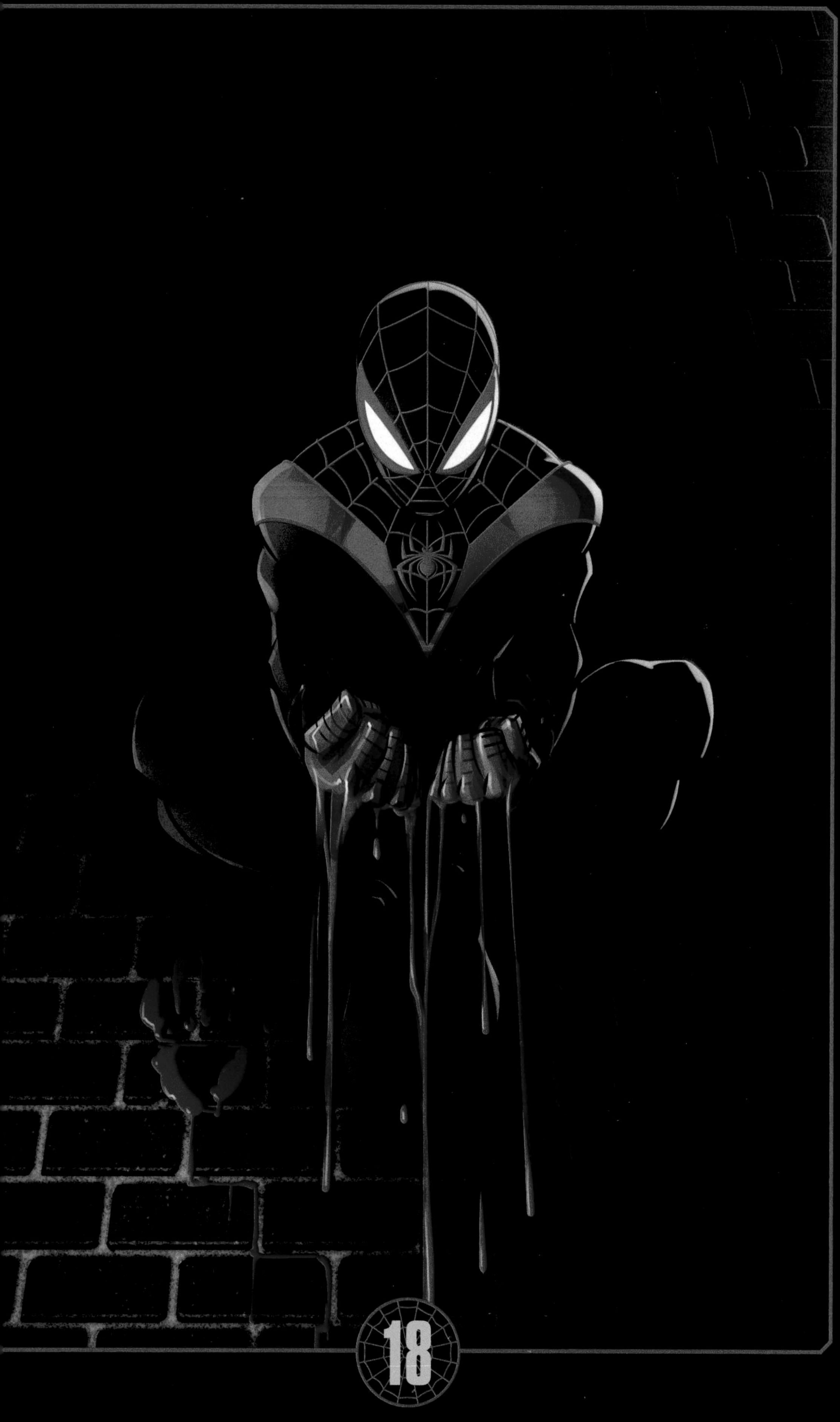

18

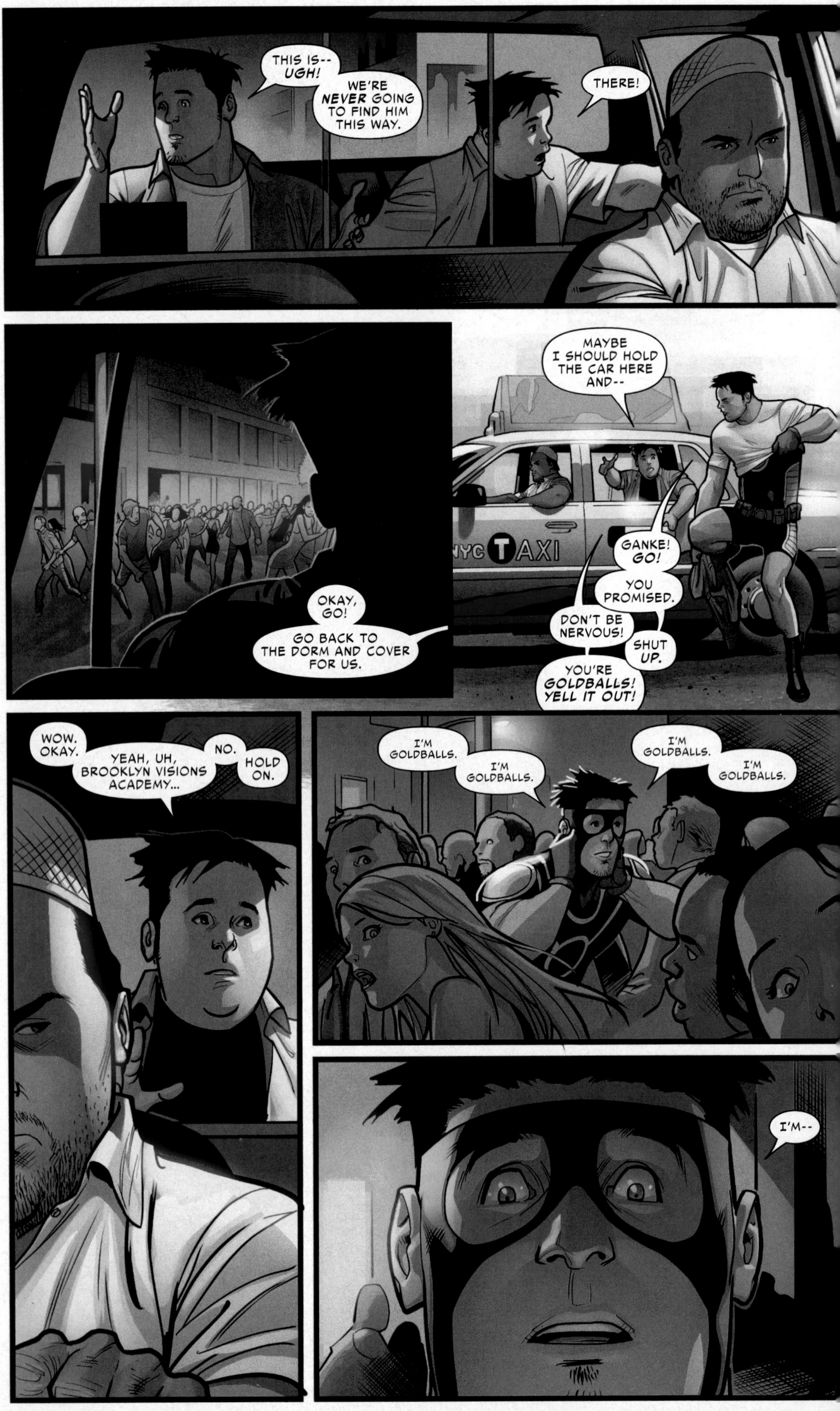
THIS IS-- UGH!
WE'RE NEVER GOING TO FIND HIM THIS WAY.
THERE!
MAYBE I SHOULD HOLD THE CAR HERE AND--
NYC TAXI
GANKE! GO!
YOU PROMISED.
DON'T BE NERVOUS!
SHUT UP.
YOU'RE GOLDBALLS! YELL IT OUT!
OKAY, GO!
GO BACK TO THE DORM AND COVER FOR US.
WOW. OKAY.
YEAH, UH, BROOKLYN VISIONS ACADEMY...
NO.
HOLD ON.
I'M GOLDBALLS.
I'M GOLDBALLS.
I'M GOLDBALLS.
I'M GOLDBALLS.
I'M--

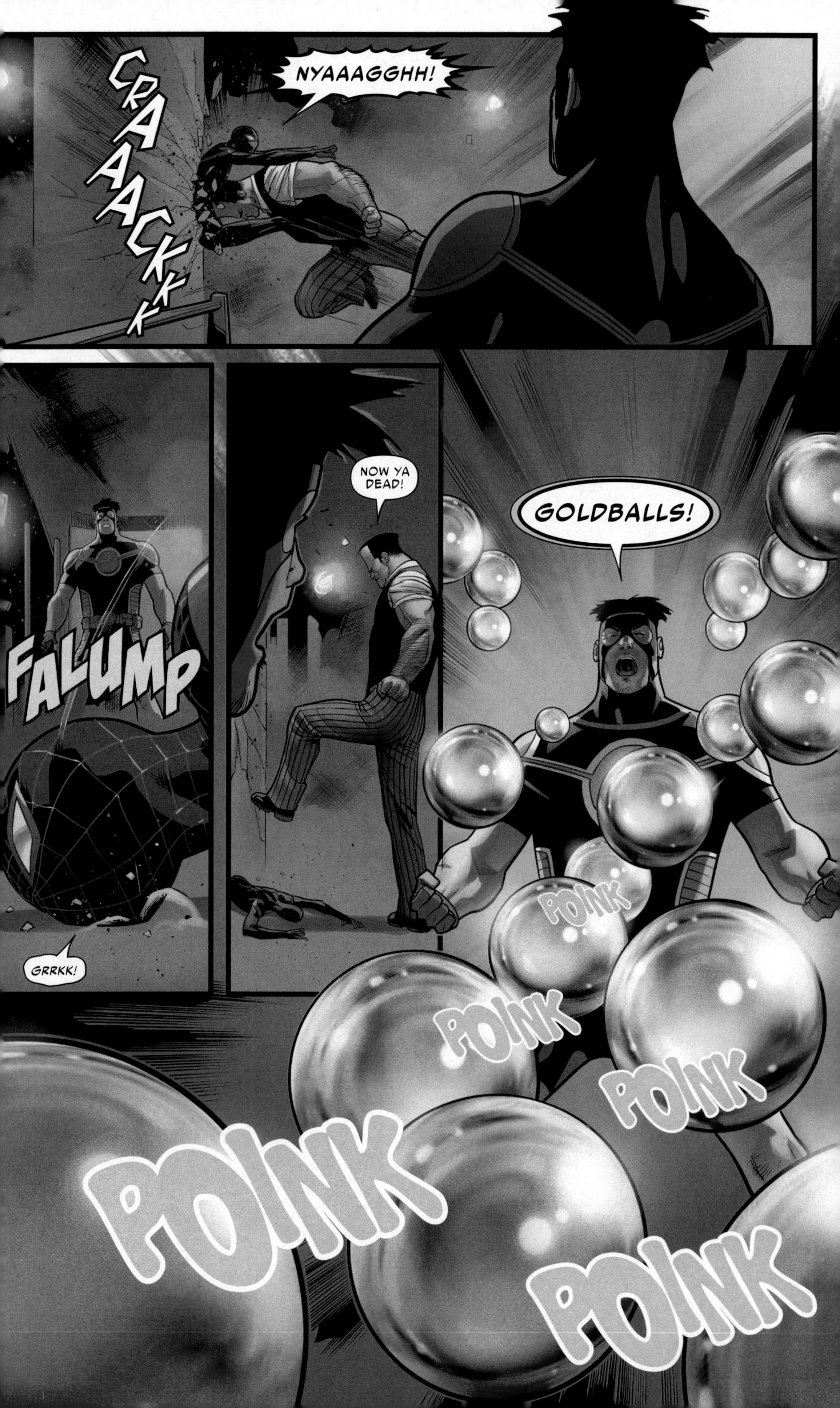

CRAAACKKK
NYAAAGGHH!
FALUMP
GRRKK!
NOW YA DEAD!
GOLDBALLS!
POINK
POINK
POINK
POINK
POINK

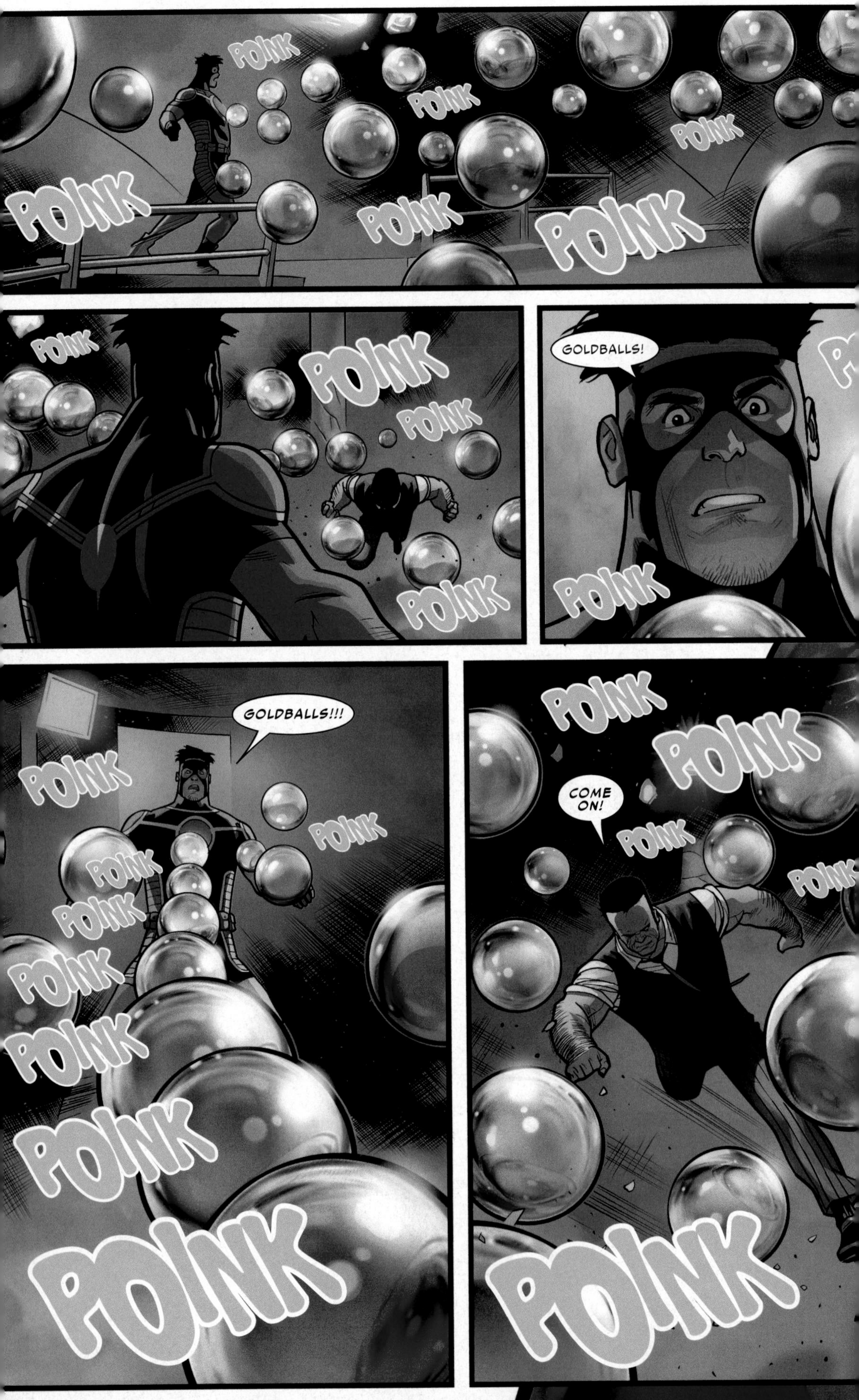
POINK
POINK
POINK
POINK
POINK
POINK
POINK
POINK
POINK
POINK
GOLDBALLS!
POINK
GOLDBALLS!!!
POINK
POINK
POINK
POINK
POINK
POINK
POINK
POINK
POINK
POINK
COME ON!
POINK
POINK
POINK

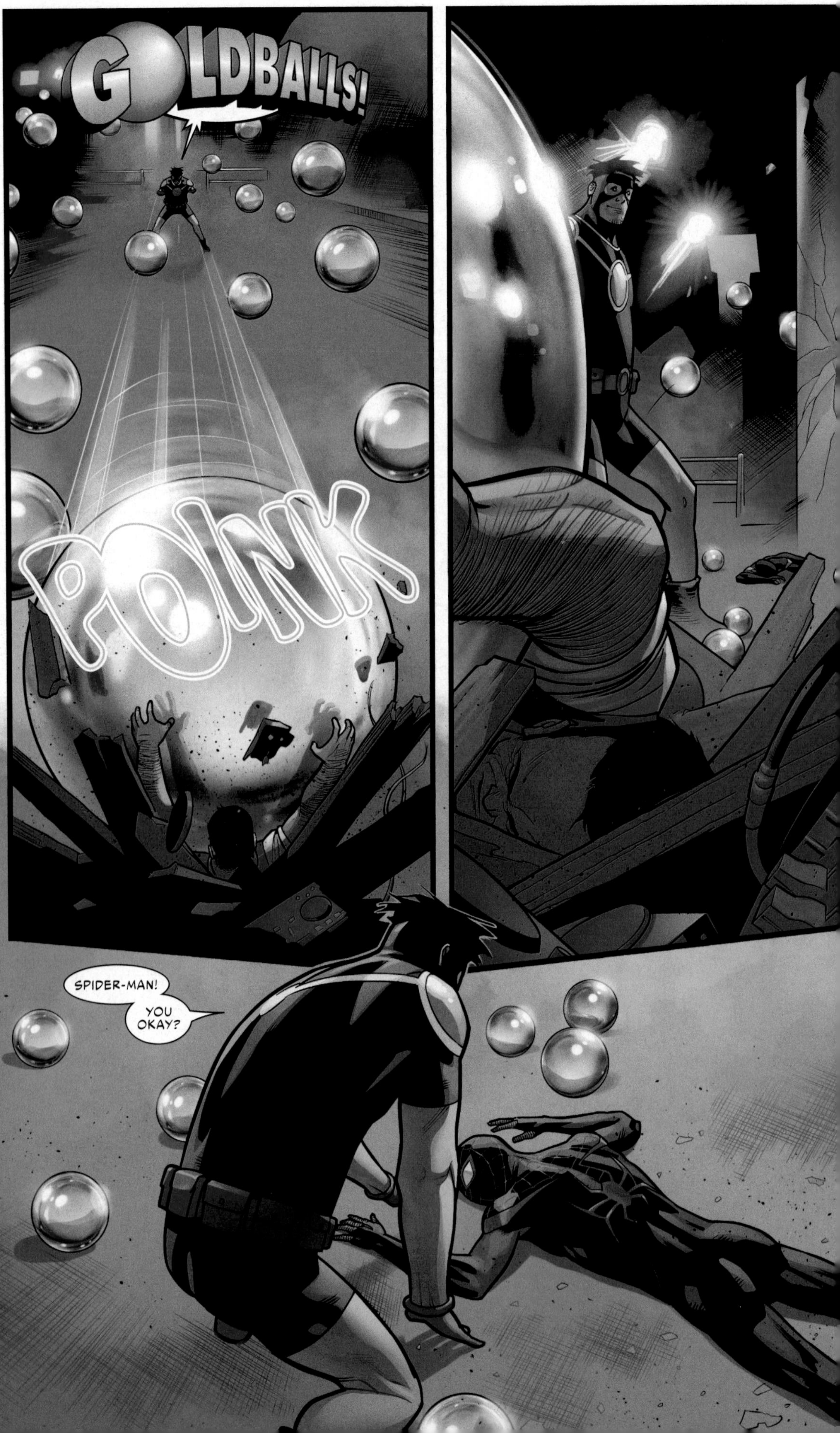
GOLDBALLS!
POINK
SPIDER-MAN!
YOU OKAY?

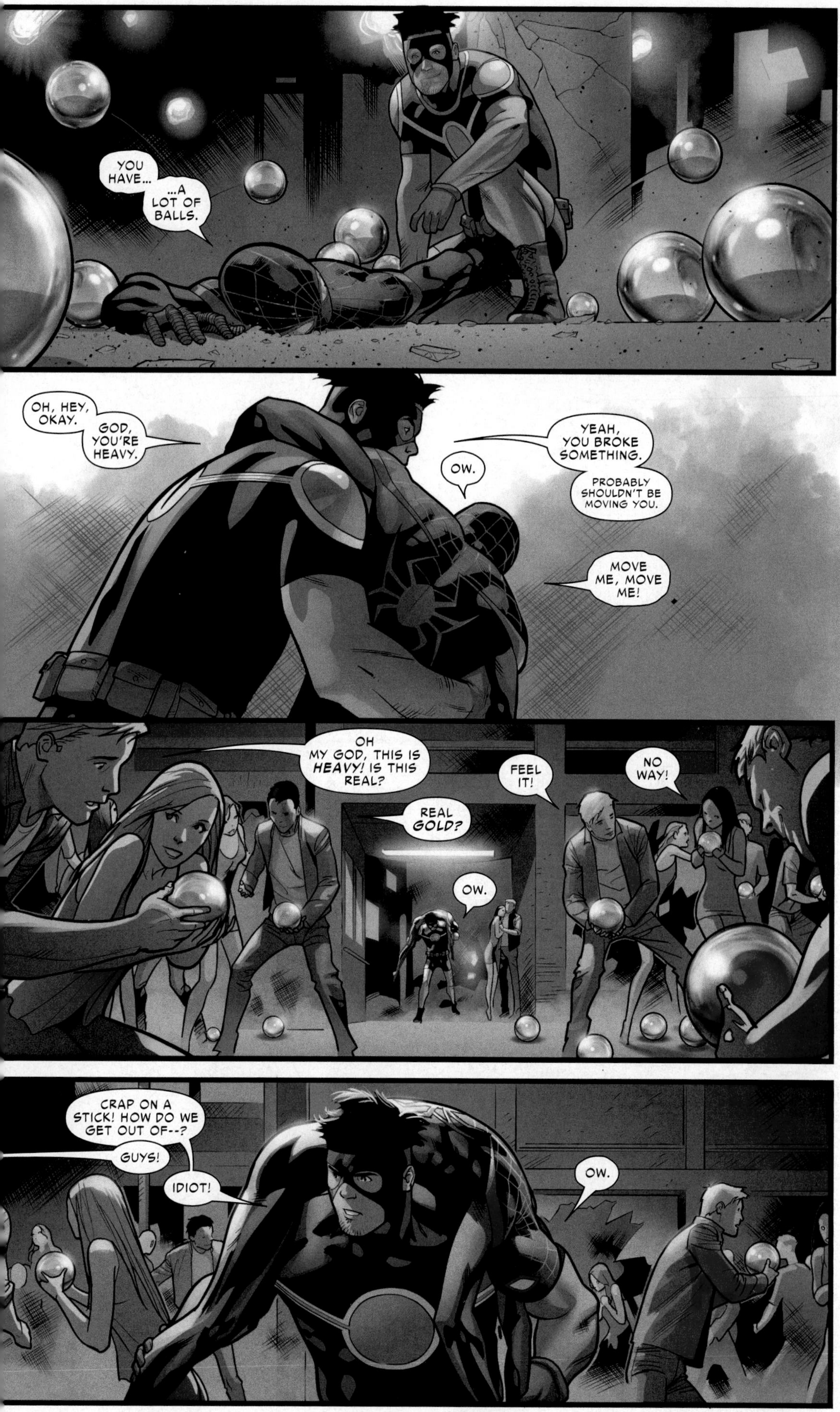
YOU HAVE...
...A LOT OF BALLS.
OH, HEY, OKAY.
GOD, YOU'RE HEAVY.
OW.
YEAH, YOU BROKE SOMETHING.
PROBABLY SHOULDN'T BE MOVING YOU.
MOVE ME, MOVE ME!
OH MY GOD, THIS IS *HEAVY!* IS THIS REAL?
REAL *GOLD?*
FEEL IT!
NO WAY!
OW.
CRAP ON A STICK! HOW DO WE GET OUT OF--?
GUYS!
IDIOT!
OW.

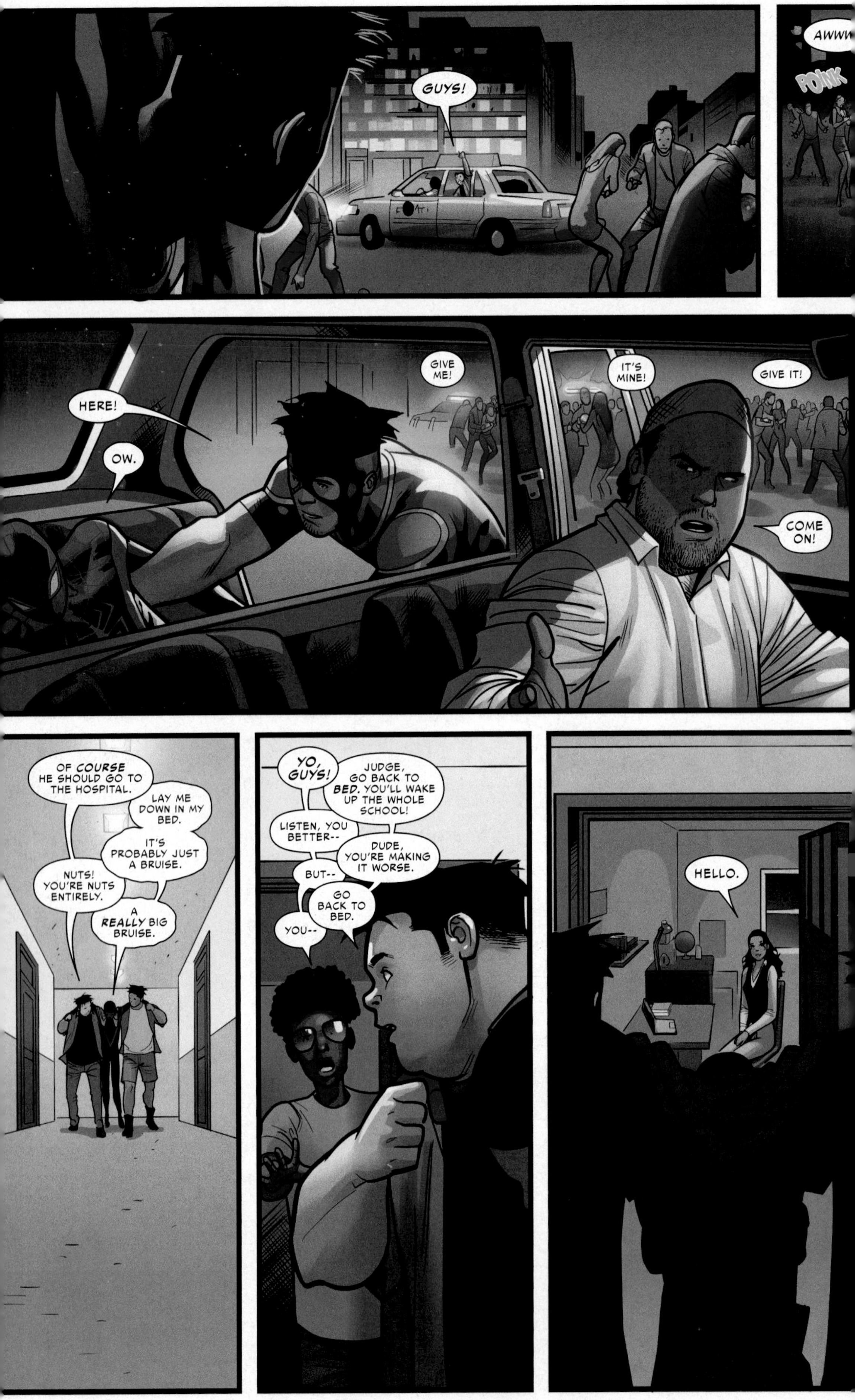
GUYS!
AWWW
POINK
HERE!
OW.
GIVE ME!
IT'S MINE!
GIVE IT!
COME ON!
OF *COURSE* HE SHOULD GO TO THE HOSPITAL.
LAY ME DOWN IN MY BED.
IT'S PROBABLY JUST A BRUISE.
NUTS! YOU'RE NUTS ENTIRELY.
A *REALLY* BIG BRUISE.
YO, GUYS!
JUDGE, GO BACK TO *BED.* YOU'LL WAKE UP THE WHOLE SCHOOL!
LISTEN, YOU BETTER--
DUDE, YOU'RE MAKING IT WORSE.
BUT--
GO BACK TO BED.
YOU--
HELLO.

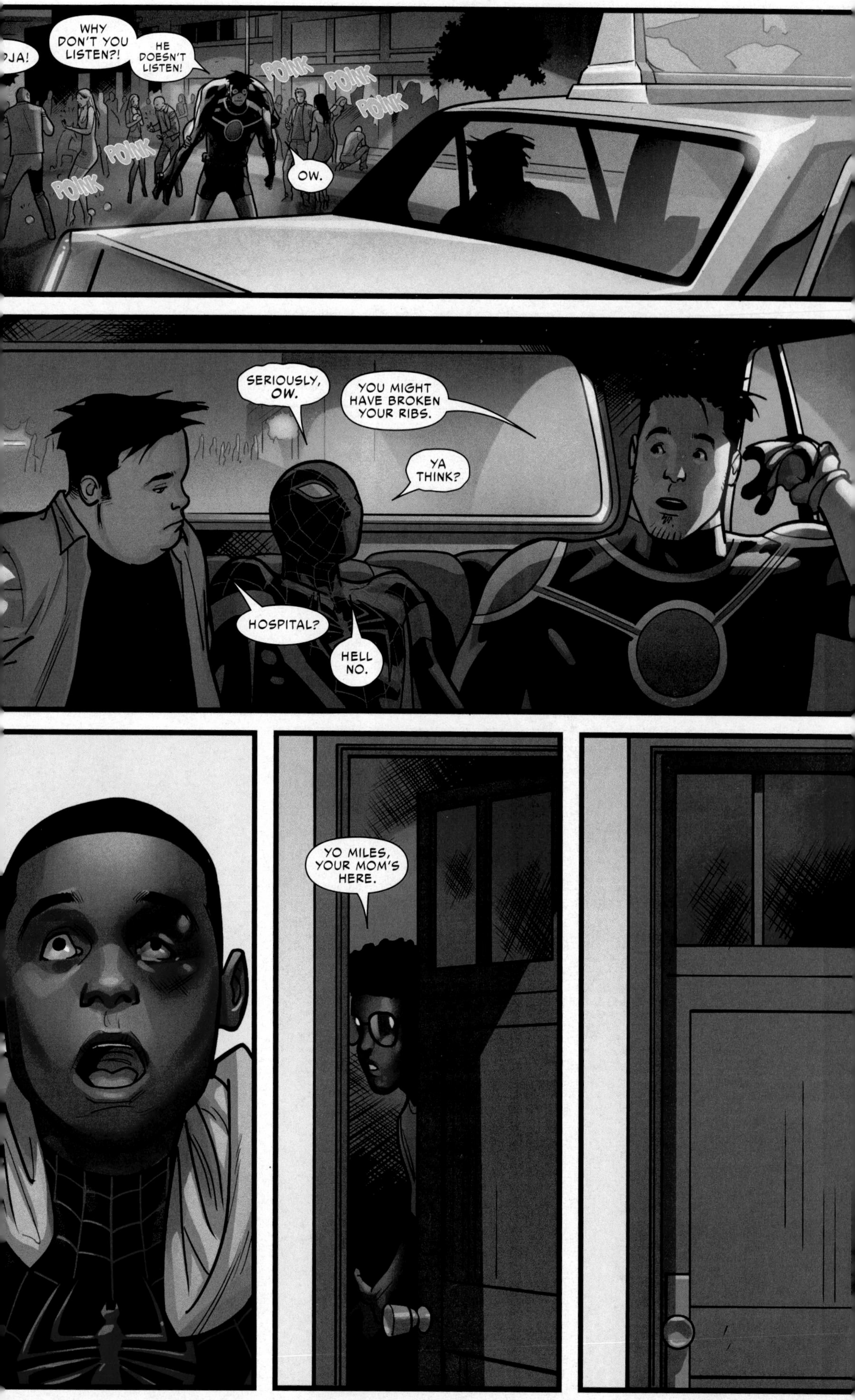

...JA!
WHY DON'T YOU LISTEN?!
HE DOESN'T LISTEN!
POINK
POINK
POINK
POINK
POINK
OW.
SERIOUSLY, OW.
YOU MIGHT HAVE BROKEN YOUR RIBS.
YA THINK?
HOSPITAL?
HELL NO.
YO MILES, YOUR MOM'S HERE.

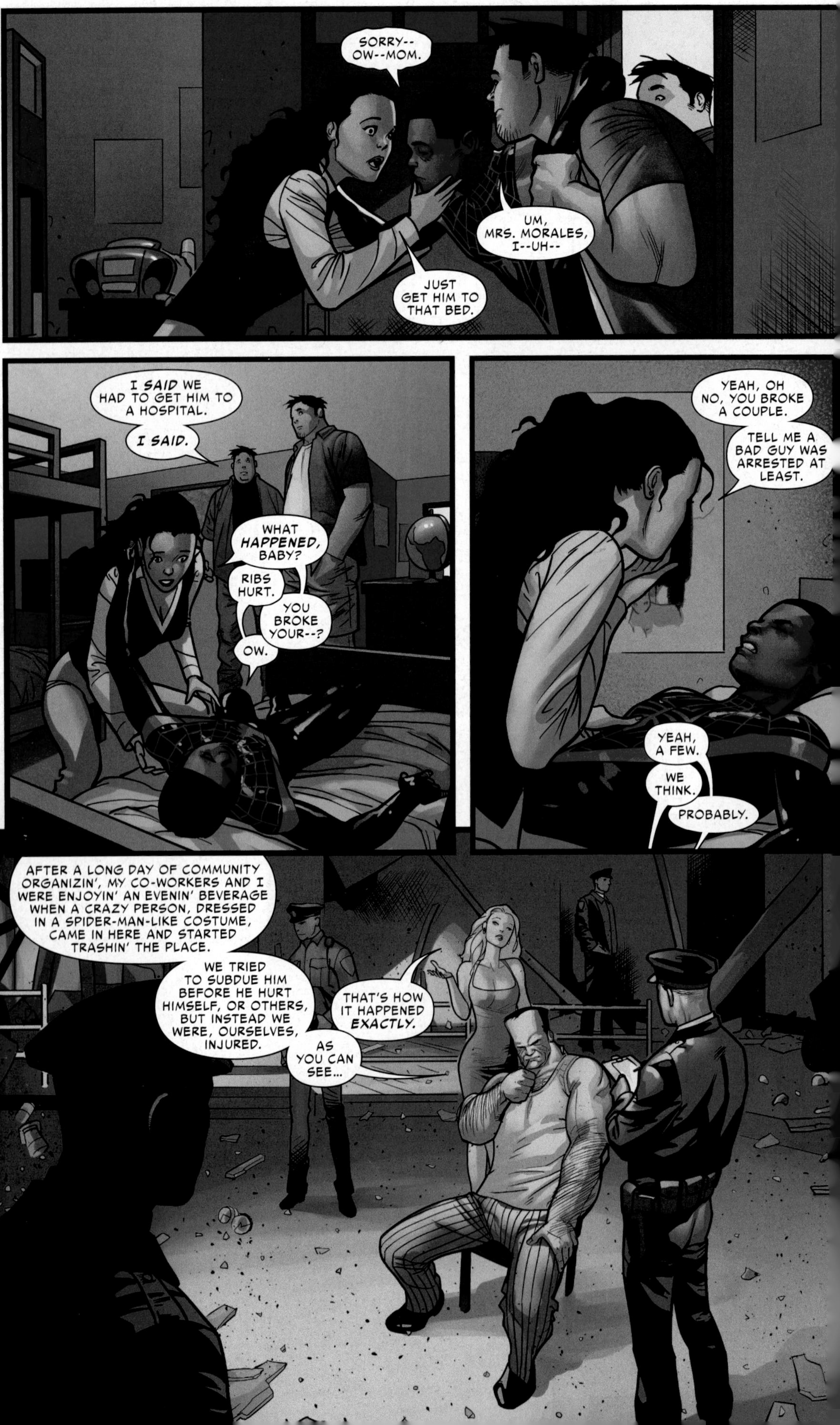
SORRY--
OW--MOM.
UM, MRS. MORALES, I--UH--
JUST GET HIM TO THAT BED.
I *SAID* WE HAD TO GET HIM TO A HOSPITAL.
I SAID.
WHAT *HAPPENED,* BABY?
RIBS HURT.
YOU BROKE YOUR--?
OW.
YEAH, OH NO, YOU BROKE A COUPLE.
TELL ME A BAD GUY WAS ARRESTED AT LEAST.
YEAH, A FEW.
WE THINK.
PROBABLY.
AFTER A LONG DAY OF COMMUNITY ORGANIZIN', MY CO-WORKERS AND I WERE ENJOYIN' AN EVENIN' BEVERAGE WHEN A CRAZY PERSON, DRESSED IN A SPIDER-MAN-LIKE COSTUME, CAME IN HERE AND STARTED TRASHIN' THE PLACE.
WE TRIED TO SUBDUE HIM BEFORE HE HURT HIMSELF, OR OTHERS, BUT INSTEAD WE WERE, OURSELVES, INJURED.
AS YOU CAN SEE...
THAT'S HOW IT HAPPENED *EXACTLY.*

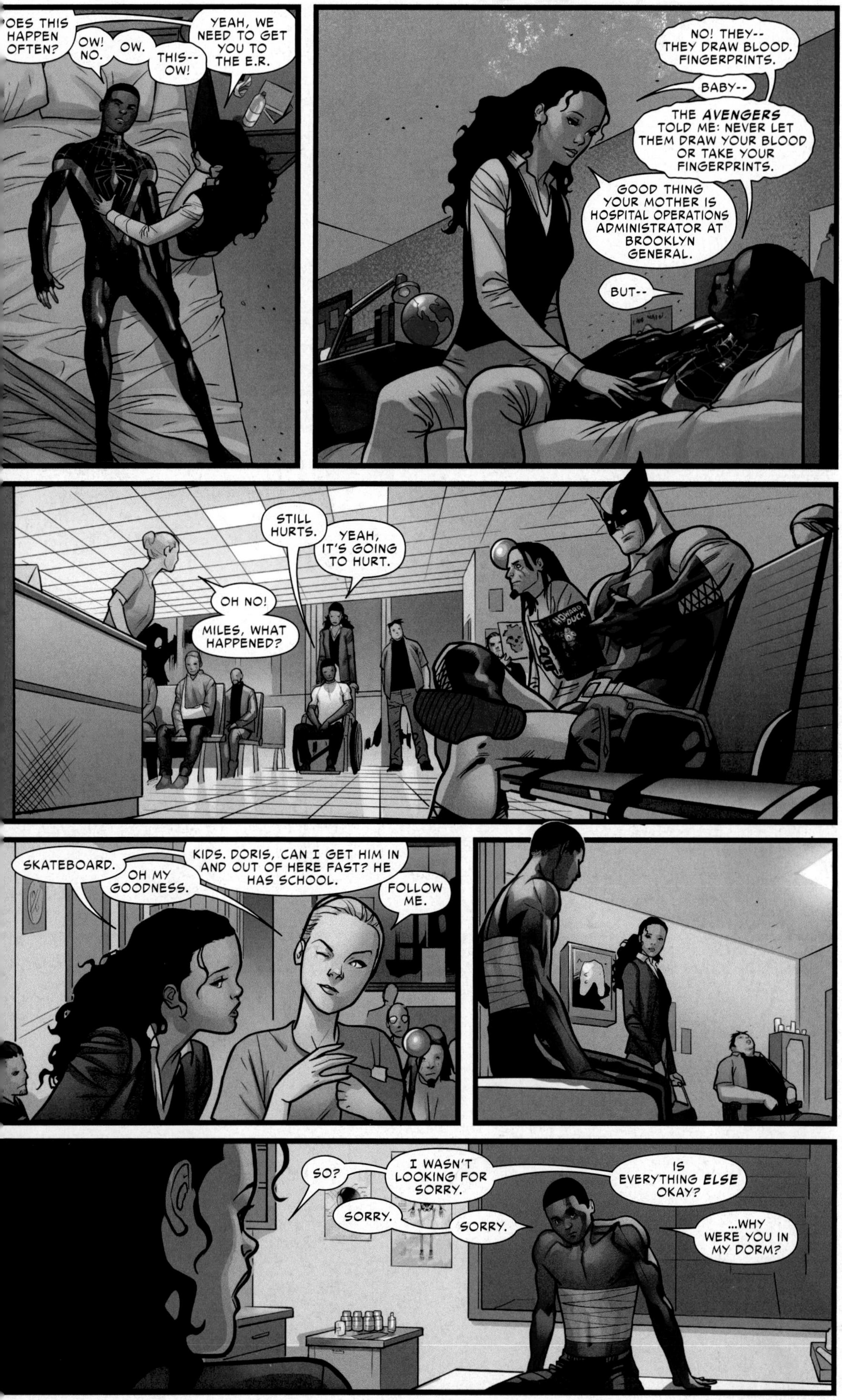

DOES THIS HAPPEN OFTEN?
OW! NO.
OW.
THIS-- OW!
YEAH, WE NEED TO GET YOU TO THE E.R.
NO! THEY-- THEY DRAW BLOOD. FINGERPRINTS.
BABY--
THE AVENGERS TOLD ME: NEVER LET THEM DRAW YOUR BLOOD OR TAKE YOUR FINGERPRINTS.
GOOD THING YOUR MOTHER IS HOSPITAL OPERATIONS ADMINISTRATOR AT BROOKLYN GENERAL.
BUT--
OH NO!
MILES, WHAT HAPPENED?
STILL HURTS.
YEAH, IT'S GOING TO HURT.
HOWARD DUCK
SKATEBOARD.
OH MY GOODNESS.
KIDS. DORIS, CAN I GET HIM IN AND OUT OF HERE FAST? HE HAS SCHOOL.
FOLLOW ME.
SO?
I WASN'T LOOKING FOR SORRY.
SORRY.
SORRY.
IS EVERYTHING ELSE OKAY?
...WHY WERE YOU IN MY DORM?

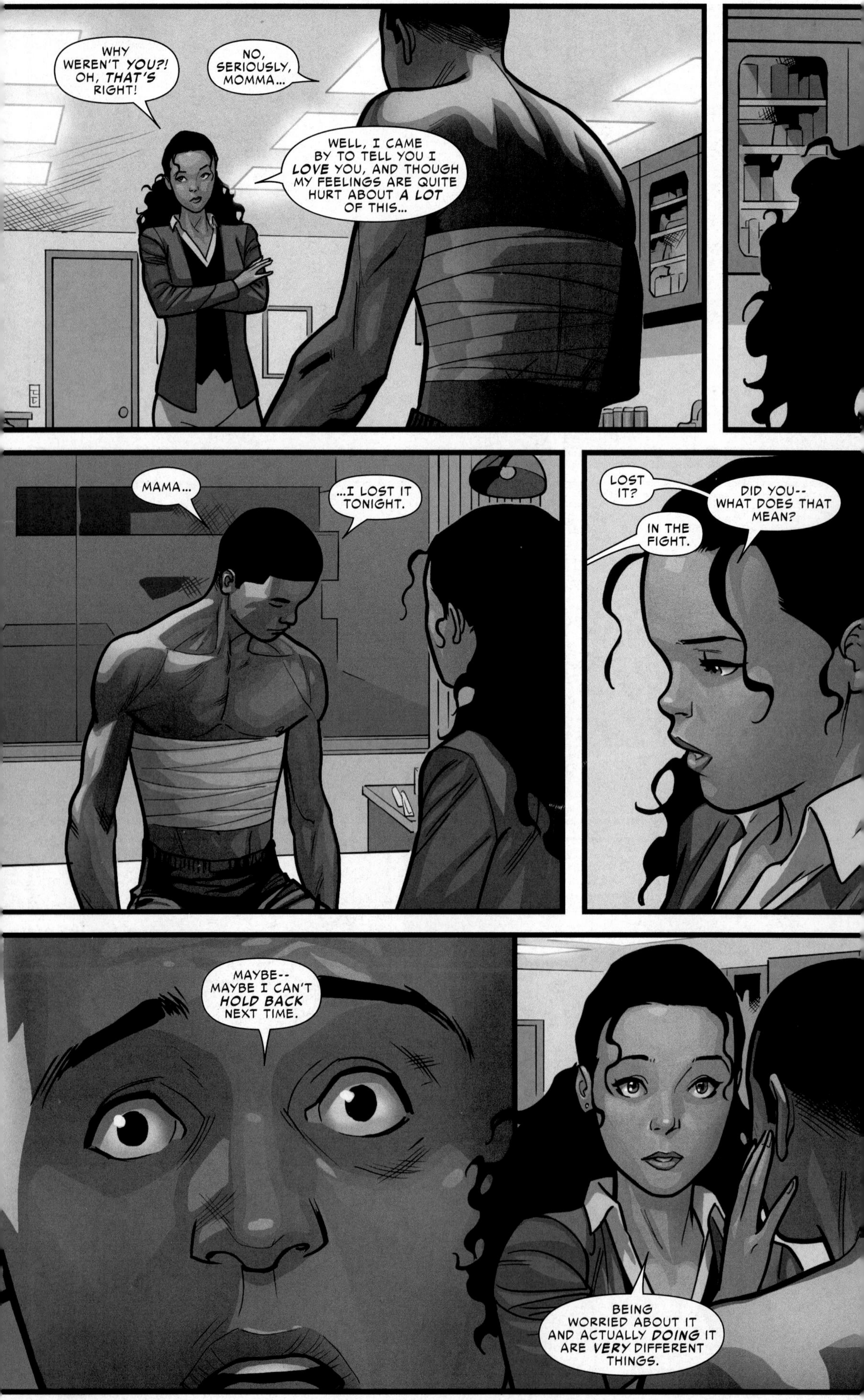

WHY WEREN'T YOU?! OH, THAT'S RIGHT!
NO, SERIOUSLY, MOMMA...
WELL, I CAME BY TO TELL YOU I LOVE YOU, AND THOUGH MY FEELINGS ARE QUITE HURT ABOUT A LOT OF THIS...
MAMA...
...I LOST IT TONIGHT.
LOST IT?
DID YOU-- WHAT DOES THAT MEAN?
IN THE FIGHT.
MAYBE-- MAYBE I CAN'T HOLD BACK NEXT TIME.
BEING WORRIED ABOUT IT AND ACTUALLY DOING IT ARE VERY DIFFERENT THINGS.

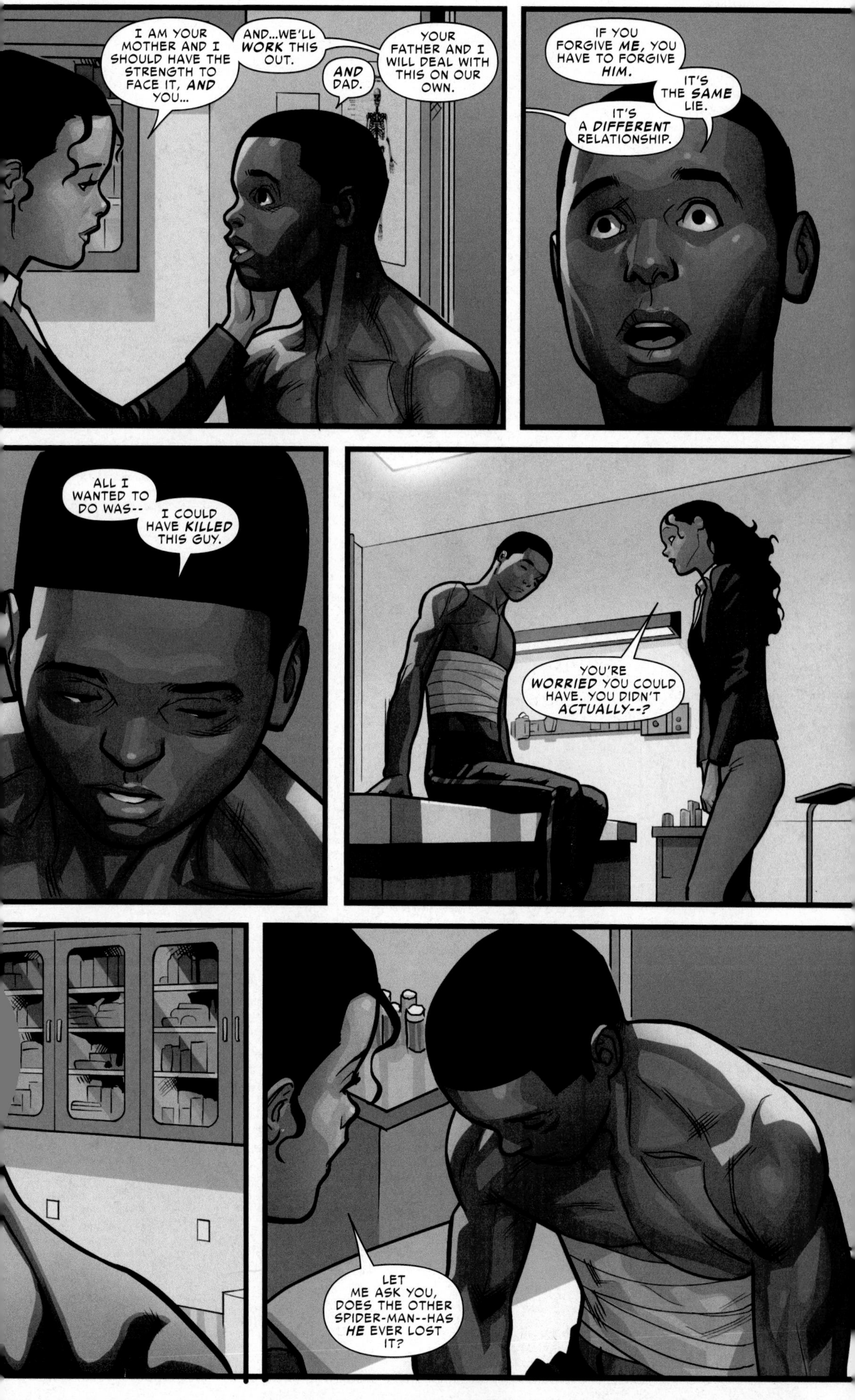
I AM YOUR MOTHER AND I SHOULD HAVE THE STRENGTH TO FACE IT, AND YOU...
AND...WE'LL WORK THIS OUT.
YOUR FATHER AND I WILL DEAL WITH THIS ON OUR OWN.
AND DAD.
IF YOU FORGIVE ME, YOU HAVE TO FORGIVE HIM.
IT'S A DIFFERENT RELATIONSHIP.
IT'S THE SAME LIE.
ALL I WANTED TO DO WAS--
I COULD HAVE KILLED THIS GUY.
YOU'RE WORRIED YOU COULD HAVE. YOU DIDN'T ACTUALLY--?
LET ME ASK YOU, DOES THE OTHER SPIDER-MAN--HAS HE EVER LOST IT?

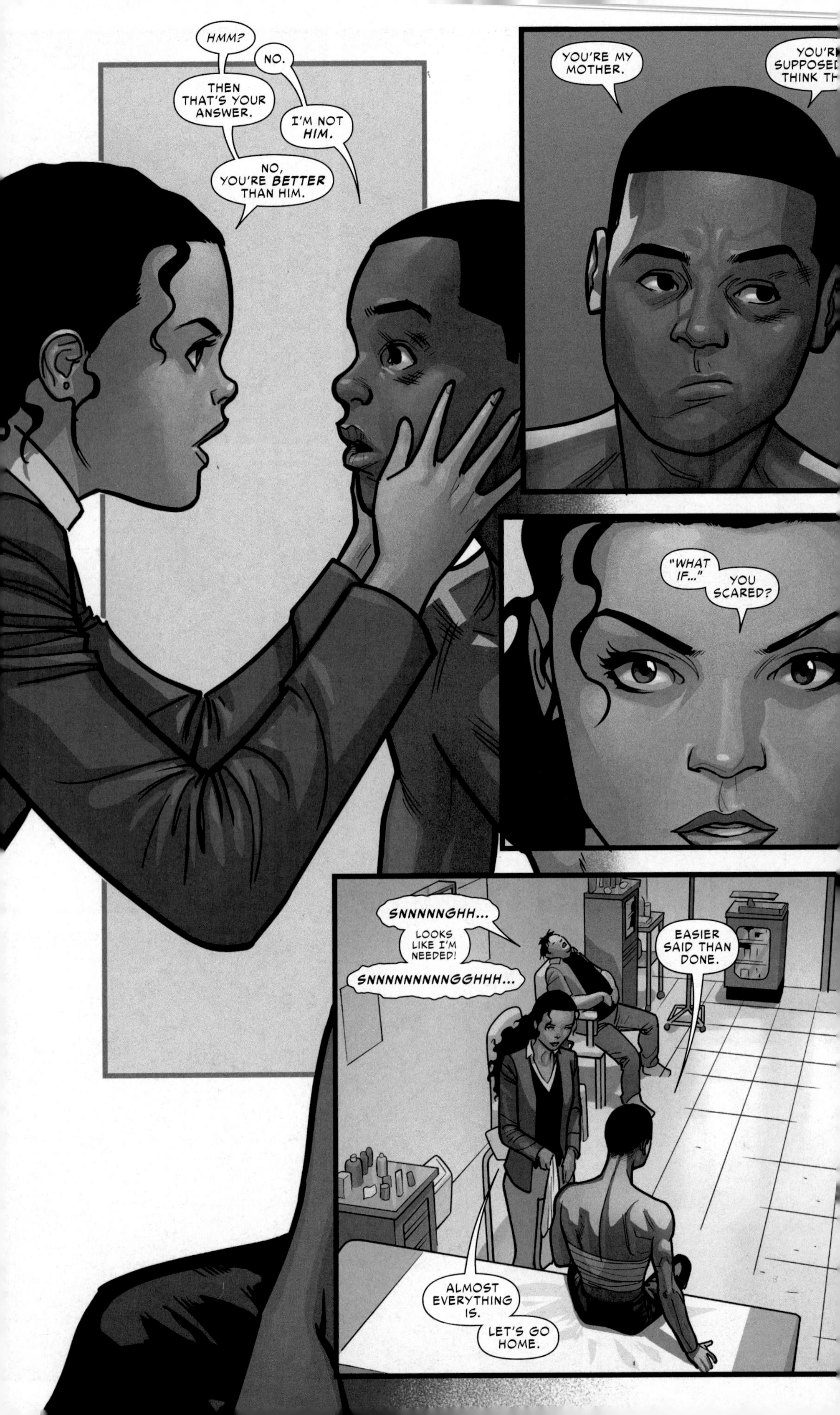
HMM?
NO.
THEN THAT'S YOUR ANSWER.
I'M NOT HIM.
NO, YOU'RE BETTER THAN HIM.
YOU'RE MY MOTHER.
"WHAT IF..."
YOU SCARED?
SNNNNNGHH...
LOOKS LIKE I'M NEEDED!
SNNNNNNNNNGGHHH...
EASIER SAID THAN DONE.
ALMOST EVERYTHING IS.
LET'S GO HOME.

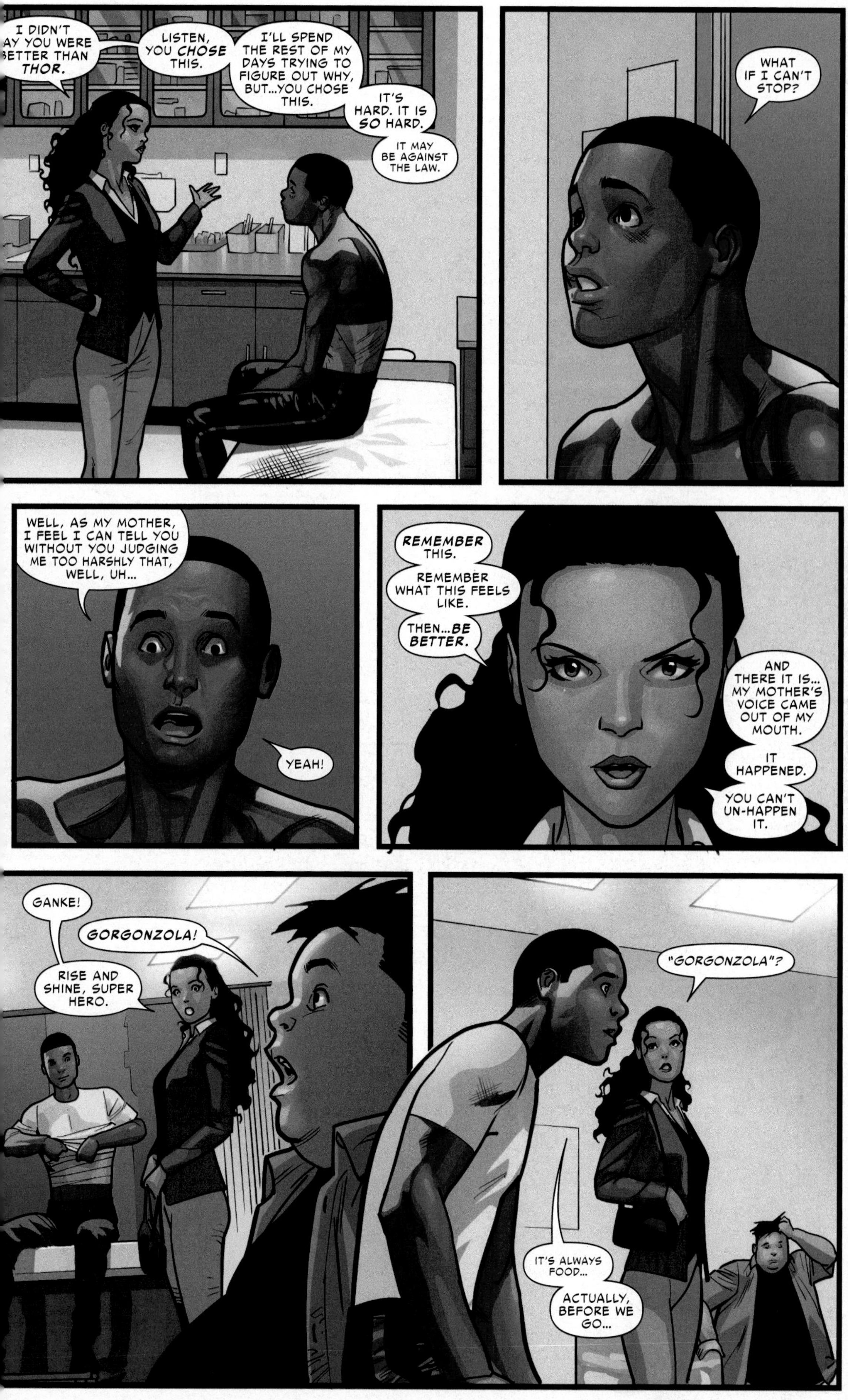
I DIDN'T SAY YOU WERE BETTER THAN *THOR.*
LISTEN, YOU *CHOSE* THIS.
I'LL SPEND THE REST OF MY DAYS TRYING TO FIGURE OUT WHY, BUT...YOU CHOSE THIS.
IT'S HARD. IT IS *SO* HARD.
IT MAY BE AGAINST THE LAW.
WHAT IF I CAN'T STOP?
WELL, AS MY MOTHER, I FEEL I CAN TELL YOU WITHOUT YOU JUDGING ME TOO HARSHLY THAT, WELL, UH...
YEAH!
REMEMBER THIS.
REMEMBER WHAT THIS FEELS LIKE.
THEN...*BE BETTER.*
AND THERE IT IS... MY MOTHER'S VOICE CAME OUT OF MY MOUTH.
IT HAPPENED.
YOU CAN'T UN-HAPPEN IT.
GANKE!
GORGONZOLA!
RISE AND SHINE, SUPER HERO.
"GORGONZOLA"?
IT'S ALWAYS FOOD...
ACTUALLY, BEFORE WE GO...

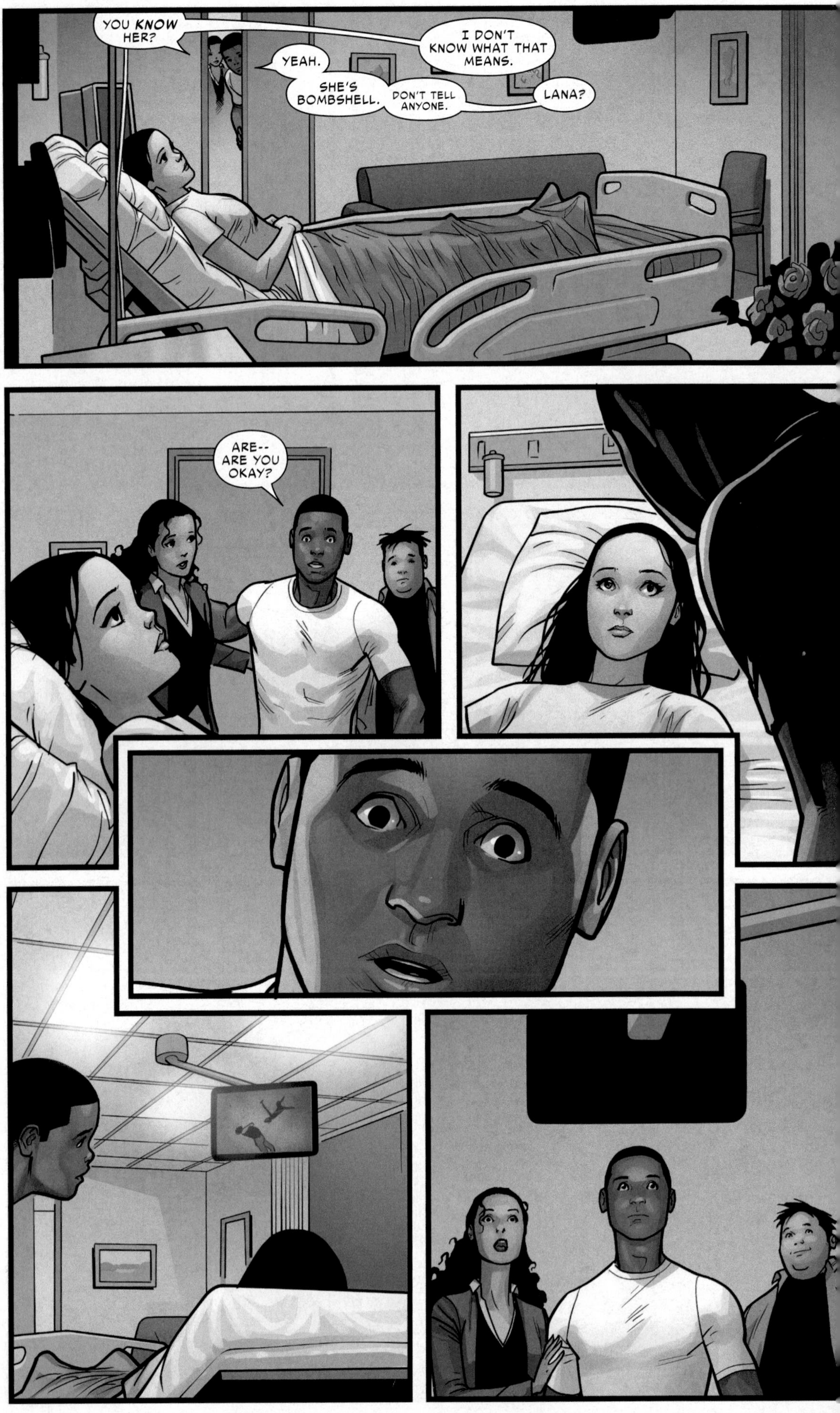

YOU KNOW HER?
YEAH.
SHE'S BOMBSHELL.
DON'T TELL ANYONE.
I DON'T KNOW WHAT THAT MEANS.
LANA?
ARE-- ARE YOU OKAY?

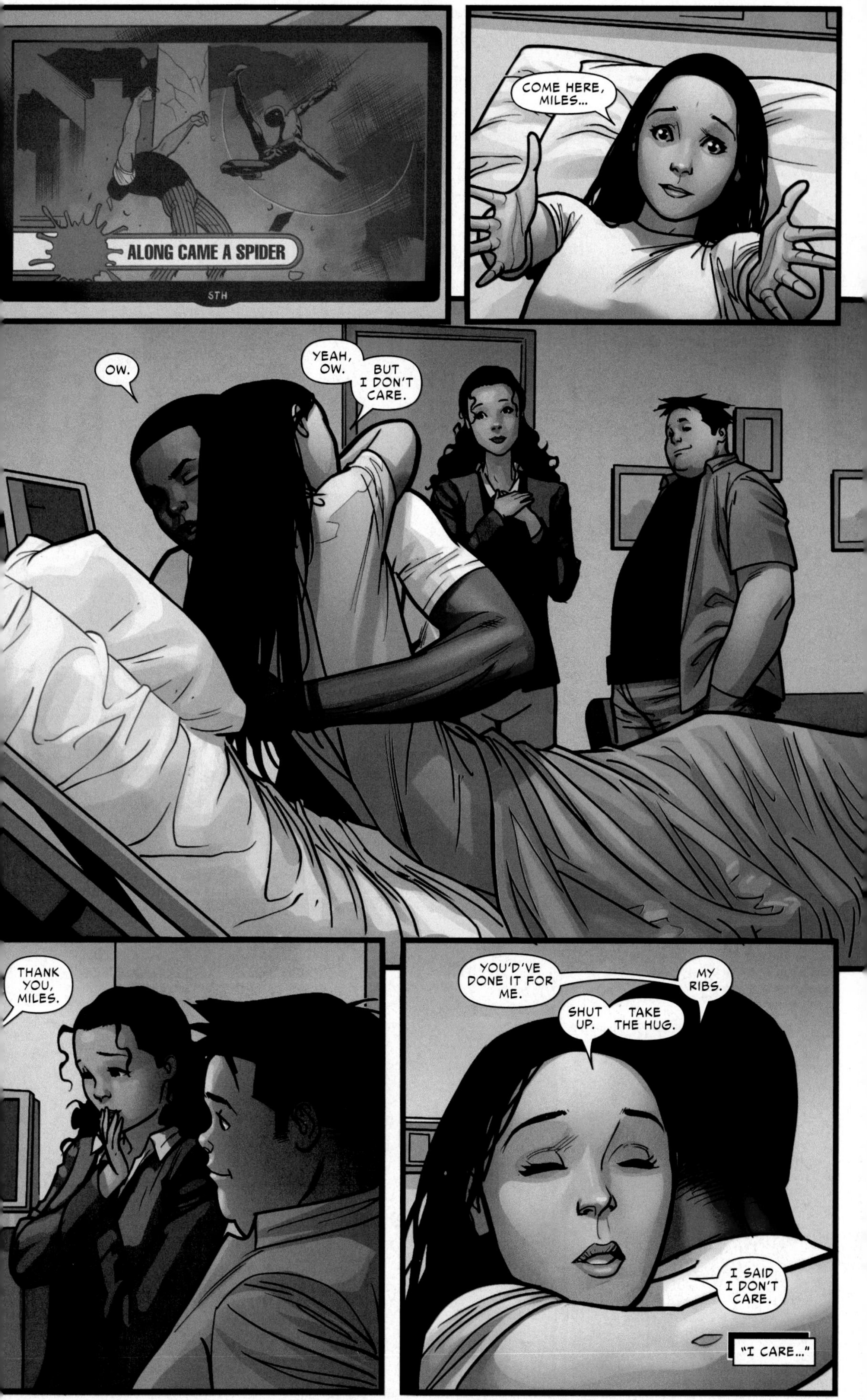

ALONG CAME A SPIDER
STH
COME HERE, MILES...
OW.
YEAH, OW.
BUT I DON'T CARE.
THANK YOU, MILES.
YOU'D'VE DONE IT FOR ME.
MY RIBS.
SHUT UP.
TAKE THE HUG.
I SAID I DON'T CARE.
"I CARE..."

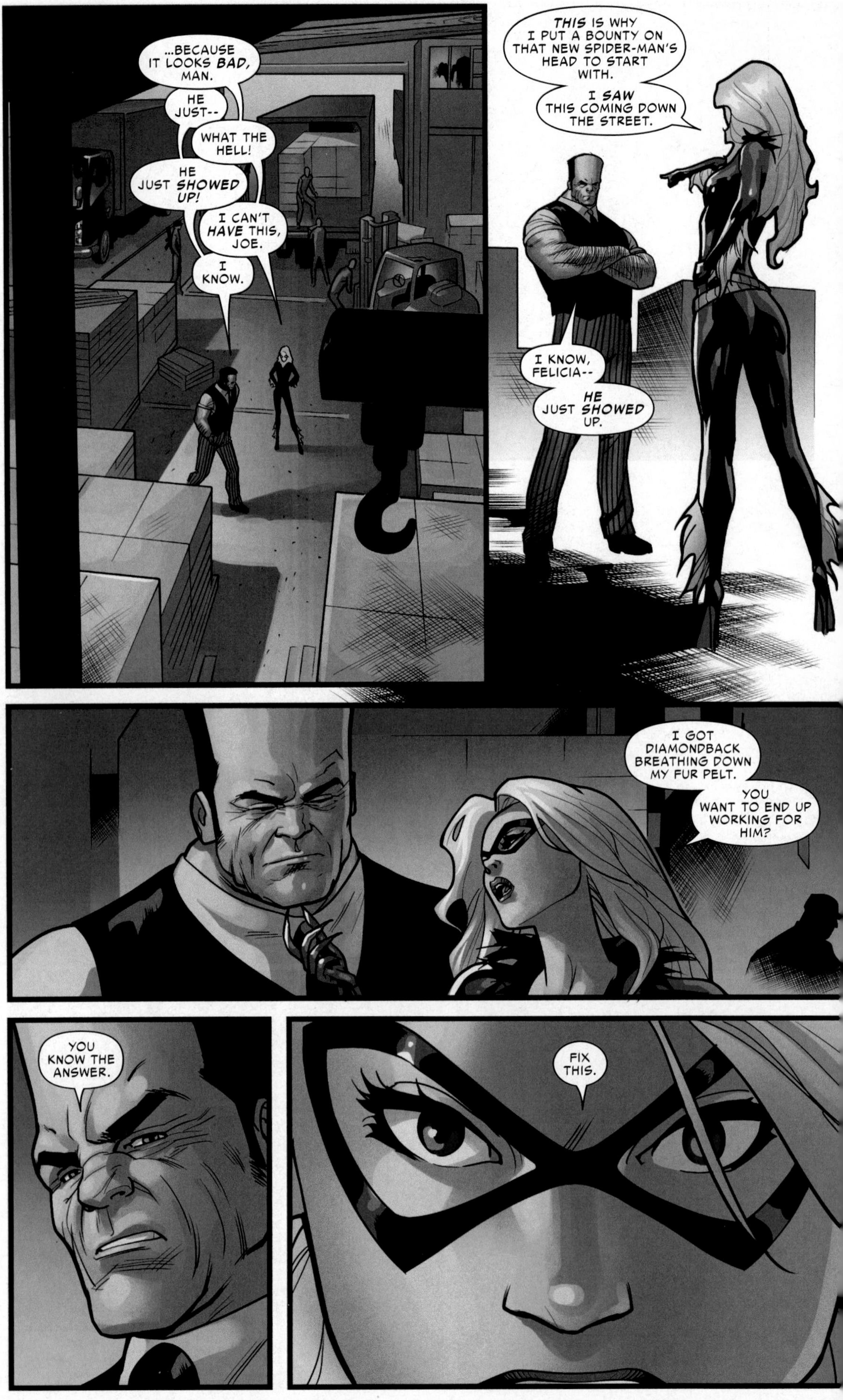

...BECAUSE IT LOOKS BAD, MAN.
HE JUST--
WHAT THE HELL!
HE JUST SHOWED UP!
I CAN'T HAVE THIS, JOE.
I KNOW.
THIS IS WHY I PUT A BOUNTY ON THAT NEW SPIDER-MAN'S HEAD TO START WITH.
I SAW THIS COMING DOWN THE STREET.
I KNOW, FELICIA--
HE JUST SHOWED UP.
I GOT DIAMONDBACK BREATHING DOWN MY FUR PELT.
YOU WANT TO END UP WORKING FOR HIM?
YOU KNOW THE ANSWER.
FIX THIS.

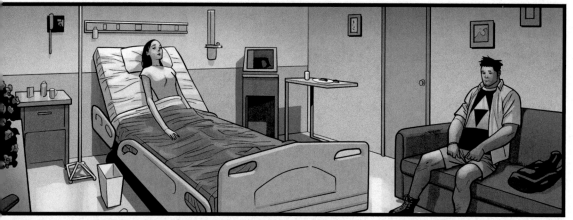

LANA?

HEEEEY...

FABIO.

YOU'RE OKAY?

NO.

I'M PRETTY BANGED UP.

YOU'RE-- I--I MEAN, YOU'RE AWAKE.

COME HERE.

I KNOW WHAT HAPPENED AT THE CLUB.

WITH HAMMERHEAD.

MILES IS AMAZING.

YEAH?

HE WENT OVER THERE AND-- AND TRASHED THE PLACE.

HE ALMOST PULLED THE ENTIRE NIGHTCLUB DOWN AROUND THAT FATHEAD GUY'S EARS!

HE DID, AND THEN--

AND I THINK THAT PROVES IT.

PROVES WHAT?

HE'S IN LOVE WITH ME.

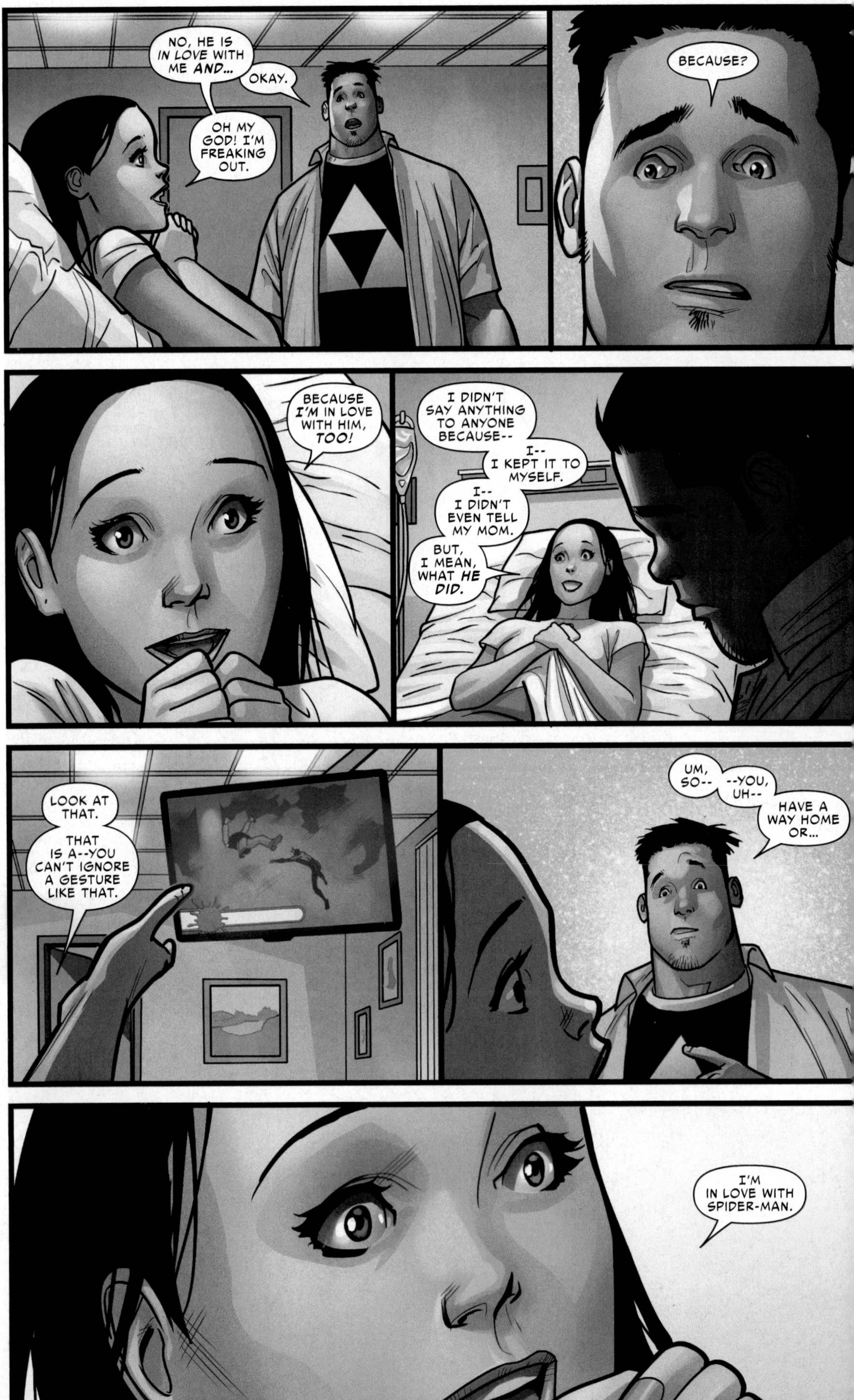

NO, HE IS IN LOVE WITH ME AND...
OKAY.
OH MY GOD! I'M FREAKING OUT.
BECAUSE?
BECAUSE I'M IN LOVE WITH HIM, TOO!
I DIDN'T SAY ANYTHING TO ANYONE BECAUSE--
I-- I KEPT IT TO MYSELF.
I-- I DIDN'T EVEN TELL MY MOM.
BUT, I MEAN, WHAT HE DID.
LOOK AT THAT.
THAT IS A--YOU CAN'T IGNORE A GESTURE LIKE THAT.
UM, SO--
--YOU, UH--
HAVE A WAY HOME OR...
I'M IN LOVE WITH SPIDER-MAN.

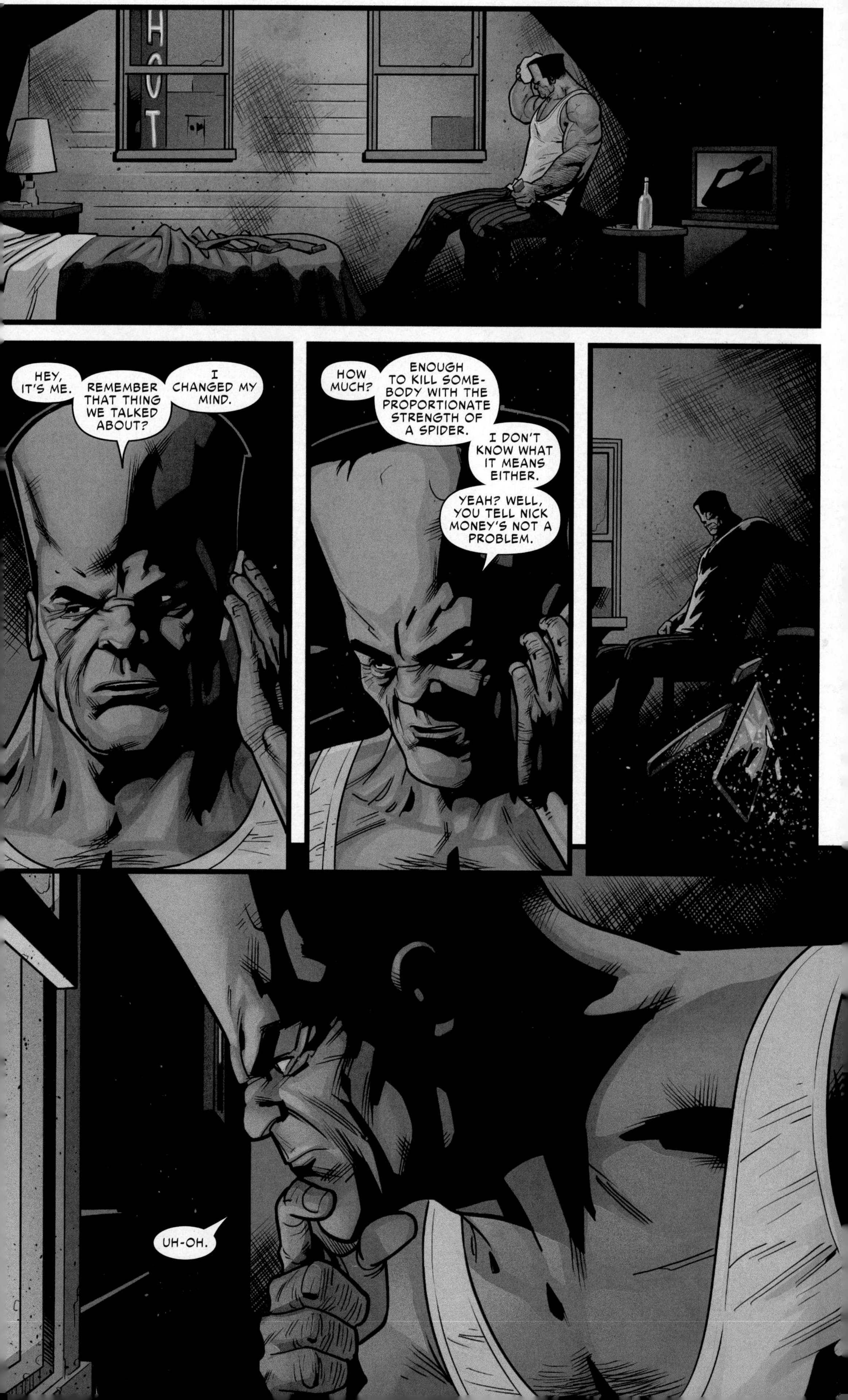
HOVT
HEY, IT'S ME.
REMEMBER THAT THING WE TALKED ABOUT?
I CHANGED MY MIND.
HOW MUCH?
ENOUGH TO KILL SOME-BODY WITH THE PROPORTIONATE STRENGTH OF A SPIDER.
I DON'T KNOW WHAT IT MEANS EITHER.
YEAH? WELL, YOU TELL NICK MONEY'S NOT A PROBLEM.
UH-OH.

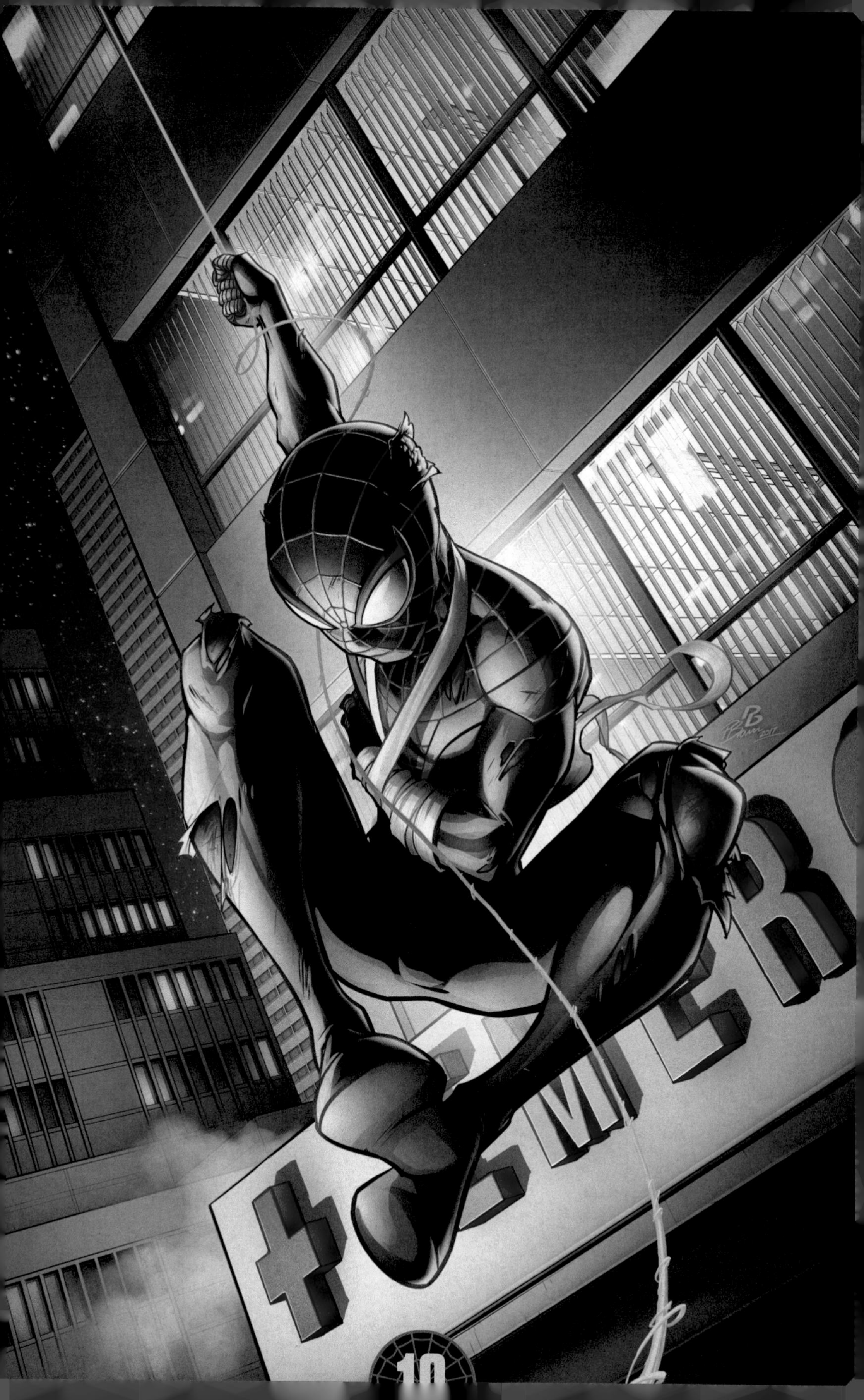

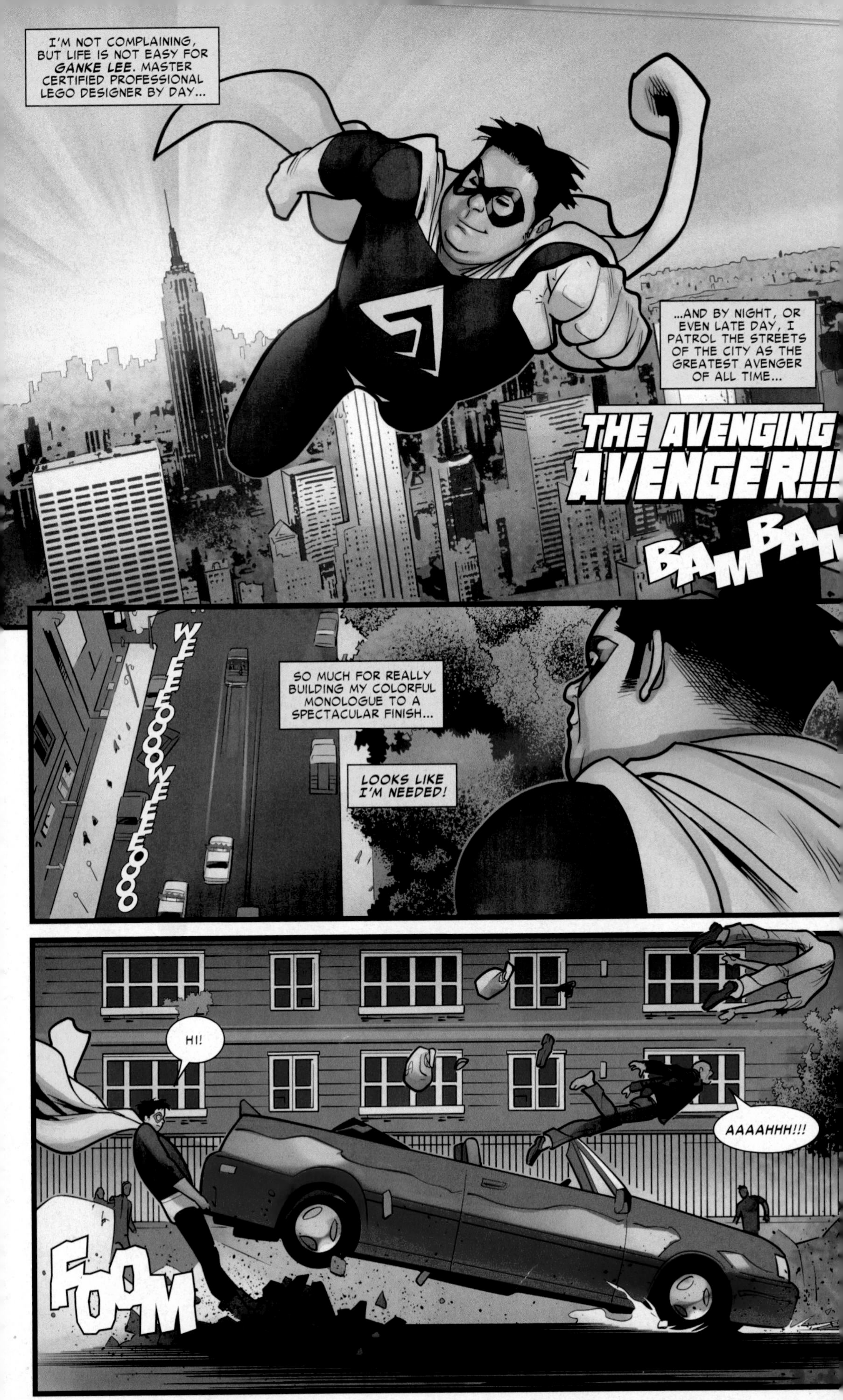
I'M NOT COMPLAINING, BUT LIFE IS NOT EASY FOR GANKE LEE. MASTER CERTIFIED PROFESSIONAL LEGO DESIGNER BY DAY...
...AND BY NIGHT, OR EVEN LATE DAY, I PATROL THE STREETS OF THE CITY AS THE GREATEST AVENGER OF ALL TIME...
THE AVENGING AVENGER!!!
BAMBAM
WEEEOOOOWEEEOOOO
SO MUCH FOR REALLY BUILDING MY COLORFUL MONOLOGUE TO A SPECTACULAR FINISH...
LOOKS LIKE I'M NEEDED!
HI!
AAAAHHH!!!
FOOM

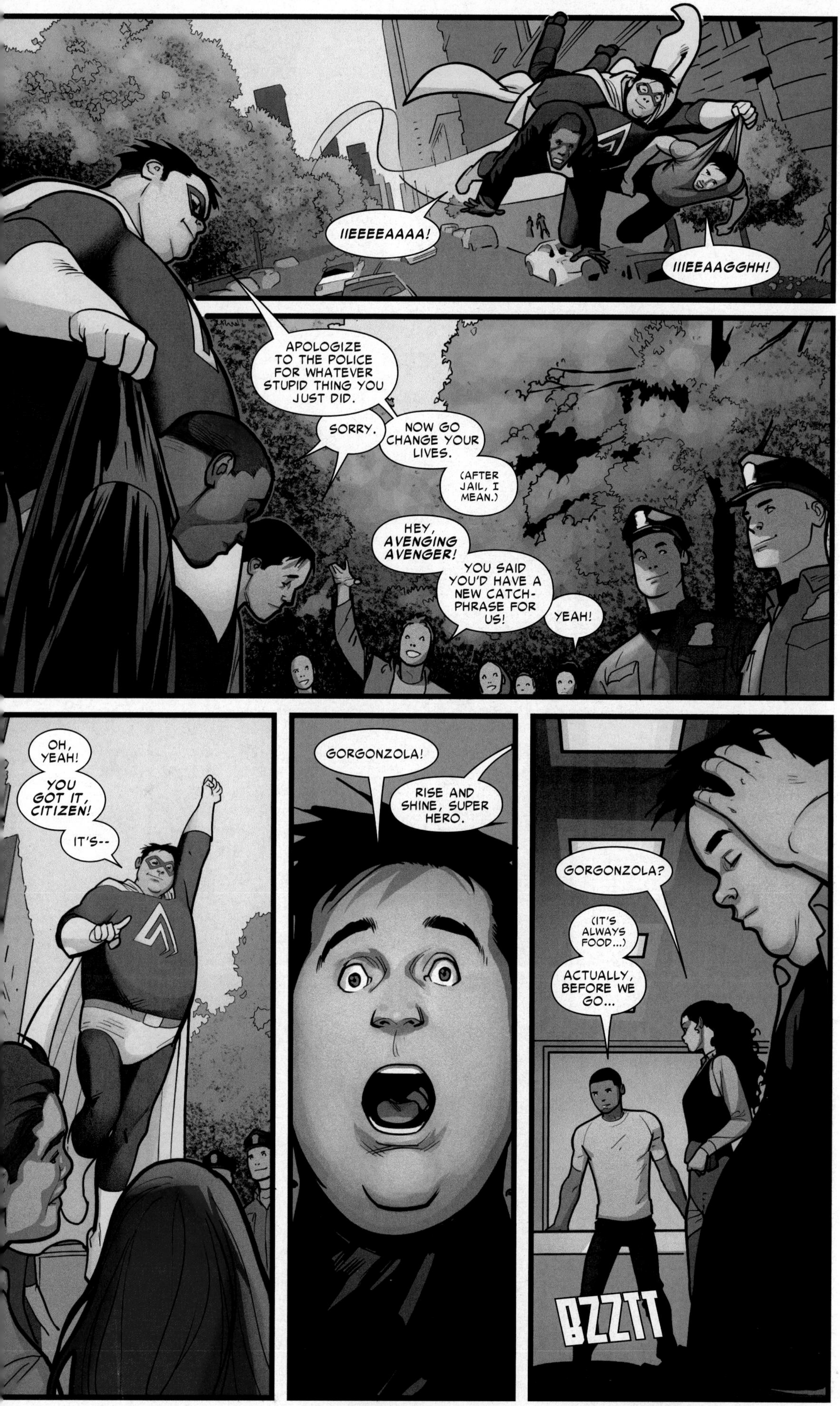
IIEEEEAAAA!
IIIEEAAGGHH!
APOLOGIZE TO THE POLICE FOR WHATEVER STUPID THING YOU JUST DID.
SORRY.
NOW GO CHANGE YOUR LIVES.
(AFTER JAIL, I MEAN.)
HEY, AVENGING AVENGER!
YOU SAID YOU'D HAVE A NEW CATCH-PHRASE FOR US!
YEAH!
OH, YEAH!
YOU GOT IT, CITIZEN!
IT'S--
GORGONZOLA!
RISE AND SHINE, SUPER HERO.
GORGONZOLA?
(IT'S ALWAYS FOOD...)
ACTUALLY, BEFORE WE GO...
BZZTT

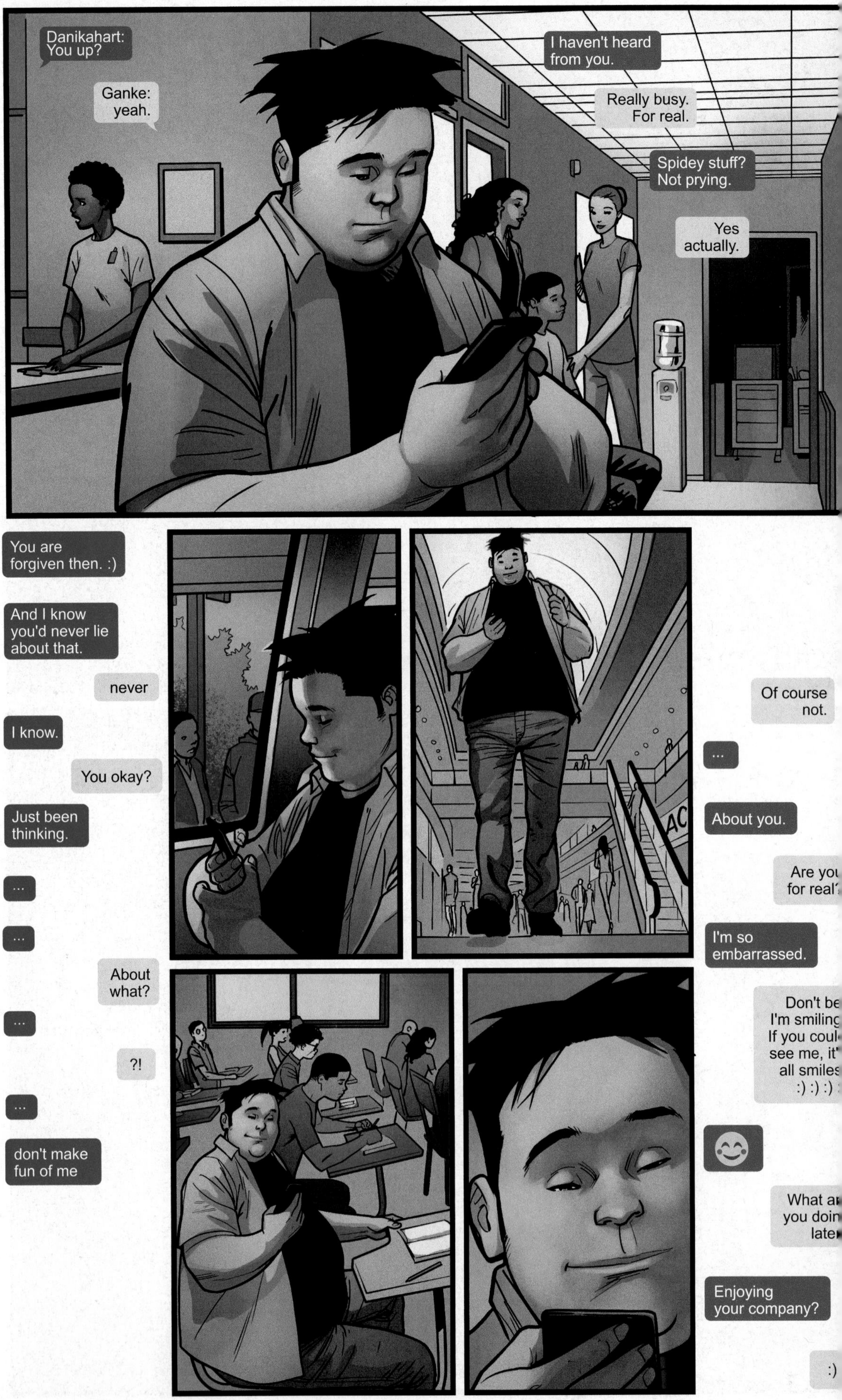

Danikahart: You up?
Ganke: yeah.
I haven't heard from you.
Really busy. For real.
Spidey stuff? Not prying.
Yes actually.
You are forgiven then. :)
And I know you'd never lie about that.
never
I know.
You okay?
Just been thinking.
...
...
About what?
...
?!
...
don't make fun of me
Of course not.
...
About you.
Are you for real
I'm so embarrassed.
Don't be I'm smiling If you coul see me, it all smiles :) :) :)
What a you doin late
Enjoying your company?
:)

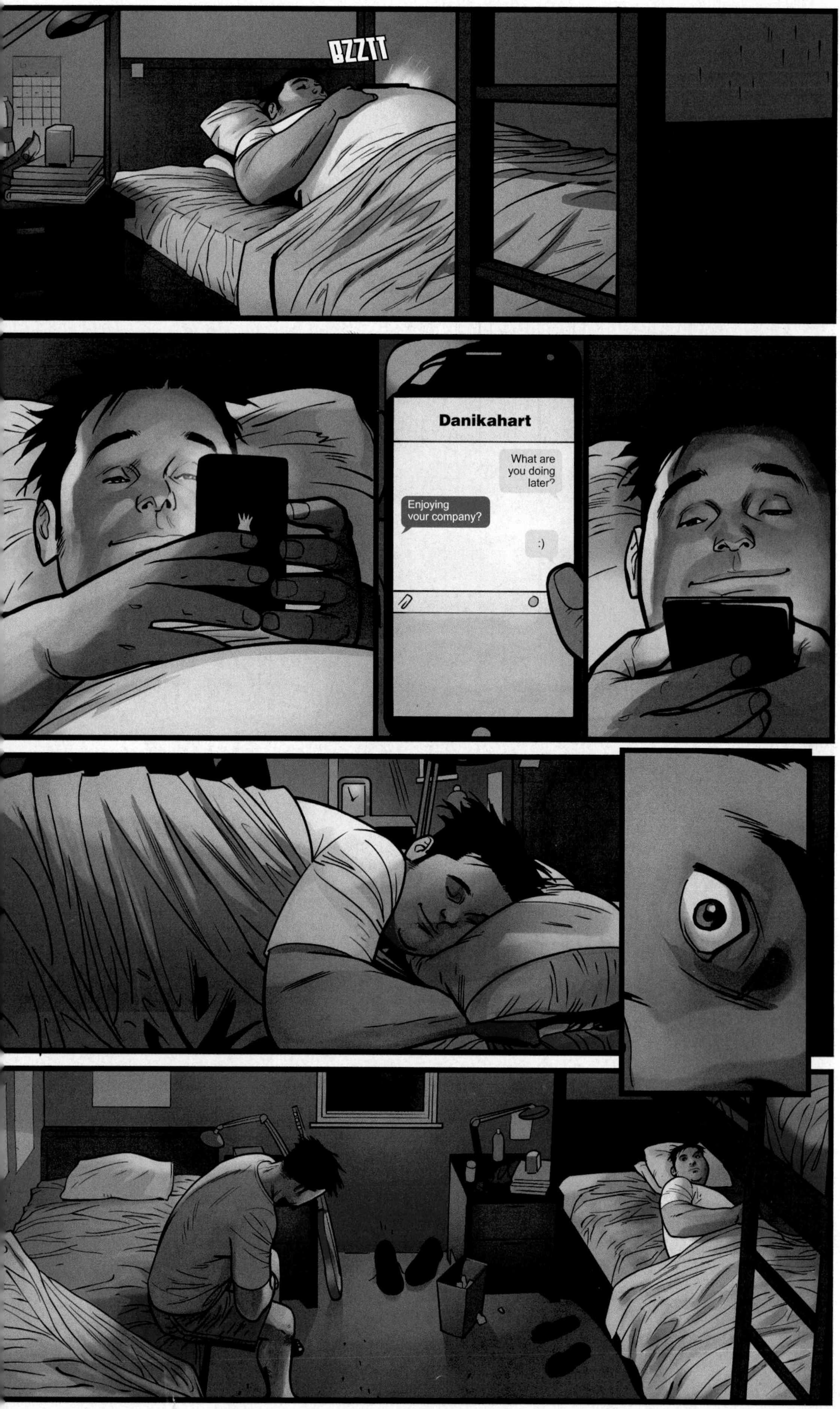
BZZTT
Danikahart
What are you doing later?
Enjoying your company?
:)

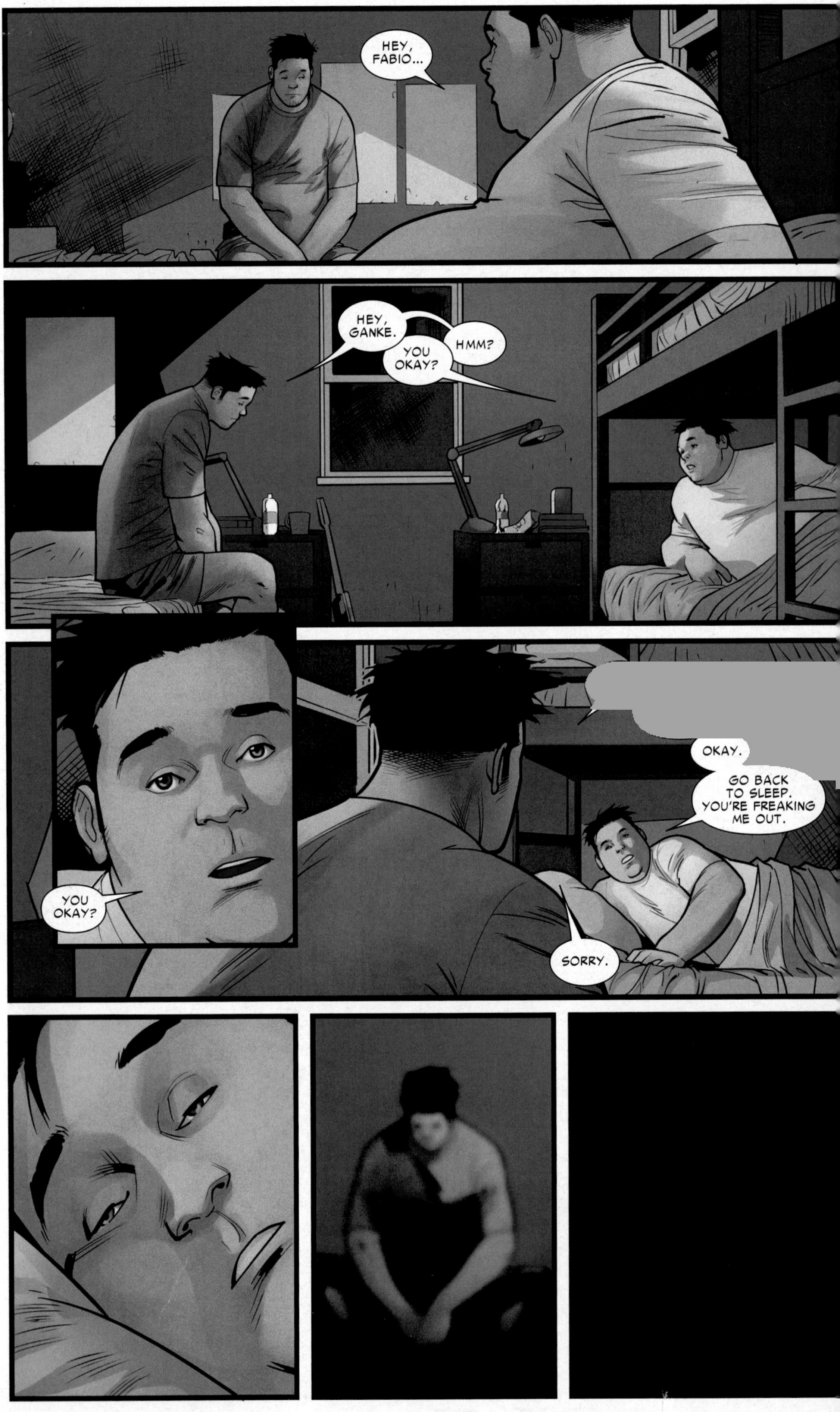

HEY, FABIO...
HEY, GANKE.
HMM?
YOU OKAY?
YOU OKAY?
OKAY.
GO BACK TO SLEEP. YOU'RE FREAKING ME OUT.
SORRY.

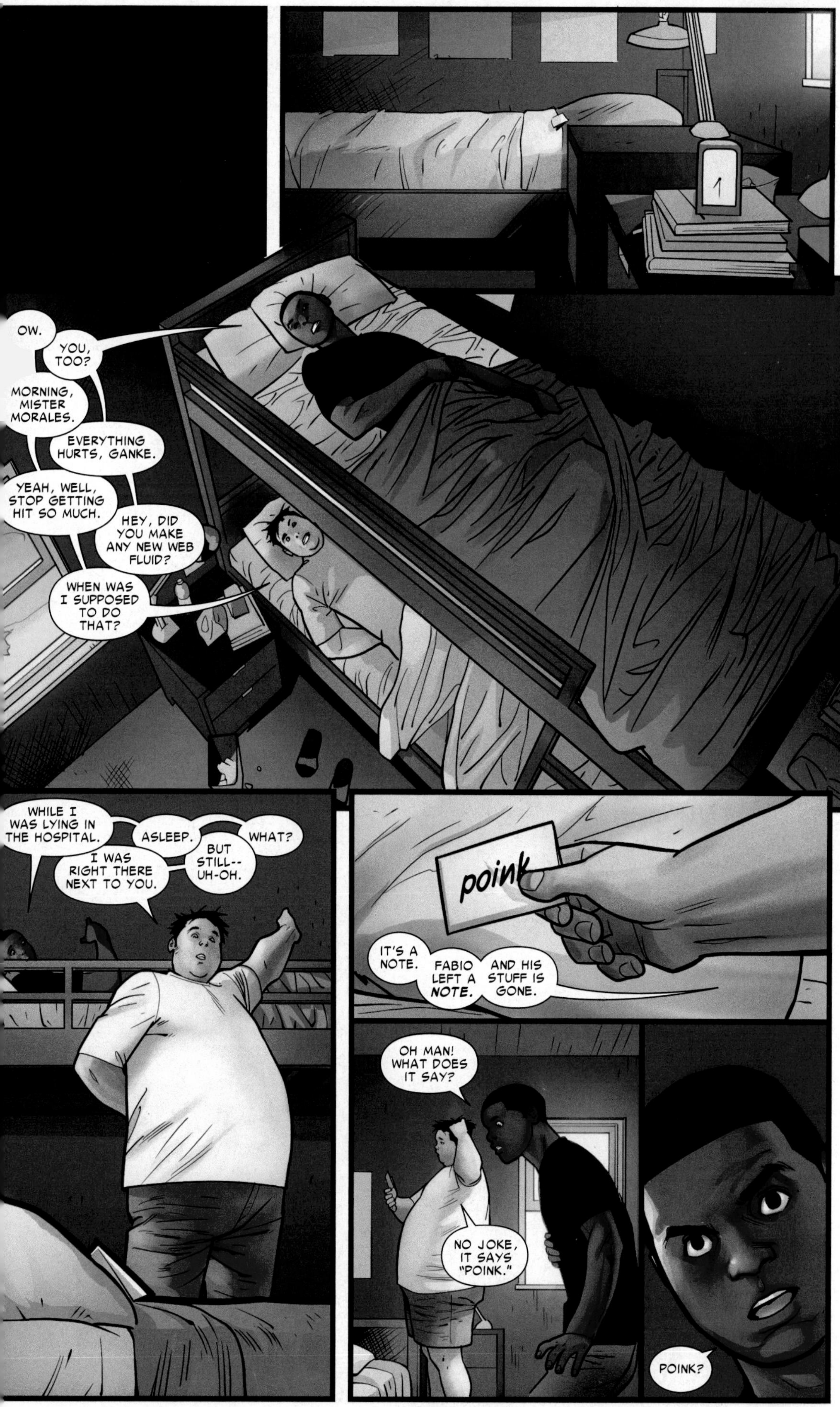
OW.
YOU, TOO?
MORNING, MISTER MORALES.
EVERYTHING HURTS, GANKE.
YEAH, WELL, STOP GETTING HIT SO MUCH.
HEY, DID YOU MAKE ANY NEW WEB FLUID?
WHEN WAS I SUPPOSED TO DO THAT?
WHILE I WAS LYING IN THE HOSPITAL.
ASLEEP.
I WAS RIGHT THERE NEXT TO YOU.
BUT STILL-- UH-OH.
WHAT?
poink
IT'S A NOTE.
FABIO LEFT A *NOTE.*
AND HIS STUFF IS GONE.
OH MAN! WHAT DOES IT SAY?
NO JOKE, IT SAYS "POINK."
POINK?

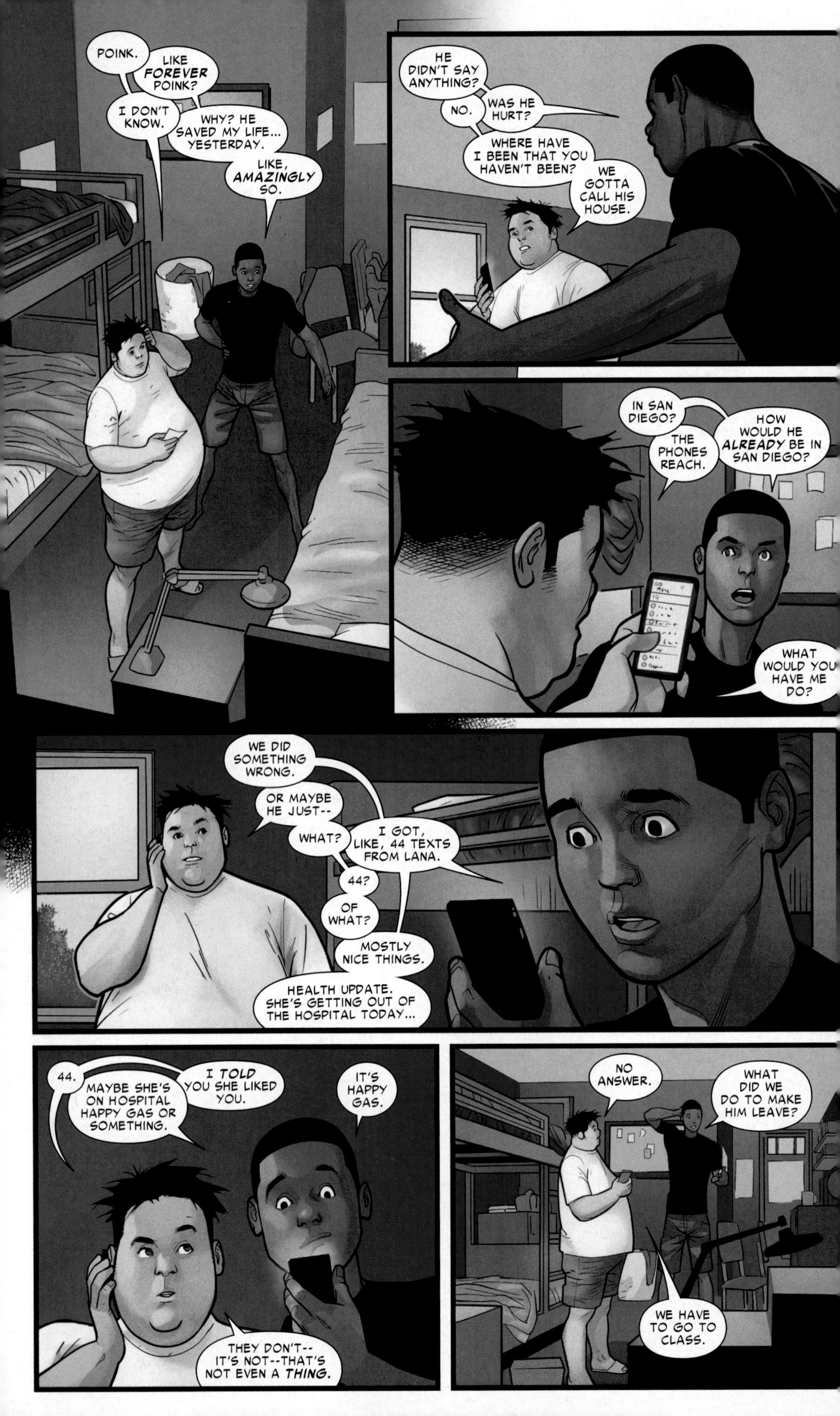
POINK.
LIKE *FOREVER* POINK?
I DON'T KNOW.
WHY? HE SAVED MY LIFE... YESTERDAY.
LIKE, *AMAZINGLY* SO.
HE DIDN'T SAY ANYTHING?
NO.
WAS HE HURT?
WHERE HAVE I BEEN THAT YOU HAVEN'T BEEN?
WE GOTTA CALL HIS HOUSE.
IN SAN DIEGO?
THE PHONES REACH.
HOW WOULD HE *ALREADY* BE IN SAN DIEGO?
WHAT WOULD YOU HAVE ME DO?
WE DID SOMETHING WRONG.
OR MAYBE HE JUST--
WHAT?
I GOT, LIKE, 44 TEXTS FROM LANA.
44?
OF WHAT?
MOSTLY NICE THINGS.
HEALTH UPDATE. SHE'S GETTING OUT OF THE HOSPITAL TODAY...
44.
MAYBE SHE'S ON HOSPITAL HAPPY GAS OR SOMETHING.
I *TOLD* YOU SHE LIKED YOU.
IT'S HAPPY GAS.
THEY DON'T-- IT'S NOT--THAT'S NOT EVEN A *THING*.
NO ANSWER.
WHAT DID WE DO TO MAKE HIM LEAVE?
WE HAVE TO GO TO CLASS.

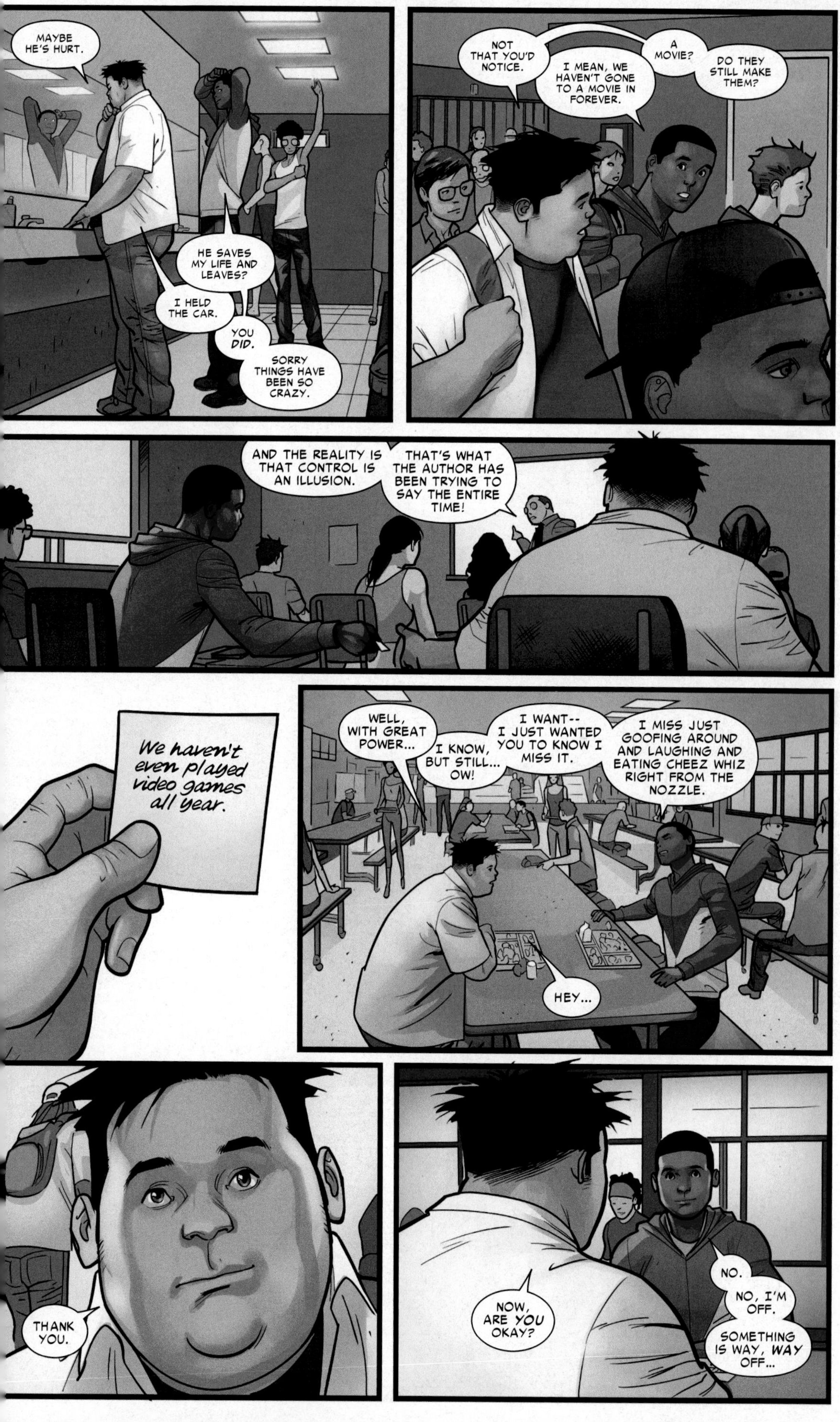
MAYBE HE'S HURT.
HE SAVES MY LIFE AND LEAVES?
I HELD THE CAR.
YOU DID.
SORRY THINGS HAVE BEEN SO CRAZY.
NOT THAT YOU'D NOTICE.
I MEAN, WE HAVEN'T GONE TO A MOVIE IN FOREVER.
A MOVIE?
DO THEY STILL MAKE THEM?
AND THE REALITY IS THAT CONTROL IS AN ILLUSION.
THAT'S WHAT THE AUTHOR HAS BEEN TRYING TO SAY THE ENTIRE TIME!
We haven't even played video games all year.
WELL, WITH GREAT POWER...
I KNOW, BUT STILL... OW!
I WANT-- I JUST WANTED YOU TO KNOW I MISS IT.
I MISS JUST GOOFING AROUND AND LAUGHING AND EATING CHEEZ WHIZ RIGHT FROM THE NOZZLE.
HEY...
THANK YOU.
NOW, ARE YOU OKAY?
NO.
NO, I'M OFF.
SOMETHING IS WAY, WAY OFF...

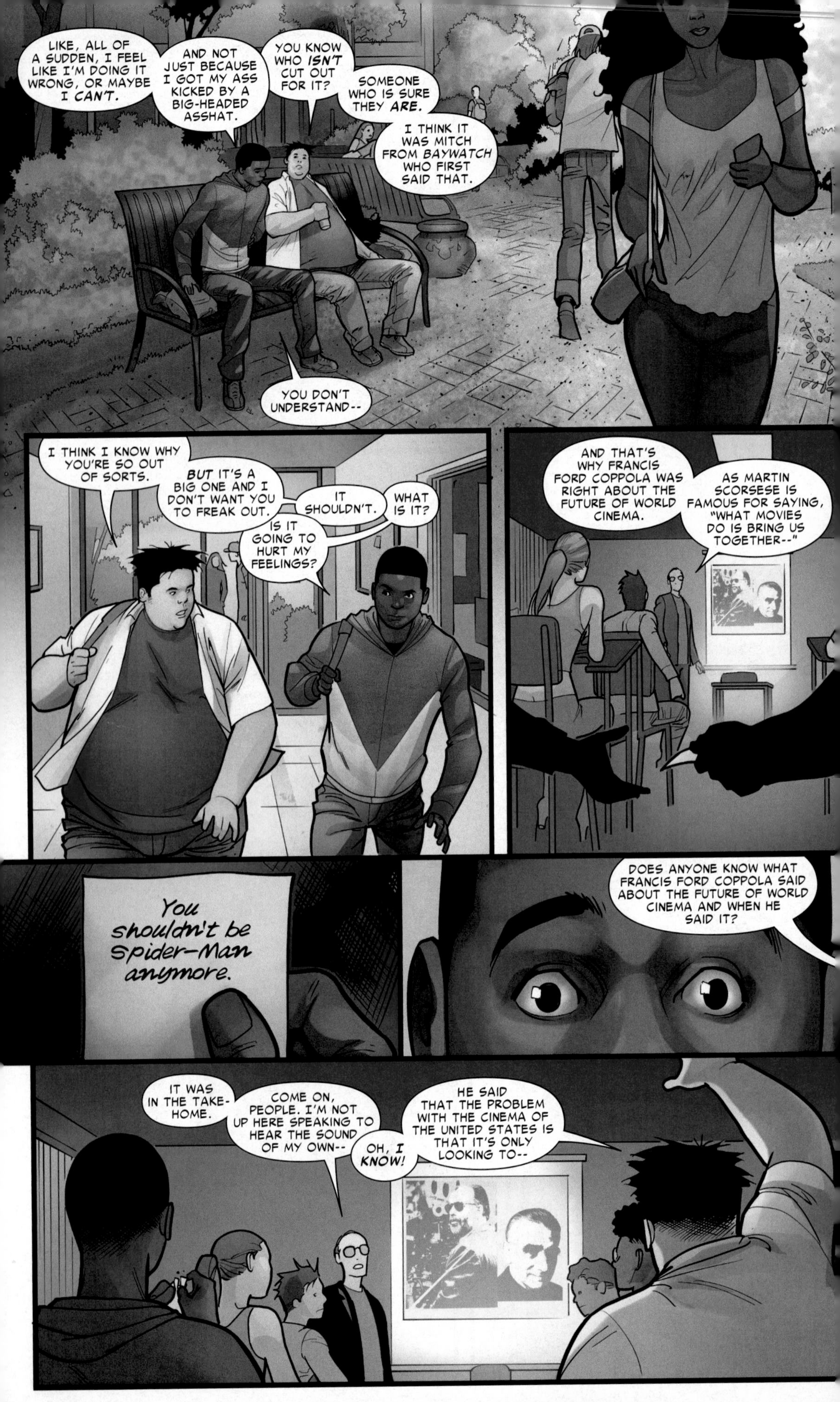
LIKE, ALL OF A SUDDEN, I FEEL LIKE I'M DOING IT WRONG, OR MAYBE I CAN'T.
AND NOT JUST BECAUSE I GOT MY ASS KICKED BY A BIG-HEADED ASSHAT.
YOU KNOW WHO ISN'T CUT OUT FOR IT?
SOMEONE WHO IS SURE THEY ARE.
I THINK IT WAS MITCH FROM BAYWATCH WHO FIRST SAID THAT.
YOU DON'T UNDERSTAND--
I THINK I KNOW WHY YOU'RE SO OUT OF SORTS.
BUT IT'S A BIG ONE AND I DON'T WANT YOU TO FREAK OUT.
IT SHOULDN'T.
WHAT IS IT?
IS IT GOING TO HURT MY FEELINGS?
AND THAT'S WHY FRANCIS FORD COPPOLA WAS RIGHT ABOUT THE FUTURE OF WORLD CINEMA.
AS MARTIN SCORSESE IS FAMOUS FOR SAYING, "WHAT MOVIES DO IS BRING US TOGETHER--"
You shouldn't be Spider-Man anymore.
DOES ANYONE KNOW WHAT FRANCIS FORD COPPOLA SAID ABOUT THE FUTURE OF WORLD CINEMA AND WHEN HE SAID IT?
IT WAS IN THE TAKE-HOME.
COME ON, PEOPLE. I'M NOT UP HERE SPEAKING TO HEAR THE SOUND OF MY OWN--
OH, I KNOW!
HE SAID THAT THE PROBLEM WITH THE CINEMA OF THE UNITED STATES IS THAT IT'S ONLY LOOKING TO--

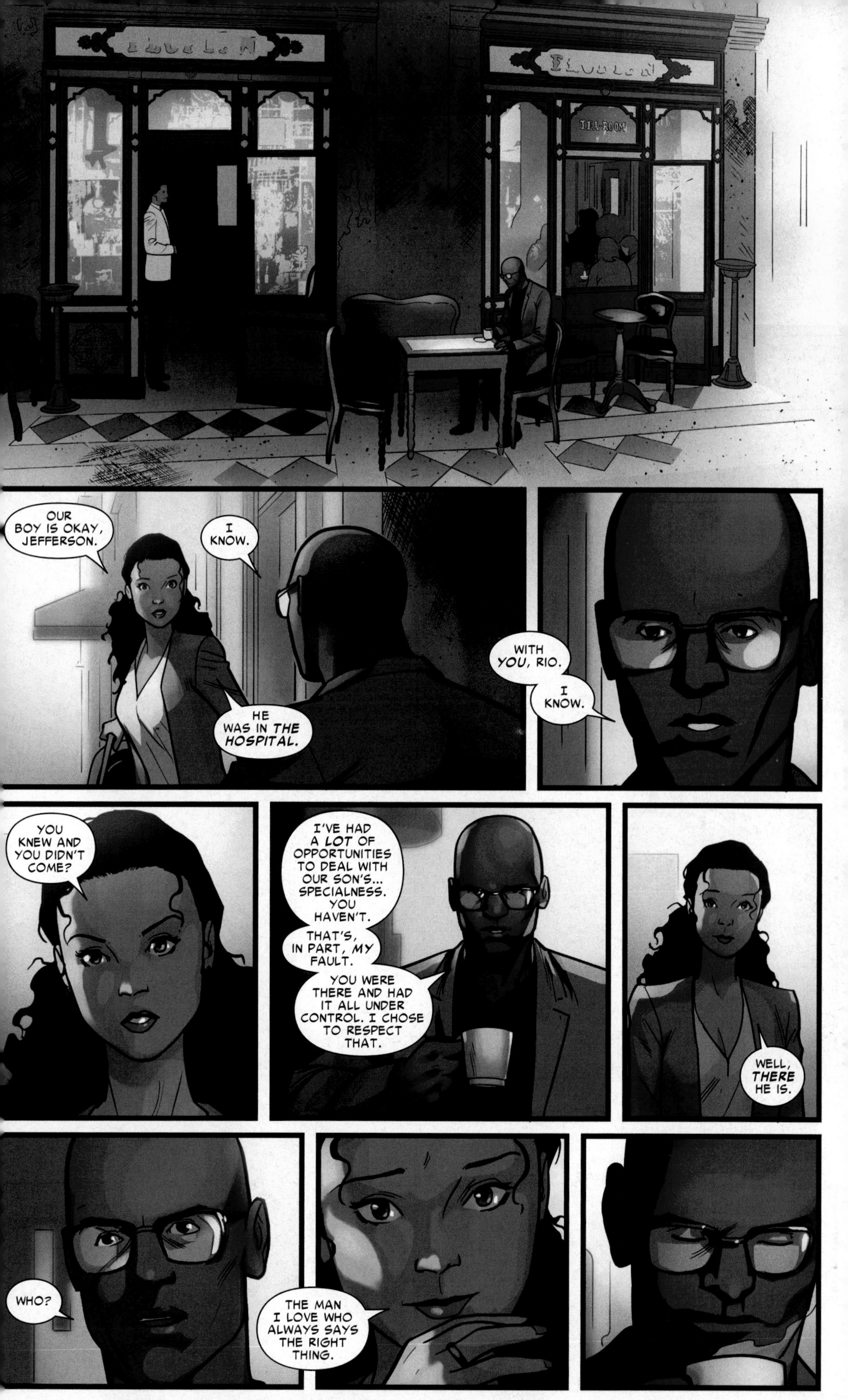
TEA-ROOM
OUR BOY IS OKAY, JEFFERSON.
I KNOW.
HE WAS IN THE HOSPITAL.
WITH YOU, RIO.
I KNOW.
YOU KNEW AND YOU DIDN'T COME?
I'VE HAD A LOT OF OPPORTUNITIES TO DEAL WITH OUR SON'S... SPECIALNESS. YOU HAVEN'T.
THAT'S, IN PART, MY FAULT.
YOU WERE THERE AND HAD IT ALL UNDER CONTROL. I CHOSE TO RESPECT THAT.
WELL, THERE HE IS.
WHO?
THE MAN I LOVE WHO ALWAYS SAYS THE RIGHT THING.

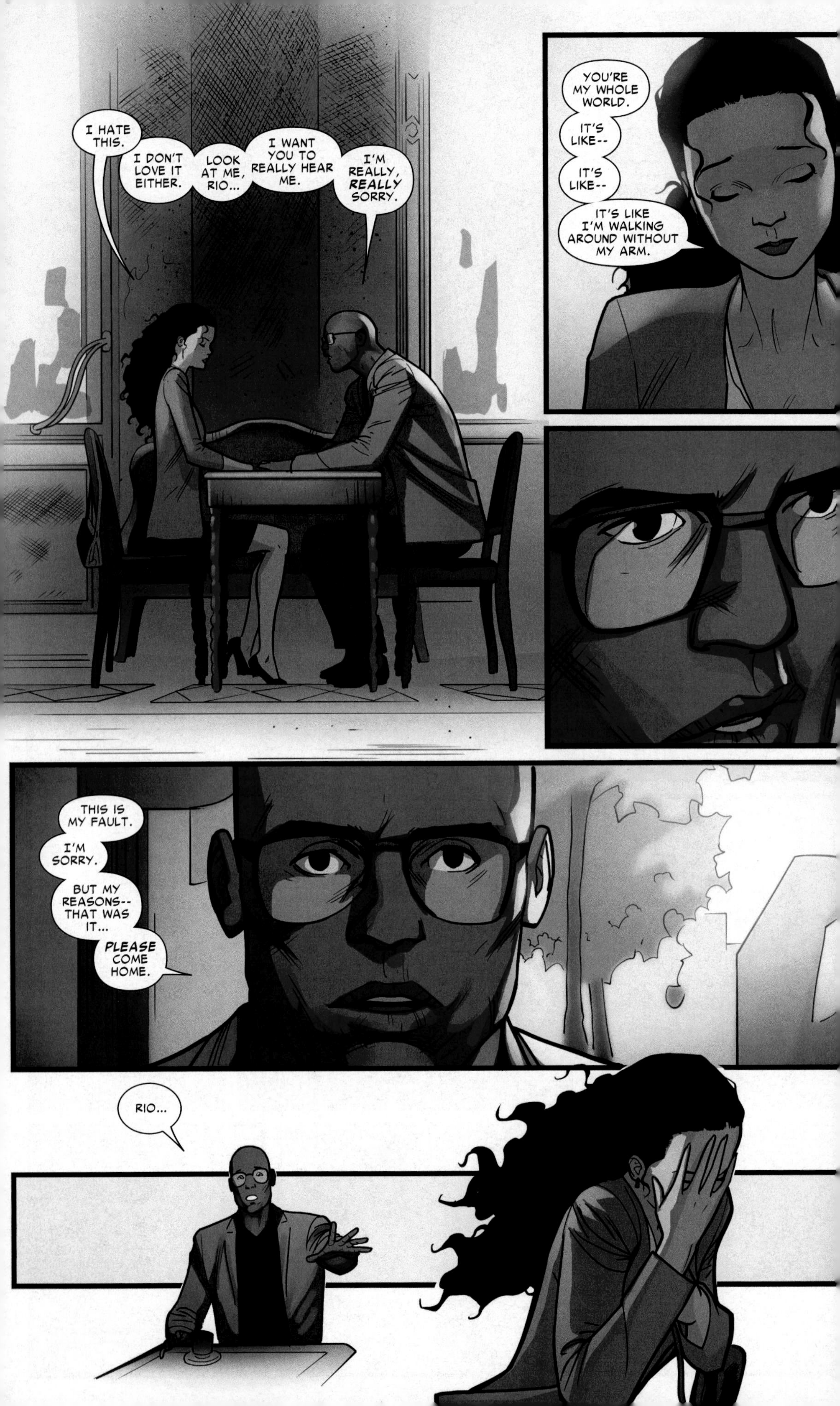

I HATE THIS.
I DON'T LOVE IT EITHER.
LOOK AT ME, RIO...
I WANT YOU TO REALLY HEAR ME.
I'M REALLY, *REALLY* SORRY.
YOU'RE MY WHOLE WORLD.
IT'S LIKE--
IT'S LIKE--
IT'S LIKE I'M WALKING AROUND WITHOUT MY ARM.
THIS IS MY FAULT.
I'M SORRY.
BUT MY REASONS-- THAT WAS IT...
PLEASE COME HOME.
RIO...

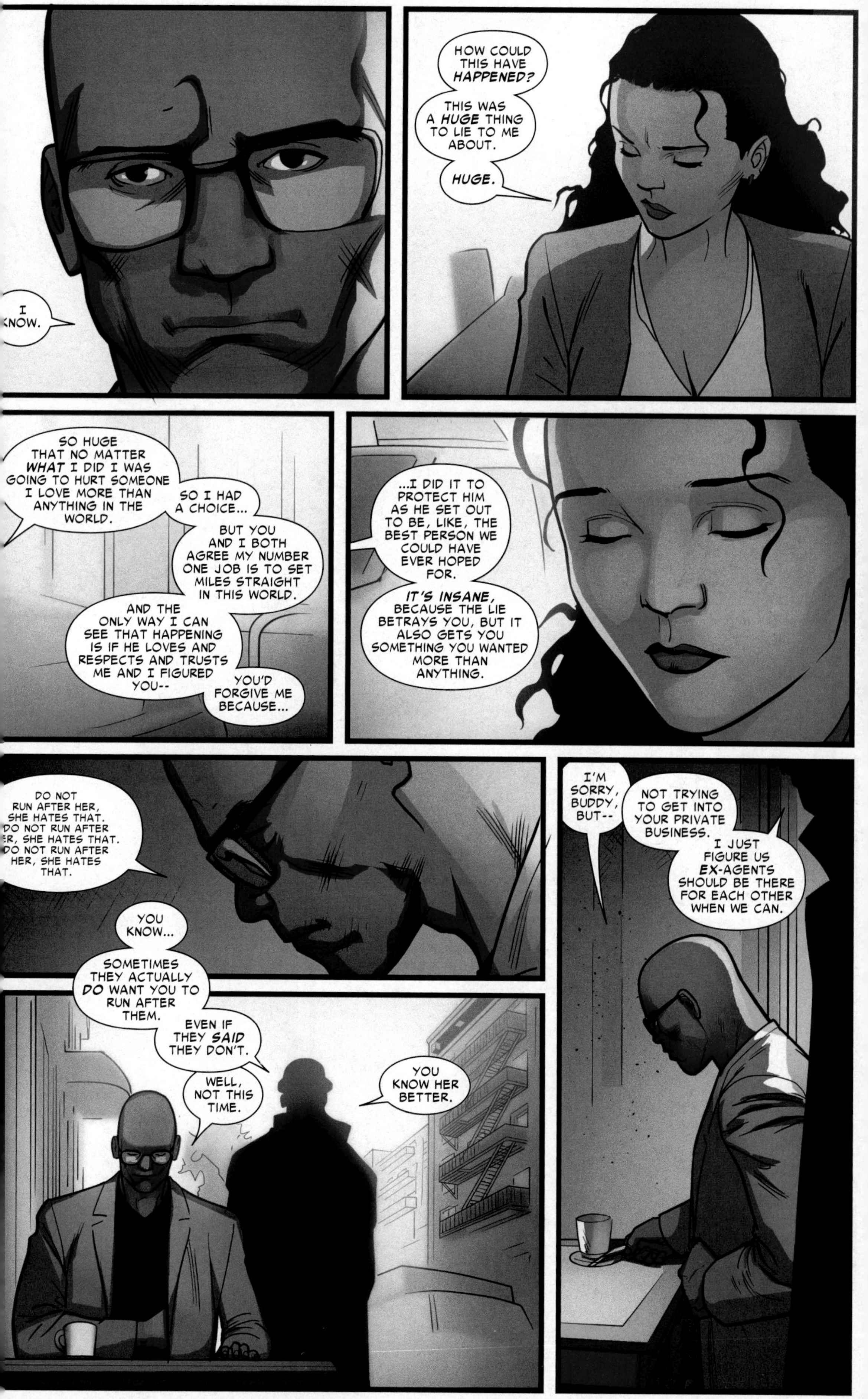
I KNOW.
HOW COULD THIS HAVE HAPPENED?
THIS WAS A HUGE THING TO LIE TO ME ABOUT.
HUGE.
SO HUGE THAT NO MATTER WHAT I DID I WAS GOING TO HURT SOMEONE I LOVE MORE THAN ANYTHING IN THE WORLD.
SO I HAD A CHOICE...
BUT YOU AND I BOTH AGREE MY NUMBER ONE JOB IS TO SET MILES STRAIGHT IN THIS WORLD.
AND THE ONLY WAY I CAN SEE THAT HAPPENING IS IF HE LOVES AND RESPECTS AND TRUSTS ME AND I FIGURED YOU--
YOU'D FORGIVE ME BECAUSE...
...I DID IT TO PROTECT HIM AS HE SET OUT TO BE, LIKE, THE BEST PERSON WE COULD HAVE EVER HOPED FOR.
IT'S INSANE, BECAUSE THE LIE BETRAYS YOU, BUT IT ALSO GETS YOU SOMETHING YOU WANTED MORE THAN ANYTHING.
DO NOT RUN AFTER HER, SHE HATES THAT. DO NOT RUN AFTER ER, SHE HATES THAT. DO NOT RUN AFTER HER, SHE HATES THAT.
YOU KNOW...
SOMETIMES THEY ACTUALLY DO WANT YOU TO RUN AFTER THEM.
EVEN IF THEY SAID THEY DON'T.
WELL, NOT THIS TIME.
YOU KNOW HER BETTER.
I'M SORRY, BUDDY, BUT--
NOT TRYING TO GET INTO YOUR PRIVATE BUSINESS.
I JUST FIGURE US EX-AGENTS SHOULD BE THERE FOR EACH OTHER WHEN WE CAN.

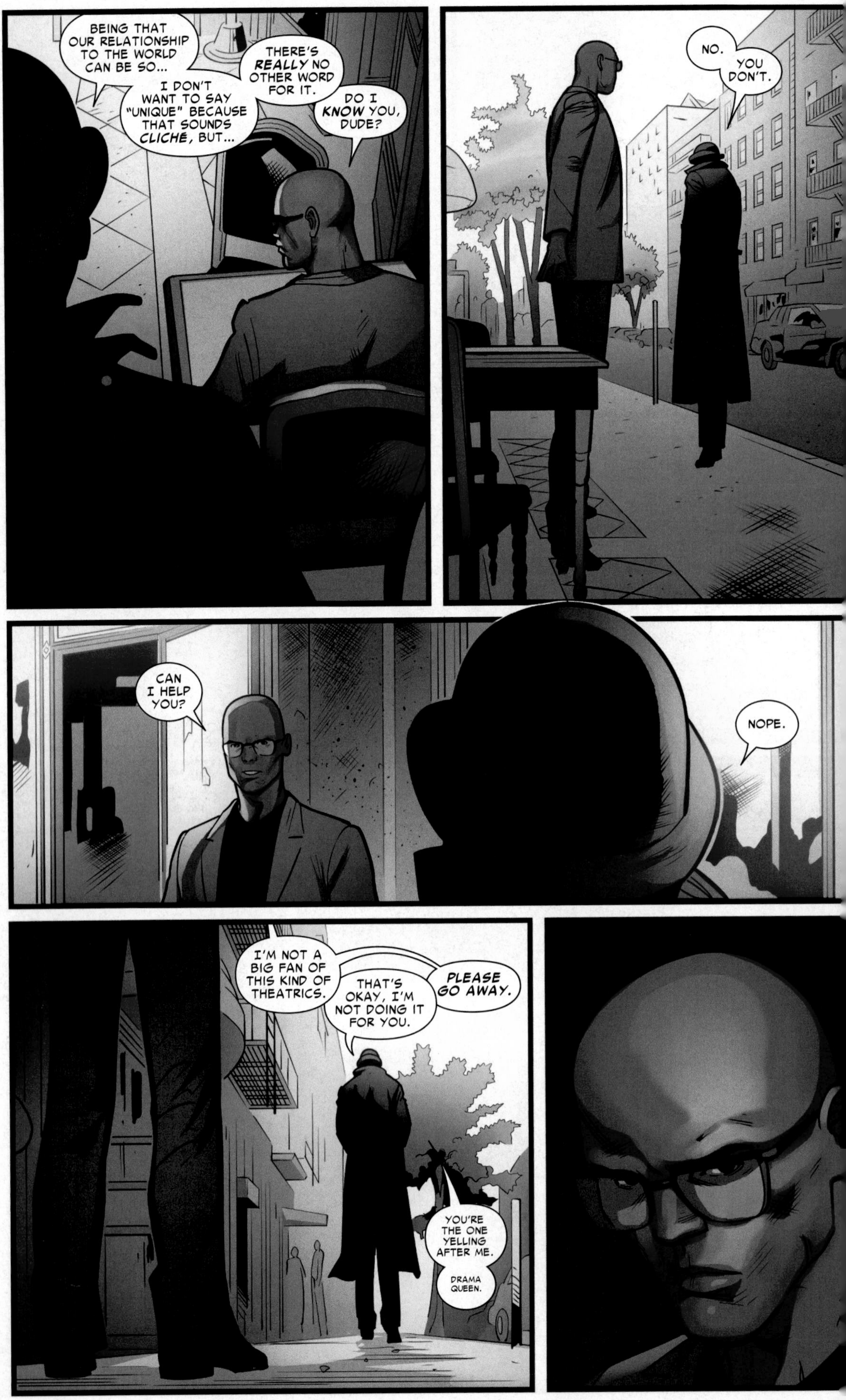

BEING THAT OUR RELATIONSHIP TO THE WORLD CAN BE SO...
I DON'T WANT TO SAY "UNIQUE" BECAUSE THAT SOUNDS *CLICHÉ*, BUT...
THERE'S *REALLY* NO OTHER WORD FOR IT.
DO I *KNOW* YOU, DUDE?
NO.
YOU DON'T.
CAN I HELP YOU?
NOPE.
I'M NOT A BIG FAN OF THIS KIND OF THEATRICS.
PLEASE GO AWAY.
THAT'S OKAY, I'M NOT DOING IT FOR YOU.
YOU'RE THE ONE YELLING AFTER ME.
DRAMA QUEEN.

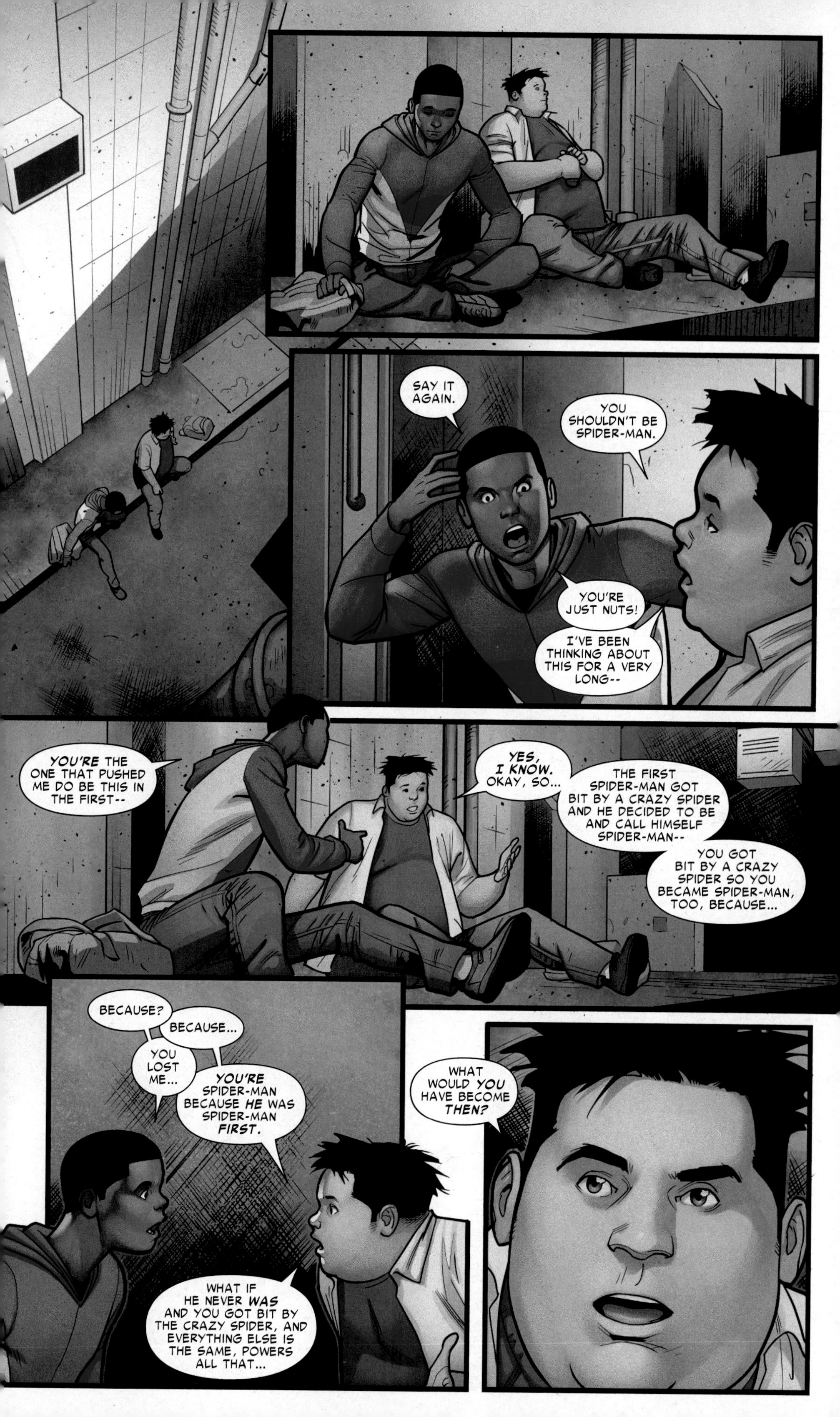
SAY IT AGAIN.
YOU SHOULDN'T BE SPIDER-MAN.
YOU'RE JUST NUTS!
I'VE BEEN THINKING ABOUT THIS FOR A VERY LONG--
YOU'RE THE ONE THAT PUSHED ME DO BE THIS IN THE FIRST--
YES, I KNOW. OKAY, SO...
THE FIRST SPIDER-MAN GOT BIT BY A CRAZY SPIDER AND HE DECIDED TO BE AND CALL HIMSELF SPIDER-MAN--
YOU GOT BIT BY A CRAZY SPIDER SO YOU BECAME SPIDER-MAN, TOO, BECAUSE...
BECAUSE?
BECAUSE...
YOU LOST ME...
YOU'RE SPIDER-MAN BECAUSE HE WAS SPIDER-MAN FIRST.
WHAT IF HE NEVER WAS AND YOU GOT BIT BY THE CRAZY SPIDER, AND EVERYTHING ELSE IS THE SAME, POWERS ALL THAT...
WHAT WOULD YOU HAVE BECOME THEN?

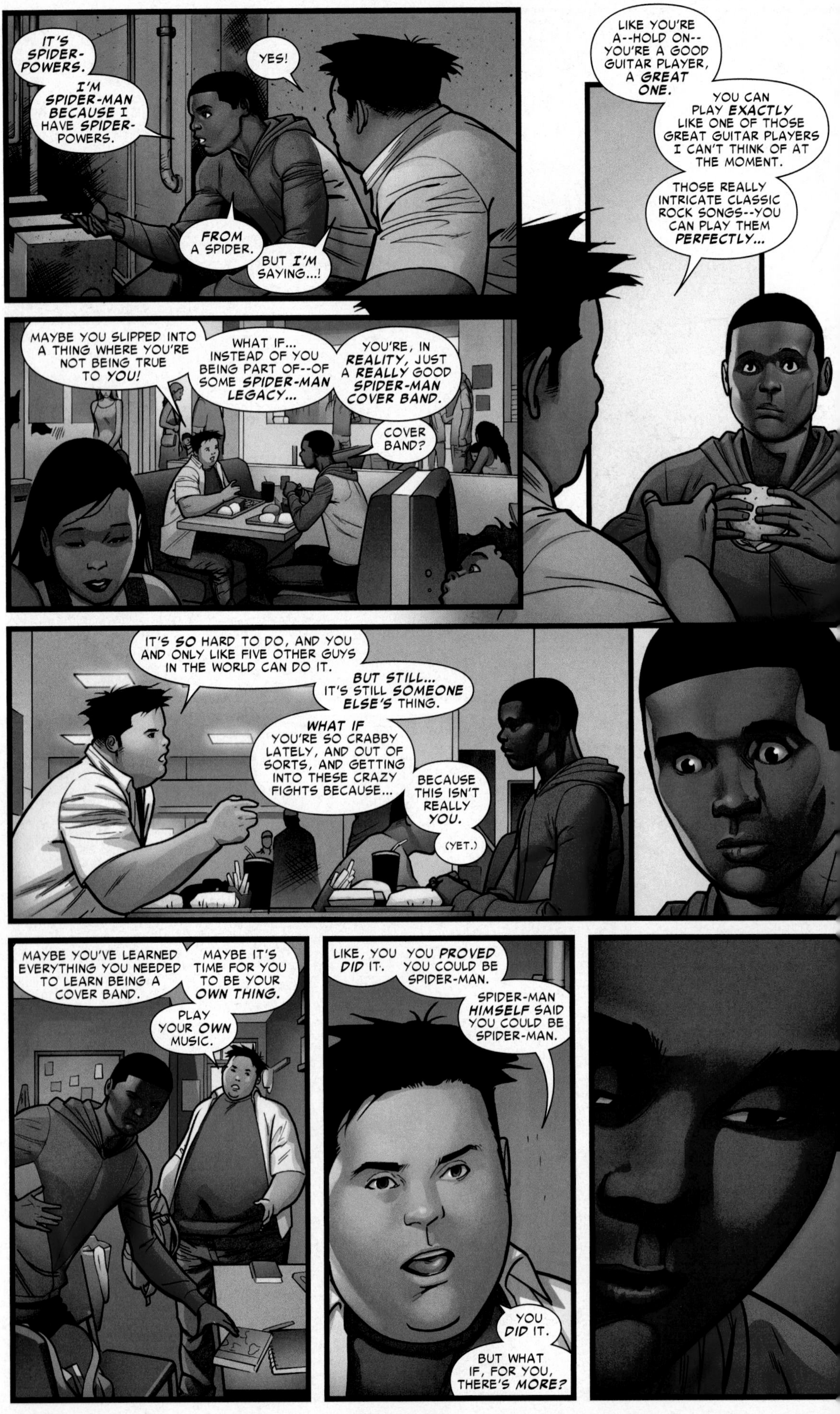
IT'S SPIDER-POWERS.
I'M SPIDER-MAN BECAUSE I HAVE SPIDER-POWERS.
YES!
FROM A SPIDER.
BUT I'M SAYING...!
LIKE YOU'RE A--HOLD ON-- YOU'RE A GOOD GUITAR PLAYER, A GREAT ONE.
YOU CAN PLAY EXACTLY LIKE ONE OF THOSE GREAT GUITAR PLAYERS I CAN'T THINK OF AT THE MOMENT.
THOSE REALLY INTRICATE CLASSIC ROCK SONGS--YOU CAN PLAY THEM PERFECTLY...
MAYBE YOU SLIPPED INTO A THING WHERE YOU'RE NOT BEING TRUE TO YOU!
WHAT IF... INSTEAD OF YOU BEING PART OF--OF SOME SPIDER-MAN LEGACY...
YOU'RE, IN REALITY, JUST A REALLY GOOD SPIDER-MAN COVER BAND.
COVER BAND?
IT'S SO HARD TO DO, AND YOU AND ONLY LIKE FIVE OTHER GUYS IN THE WORLD CAN DO IT.
BUT STILL... IT'S STILL SOMEONE ELSE'S THING.
WHAT IF YOU'RE SO CRABBY LATELY, AND OUT OF SORTS, AND GETTING INTO THESE CRAZY FIGHTS BECAUSE...
BECAUSE THIS ISN'T REALLY YOU.
(YET.)
MAYBE YOU'VE LEARNED EVERYTHING YOU NEEDED TO LEARN BEING A COVER BAND.
MAYBE IT'S TIME FOR YOU TO BE YOUR OWN THING.
PLAY YOUR OWN MUSIC.
LIKE, YOU DID IT.
YOU PROVED YOU COULD BE SPIDER-MAN.
SPIDER-MAN HIMSELF SAID YOU COULD BE SPIDER-MAN.
YOU DID IT.
BUT WHAT IF, FOR YOU, THERE'S MORE?

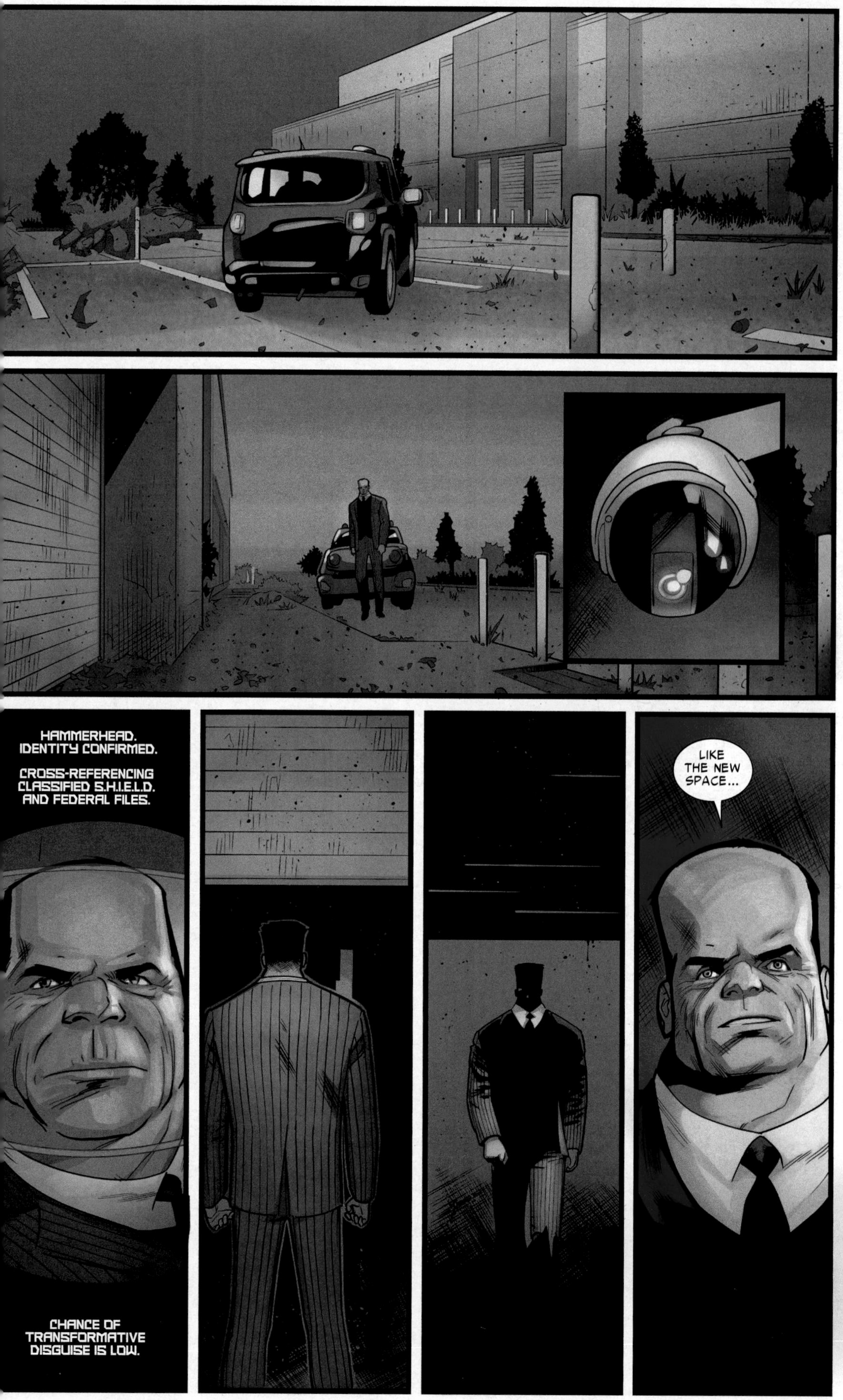
HAMMERHEAD. IDENTITY CONFIRMED.
CROSS-REFERENCING CLASSIFIED S.H.I.E.L.D. AND FEDERAL FILES.
CHANCE OF TRANSFORMATIVE DISGUISE IS LOW.
LIKE THE NEW SPACE...

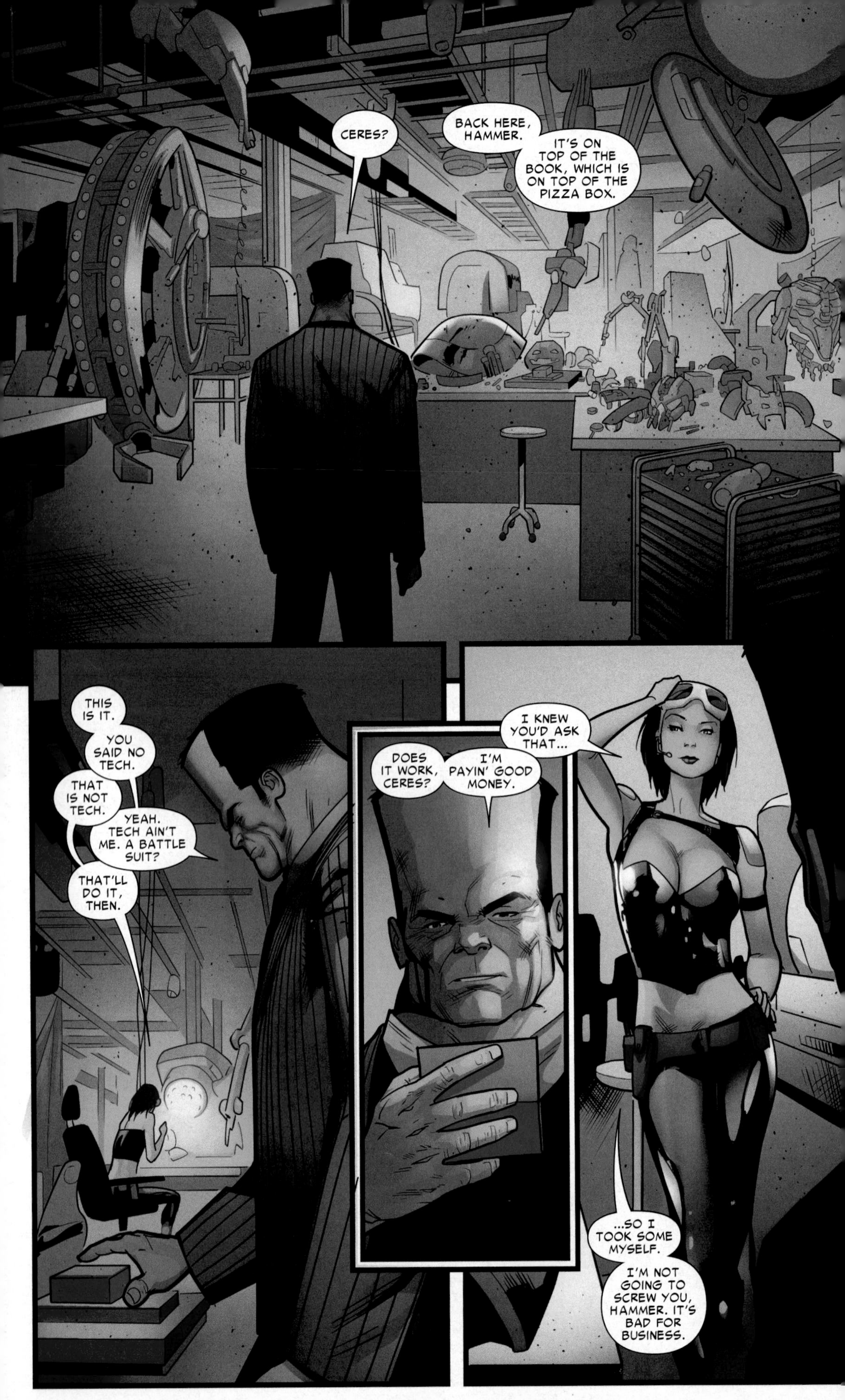
CERES?
BACK HERE, HAMMER.
IT'S ON TOP OF THE BOOK, WHICH IS ON TOP OF THE PIZZA BOX.
THIS IS IT.
YOU SAID NO TECH.
THAT IS NOT TECH.
YEAH. TECH AIN'T ME. A BATTLE SUIT?
THAT'LL DO IT, THEN.
DOES IT WORK, CERES?
I'M PAYIN' GOOD MONEY.
I KNEW YOU'D ASK THAT...
...SO I TOOK SOME MYSELF.
I'M NOT GOING TO SCREW YOU, HAMMER. IT'S BAD FOR BUSINESS.

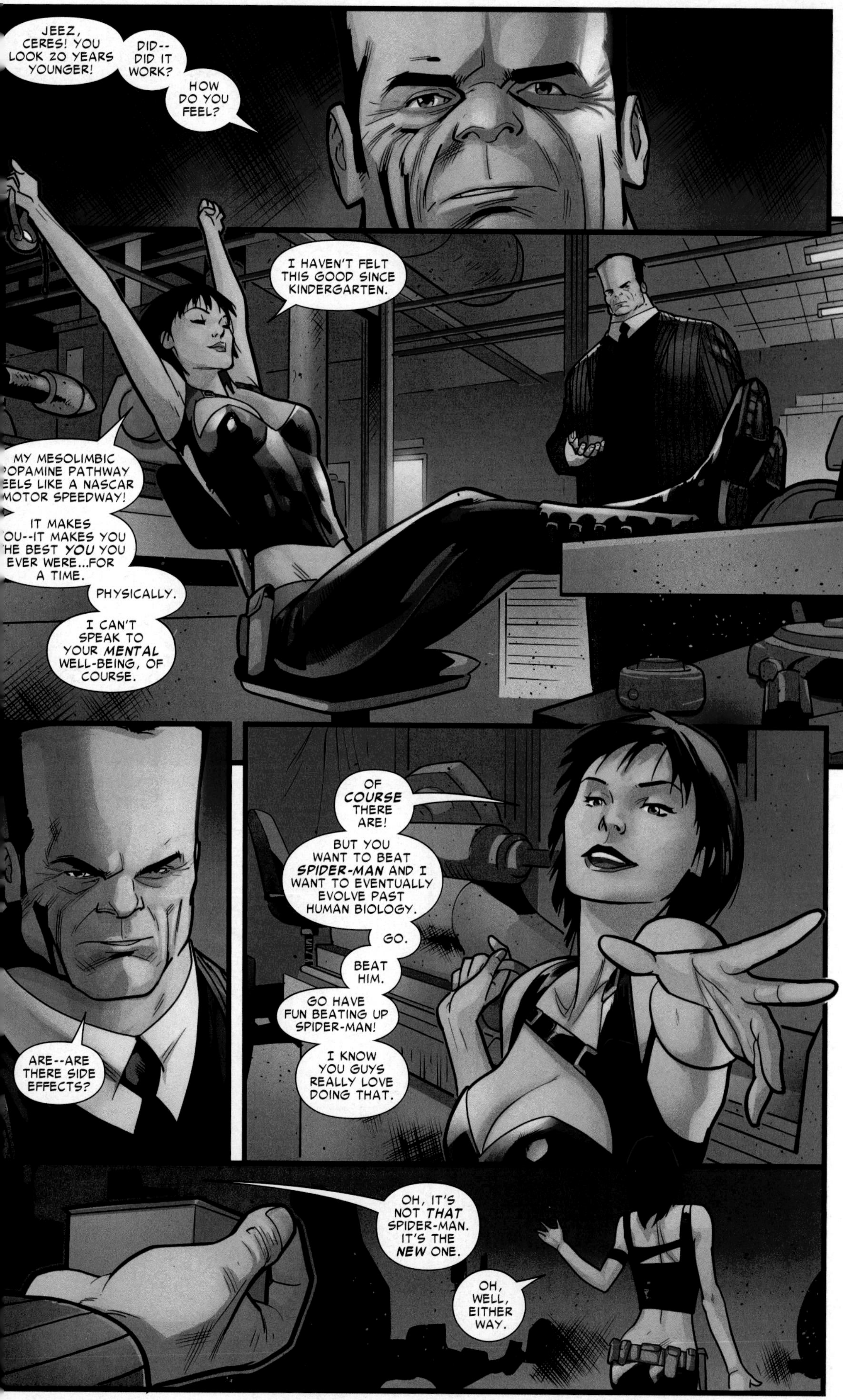

JEEZ, CERES! YOU LOOK 20 YEARS YOUNGER!
DID-- DID IT WORK?
HOW DO YOU FEEL?
I HAVEN'T FELT THIS GOOD SINCE KINDERGARTEN.
MY MESOLIMBIC DOPAMINE PATHWAY FEELS LIKE A NASCAR MOTOR SPEEDWAY!
IT MAKES YOU--IT MAKES YOU THE BEST YOU YOU EVER WERE...FOR A TIME.
PHYSICALLY.
I CAN'T SPEAK TO YOUR MENTAL WELL-BEING, OF COURSE.
ARE--ARE THERE SIDE EFFECTS?
OF COURSE THERE ARE!
BUT YOU WANT TO BEAT SPIDER-MAN AND I WANT TO EVENTUALLY EVOLVE PAST HUMAN BIOLOGY.
GO.
BEAT HIM.
GO HAVE FUN BEATING UP SPIDER-MAN!
I KNOW YOU GUYS REALLY LOVE DOING THAT.
OH, IT'S NOT THAT SPIDER-MAN. IT'S THE NEW ONE.
OH, WELL, EITHER WAY.

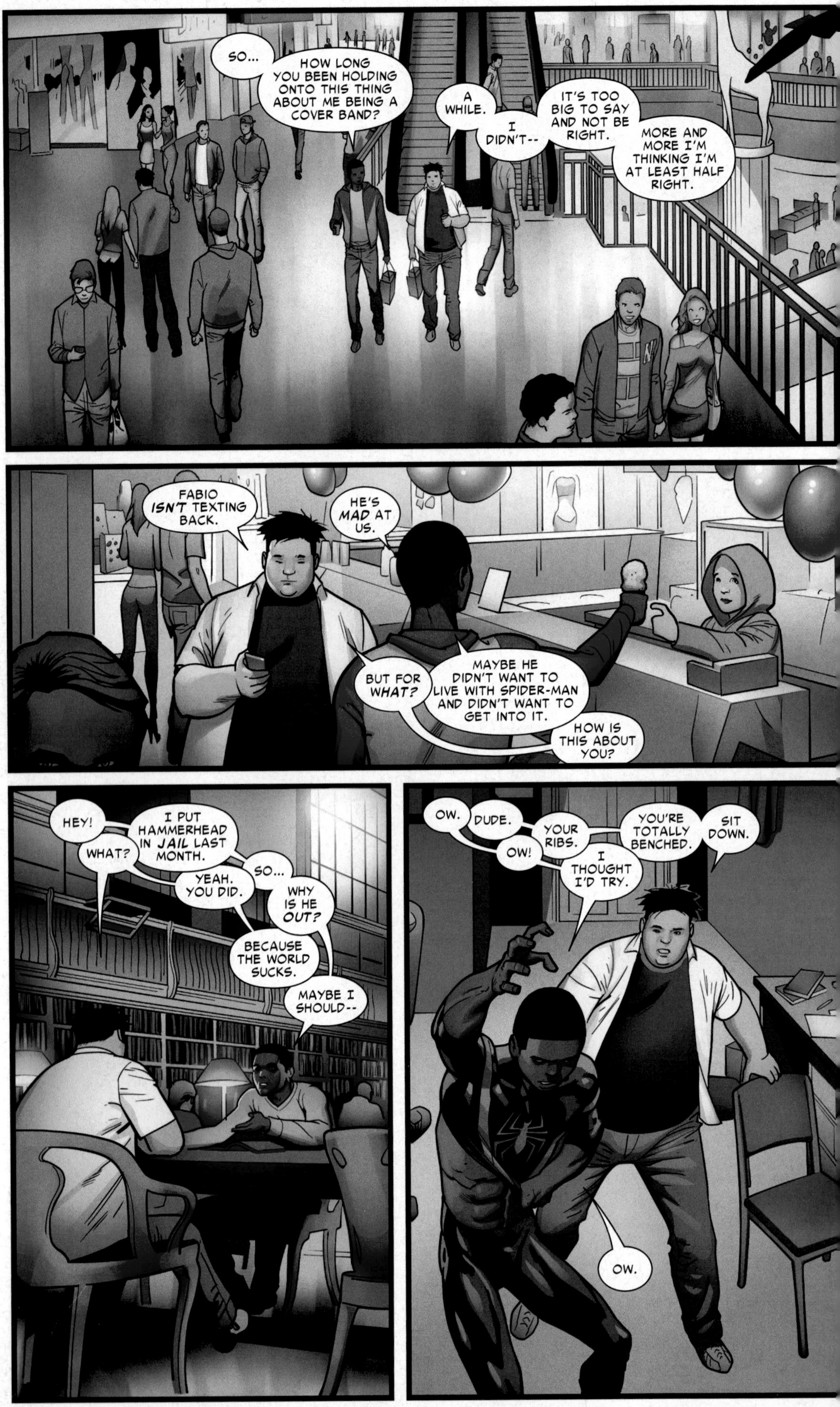
SO...
HOW LONG YOU BEEN HOLDING ONTO THIS THING ABOUT ME BEING A COVER BAND?
A WHILE.
I DIDN'T--
IT'S TOO BIG TO SAY AND NOT BE RIGHT.
MORE AND MORE I'M THINKING I'M AT LEAST HALF RIGHT.
FABIO ISN'T TEXTING BACK.
HE'S MAD AT US.
BUT FOR WHAT?
MAYBE HE DIDN'T WANT TO LIVE WITH SPIDER-MAN AND DIDN'T WANT TO GET INTO IT.
HOW IS THIS ABOUT YOU?
HEY!
WHAT?
I PUT HAMMERHEAD IN JAIL LAST MONTH.
YEAH. YOU DID.
SO...
WHY IS HE OUT?
BECAUSE THE WORLD SUCKS.
MAYBE I SHOULD--
OW.
DUDE.
OW!
YOUR RIBS.
I THOUGHT I'D TRY.
YOU'RE TOTALLY BENCHED.
SIT DOWN.
OW.

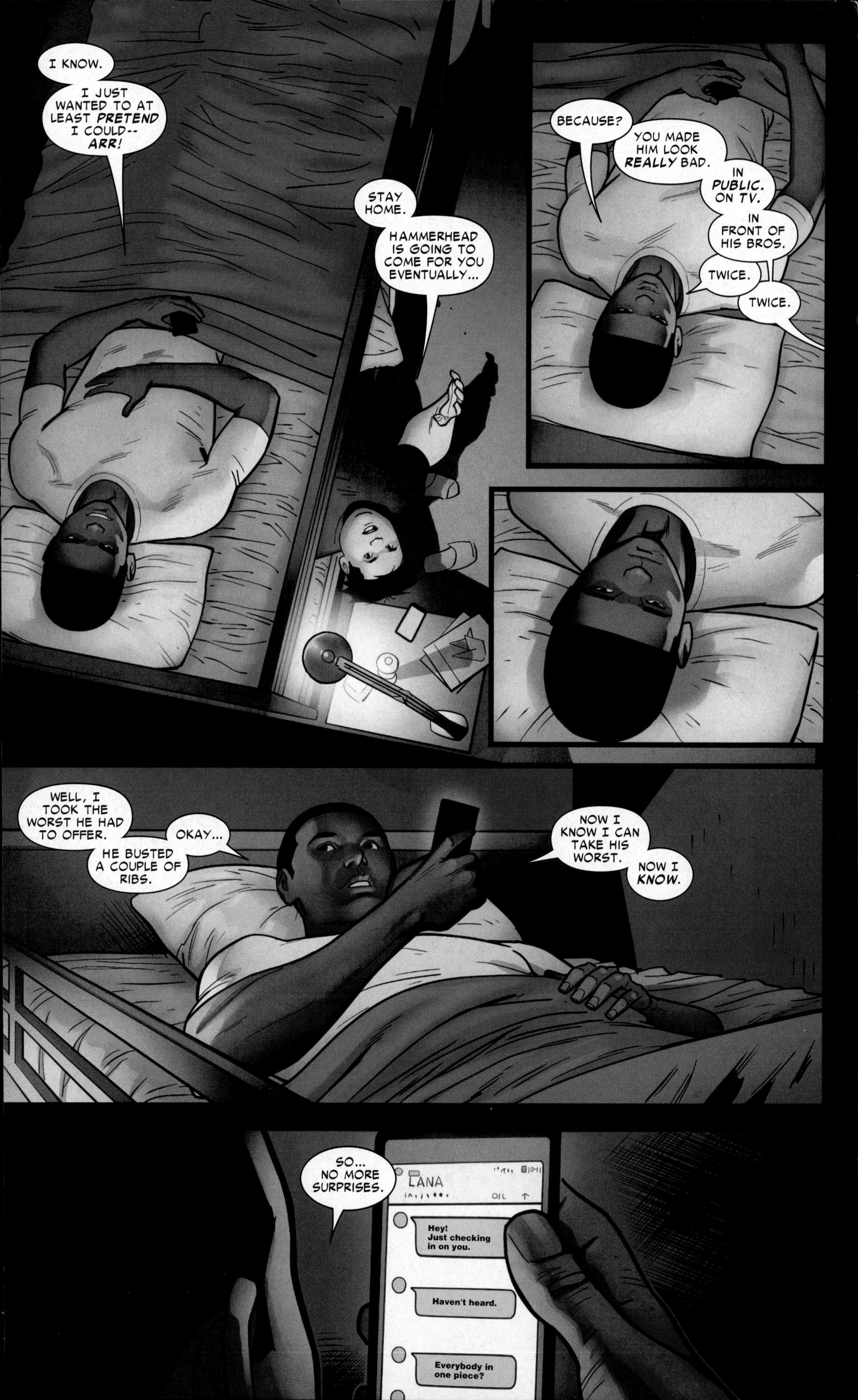
I KNOW.
I JUST WANTED TO AT LEAST *PRETEND* I COULD-- *ARR!*
STAY HOME.
HAMMERHEAD IS GOING TO COME FOR YOU EVENTUALLY...
BECAUSE?
YOU MADE HIM LOOK *REALLY* BAD.
IN *PUBLIC.* ON *TV.*
IN FRONT OF HIS BROS.
TWICE.
TWICE.
WELL, I TOOK THE WORST HE HAD TO OFFER.
OKAY...
HE BUSTED A COUPLE OF RIBS.
NOW I KNOW I CAN TAKE HIS WORST.
NOW I *KNOW.*
SO... NO MORE SURPRISES.
LANA
Hey! Just checking in on you.
Haven't heard.
Everybody in one piece?

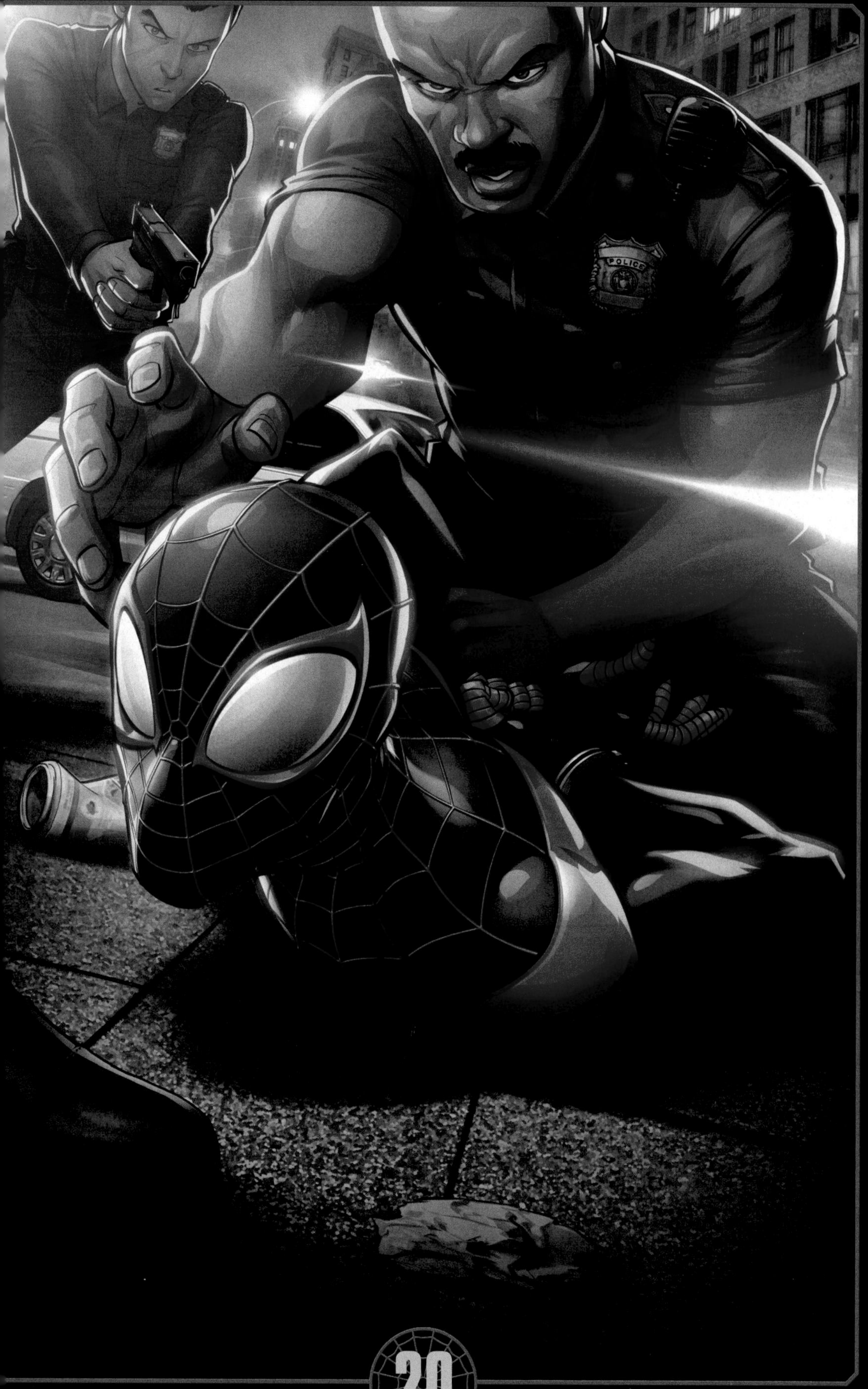
POLICE

20

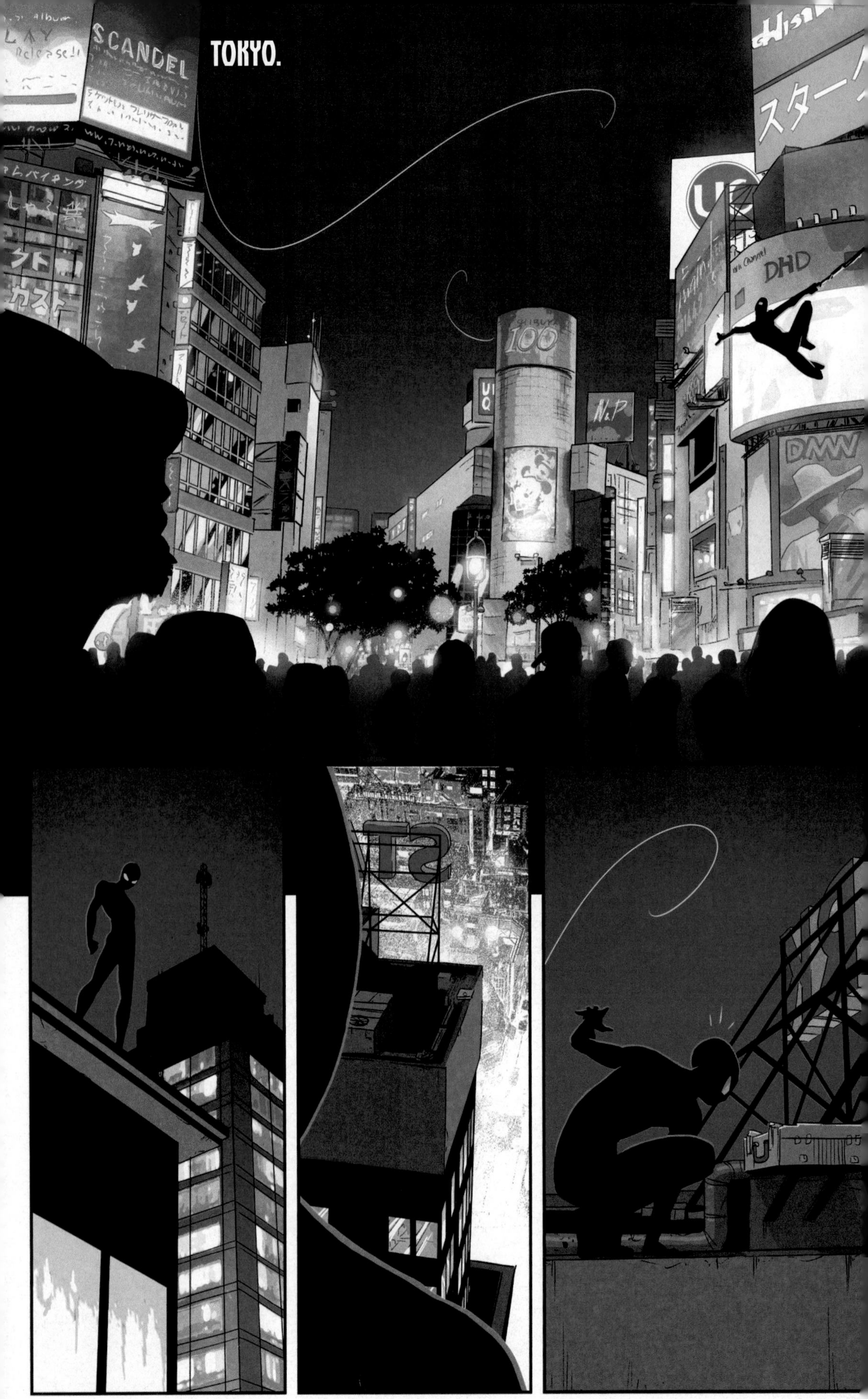
TOKYO.
SCANDEL
SHIBUYA
100
UQ
DHD

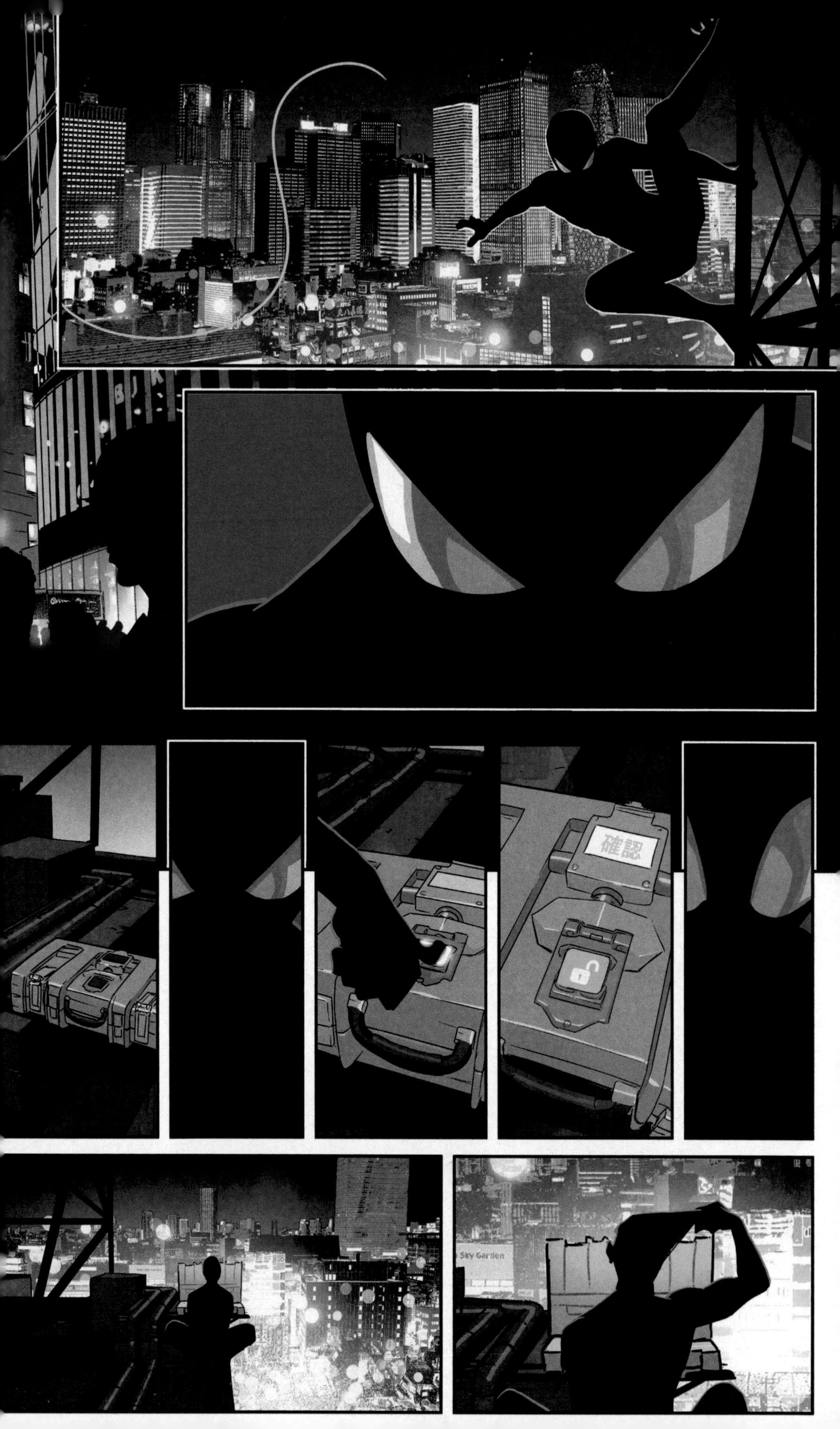
確認
Sky Garden

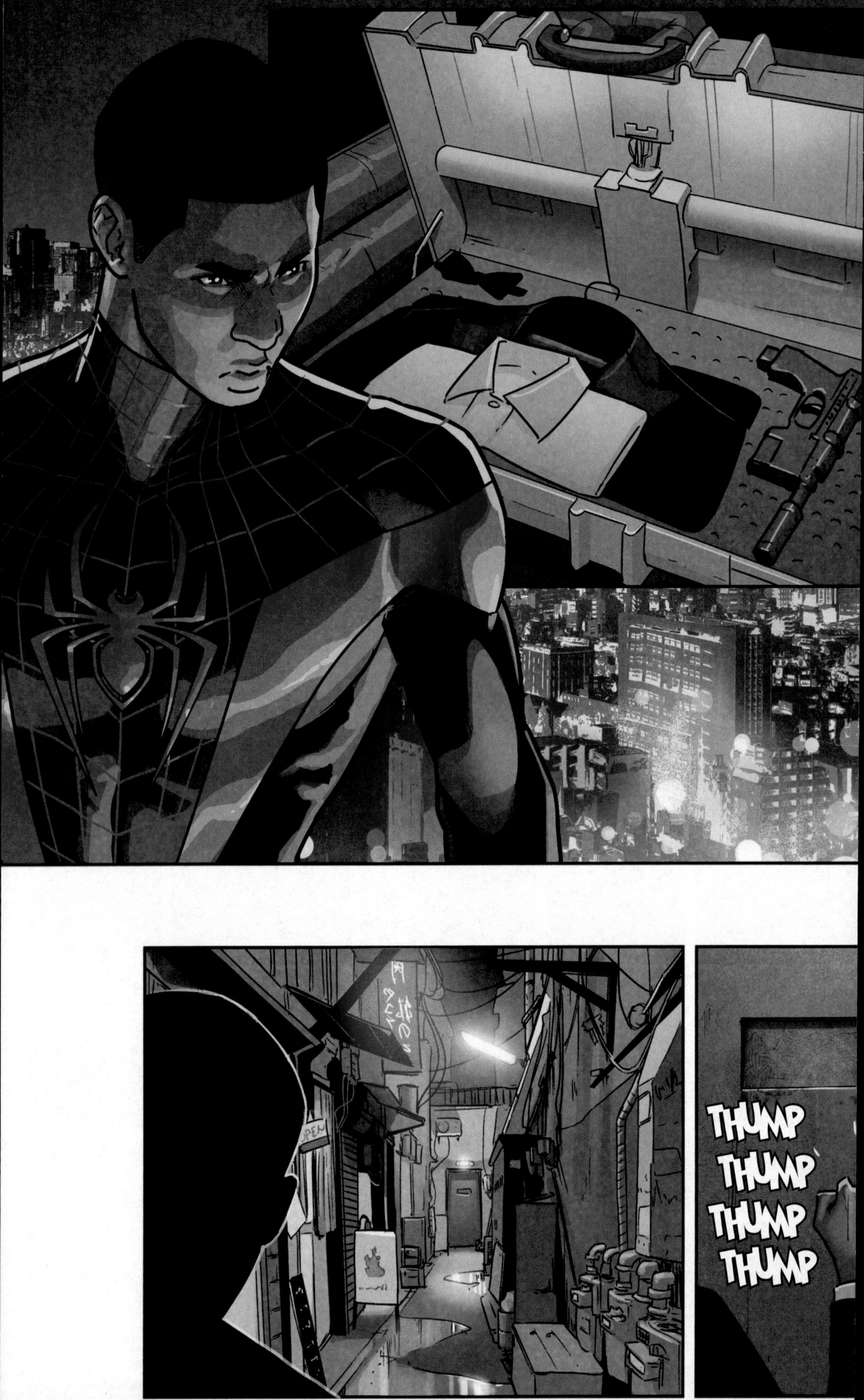
THUMP
THUMP
THUMP
THUMP

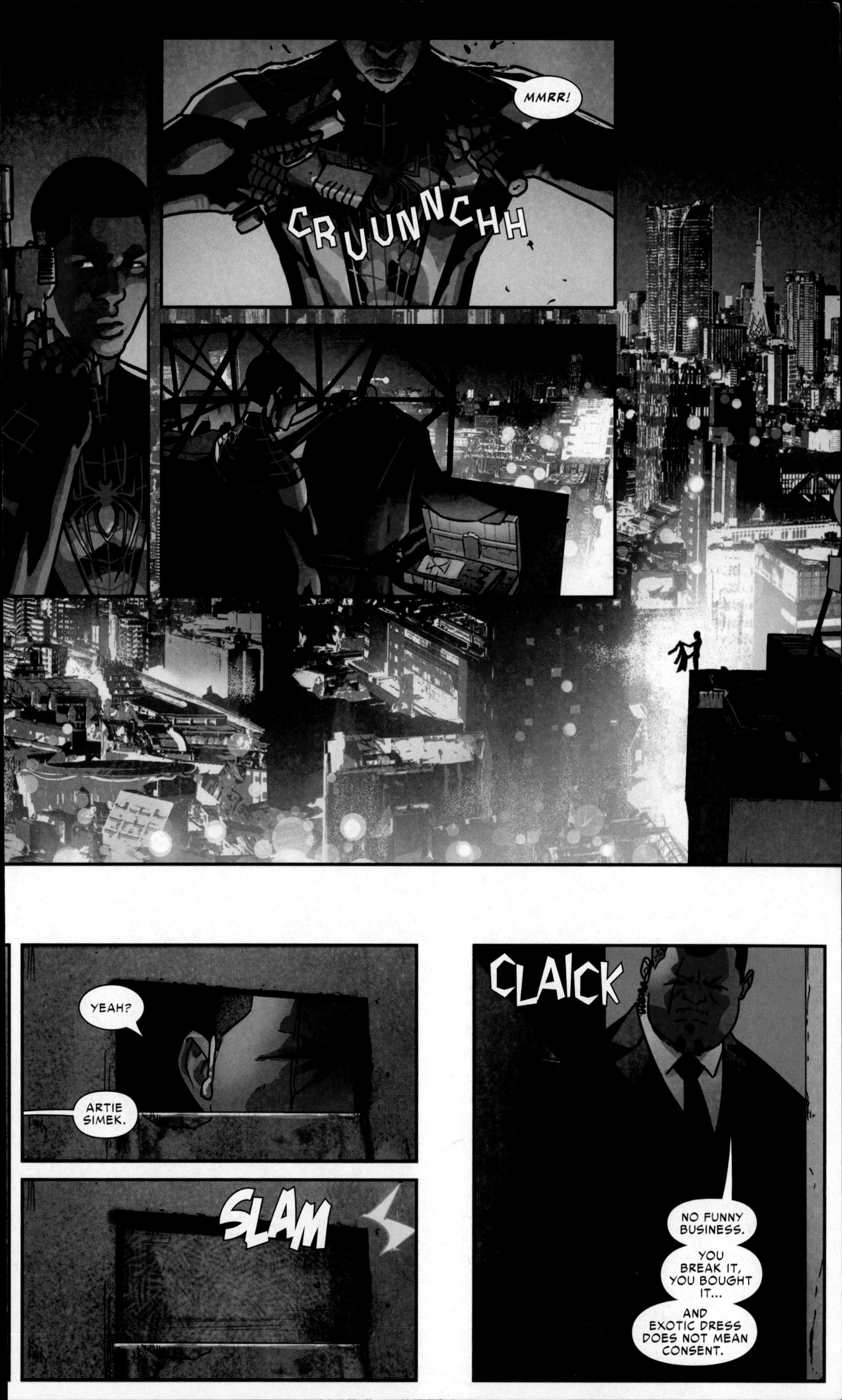
MMRR!
CRUUNNCHH
YEAH?
ARTIE SIMEK.
SLAM
CLAICK
NO FUNNY BUSINESS.
YOU BREAK IT, YOU BOUGHT IT...
AND EXOTIC DRESS DOES NOT MEAN CONSENT.

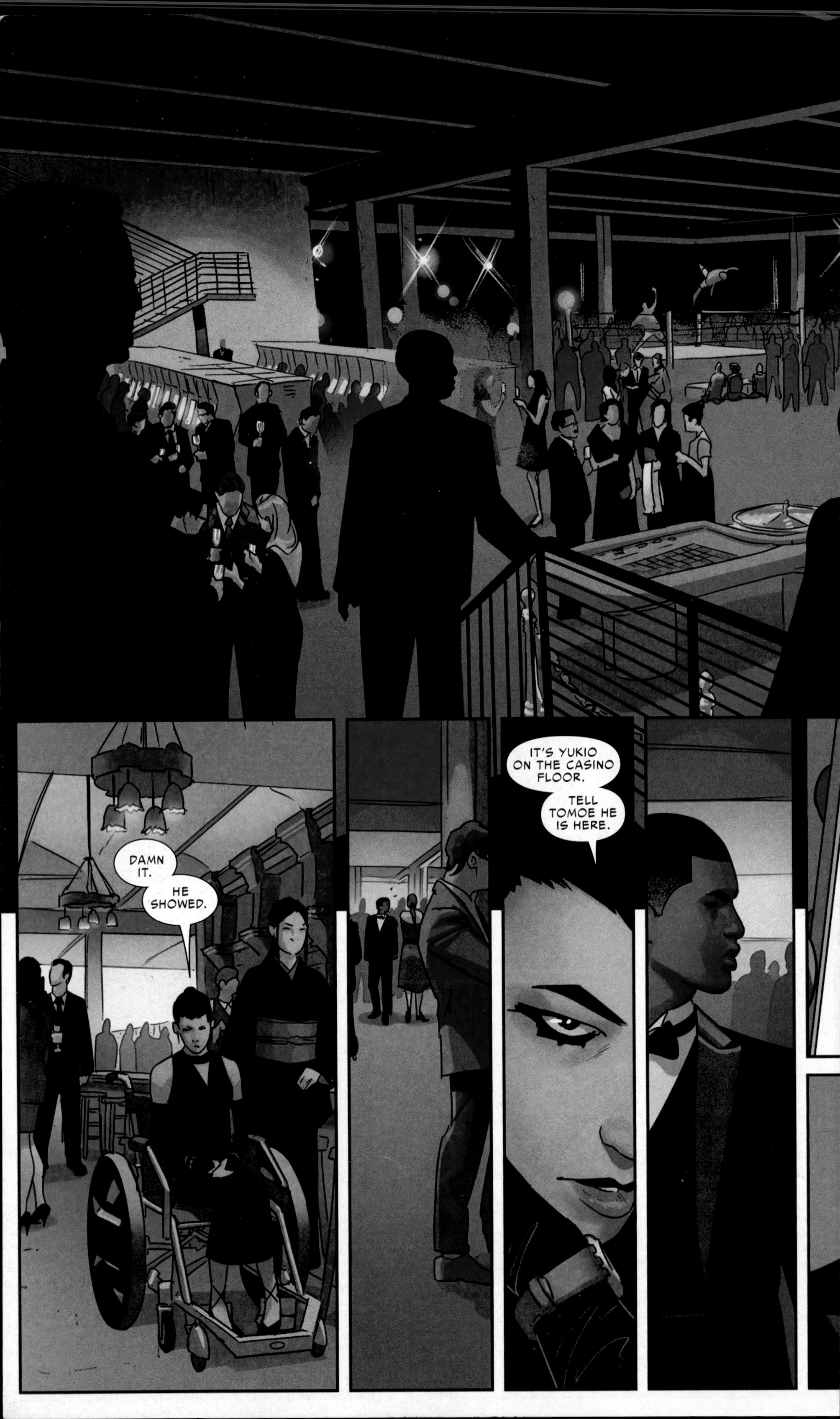
DAMN IT.
HE SHOWED.
IT'S YUKIO ON THE CASINO FLOOR.
TELL TOMOE HE IS HERE.

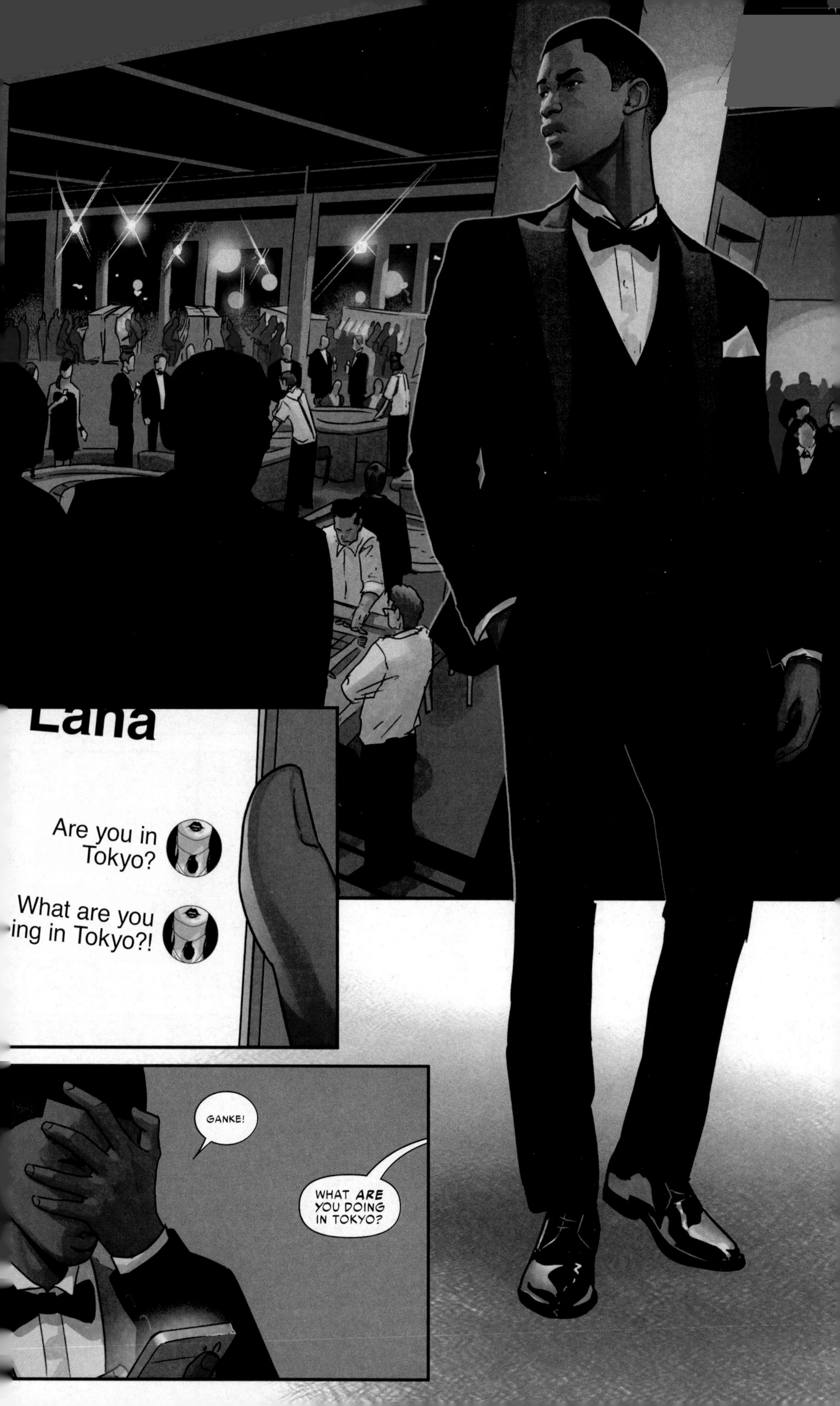

Lana
Are you in Tokyo?
What are you
ing in Tokyo?!
GANKE!
WHAT ARE YOU DOING IN TOKYO?

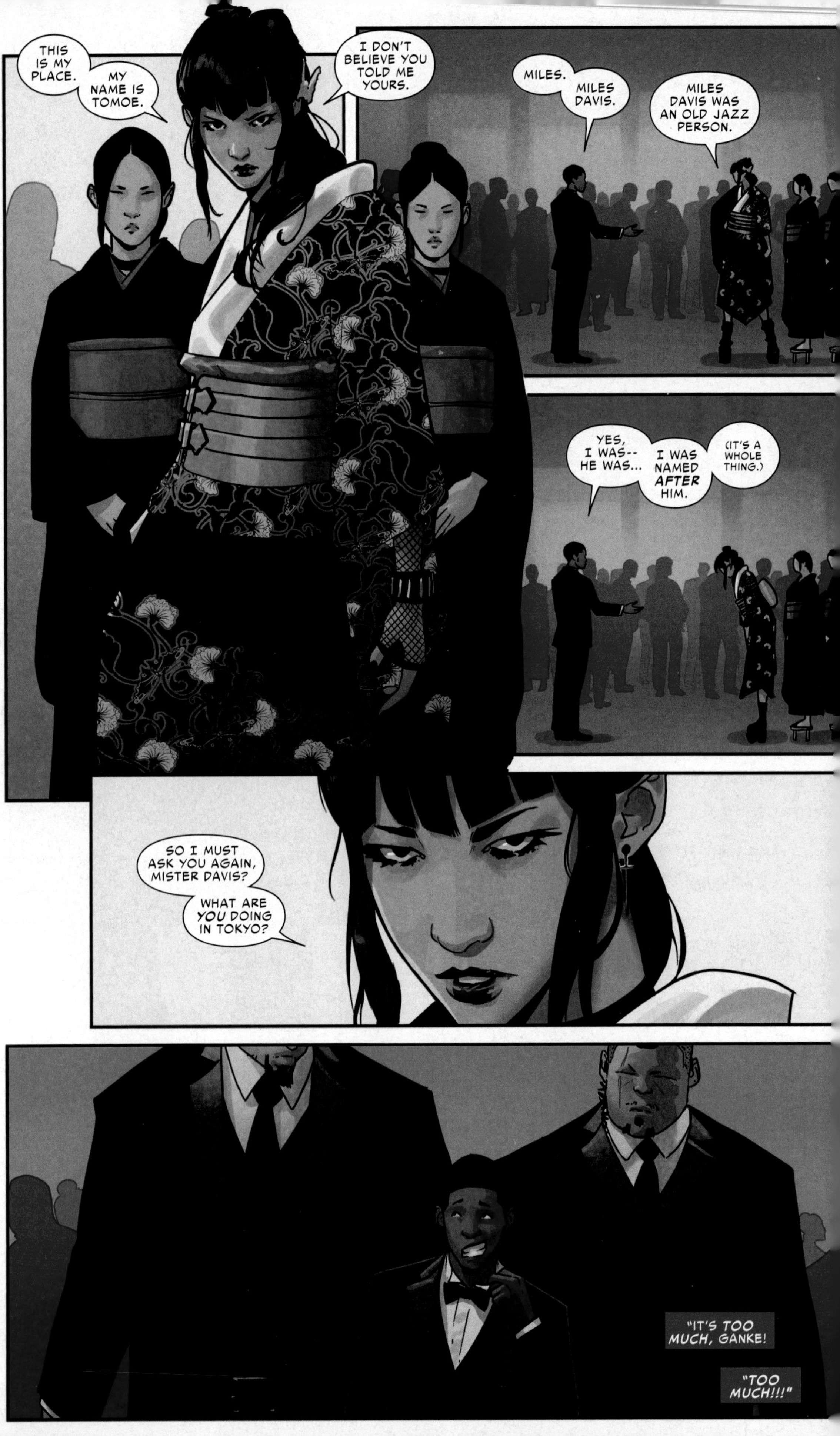

THIS IS MY PLACE.
MY NAME IS TOMOE.
I DON'T BELIEVE YOU TOLD ME YOURS.
MILES.
MILES DAVIS.
MILES DAVIS WAS AN OLD JAZZ PERSON.
YES, I WAS-- HE WAS...
I WAS NAMED *AFTER* HIM.
(IT'S A WHOLE THING.)
SO I MUST ASK YOU AGAIN, MISTER DAVIS?
WHAT ARE *YOU* DOING IN TOKYO?
"IT'S *TOO* MUCH, GANKE!
"TOO MUCH!!!"

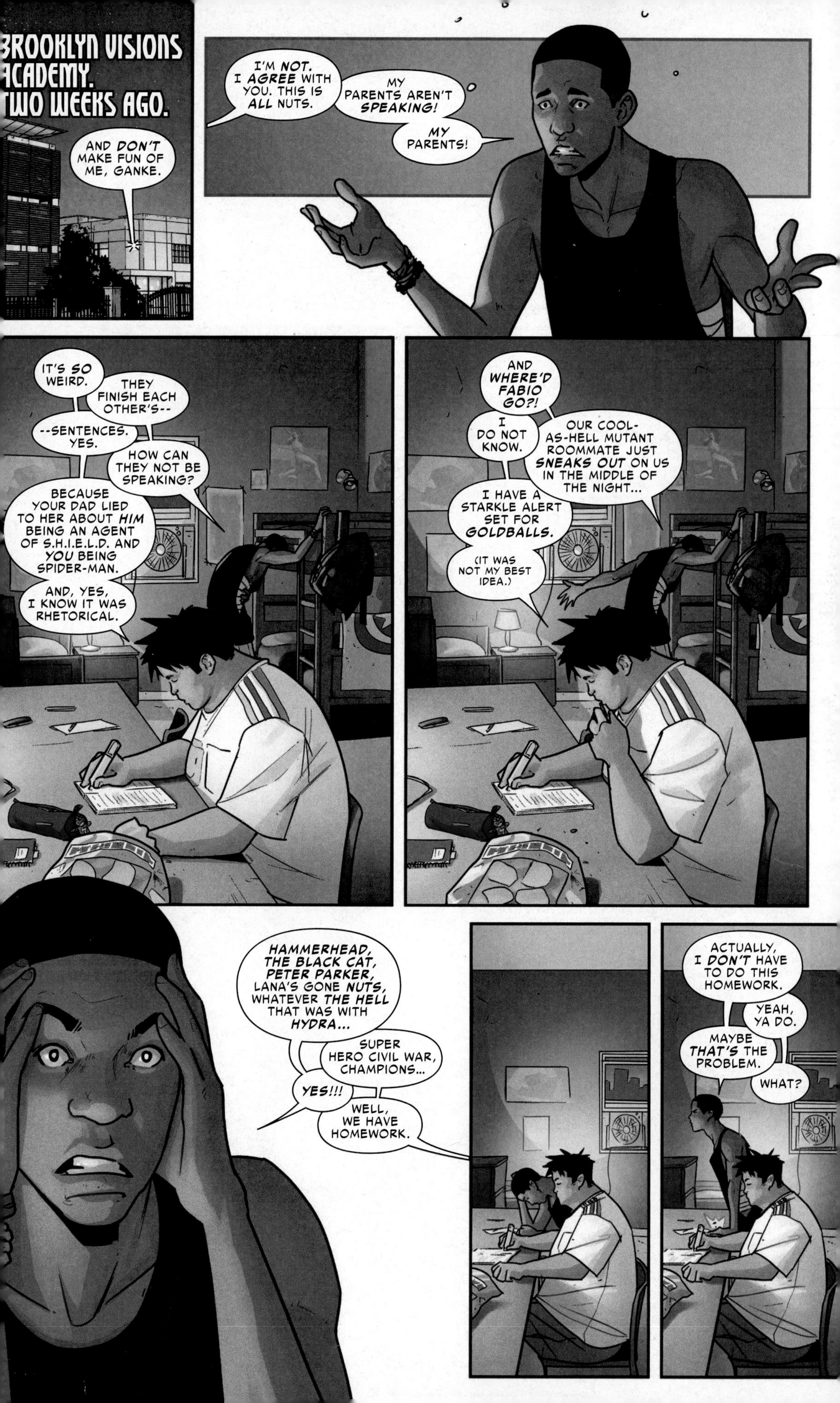

BROOKLYN VISIONS ACADEMY. TWO WEEKS AGO.
AND DON'T MAKE FUN OF ME, GANKE.
I'M NOT. I AGREE WITH YOU. THIS IS ALL NUTS.
MY PARENTS AREN'T SPEAKING!
MY PARENTS!
IT'S SO WEIRD.
THEY FINISH EACH OTHER'S--
--SENTENCES. YES.
HOW CAN THEY NOT BE SPEAKING?
BECAUSE YOUR DAD LIED TO HER ABOUT HIM BEING AN AGENT OF S.H.I.E.L.D. AND YOU BEING SPIDER-MAN.
AND, YES, I KNOW IT WAS RHETORICAL.
AND WHERE'D FABIO GO?!
I DO NOT KNOW.
OUR COOL-AS-HELL MUTANT ROOMMATE JUST SNEAKS OUT ON US IN THE MIDDLE OF THE NIGHT...
I HAVE A STARKLE ALERT SET FOR GOLDBALLS.
(IT WAS NOT MY BEST IDEA.)
HAMMERHEAD, THE BLACK CAT, PETER PARKER, LANA'S GONE NUTS, WHATEVER THE HELL THAT WAS WITH HYDRA...
SUPER HERO CIVIL WAR, CHAMPIONS...
YES!!!
WELL, WE HAVE HOMEWORK.
ACTUALLY, I DON'T HAVE TO DO THIS HOMEWORK.
YEAH, YA DO.
MAYBE THAT'S THE PROBLEM.
WHAT?

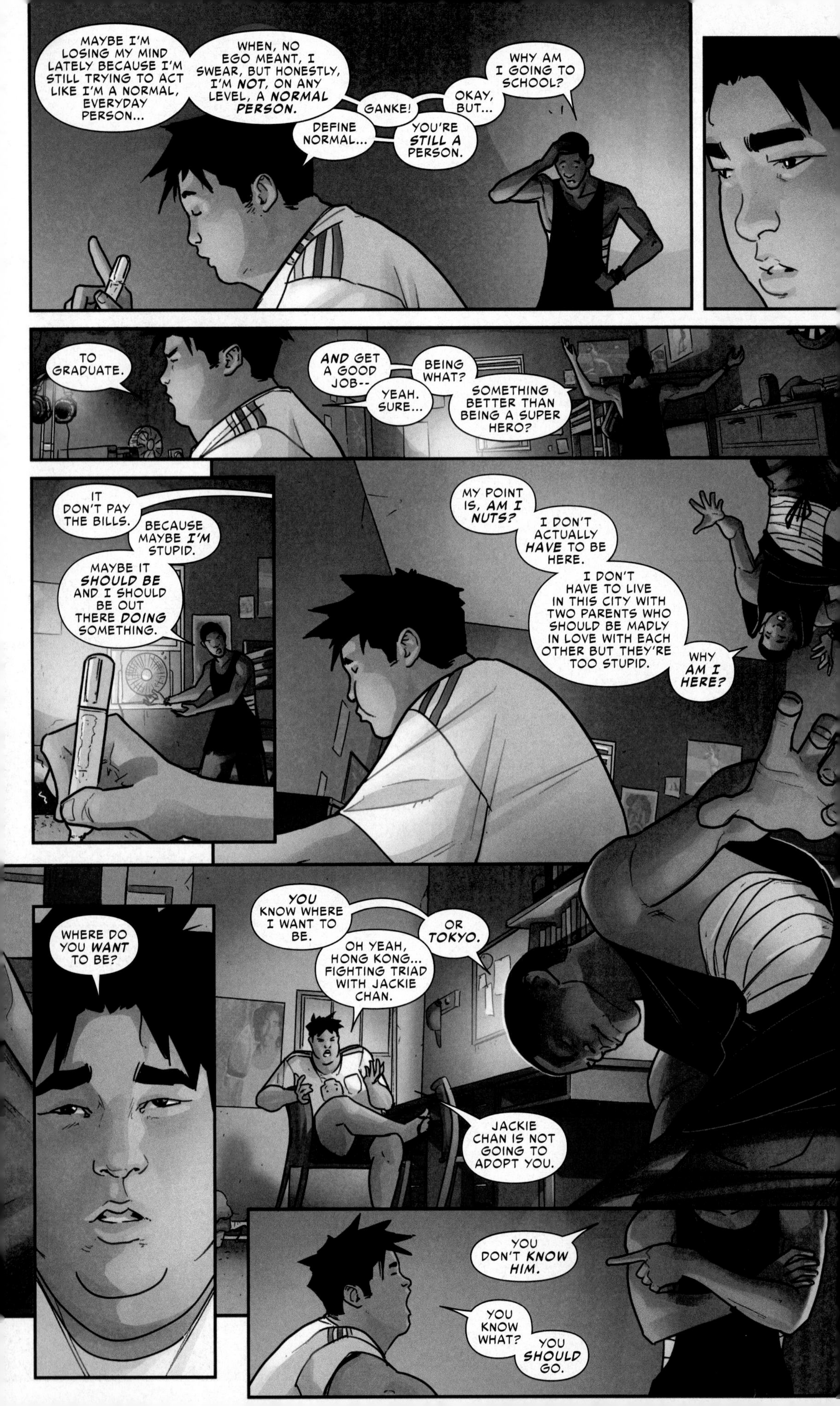
MAYBE I'M LOSING MY MIND LATELY BECAUSE I'M STILL TRYING TO ACT LIKE I'M A NORMAL, EVERYDAY PERSON...
WHEN, NO EGO MEANT, I SWEAR, BUT HONESTLY, I'M NOT, ON ANY LEVEL, A NORMAL PERSON.
DEFINE NORMAL...
GANKE!
YOU'RE STILL A PERSON.
OKAY, BUT...
WHY AM I GOING TO SCHOOL?
TO GRADUATE.
AND GET A GOOD JOB--
BEING WHAT?
YEAH. SURE...
SOMETHING BETTER THAN BEING A SUPER HERO?
IT DON'T PAY THE BILLS.
BECAUSE MAYBE I'M STUPID.
MAYBE IT SHOULD BE AND I SHOULD BE OUT THERE DOING SOMETHING.
MY POINT IS, AM I NUTS?
I DON'T ACTUALLY HAVE TO BE HERE.
I DON'T HAVE TO LIVE IN THIS CITY WITH TWO PARENTS WHO SHOULD BE MADLY IN LOVE WITH EACH OTHER BUT THEY'RE TOO STUPID.
WHY AM I HERE?
WHERE DO YOU WANT TO BE?
YOU KNOW WHERE I WANT TO BE.
OH YEAH, HONG KONG... FIGHTING TRIAD WITH JACKIE CHAN.
OR TOKYO.
JACKIE CHAN IS NOT GOING TO ADOPT YOU.
YOU DON'T KNOW HIM.
YOU KNOW WHAT?
YOU SHOULD GO.

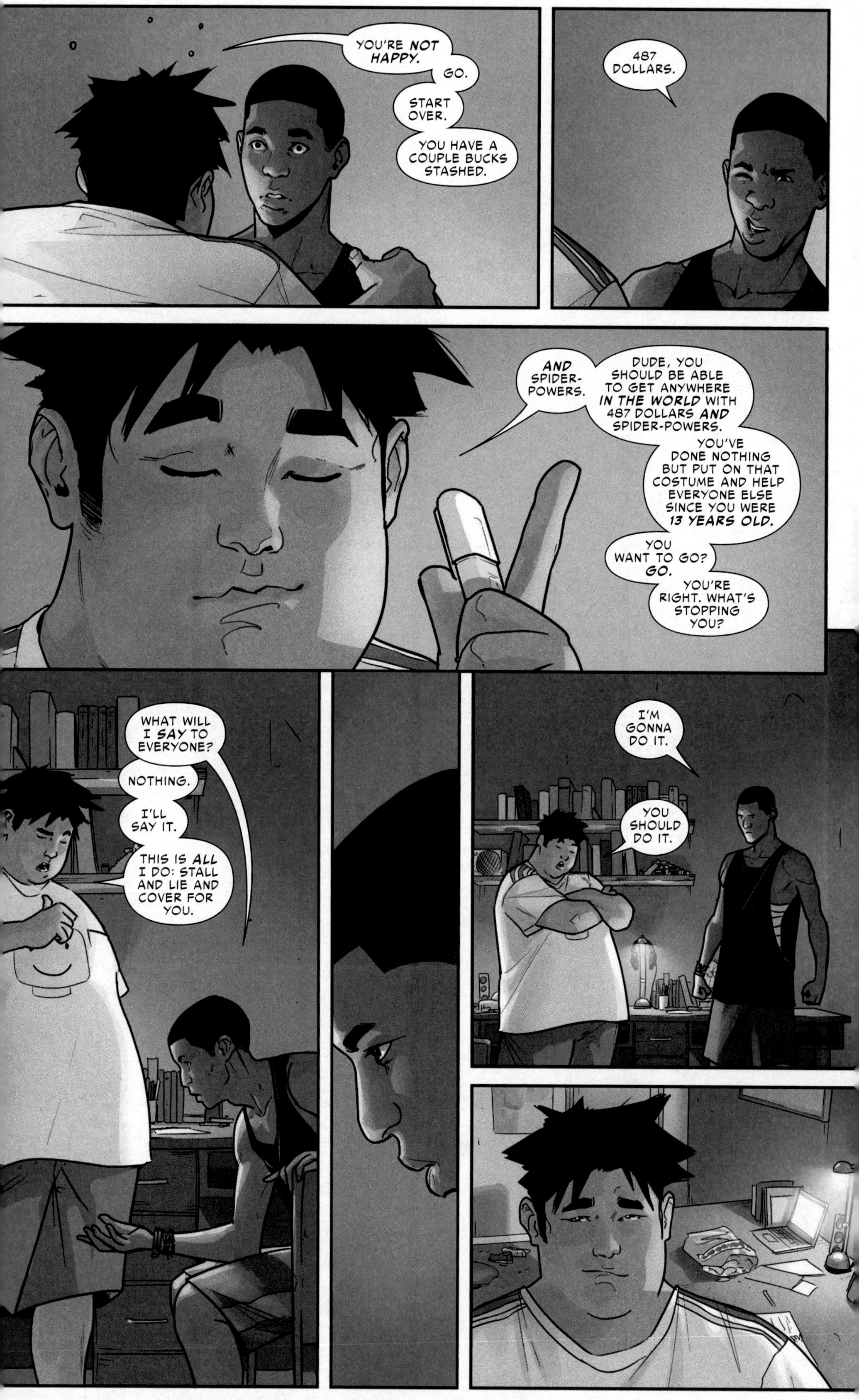

YOU'RE NOT HAPPY.
GO.
START OVER.
YOU HAVE A COUPLE BUCKS STASHED.
487 DOLLARS.
DUDE, YOU SHOULD BE ABLE TO GET ANYWHERE IN THE WORLD WITH 487 DOLLARS AND SPIDER-POWERS.
AND SPIDER-POWERS.
YOU'VE DONE NOTHING BUT PUT ON THAT COSTUME AND HELP EVERYONE ELSE SINCE YOU WERE 13 YEARS OLD.
YOU WANT TO GO? GO.
YOU'RE RIGHT. WHAT'S STOPPING YOU?
WHAT WILL I SAY TO EVERYONE?
NOTHING.
I'LL SAY IT.
THIS IS ALL I DO: STALL AND LIE AND COVER FOR YOU.
I'M GONNA DO IT.
YOU SHOULD DO IT.

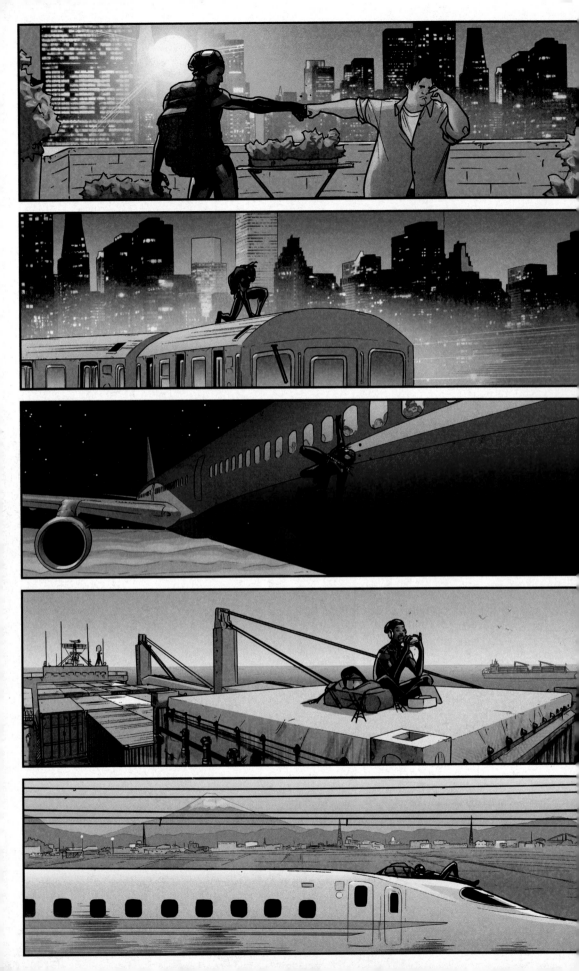

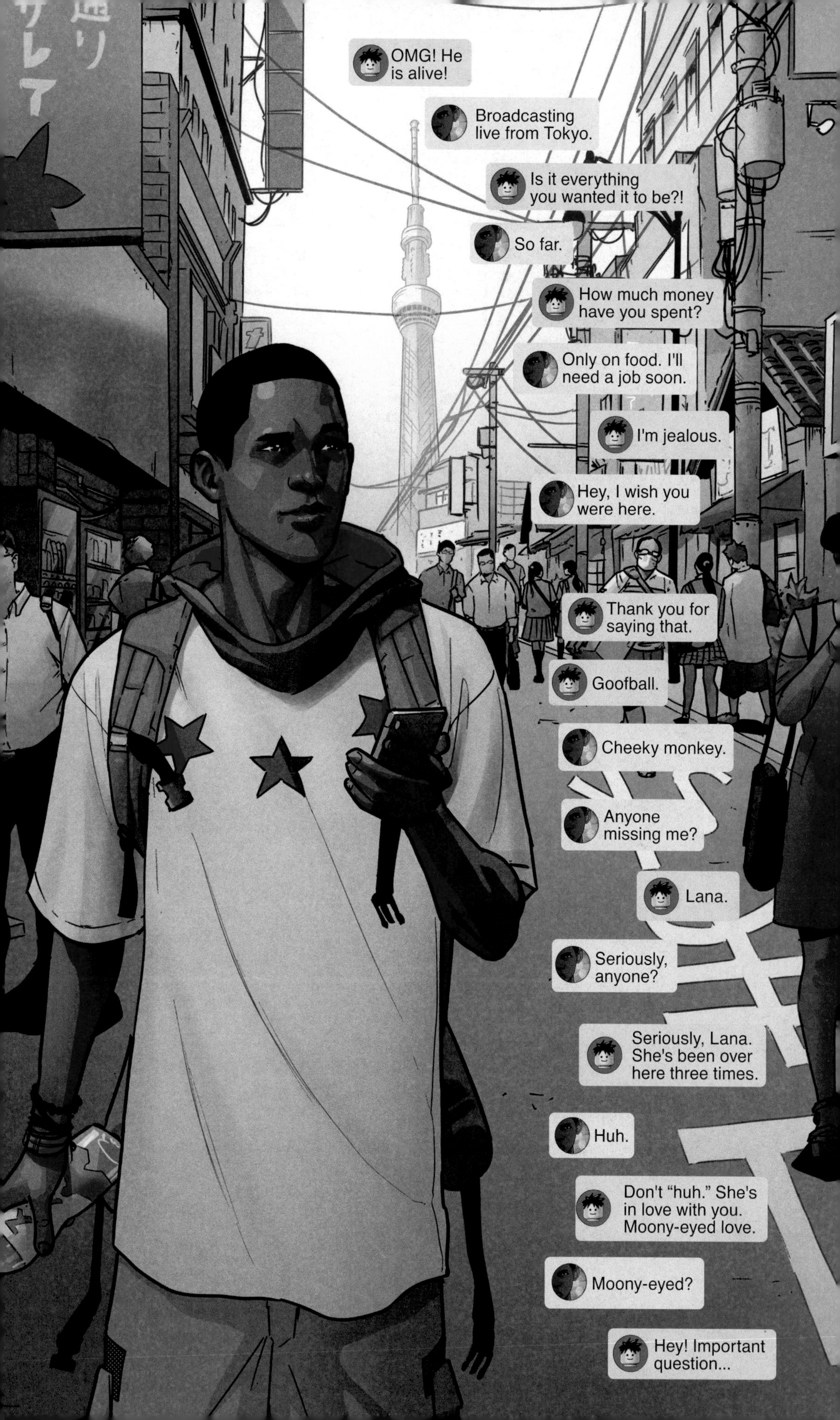
OMG! He is alive!
Broadcasting live from Tokyo.
Is it everything you wanted it to be?!
So far.
How much money have you spent?
Only on food. I'll need a job soon.
I'm jealous.
Hey, I wish you were here.
Thank you for saying that.
Goofball.
Cheeky monkey.
Anyone missing me?
Lana.
Seriously, anyone?
Seriously, Lana. She's been over here three times.
Huh.
Don't "huh." She's in love with you. Moony-eyed love.
Moony-eyed?
Hey! Important question...

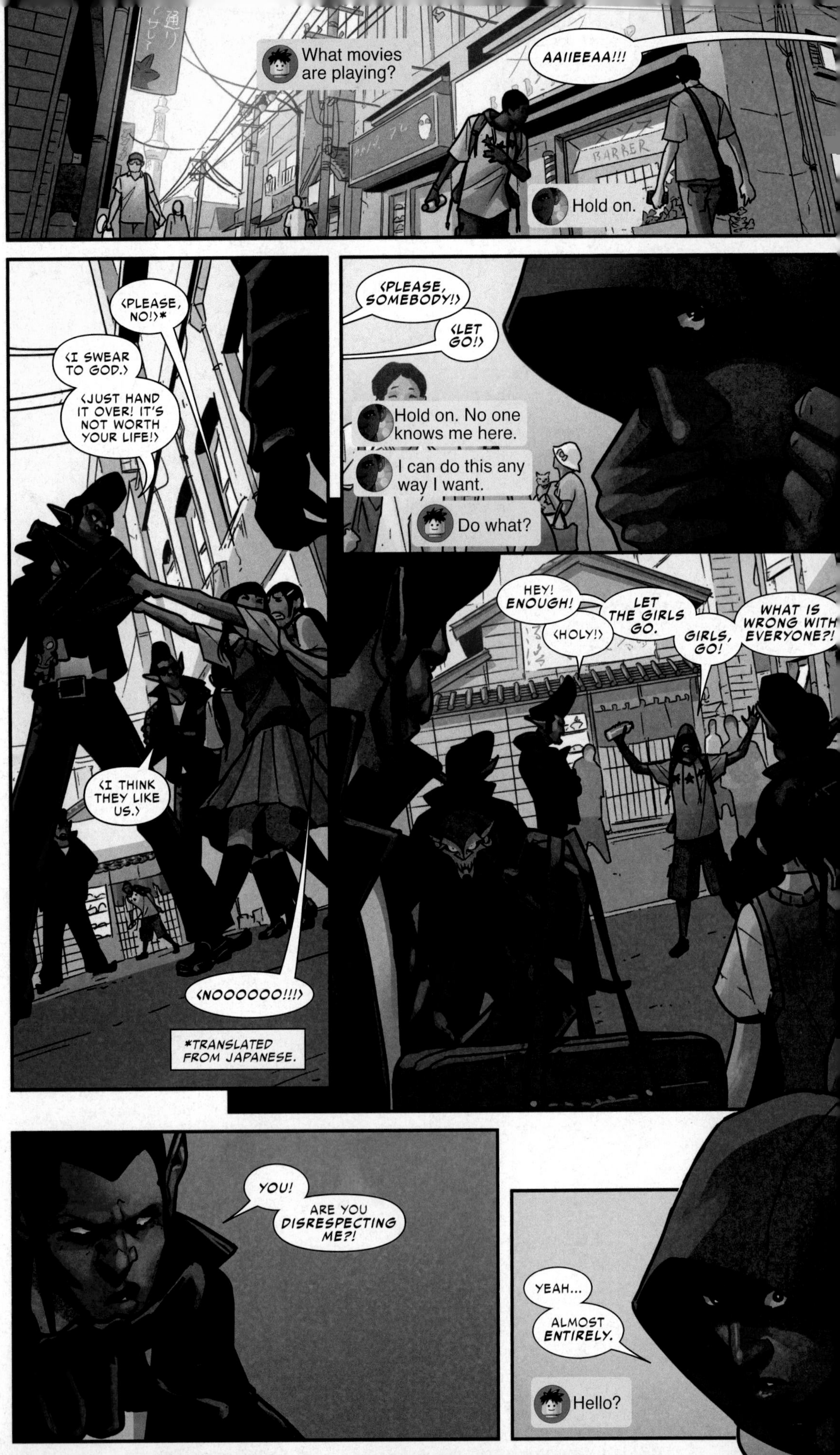
What movies are playing?
AAIIEEAA!!!
Hold on.
<PLEASE, NO!>*
<I SWEAR TO GOD.>
<JUST HAND IT OVER! IT'S NOT WORTH YOUR LIFE!>
<I THINK THEY LIKE US.>
<NOOOOOO!!!>
*TRANSLATED FROM JAPANESE.
<PLEASE, SOMEBODY!>
<LET GO!>
Hold on. No one knows me here.
I can do this any way I want.
Do what?
HEY! ENOUGH!
<HOLY!>
LET THE GIRLS GO.
GIRLS, GO!
WHAT IS WRONG WITH EVERYONE?!
YOU!
ARE YOU DISRESPECTING ME?!
YEAH...
ALMOST ENTIRELY.
Hello?

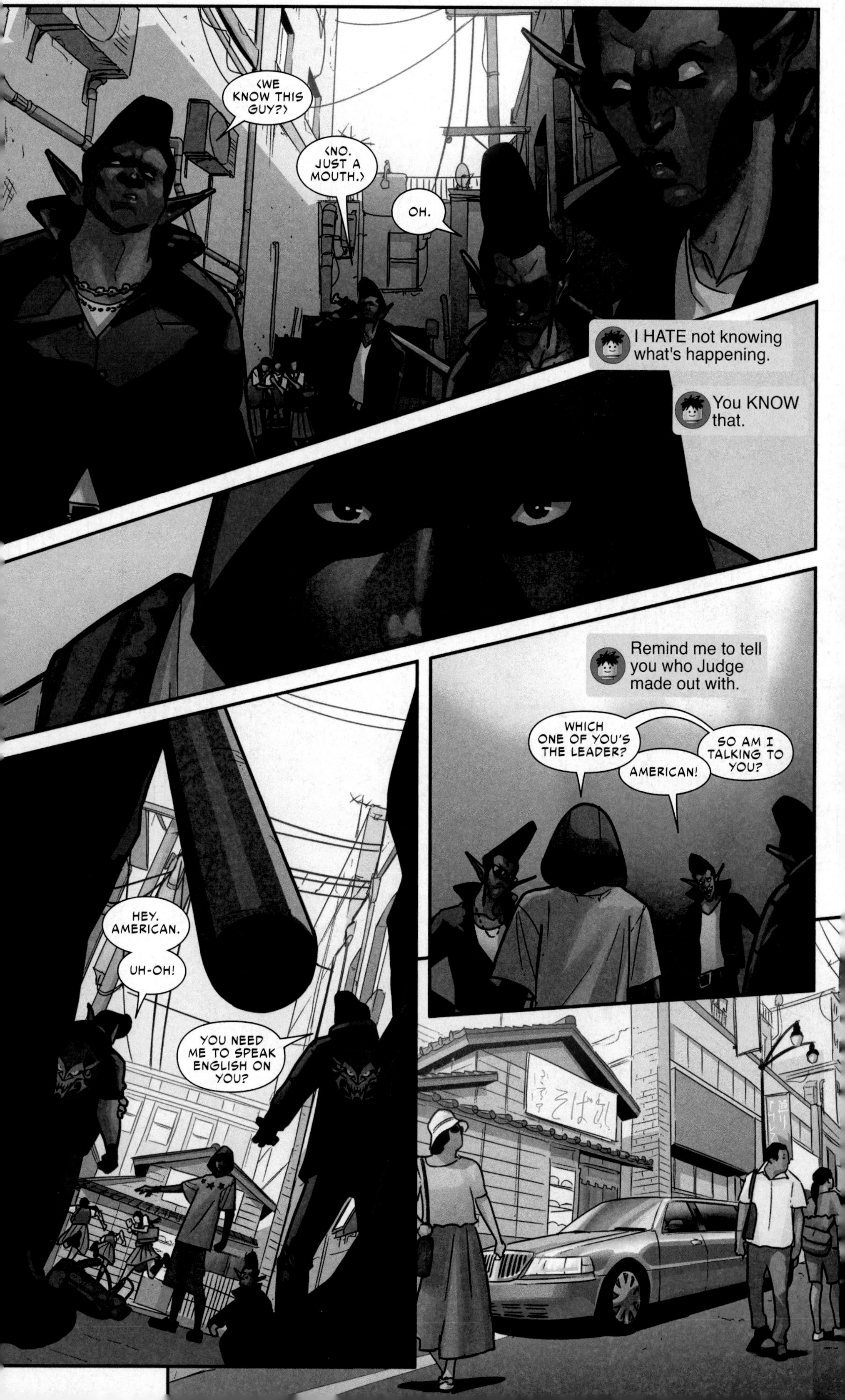

‹WE KNOW THIS GUY?›
‹NO. JUST A MOUTH.›
OH.
I HATE not knowing what's happening.
You KNOW that.
Remind me to tell you who Judge made out with.
WHICH ONE OF YOU'S THE LEADER?
SO AM I TALKING TO YOU?
AMERICAN!
HEY. AMERICAN.
UH-OH!
YOU NEED ME TO SPEAK ENGLISH ON YOU?

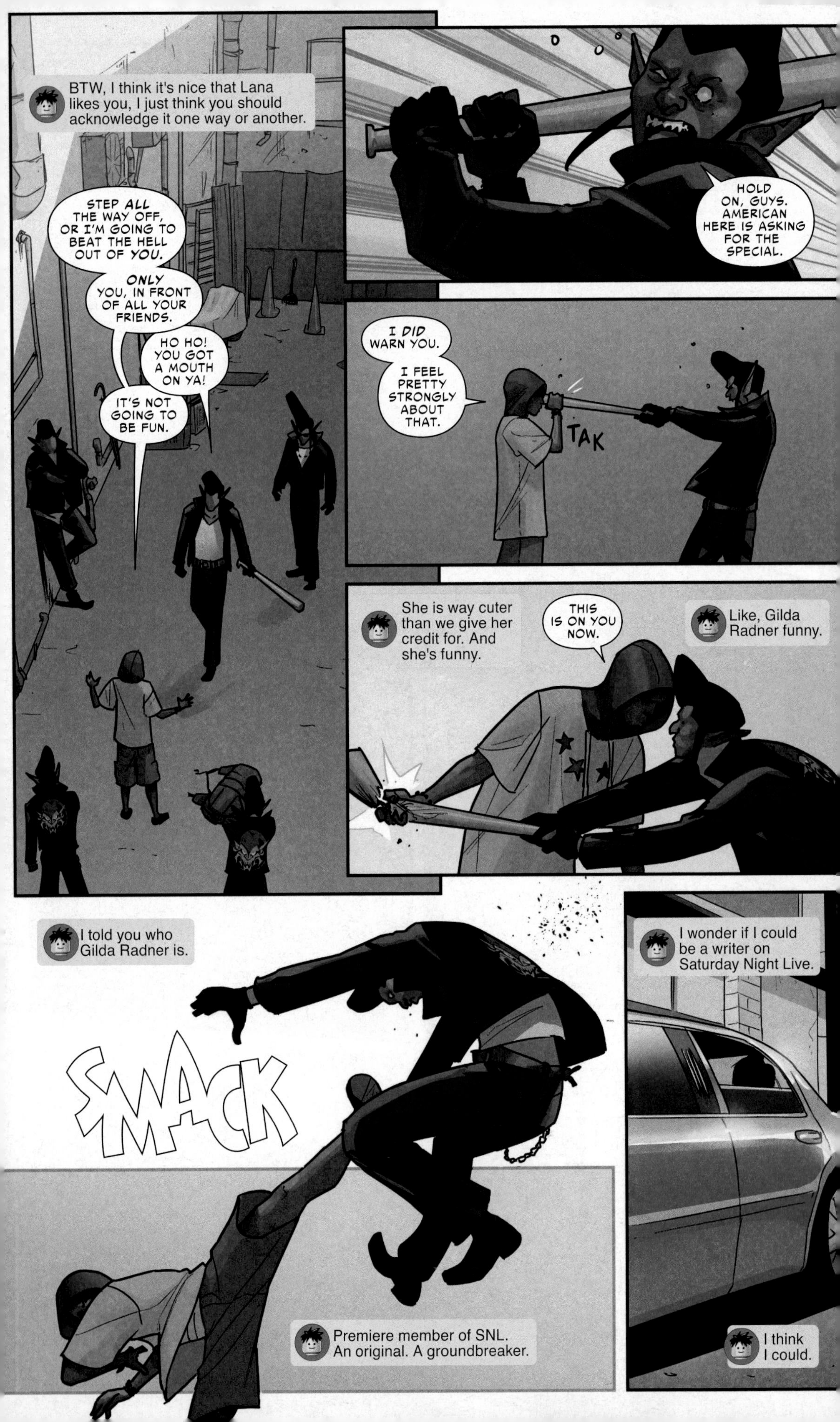
BTW, I think it's nice that Lana likes you, I just think you should acknowledge it one way or another.
STEP ALL THE WAY OFF, OR I'M GOING TO BEAT THE HELL OUT OF YOU.
ONLY YOU, IN FRONT OF ALL YOUR FRIENDS.
HO HO! YOU GOT A MOUTH ON YA!
IT'S NOT GOING TO BE FUN.
HOLD ON, GUYS. AMERICAN HERE IS ASKING FOR THE SPECIAL.
I DID WARN YOU.
I FEEL PRETTY STRONGLY ABOUT THAT.
TAK
She is way cuter than we give her credit for. And she's funny.
THIS IS ON YOU NOW.
Like, Gilda Radner funny.
I told you who Gilda Radner is.
SMACK
Premiere member of SNL. An original. A groundbreaker.
I wonder if I could be a writer on Saturday Night Live.
I think I could.

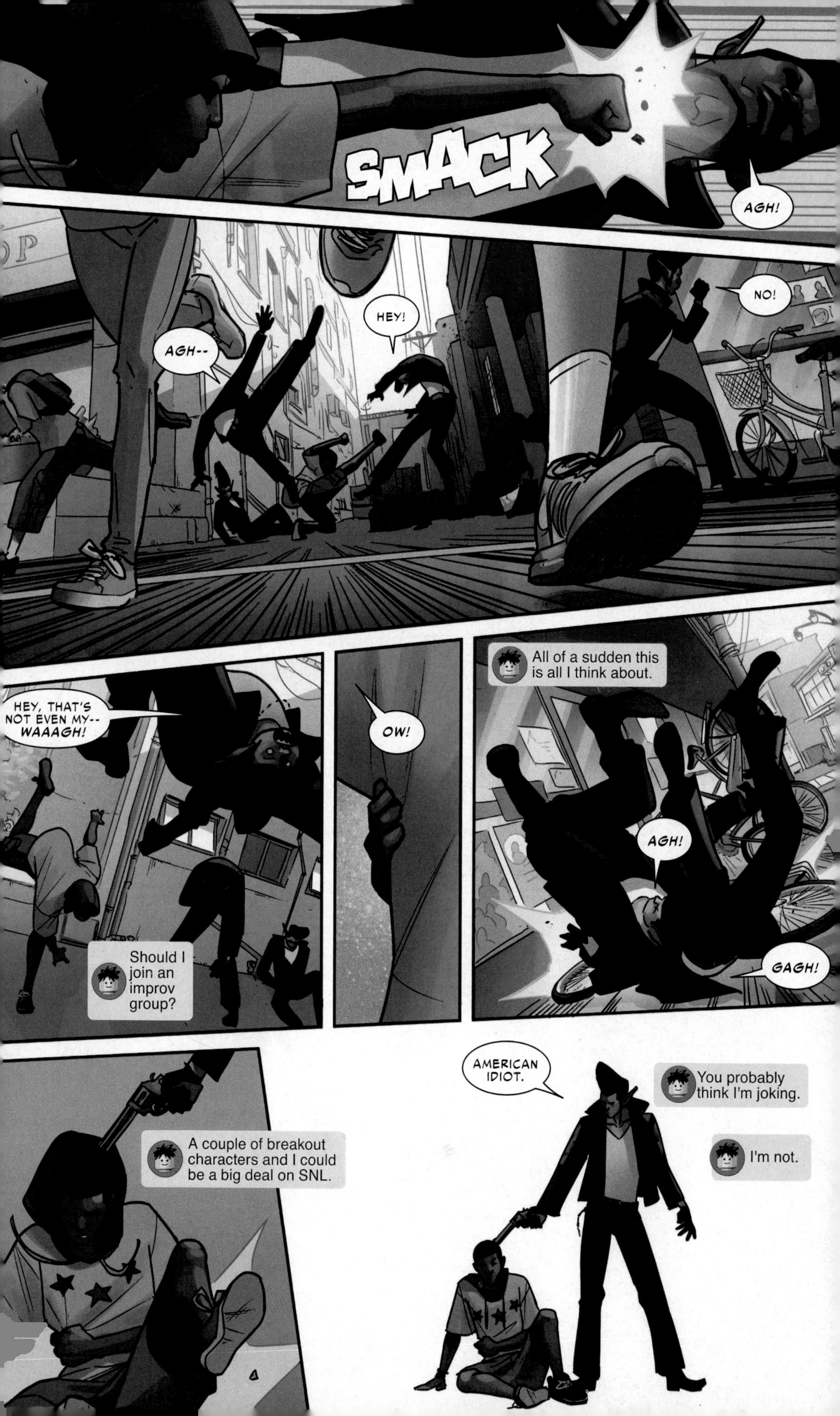
SMACK
AGH!
AGH--
HEY!
NO!
HEY, THAT'S NOT EVEN MY-- WAAAGH!
Should I join an improv group?
OW!
All of a sudden this is all I think about.
AGH!
GAGH!
A couple of breakout characters and I could be a big deal on SNL.
AMERICAN IDIOT.
You probably think I'm joking.
I'm not.

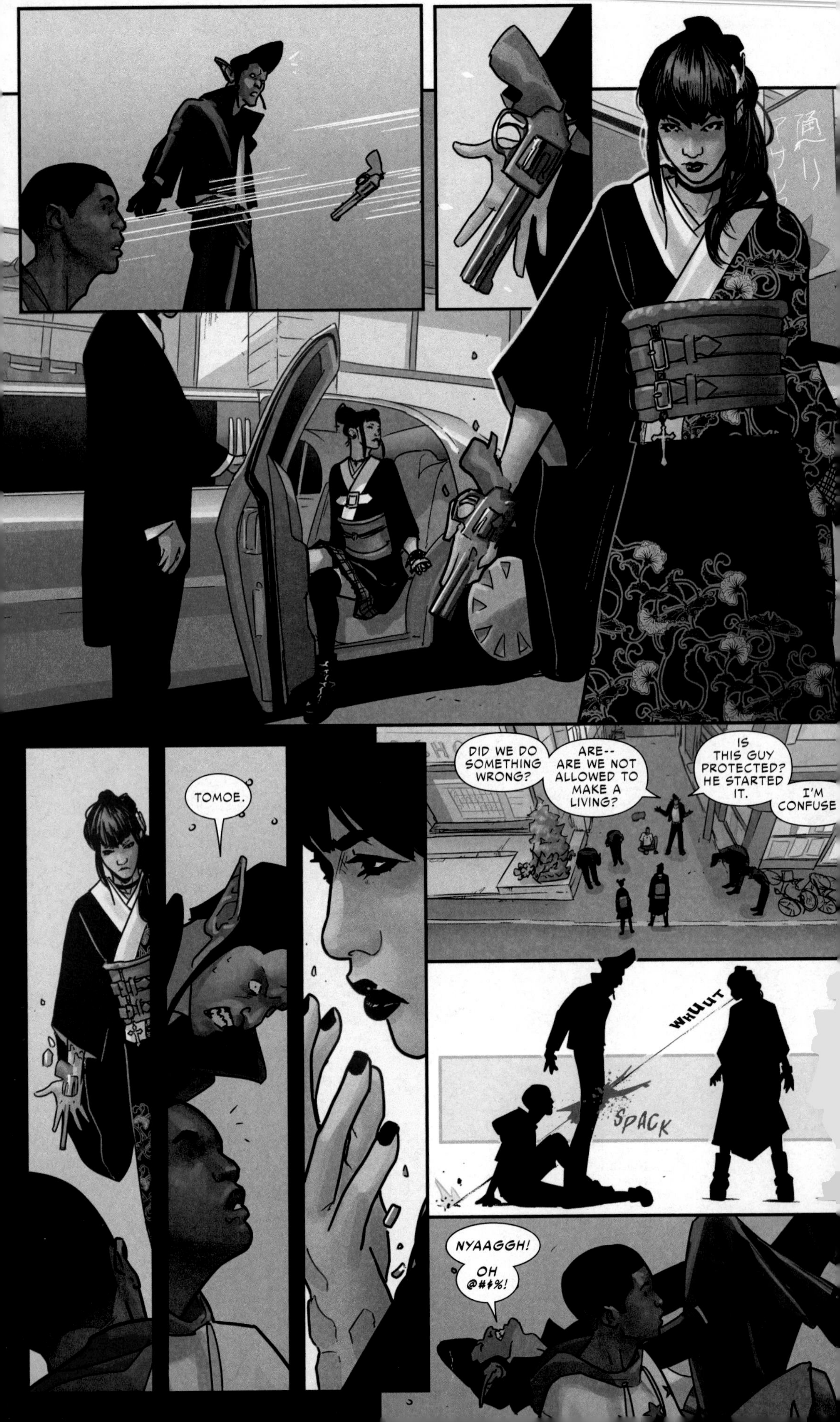
TOMOE.
DID WE DO SOMETHING WRONG?
ARE-- ARE WE NOT ALLOWED TO MAKE A LIVING?
IS THIS GUY PROTECTED? HE STARTED IT.
I'M CONFUSE
WHUUT
SPACK
NYAAGGH!
OH @#$%!

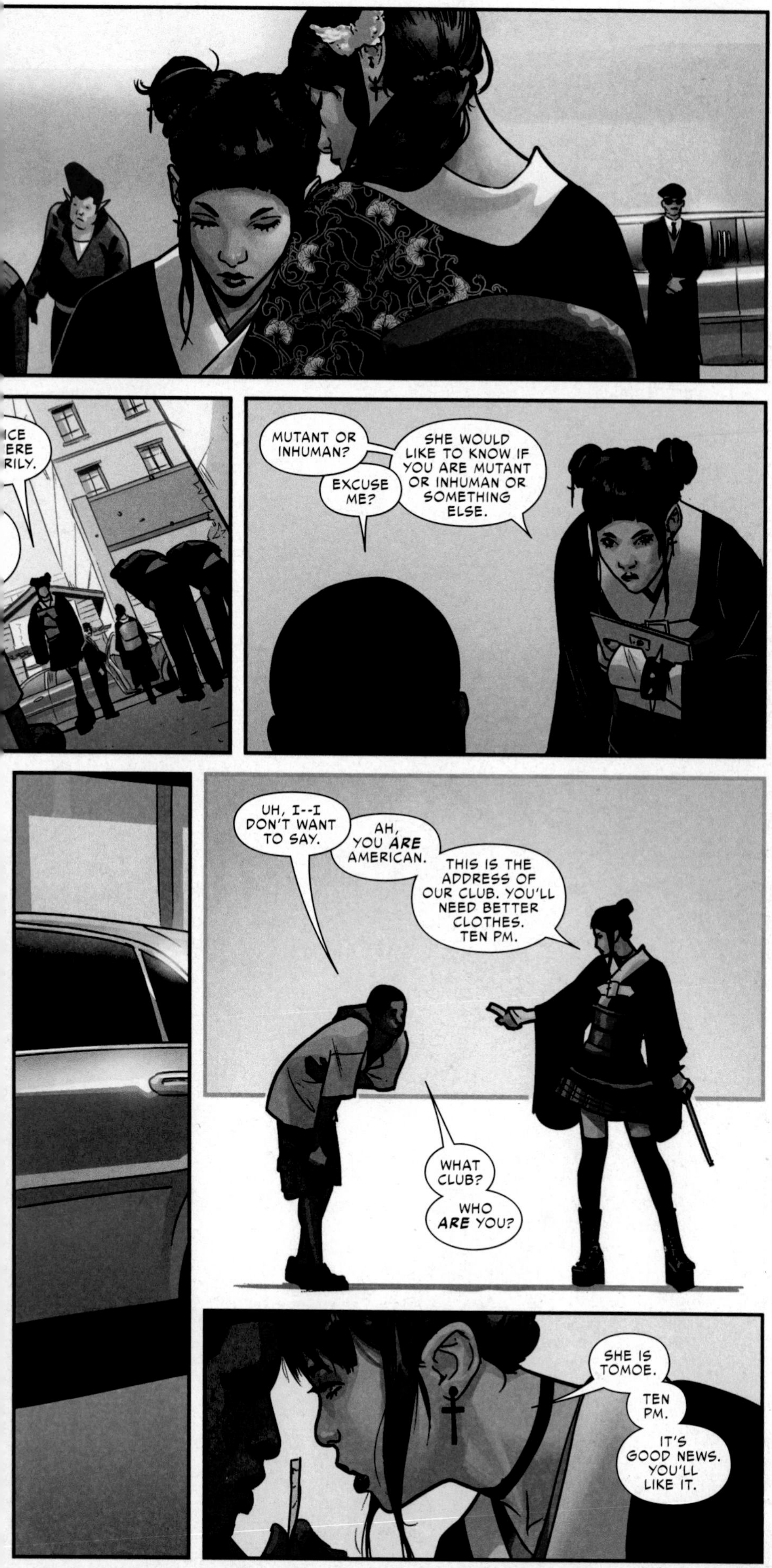
MUTANT OR INHUMAN?
SHE WOULD LIKE TO KNOW IF YOU ARE MUTANT OR INHUMAN OR SOMETHING ELSE.
EXCUSE ME?
UH, I--I DON'T WANT TO SAY.
AH, YOU *ARE* AMERICAN.
THIS IS THE ADDRESS OF OUR CLUB. YOU'LL NEED BETTER CLOTHES. TEN PM.
WHAT CLUB?
WHO *ARE* YOU?
SHE IS TOMOE.
TEN PM.
IT'S GOOD NEWS. YOU'LL LIKE IT.

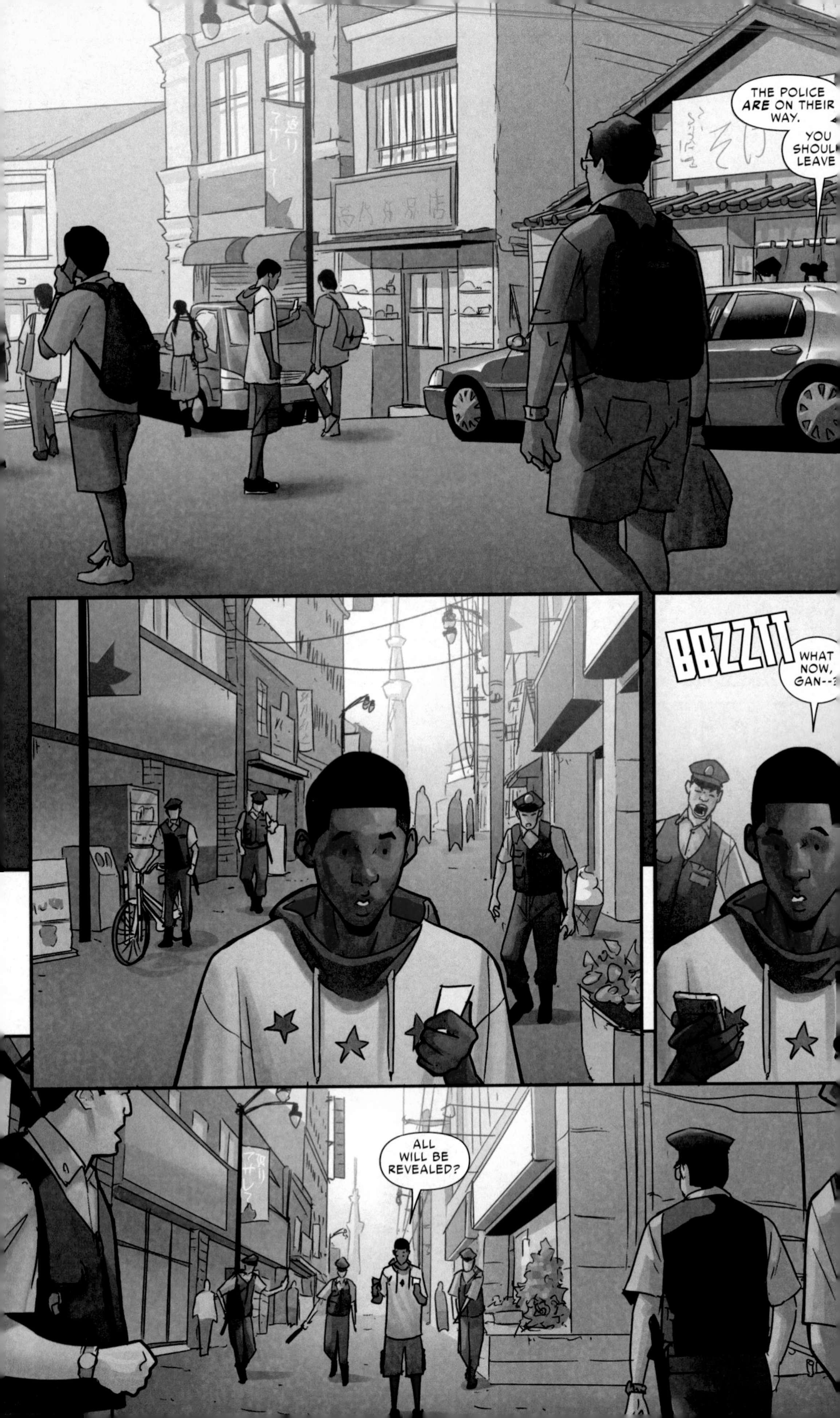
THE POLICE ARE ON THEIR WAY.
YOU SHOUL LEAVE
BBZZTT
WHAT NOW, GAN--?
ALL WILL BE REVEALED?

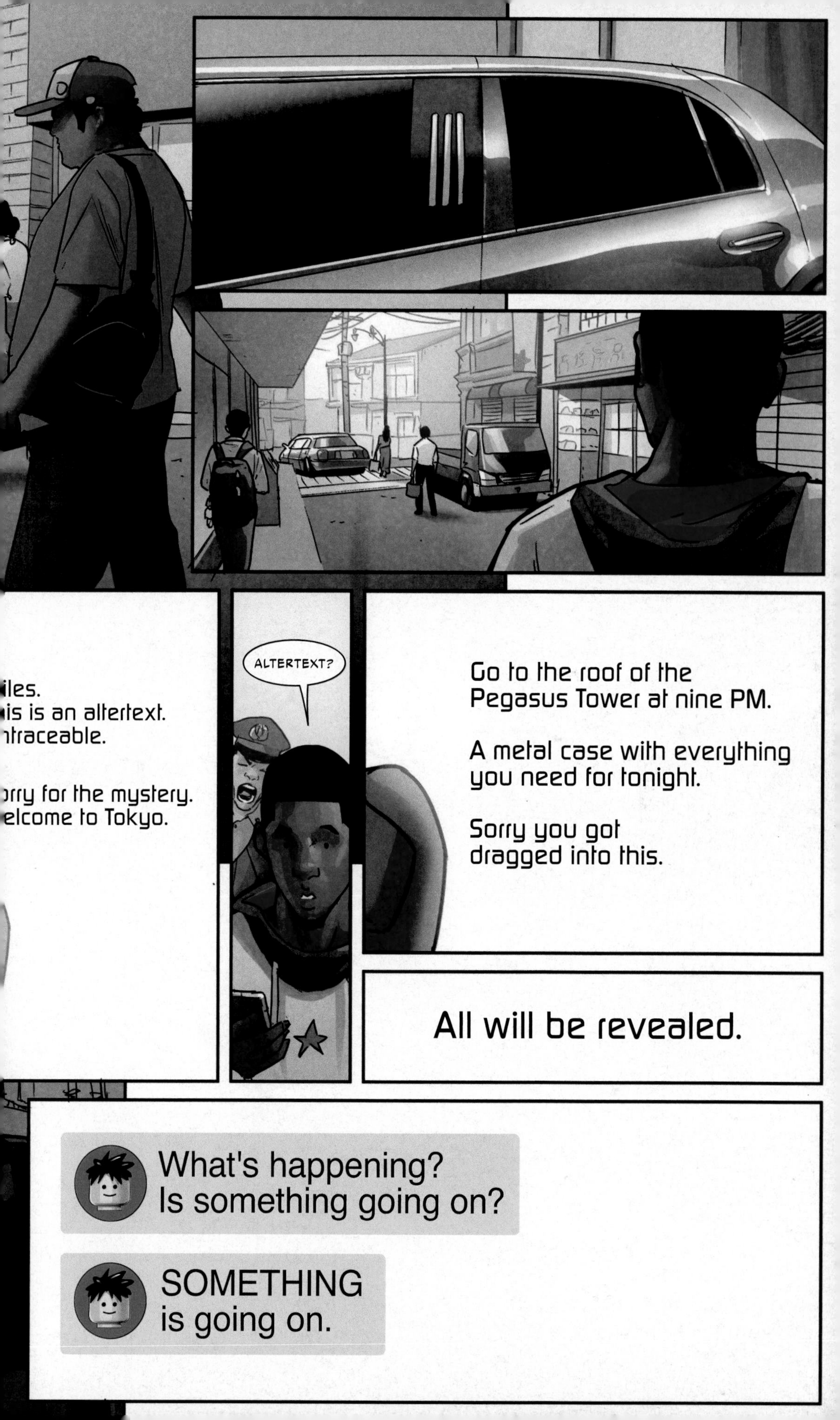
ALTERTEXT?
iles.
is is an altertext.
ntraceable.
orry for the mystery.
elcome to Tokyo.
Go to the roof of the Pegasus Tower at nine PM.
A metal case with everything you need for tonight.
Sorry you got dragged into this.
All will be revealed.
What's happening? Is something going on?
SOMETHING is going on.

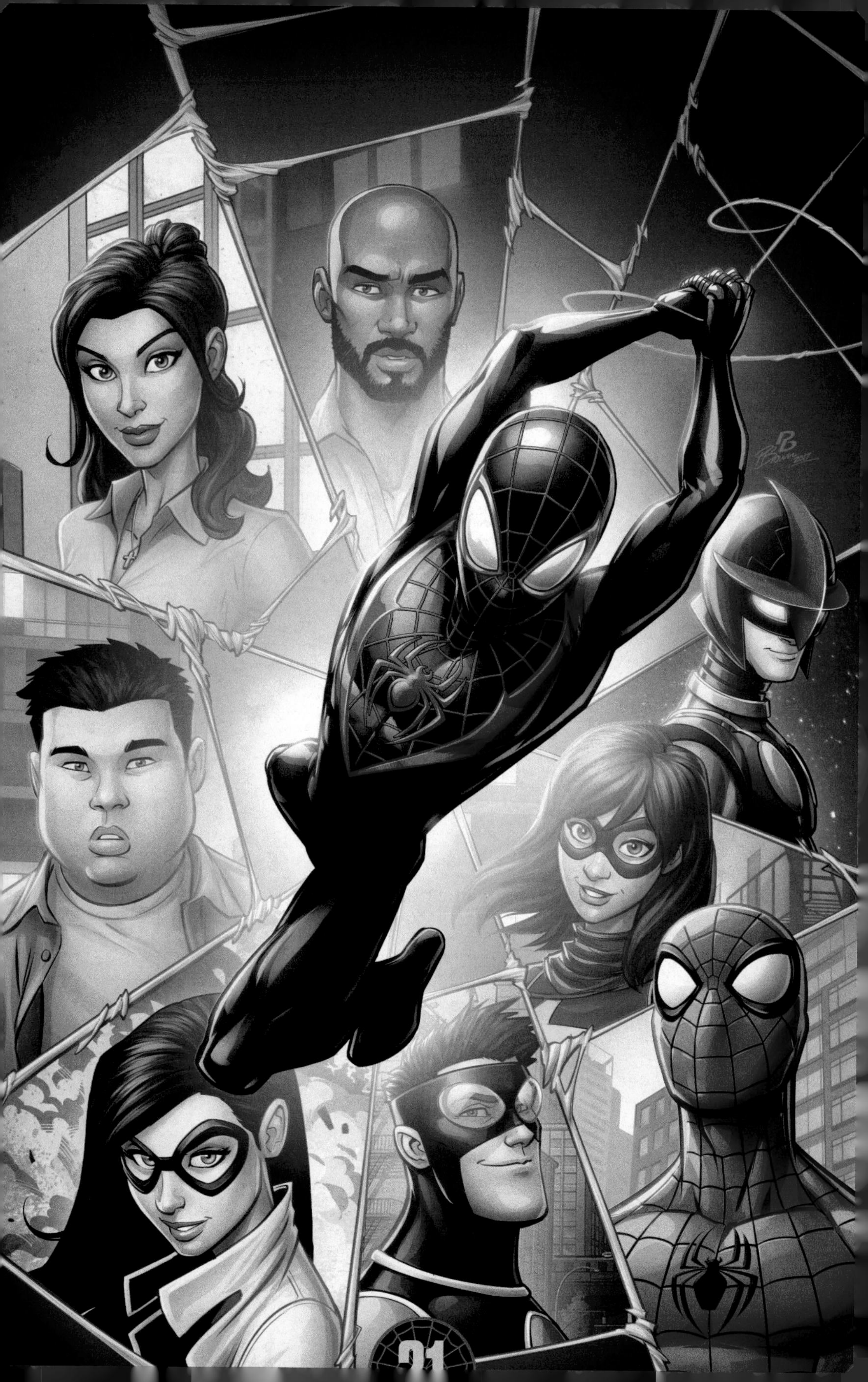

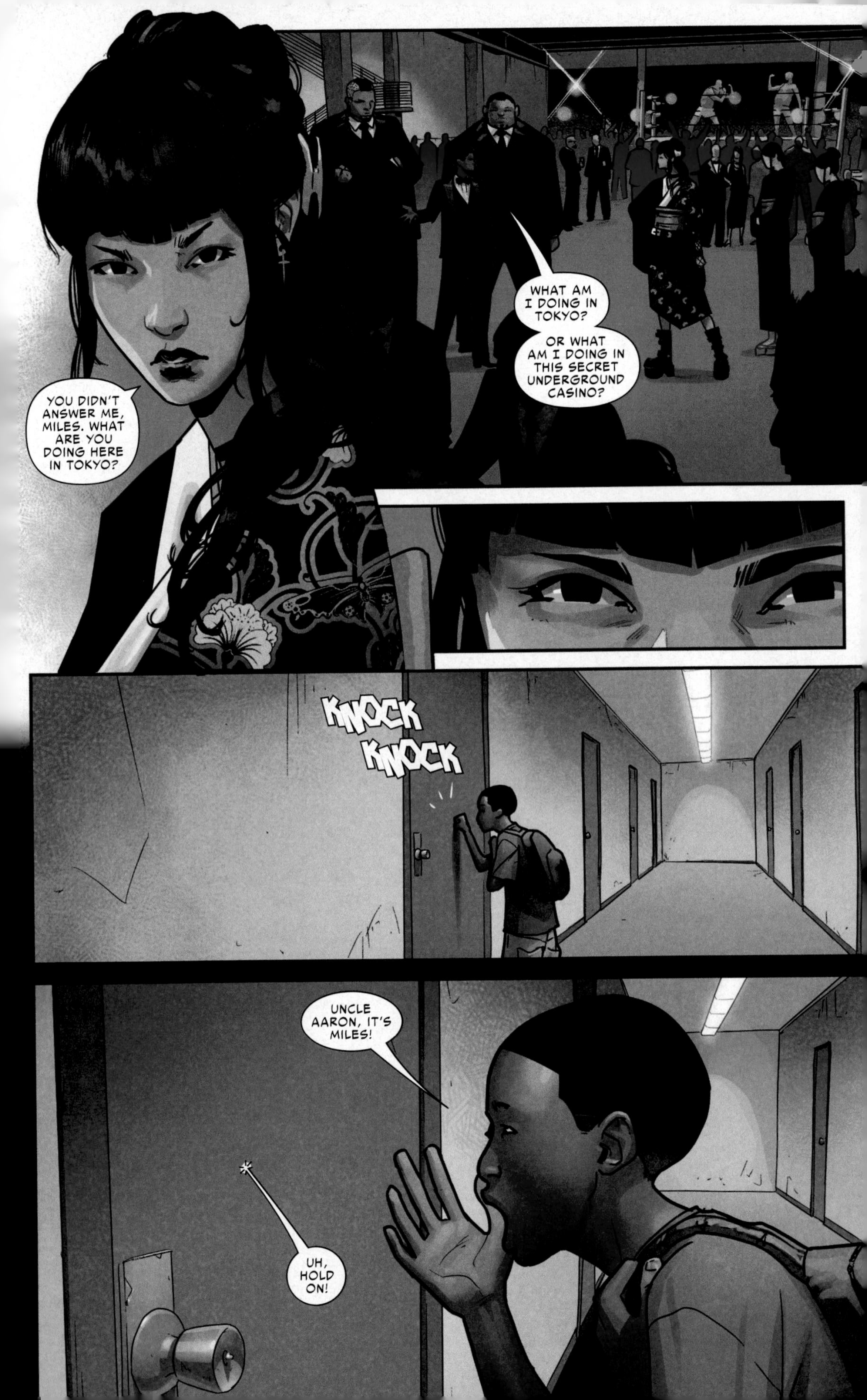
YOU DIDN'T ANSWER ME, MILES. WHAT ARE YOU DOING HERE IN TOKYO?
WHAT AM I DOING IN TOKYO?
OR WHAT AM I DOING IN THIS SECRET UNDERGROUND CASINO?
KNOCK KNOCK
UNCLE AARON, IT'S MILES!
UH, HOLD ON!

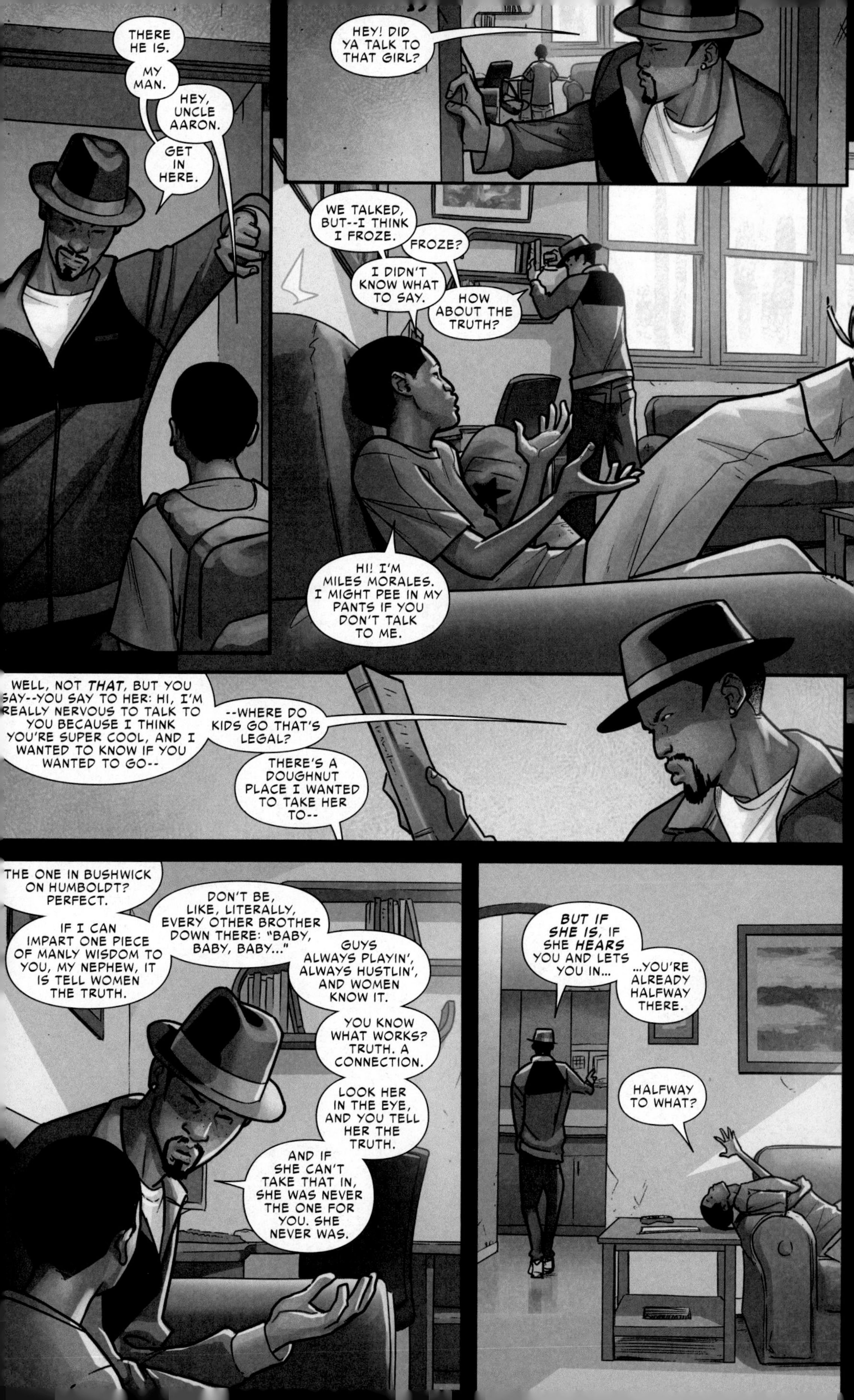

THERE HE IS.
MY MAN.
HEY, UNCLE AARON.
GET IN HERE.
HEY! DID YA TALK TO THAT GIRL?
WE TALKED, BUT--I THINK I FROZE.
FROZE?
I DIDN'T KNOW WHAT TO SAY.
HOW ABOUT THE TRUTH?
HI! I'M MILES MORALES. I MIGHT PEE IN MY PANTS IF YOU DON'T TALK TO ME.
WELL, NOT *THAT*, BUT YOU SAY--YOU SAY TO HER: HI, I'M REALLY NERVOUS TO TALK TO YOU BECAUSE I THINK YOU'RE SUPER COOL, AND I WANTED TO KNOW IF YOU WANTED TO GO--
--WHERE DO KIDS GO THAT'S LEGAL?
THERE'S A DOUGHNUT PLACE I WANTED TO TAKE HER TO--
THE ONE IN BUSHWICK ON HUMBOLDT? PERFECT.
IF I CAN IMPART ONE PIECE OF MANLY WISDOM TO YOU, MY NEPHEW, IT IS TELL WOMEN THE TRUTH.
DON'T BE, LIKE, LITERALLY, EVERY OTHER BROTHER DOWN THERE: "BABY, BABY, BABY..."
GUYS ALWAYS PLAYIN', ALWAYS HUSTLIN', AND WOMEN KNOW IT.
YOU KNOW WHAT WORKS? TRUTH. A CONNECTION.
LOOK HER IN THE EYE, AND YOU TELL HER THE TRUTH.
AND IF SHE CAN'T TAKE THAT IN, SHE WAS NEVER THE ONE FOR YOU. SHE NEVER WAS.
BUT IF SHE IS, IF SHE *HEARS* YOU AND LETS YOU IN...
...YOU'RE ALREADY HALFWAY THERE.
HALFWAY TO WHAT?

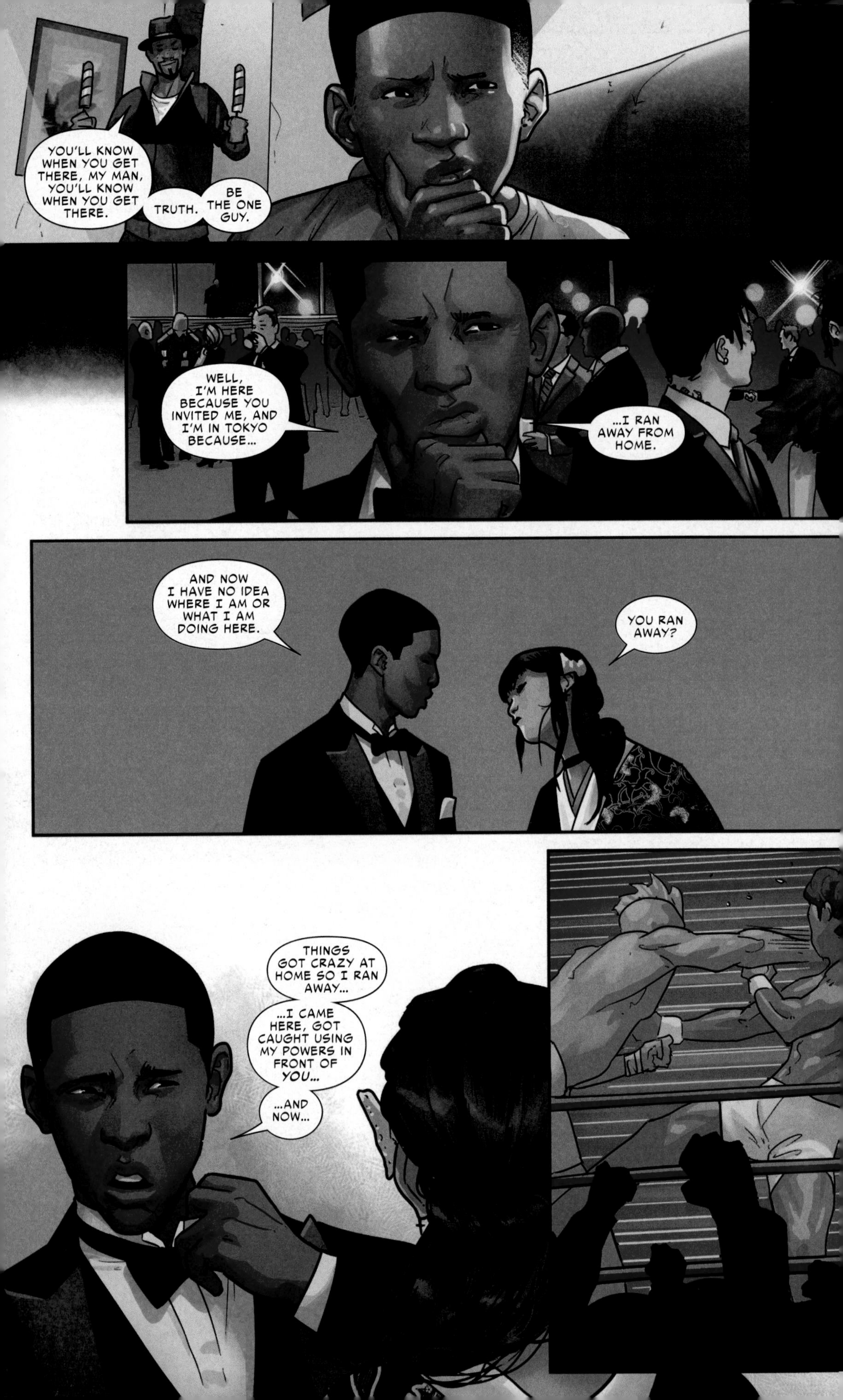
YOU'LL KNOW WHEN YOU GET THERE, MY MAN, YOU'LL KNOW WHEN YOU GET THERE.
TRUTH.
BE THE ONE GUY.
WELL, I'M HERE BECAUSE YOU INVITED ME, AND I'M IN TOKYO BECAUSE...
...I RAN AWAY FROM HOME.
AND NOW I HAVE NO IDEA WHERE I AM OR WHAT I AM DOING HERE.
YOU RAN AWAY?
THINGS GOT CRAZY AT HOME SO I RAN AWAY...
...I CAME HERE, GOT CAUGHT USING MY POWERS IN FRONT OF YOU...
...AND NOW...

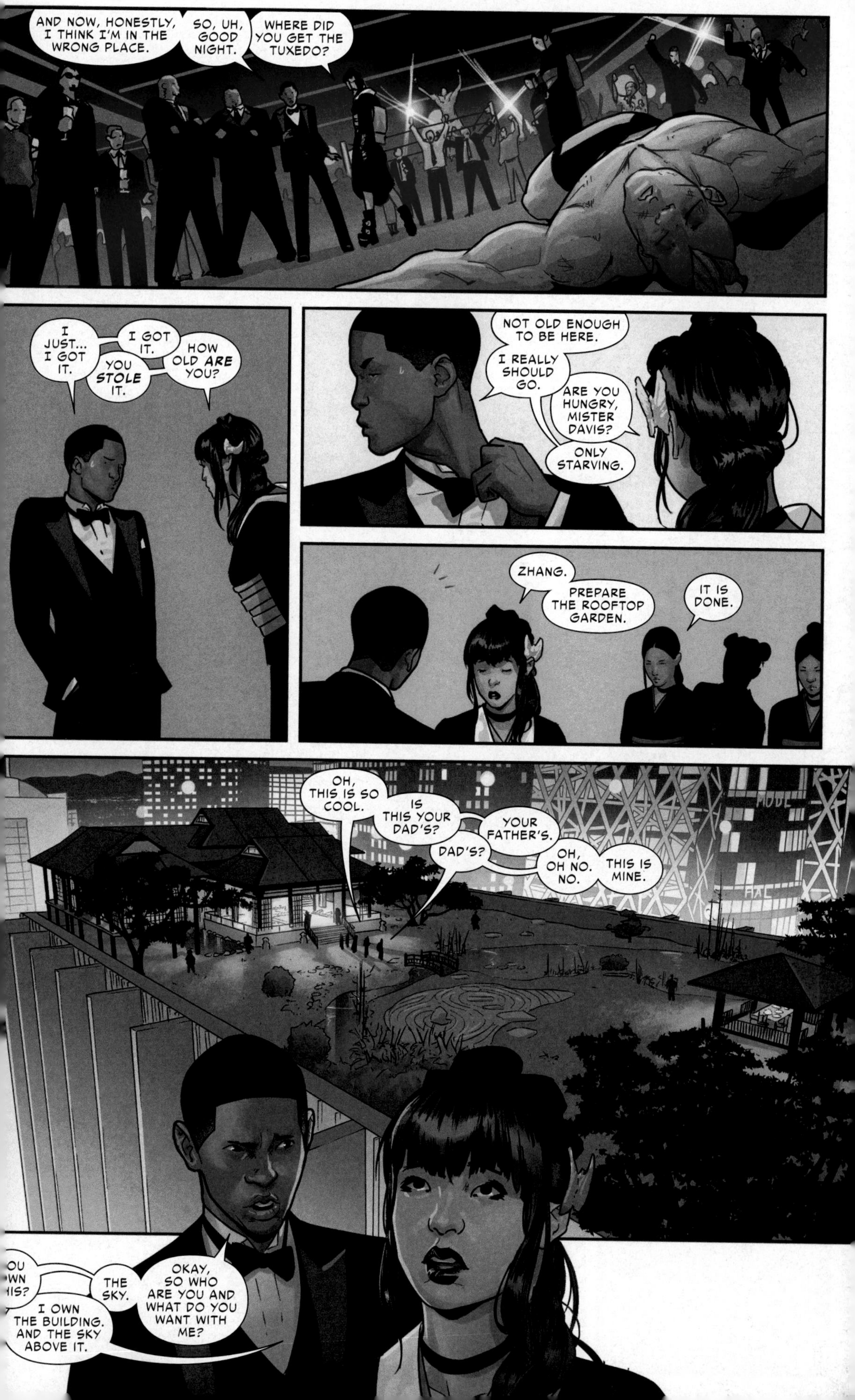
AND NOW, HONESTLY, I THINK I'M IN THE WRONG PLACE.
SO, UH, GOOD NIGHT.
WHERE DID YOU GET THE TUXEDO?
I JUST... I GOT IT.
I GOT IT.
YOU STOLE IT.
HOW OLD ARE YOU?
NOT OLD ENOUGH TO BE HERE.
I REALLY SHOULD GO.
ARE YOU HUNGRY, MISTER DAVIS?
ONLY STARVING.
ZHANG.
PREPARE THE ROOFTOP GARDEN.
IT IS DONE.
OH, THIS IS SO COOL.
IS THIS YOUR DAD'S?
YOUR FATHER'S.
DAD'S?
OH, OH NO. NO.
THIS IS MINE.
THE SKY.
I OWN THE BUILDING. AND THE SKY ABOVE IT.
OKAY, SO WHO ARE YOU AND WHAT DO YOU WANT WITH ME?

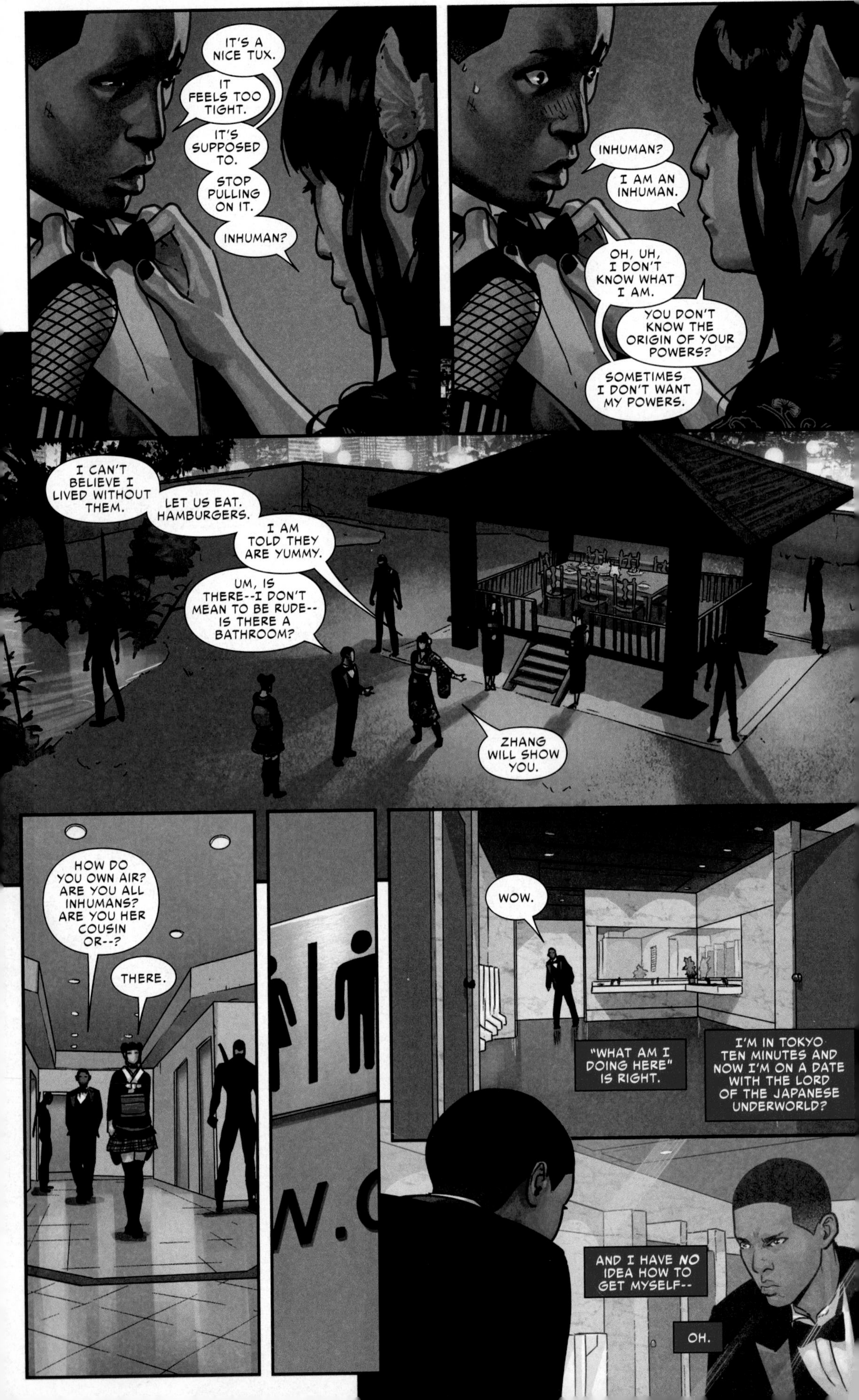
IT'S A NICE TUX.
IT FEELS TOO TIGHT.
IT'S SUPPOSED TO.
STOP PULLING ON IT.
INHUMAN?
INHUMAN?
I AM AN INHUMAN.
OH, UH, I DON'T KNOW WHAT I AM.
YOU DON'T KNOW THE ORIGIN OF YOUR POWERS?
SOMETIMES I DON'T WANT MY POWERS.
I CAN'T BELIEVE I LIVED WITHOUT THEM.
LET US EAT. HAMBURGERS.
I AM TOLD THEY ARE YUMMY.
UM, IS THERE--I DON'T MEAN TO BE RUDE--IS THERE A BATHROOM?
ZHANG WILL SHOW YOU.
HOW DO YOU OWN AIR? ARE YOU ALL INHUMANS? ARE YOU HER COUSIN OR--?
THERE.
W.C
WOW.
"WHAT AM I DOING HERE" IS RIGHT.
I'M IN TOKYO TEN MINUTES AND NOW I'M ON A DATE WITH THE LORD OF THE JAPANESE UNDERWORLD?
AND I HAVE NO IDEA HOW TO GET MYSELF--
OH.

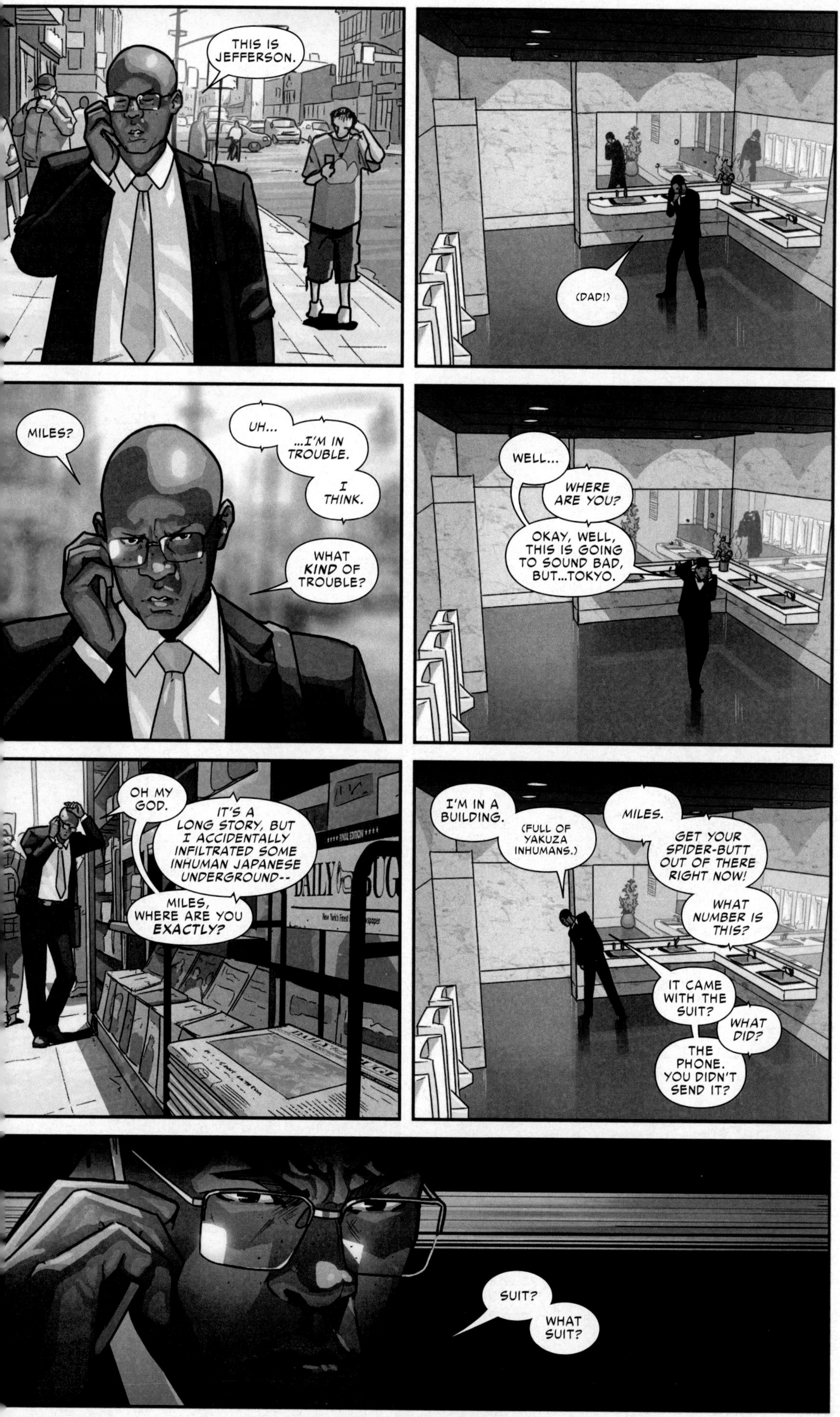
THIS IS JEFFERSON.
(DAD!)
MILES?
UH...
...I'M IN TROUBLE.
I THINK.
WHAT *KIND* OF TROUBLE?
WELL...
WHERE ARE YOU?
OKAY, WELL, THIS IS GOING TO SOUND BAD, BUT...TOKYO.
OH MY GOD.
IT'S A LONG STORY, BUT I ACCIDENTALLY INFILTRATED SOME INHUMAN JAPANESE UNDERGROUND--
MILES, WHERE ARE YOU *EXACTLY?*
I'M IN A BUILDING.
(FULL OF YAKUZA INHUMANS.)
MILES.
GET YOUR SPIDER-BUTT OUT OF THERE RIGHT NOW!
WHAT NUMBER IS THIS?
IT CAME WITH THE SUIT?
WHAT DID?
THE PHONE. YOU DIDN'T SEND IT?
SUIT?
WHAT SUIT?

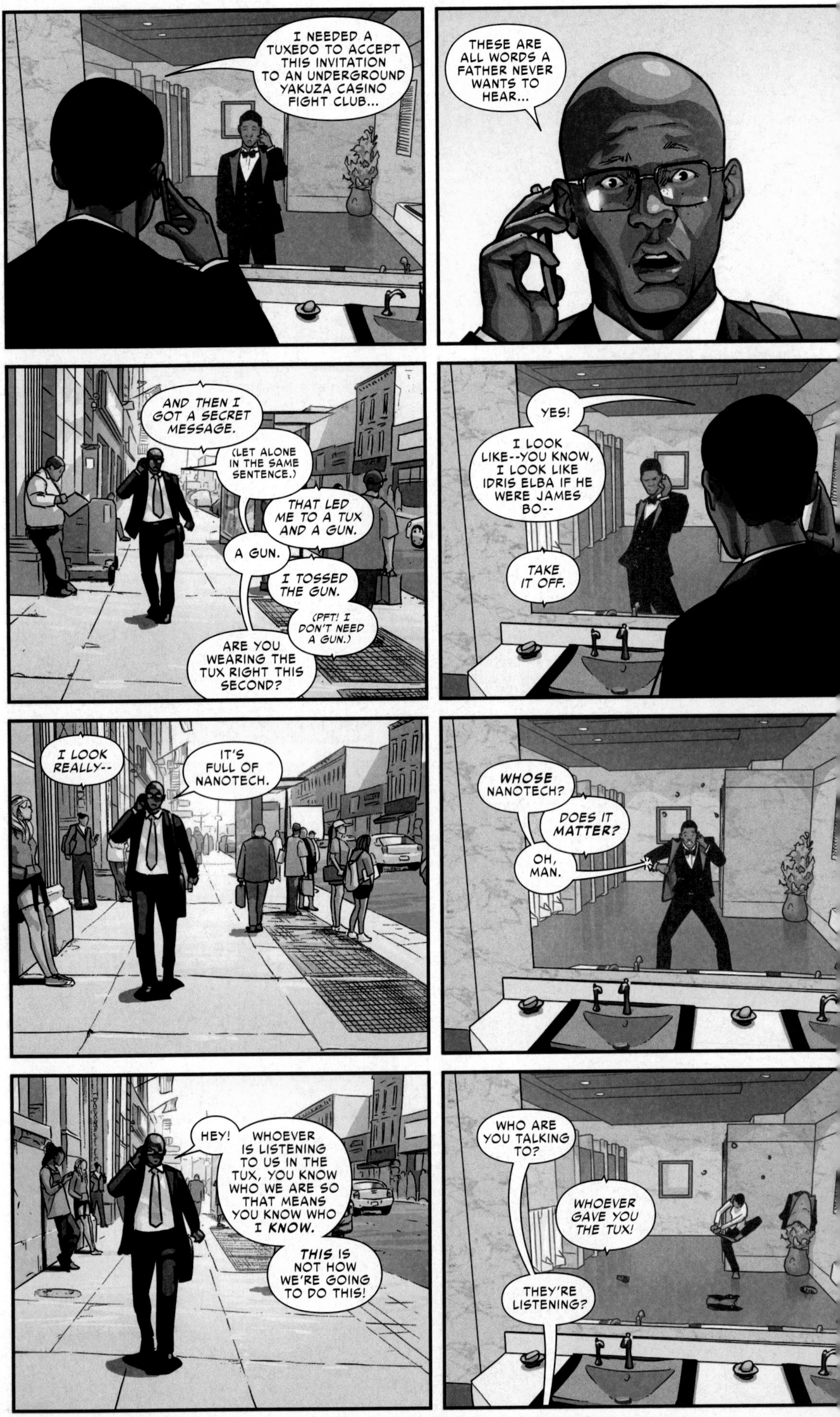

I NEEDED A TUXEDO TO ACCEPT THIS INVITATION TO AN UNDERGROUND YAKUZA CASINO FIGHT CLUB...
THESE ARE ALL WORDS A FATHER NEVER WANTS TO HEAR...
AND THEN I GOT A SECRET MESSAGE.
(LET ALONE IN THE SAME SENTENCE.)
THAT LED ME TO A TUX AND A GUN.
A GUN.
I TOSSED THE GUN.
(PFT! I DON'T NEED A GUN.)
ARE YOU WEARING THE TUX RIGHT THIS SECOND?
YES!
I LOOK LIKE--YOU KNOW, I LOOK LIKE IDRIS ELBA IF HE WERE JAMES BO--
TAKE IT OFF.
I LOOK REALLY--
IT'S FULL OF NANOTECH.
WHOSE NANOTECH?
DOES IT *MATTER?*
OH, MAN.
HEY!
WHOEVER IS LISTENING TO US IN THE TUX, YOU KNOW WHO WE ARE SO THAT MEANS YOU KNOW WHO I *KNOW*.
THIS IS NOT HOW WE'RE GOING TO DO THIS!
WHO ARE YOU TALKING TO?
WHOEVER GAVE YOU THE TUX!
THEY'RE LISTENING?

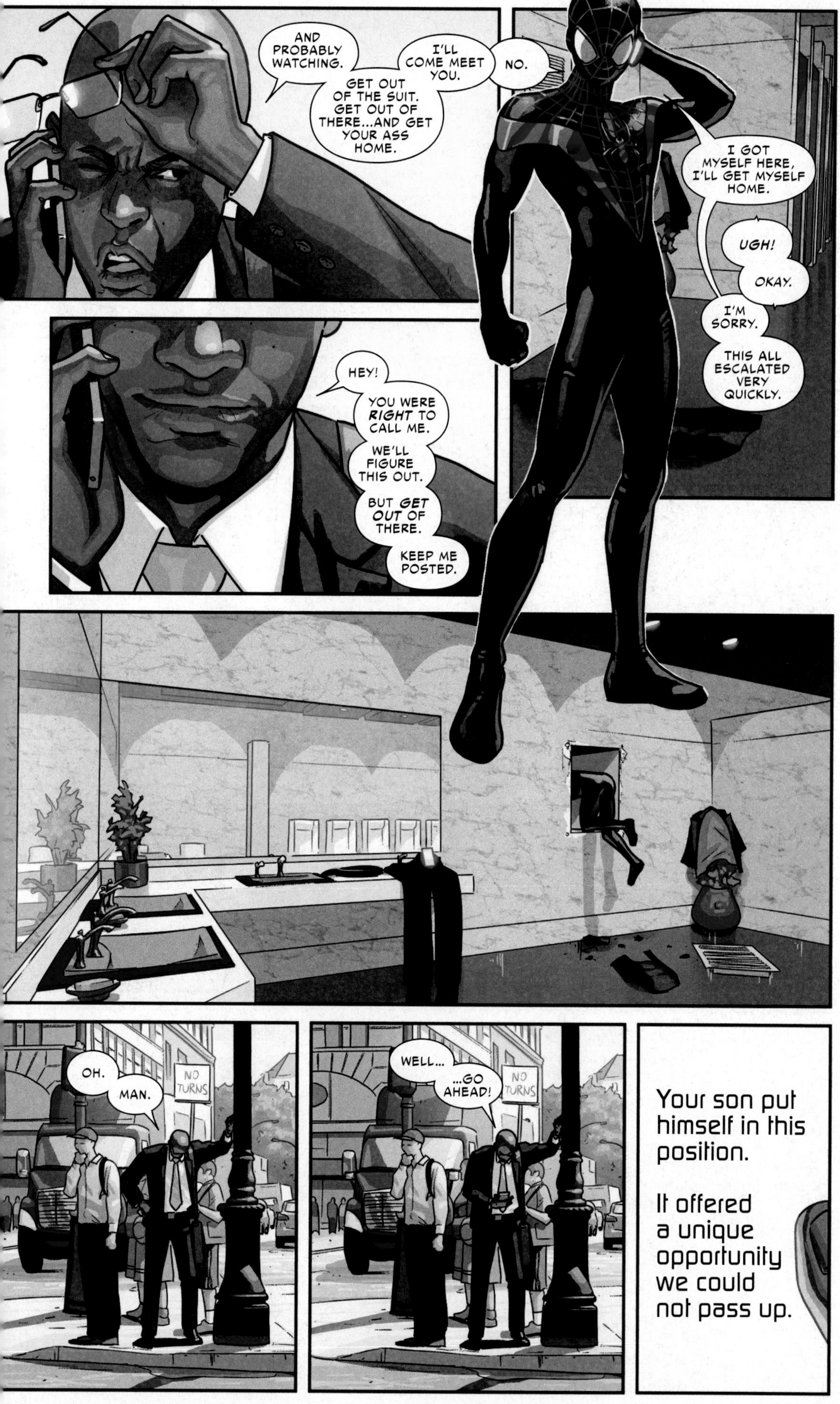
AND PROBABLY WATCHING.
I'LL COME MEET YOU.
NO.
GET OUT OF THE SUIT. GET OUT OF THERE...AND GET YOUR ASS HOME.
I GOT MYSELF HERE, I'LL GET MYSELF HOME.
UGH!
OKAY.
I'M SORRY.
THIS ALL ESCALATED VERY QUICKLY.
HEY!
YOU WERE RIGHT TO CALL ME.
WE'LL FIGURE THIS OUT.
BUT GET OUT OF THERE.
KEEP ME POSTED.
OH.
MAN.
NO TURNS
WELL...
...GO AHEAD!
NO TURNS
Your son put himself in this position.
It offered a unique opportunity we could not pass up.

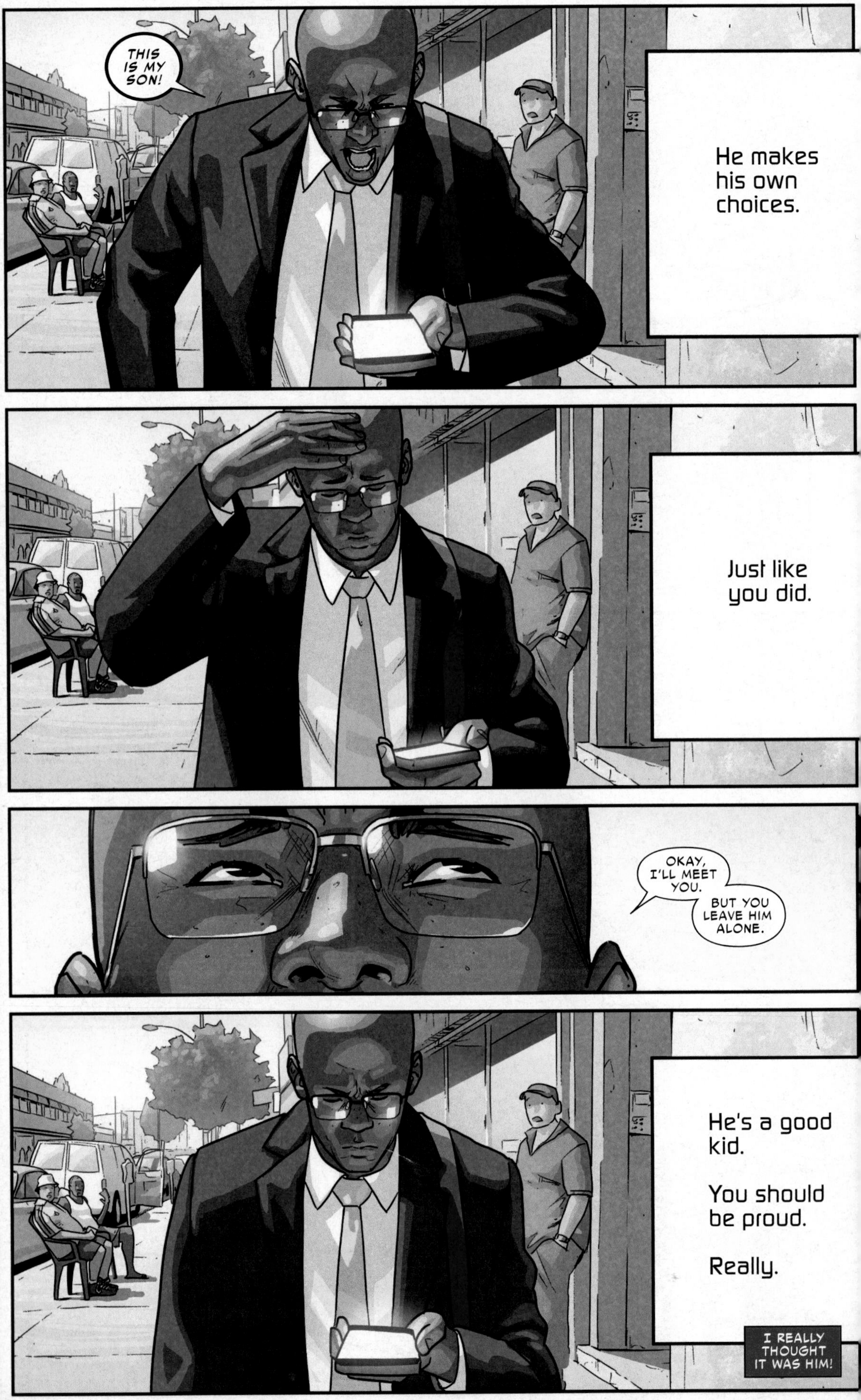
THIS IS MY SON!
He makes his own choices.
Just like you did.
OKAY, I'LL MEET YOU.
BUT YOU LEAVE HIM ALONE.
He's a good kid.
You should be proud.
Really.
I REALLY THOUGHT IT WAS HIM!

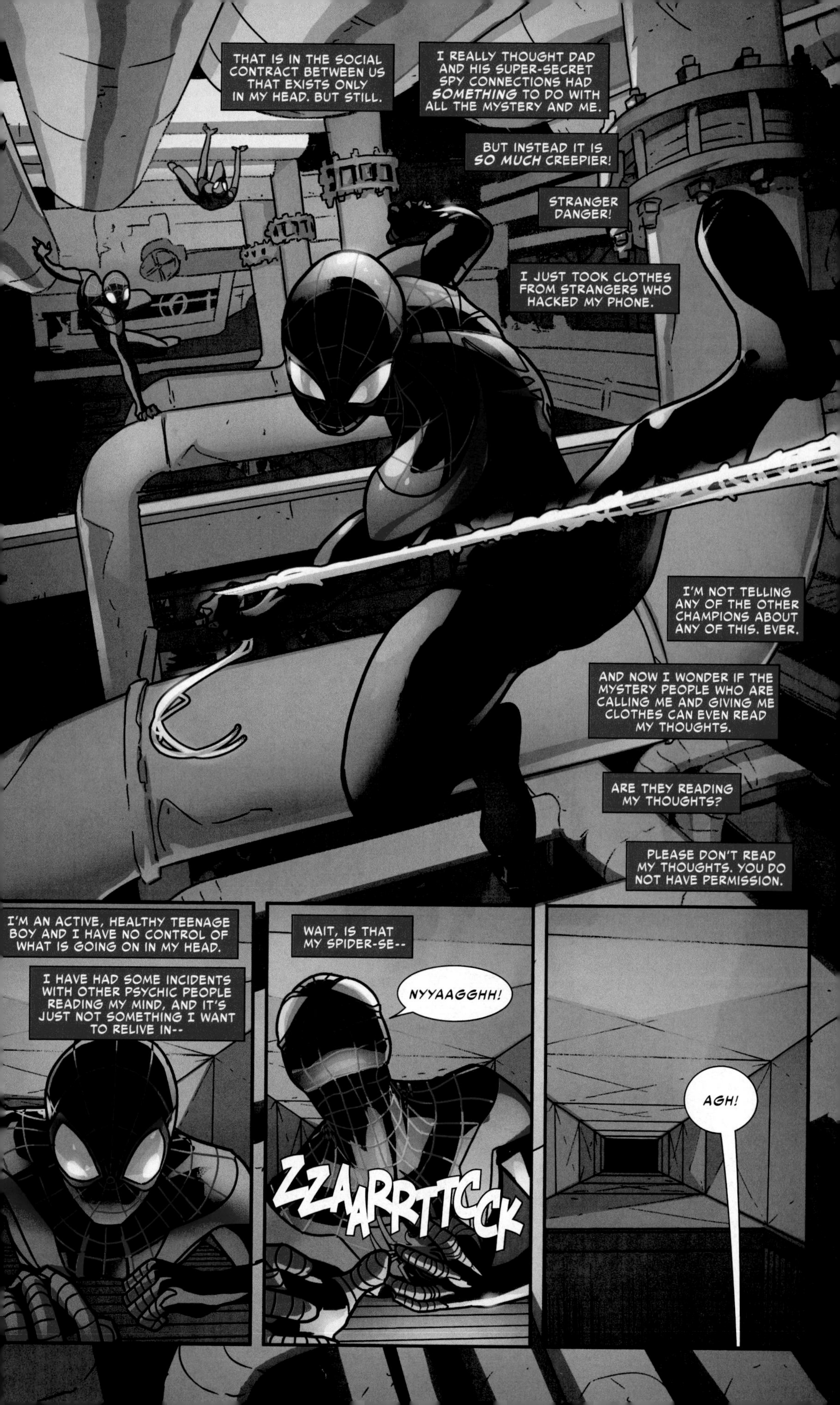
THAT IS IN THE SOCIAL CONTRACT BETWEEN US THAT EXISTS ONLY IN MY HEAD. BUT STILL.
I REALLY THOUGHT DAD AND HIS SUPER-SECRET SPY CONNECTIONS HAD *SOMETHING* TO DO WITH ALL THE MYSTERY AND ME.
BUT INSTEAD IT IS *SO MUCH* CREEPIER!
STRANGER DANGER!
I JUST TOOK CLOTHES FROM STRANGERS WHO HACKED MY PHONE.
I'M NOT TELLING ANY OF THE OTHER CHAMPIONS ABOUT ANY OF THIS. EVER.
AND NOW I WONDER IF THE MYSTERY PEOPLE WHO ARE CALLING ME AND GIVING ME CLOTHES CAN EVEN READ MY THOUGHTS.
ARE THEY READING MY THOUGHTS?
PLEASE DON'T READ MY THOUGHTS. YOU DO NOT HAVE PERMISSION.
I'M AN ACTIVE, HEALTHY TEENAGE BOY AND I HAVE NO CONTROL OF WHAT IS GOING ON IN MY HEAD.
I HAVE HAD SOME INCIDENTS WITH OTHER PSYCHIC PEOPLE READING MY MIND, AND IT'S JUST NOT SOMETHING I WANT TO RELIVE IN--
WAIT, IS THAT MY SPIDER-SE--
NYYAAGGHH!
ZZAARRTTCCK
AGH!

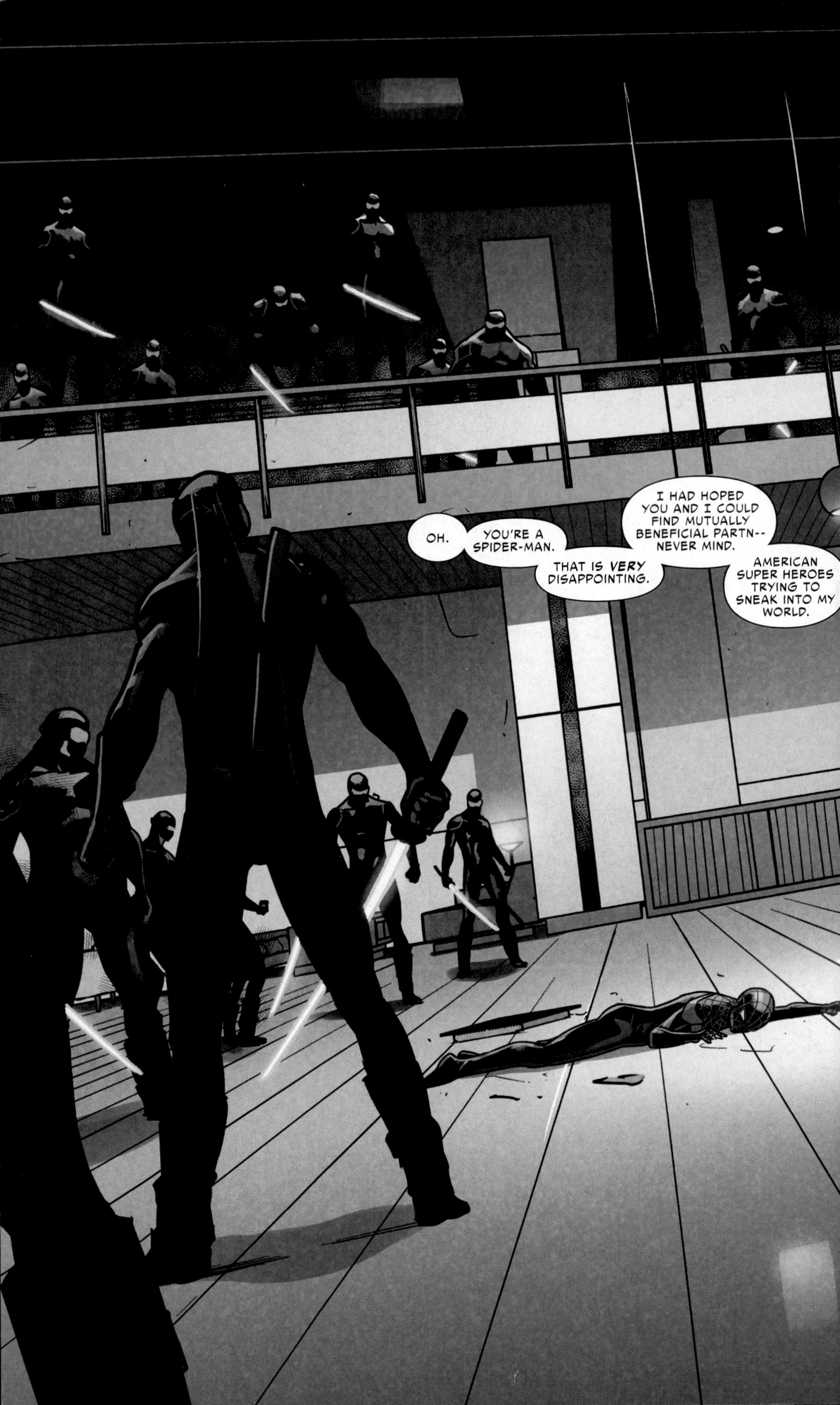
OH.
YOU'RE A SPIDER-MAN.
THAT IS VERY DISAPPOINTING.
I HAD HOPED YOU AND I COULD FIND MUTUALLY BENEFICIAL PARTN-- NEVER MIND.
AMERICAN SUPER HEROES TRYING TO SNEAK INTO MY WORLD.

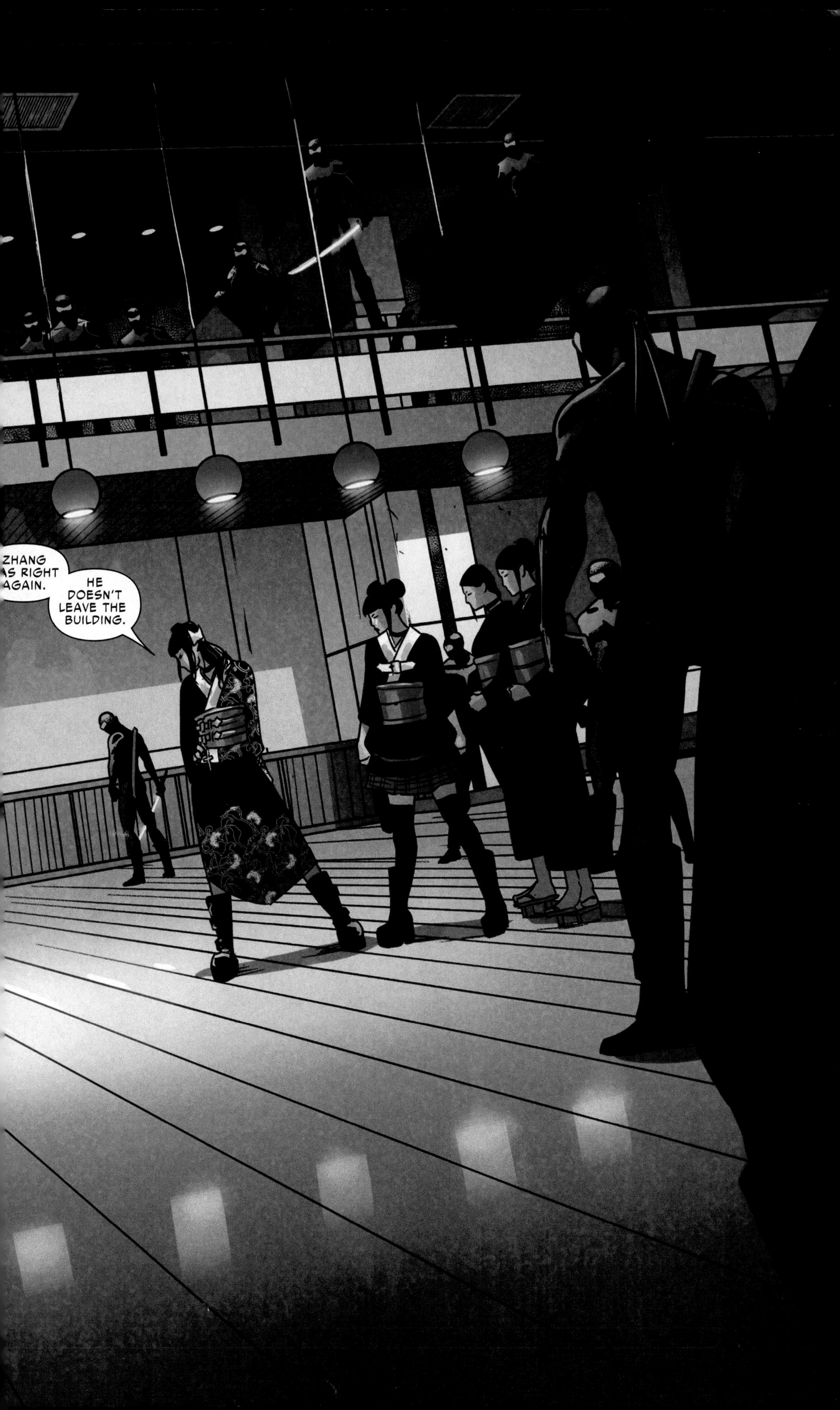
ZHANG
AS RIGHT
AGAIN.
HE DOESN'T LEAVE THE BUILDING.

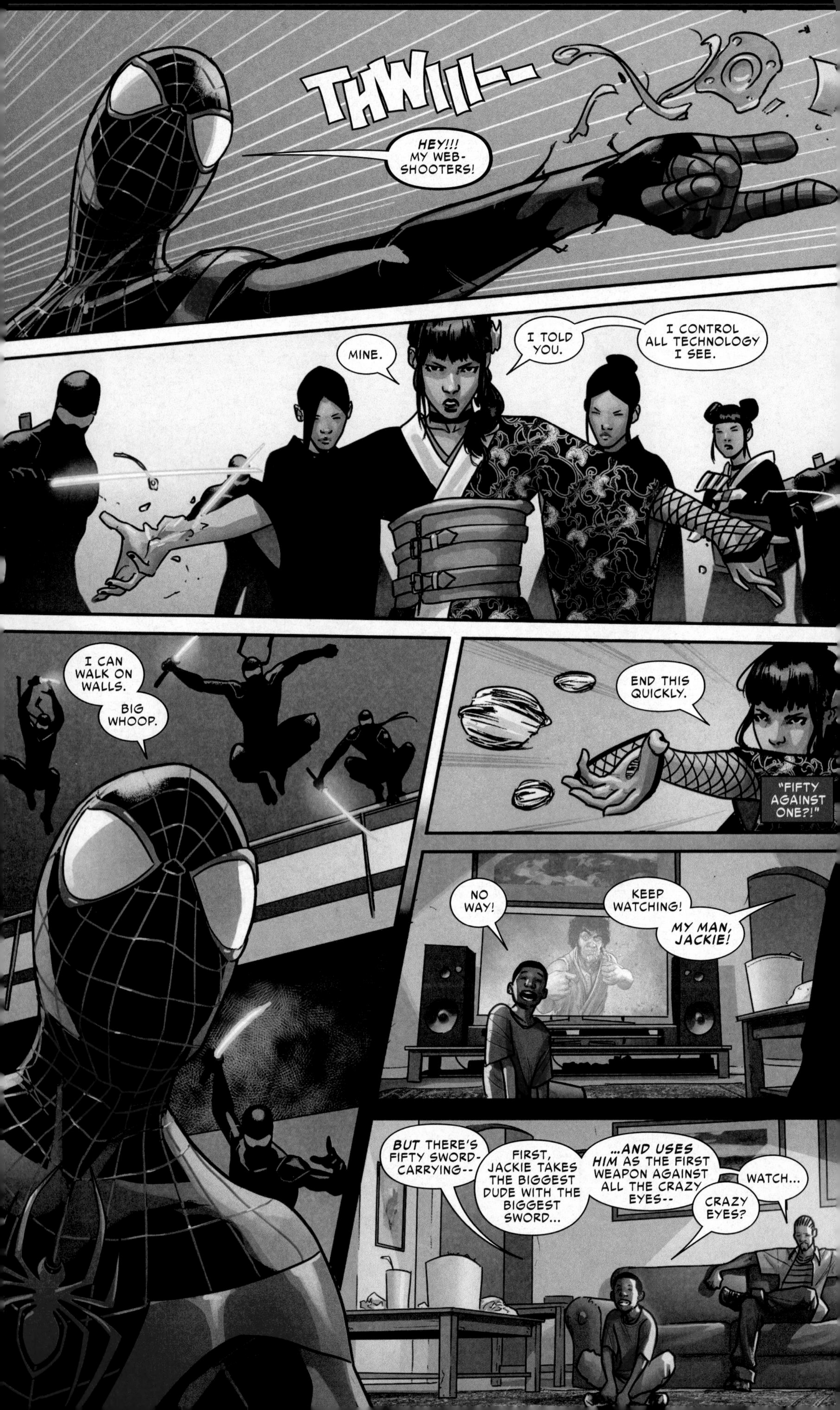

THWIII--
HEY!!! MY WEB-SHOOTERS!
MINE.
I TOLD YOU.
I CONTROL ALL TECHNOLOGY I SEE.
I CAN WALK ON WALLS.
BIG WHOOP.
END THIS QUICKLY.
"FIFTY AGAINST ONE?!"
NO WAY!
KEEP WATCHING!
MY MAN, JACKIE!
BUT THERE'S FIFTY SWORD-CARRYING--
FIRST, JACKIE TAKES THE BIGGEST DUDE WITH THE BIGGEST SWORD...
...AND USES HIM AS THE FIRST WEAPON AGAINST ALL THE CRAZY EYES--
WATCH...
CRAZY EYES?

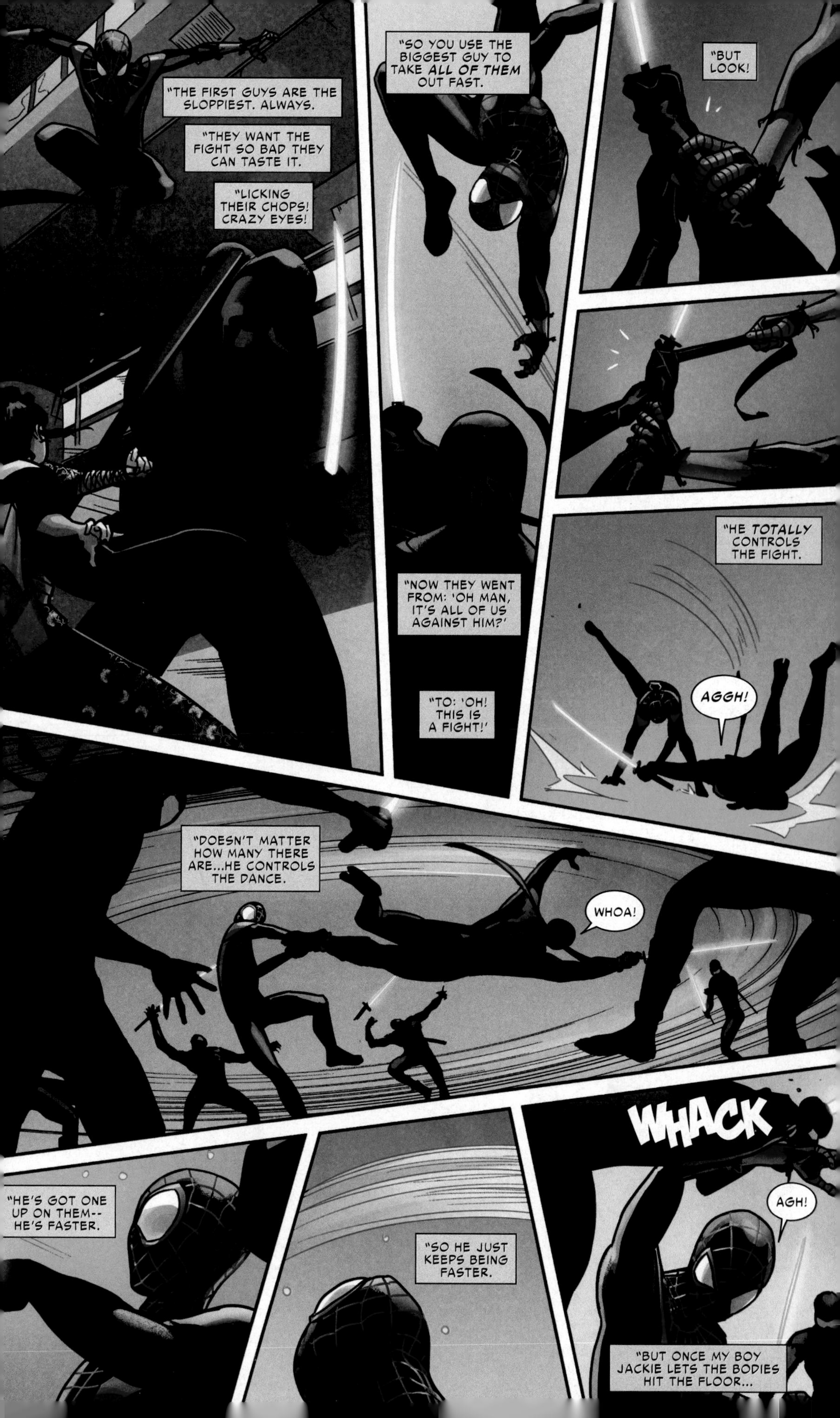
"THE FIRST GUYS ARE THE SLOPPIEST. ALWAYS.
"THEY WANT THE FIGHT SO BAD THEY CAN TASTE IT.
"LICKING THEIR CHOPS! CRAZY EYES!
"SO YOU USE THE BIGGEST GUY TO TAKE ALL OF THEM OUT FAST.
"NOW THEY WENT FROM: 'OH MAN, IT'S ALL OF US AGAINST HIM?'
"TO: 'OH! THIS IS A FIGHT!'
"BUT LOOK!
"HE TOTALLY CONTROLS THE FIGHT.
AGGH!
"DOESN'T MATTER HOW MANY THERE ARE...HE CONTROLS THE DANCE.
WHOA!
"HE'S GOT ONE UP ON THEM-- HE'S FASTER.
"SO HE JUST KEEPS BEING FASTER.
WHACK
AGH!
"BUT ONCE MY BOY JACKIE LETS THE BODIES HIT THE FLOOR...

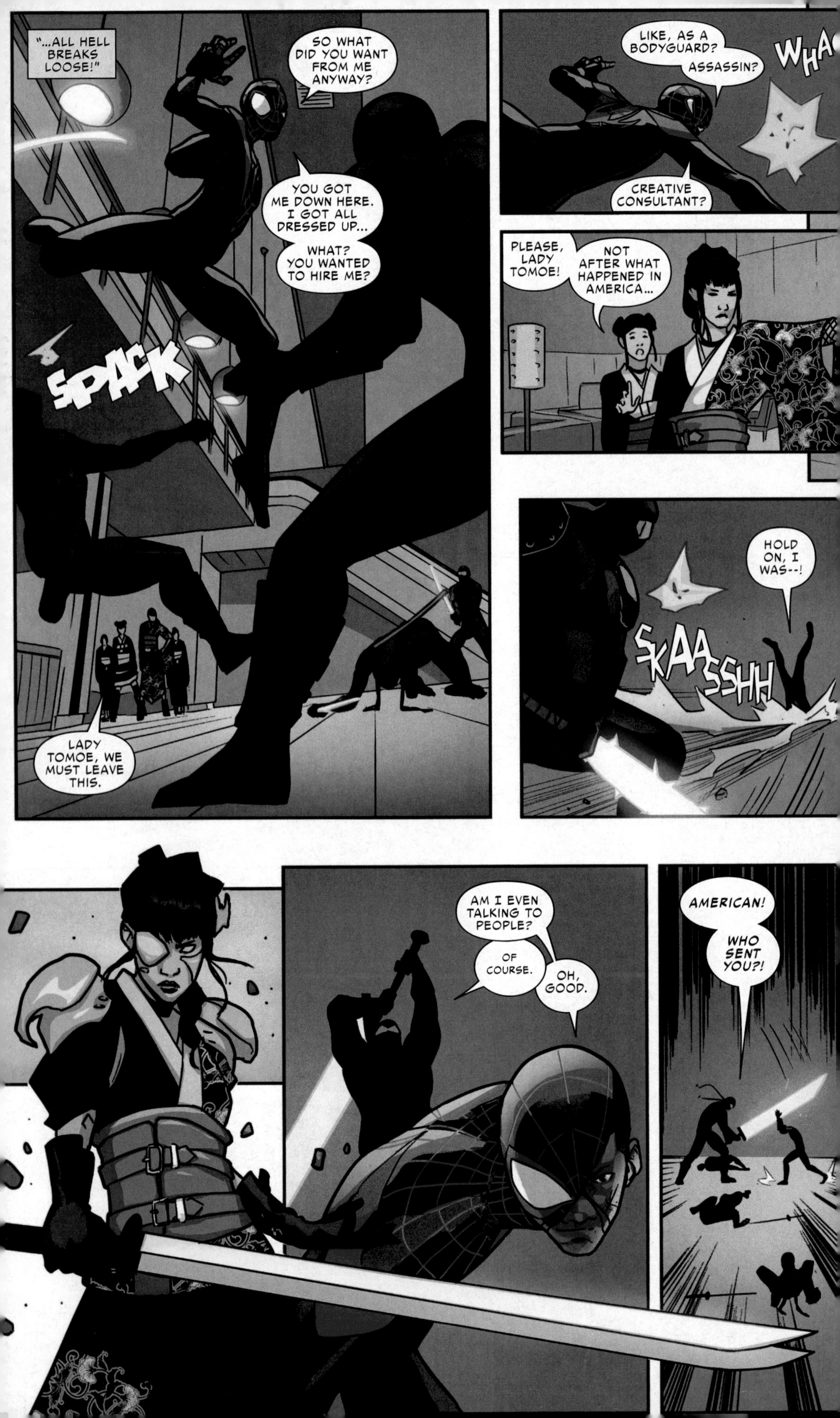
"...ALL HELL BREAKS LOOSE!"
SO WHAT DID YOU WANT FROM ME ANYWAY?
YOU GOT ME DOWN HERE. I GOT ALL DRESSED UP...
WHAT? YOU WANTED TO HIRE ME?
SPACK
LADY TOMOE, WE MUST LEAVE THIS.
LIKE, AS A BODYGUARD?
ASSASSIN?
CREATIVE CONSULTANT?
PLEASE, LADY TOMOE!
NOT AFTER WHAT HAPPENED IN AMERICA...
HOLD ON, I WAS--!
SKAASSHH
AM I EVEN TALKING TO PEOPLE?
OF COURSE.
OH, GOOD.
AMERICAN!
WHO SENT YOU?!

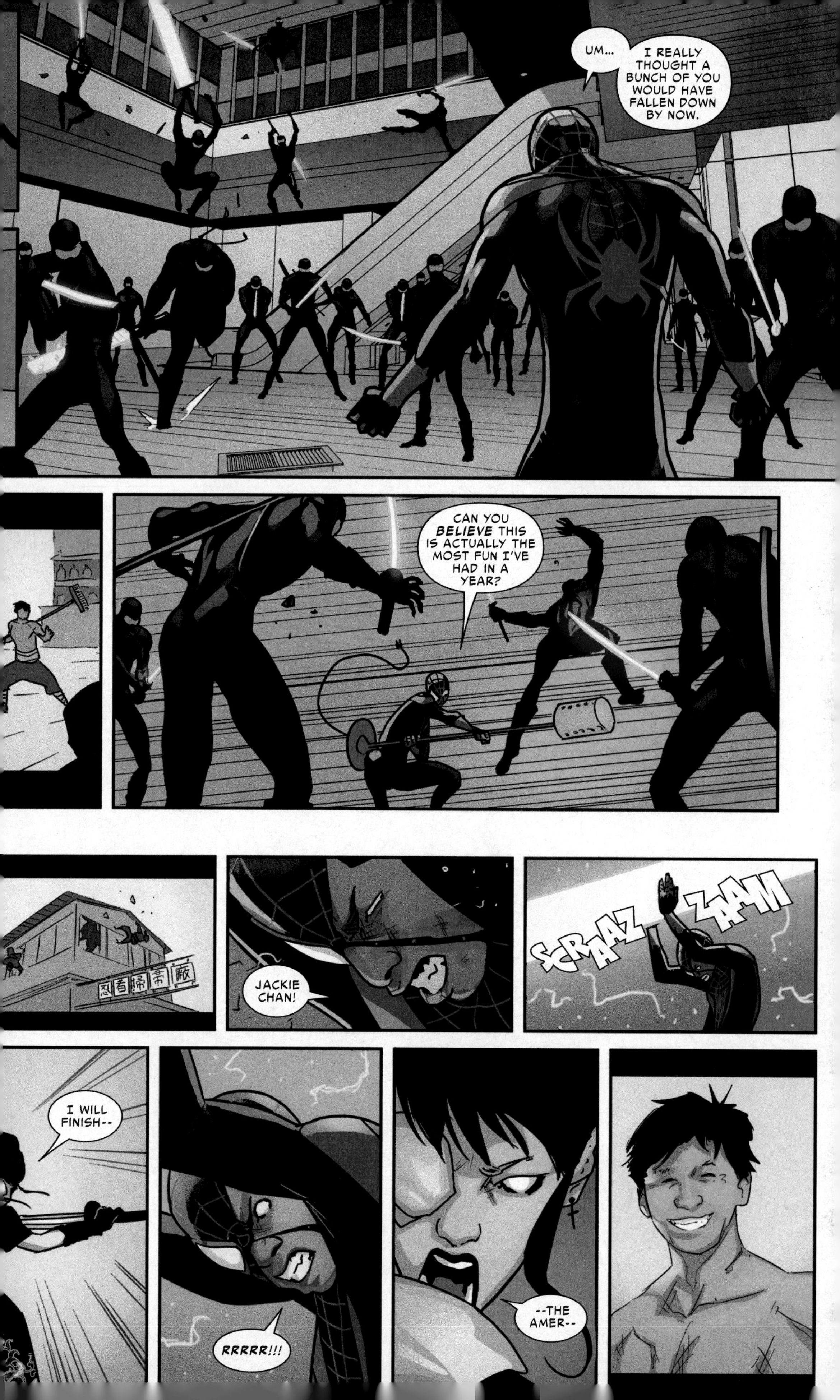
UM...
I REALLY THOUGHT A BUNCH OF YOU WOULD HAVE FALLEN DOWN BY NOW.
CAN YOU BELIEVE THIS IS ACTUALLY THE MOST FUN I'VE HAD IN A YEAR?
忍者掃帚廠
JACKIE CHAN!
SCRAAZ
ZAAM
I WILL FINISH--
RRRRR!!!
--THE AMER--

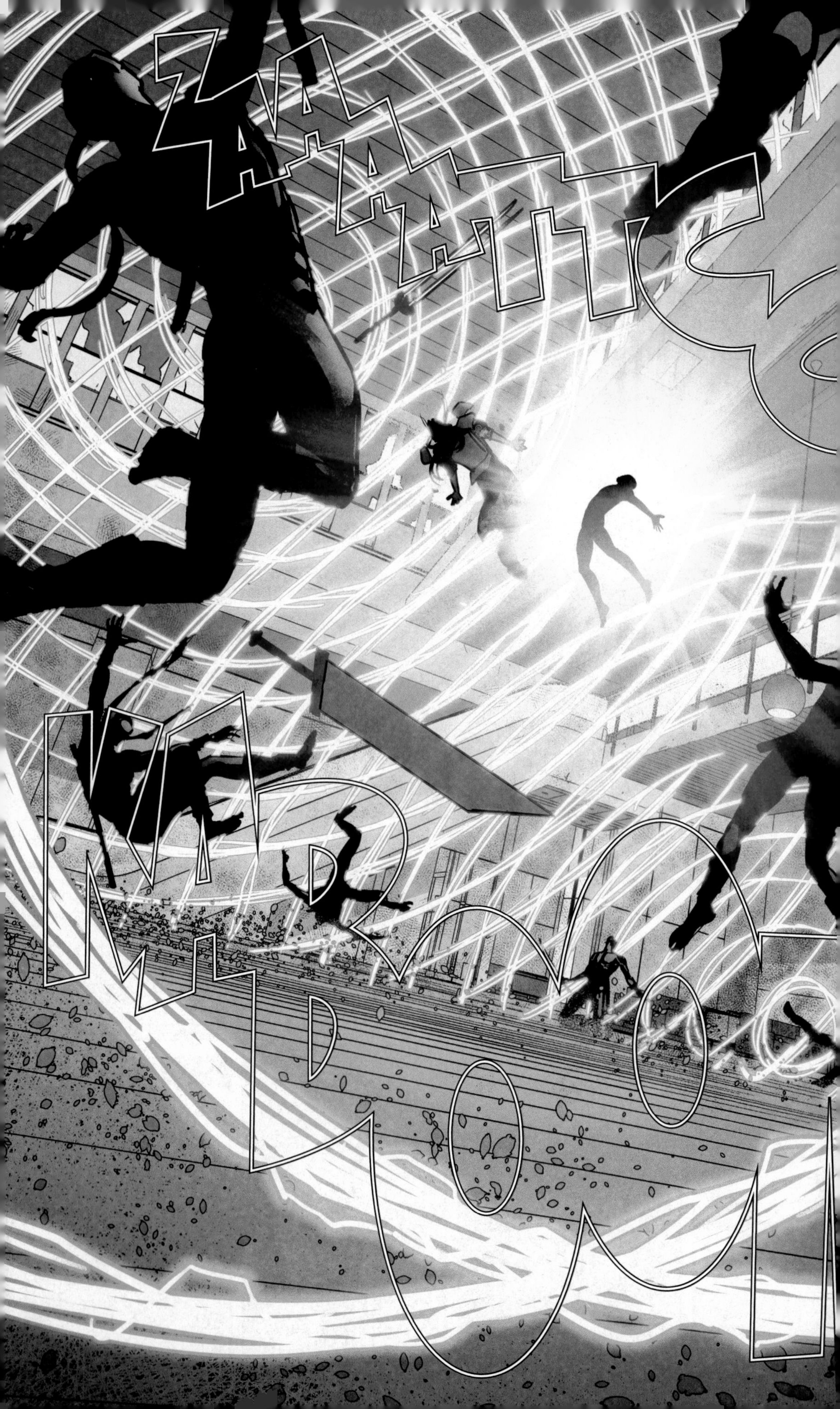

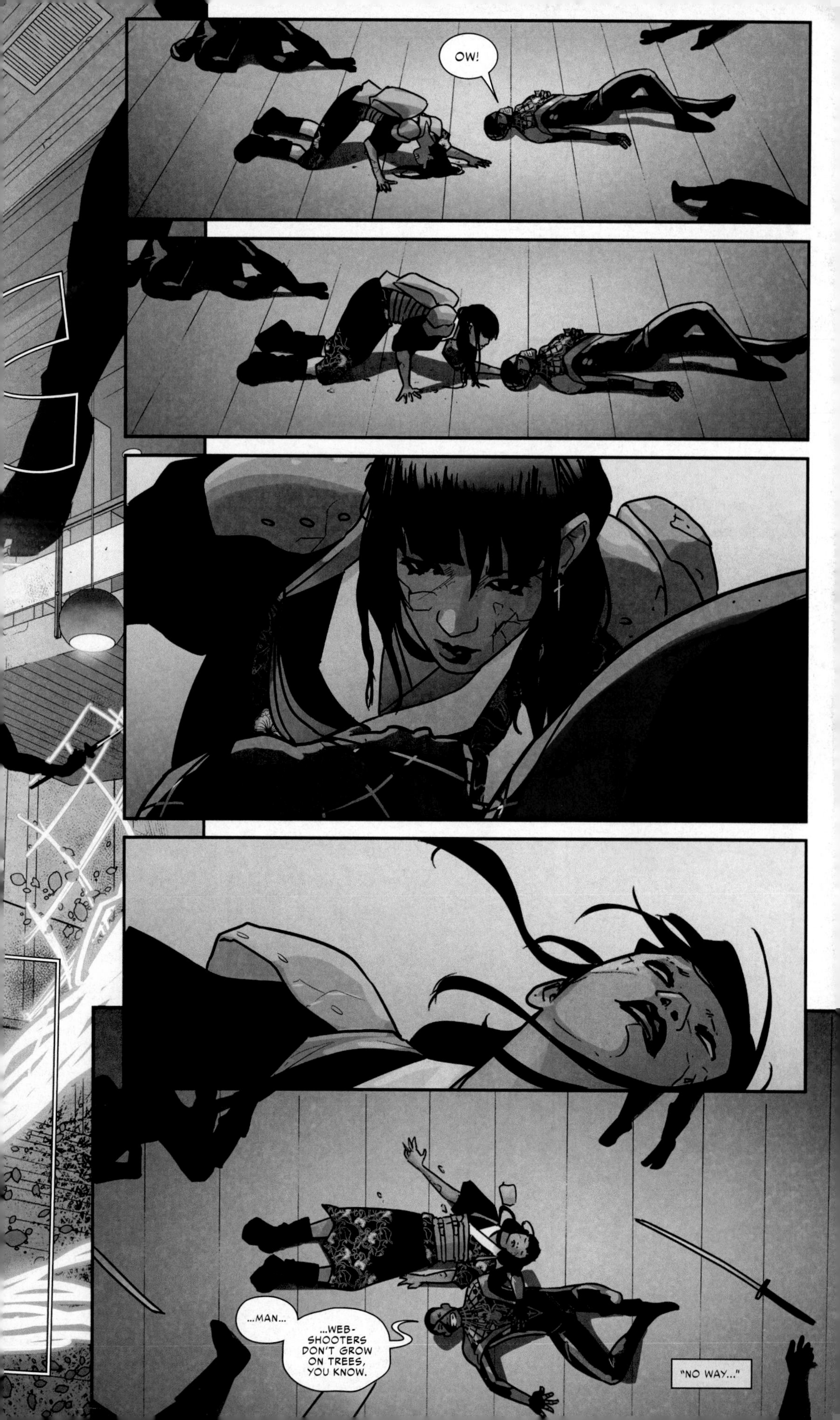
OW!
...MAN...
...WEB-SHOOTERS DON'T GROW ON TREES, YOU KNOW.
"NO WAY..."

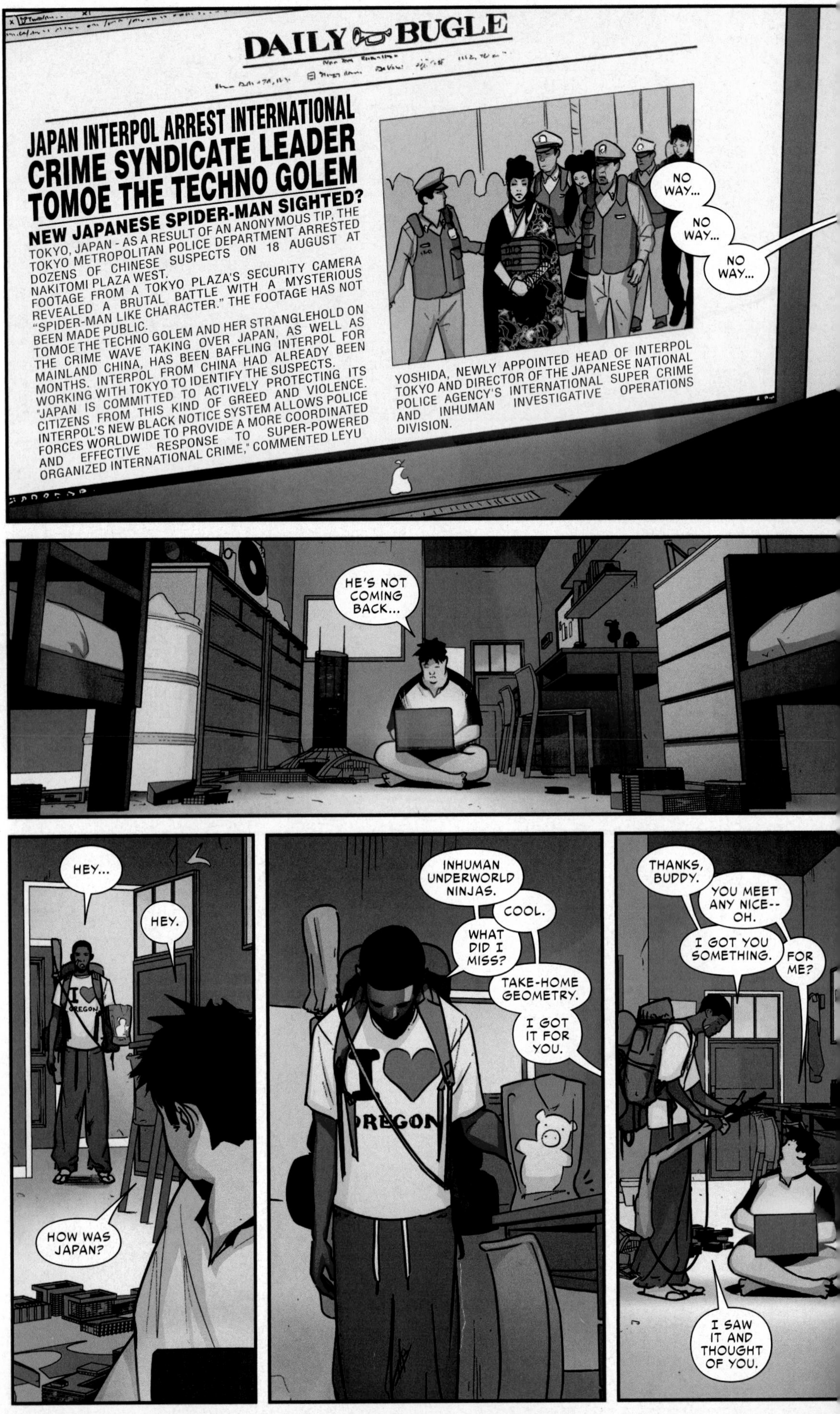
DAILY BUGLE
JAPAN INTERPOL ARREST INTERNATIONAL CRIME SYNDICATE LEADER TOMOE THE TECHNO GOLEM
NEW JAPANESE SPIDER-MAN SIGHTED?
TOKYO, JAPAN - AS A RESULT OF AN ANONYMOUS TIP, THE TOKYO METROPOLITAN POLICE DEPARTMENT ARRESTED DOZENS OF CHINESE SUSPECTS ON 18 AUGUST AT NAKITOMI PLAZA WEST.
FOOTAGE FROM A TOKYO PLAZA'S SECURITY CAMERA REVEALED A BRUTAL BATTLE WITH A MYSTERIOUS "SPIDER-MAN LIKE CHARACTER." THE FOOTAGE HAS NOT BEEN MADE PUBLIC.
TOMOE THE TECHNO GOLEM AND HER STRANGLEHOLD ON THE CRIME WAVE TAKING OVER JAPAN, AS WELL AS MAINLAND CHINA, HAS BEEN BAFFLING INTERPOL FOR MONTHS. INTERPOL FROM CHINA HAD ALREADY BEEN WORKING WITH TOKYO TO IDENTIFY THE SUSPECTS.
"JAPAN IS COMMITTED TO ACTIVELY PROTECTING ITS CITIZENS FROM THIS KIND OF GREED AND VIOLENCE. INTERPOL'S NEW BLACK NOTICE SYSTEM ALLOWS POLICE FORCES WORLDWIDE TO PROVIDE A MORE COORDINATED AND EFFECTIVE RESPONSE TO SUPER-POWERED ORGANIZED INTERNATIONAL CRIME," COMMENTED LEYU
YOSHIDA, NEWLY APPOINTED HEAD OF INTERPOL TOKYO AND DIRECTOR OF THE JAPANESE NATIONAL POLICE AGENCY'S INTERNATIONAL SUPER CRIME AND INHUMAN INVESTIGATIVE OPERATIONS DIVISION.
NO WAY...
NO WAY...
NO WAY...
HE'S NOT COMING BACK...
HEY...
HEY.
HOW WAS JAPAN?
INHUMAN UNDERWORLD NINJAS.
COOL.
WHAT DID I MISS?
TAKE-HOME GEOMETRY.
I GOT IT FOR YOU.
THANKS, BUDDY.
YOU MEET ANY NICE--OH.
I GOT YOU SOMETHING.
FOR ME?
I SAW IT AND THOUGHT OF YOU.

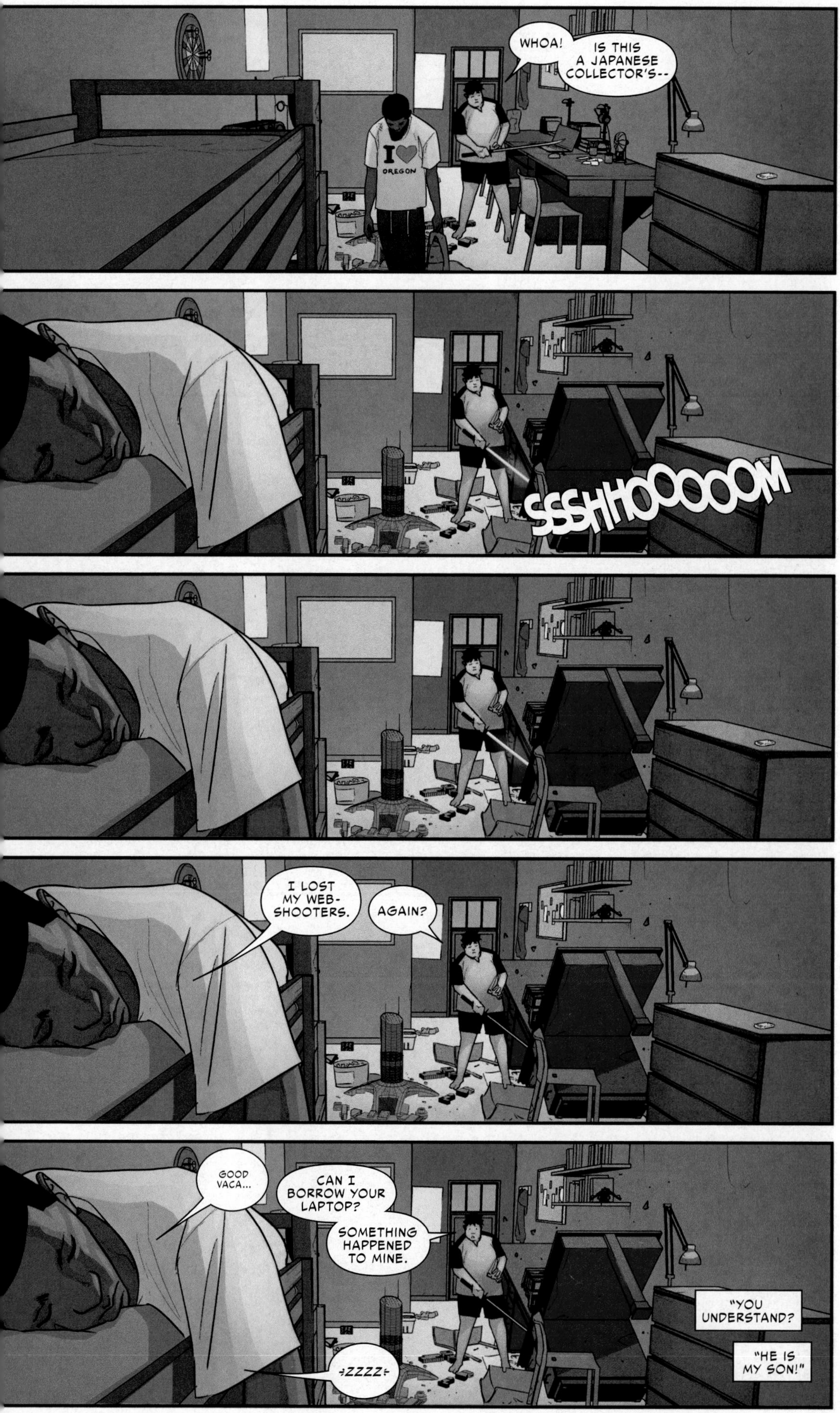
WHOA!
IS THIS A JAPANESE COLLECTOR'S--
I ♥ OREGON
SSSHHOOOOOOM
I LOST MY WEB-SHOOTERS.
AGAIN?
GOOD VACA...
CAN I BORROW YOUR LAPTOP?
SOMETHING HAPPENED TO MINE.
ZZZZ
"YOU UNDERSTAND?
"HE IS MY SON!"

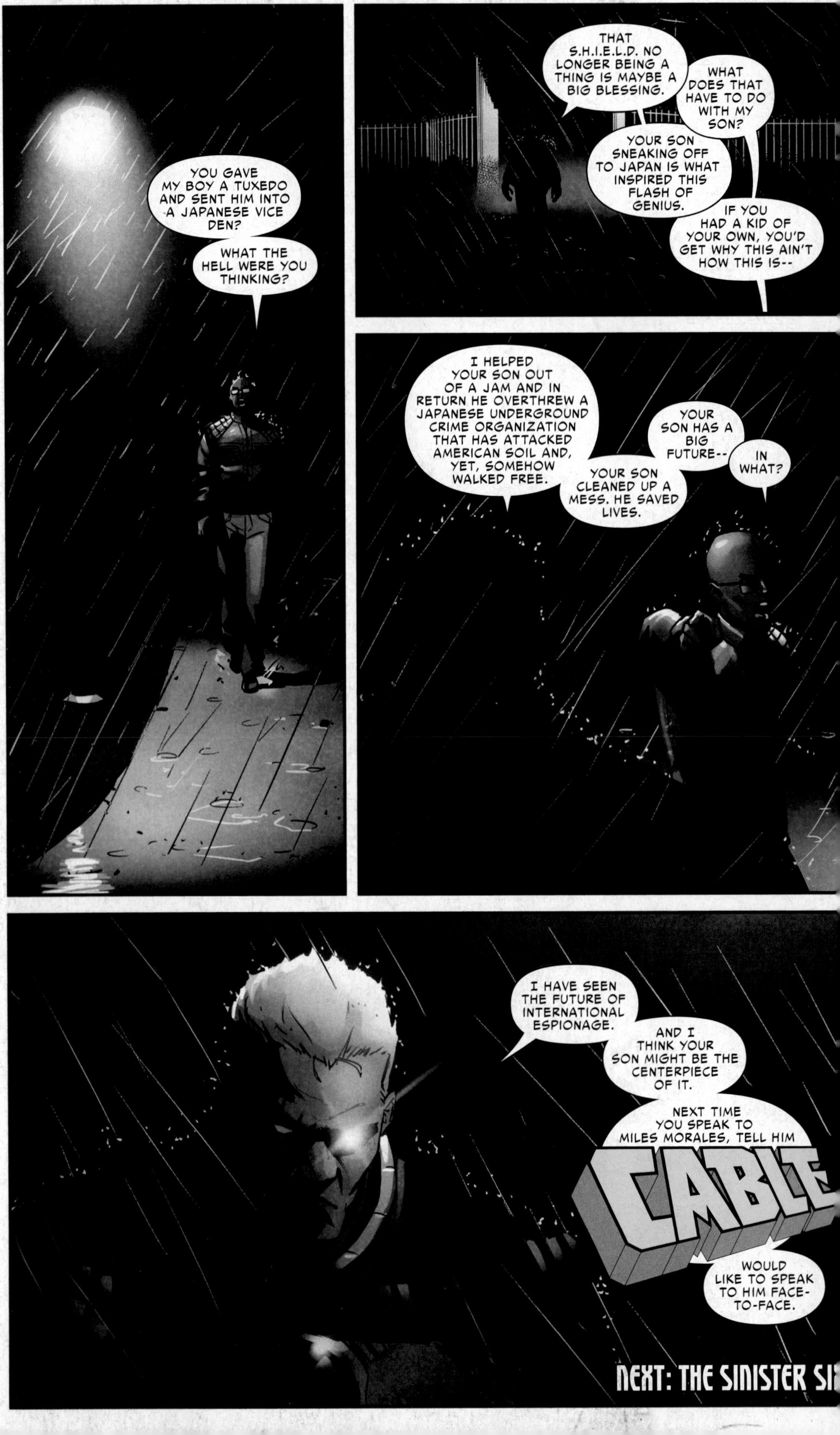
YOU GAVE MY BOY A TUXEDO AND SENT HIM INTO A JAPANESE VICE DEN?
WHAT THE HELL WERE YOU THINKING?
THAT S.H.I.E.L.D. NO LONGER BEING A THING IS MAYBE A BIG BLESSING.
WHAT DOES THAT HAVE TO DO WITH MY SON?
YOUR SON SNEAKING OFF TO JAPAN IS WHAT INSPIRED THIS FLASH OF GENIUS.
IF YOU HAD A KID OF YOUR OWN, YOU'D GET WHY THIS AIN'T HOW THIS IS--
I HELPED YOUR SON OUT OF A JAM AND IN RETURN HE OVERTHREW A JAPANESE UNDERGROUND CRIME ORGANIZATION THAT HAS ATTACKED AMERICAN SOIL AND, YET, SOMEHOW WALKED FREE.
YOUR SON CLEANED UP A MESS. HE SAVED LIVES.
YOUR SON HAS A BIG FUTURE--
IN WHAT?
I HAVE SEEN THE FUTURE OF INTERNATIONAL ESPIONAGE.
AND I THINK YOUR SON MIGHT BE THE CENTERPIECE OF IT.
NEXT TIME YOU SPEAK TO MILES MORALES, TELL HIM
CABLE
WOULD LIKE TO SPEAK TO HIM FACE-TO-FACE.
NEXT: THE SINISTER SI

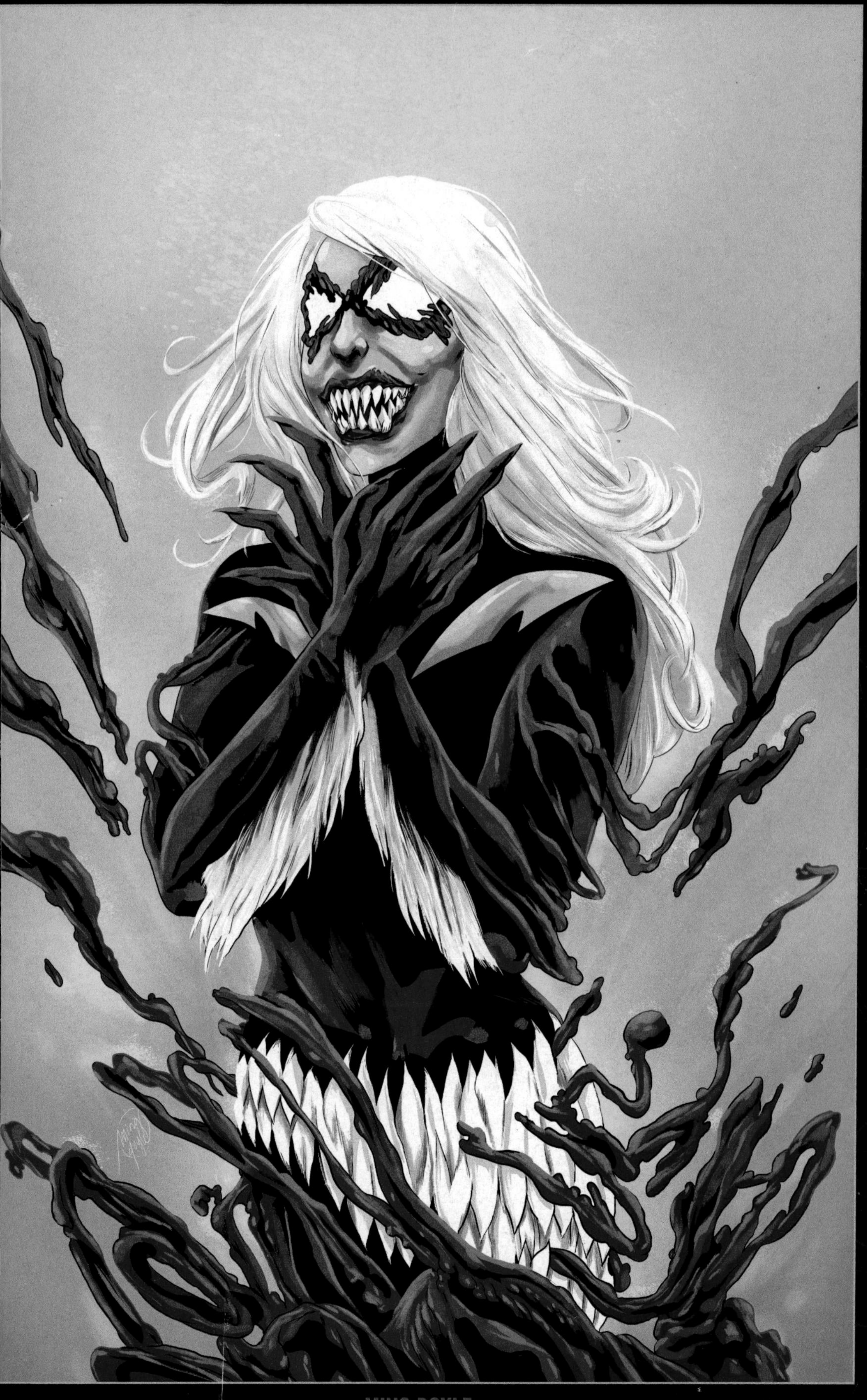

MING DOYLE
#20 VENOMIZED VILLIANS VARIANT